Ever-Moving Repose

VERITAS
Series Introduction

". . . the truth will set you free" (John 8:32)

In much contemporary discourse, Pilate's question has been taken to mark the absolute boundary of human thought. Beyond this boundary, it is often suggested, is an intellectual hinterland into which we must not venture. This terrain is an agnosticism of thought: because truth cannot be possessed, it must not be spoken. Thus, it is argued that the defenders of "truth" in our day are often traffickers in ideology, merchants of counterfeits, or anti-liberal. They are, because it is somewhat taken for granted that Nietzsche's word is final: truth is the domain of tyranny.

Is this indeed the case, or might another vision of truth offer itself? The ancient Greeks named the love of wisdom as *philia*, or friendship. The one who would become wise, they argued, would be a "friend of truth." For both philosophy and theology might be conceived as schools in the friendship of truth, as a kind of relation. For like friendship, truth is as much discovered as it is made. If truth is then so elusive, if its domain is *terra incognita*, perhaps this is because it arrives to us—unannounced—as gift, as a person, and not some thing.

The aim of the Veritas book series is to publish incisive and original current scholarly work that inhabits "the between" and "the beyond" of theology and philosophy. These volumes will all share a common aspiration to transcend the institutional divorce in which these two disciplines often find themselves, and to engage questions of pressing concern to both philosophers and theologians in such a way as to reinvigorate both disciplines with a kind of interdisciplinary desire, often so absent in contemporary academe. In a word, these volumes represent collective efforts in the befriending of truth, doing so beyond the simulacra of pretend tolerance, the violent, yet insipid reasoning of liberalism that asks with Pilate, "What is truth?"—expecting a consensus of non-commitment; one that encourages the commodification of the mind, now sedated by the civil service of career, ministered by the frightened patrons of position.

The series will therefore consist of two "wings": (1) original monographs; and (2) essay collections on a range of topics in theology and philosophy. The latter will principally be the products of the annual conferences of the Centre of Theology and Philosophy (www.theologyphilosophycentre .co.uk).

Conor Cunningham and Eric Austin Lee, *Series editors*

Ever-Moving Repose

A Contemporary Reading of
Maximus the Confessor's Theory of Time

SOTIRIS MITRALEXIS

With a foreword by
Ecumenical Patriarch Bartholomew

CASCADE *Books* · Eugene, Oregon

EVER-MOVING REPOSE
A Contemporary Reading of Maximus the Confessor's Theory of Time

Veritas Series 24

Cascade Books
An Imprint of Wipf and Stock Publishers
199 W. 8th Ave., Suite 3
Eugene, OR 97401

www.wipfandstock.com

PAPERBACK ISBN: 978-1-5326-0703-5
HARDCOVER ISBN: 978-1-5326-0705-9
EBOOK ISBN: 978-1-5326-0704-2

Cataloguing-in-Publication data:

Names: Mitralexis, Sotiris, 1988– | Bartholomew, Ecumenical Patriarch of Con
stantinople, 1940–

Title: Ever-moving repose : a contemporary reading of Maximus the Confessor's
theory of time / Sotiris Mitralexis, with a foreword by Ecumenical Patriarch
Bartholomew.

Description: Eugene, OR: Cascade Books, 2017 | Series: Veritas Series 24 | In-
cludes bibliographical references and index.

Identifiers: ISBN 978-1-5326-0703-5 (paperback) | ISBN 978-1-5326-0705-9 (hard-
cover) | ISBN 978-1-5326-0704-2 (ebook)

Subjects: LCSH: Maximus, Confessor, Saint, approximately 580–662 | Time |
Time—Philosophy

Classification: BR65.M416 M487 2017 (print) | BR65.M416 (ebook)

Manufactured in the U.S.A.   APRIL 7, 2017

Cover image: Fikos, *We Feel the Sick Body . . .* / Athens, 2012 (Mural). Fikos.gr

Table of Contents

Foreword

By His All-Holiness

ECUMENICAL PATRIARCH BARTHOLOMEW

WE ARE SINCERELY DELIGHTED to respond to the request by Dr. Sotiris Mitralexis to provide a foreword to the published edition of *Ever-Moving Repose: A Contemporary Reading of Maximus the Confessor's Theory of Time*, whose original format comprised the doctoral dissertation of the author.

It is a refreshing sign of our times that the church fathers, both of the East and West, have been explored and examined anew in scholarly circles in recent decades. St. Maximus the Confessor is a unique example among these classical giants inasmuch as his life spans East and West alike, while his writing straddles philosophy and theology. Indeed, more profoundly and more substantially, this scholar saint fought to overcome the distinction between theology and mystagogy, even as he sought to overcome divisions, among others, between intelligible and sensible, corruption and incorruptibility, material and spiritual, body and soul, as well as male and female. The human person, who is a microcosm of these contrasts, is called to serve as a mediator between heaven and earth in the cosmic liturgy that frames the entire universe.

This book by Sotiris Mitralexis focuses on other variations of these primal distinctions and philosophical dualities, namely between time and eternity as well as between mobility and stability. Indeed, it articulates the importance and impact of this monastic and mystic—both philologically and philosophically—in the medieval period, but also in modern thought, particularly in various representatives of contemporary Greek theology. In this way, this seventh-century ascetic confessor—who formulated theology with his blood and with his pen—is not approached as if from the ivory tower of dry scholasticism, but as the vibrant legacy of the faith once delivered and entrusted to the holy people of God (see Jude 3) in the organic continuity of the living church.

For, by analyzing the powerful principles of beings (*logoi*), the author reconstructs the theory of time in St. Maximus and elevates the doctrine of deification (*theosis*) to the potential and mandate of human beings, created in the image of God, in order to transcend all "divisions, dualities, and distances" in the likeness of Jesus Christ. All of this reveals the motion of life and the meaning of humanity as a vivid, personal relationship—a voluntary, affirmative response to the divine call for communion.

It is our fervent prayer that the exceptional vision and extraordinary worldview of St. Maximus the Confessor will touch and transform the hearts of those who read this publication.

At the Ecumenical Patriarchate, September 5, 2016

✠ **BARTHOLOMEW**
Archbishop of Constantinople—New Rome
and Ecumenical Patriarch

Acknowledgements

THIS BOOK IS A revised version of my doctoral dissertation in philosophy at the Freie Universität Berlin's Institute of Philosophy, written under the supervision of Prof. Dr. Wilhelm Schmidt-Biggemann (*Erstgutachter*) and Dr. Rowan Williams (*Zweitgutachter*), defended on the 24th of September 2014, and entitled *Ever-Moving Repose: The Notion of Time in Maximus the Confessor's Philosophy Through the Perspective of a Relational Ontology*. This study would not have been completed without the help of many scholars, whom I would like to thank.

I would like to express my deepest gratitude to Priv.-Doz. Dr. Sebastian Lalla, who has diligently supervised the greater part of this study's development. His patient guidance, encouragement, support, and critique, as well as his willingness to give his time so generously, acted as decisive factors in the progress of my research. I am especially thankful to my doctoral supervisor, Prof. Dr. Schmidt-Biggemann, whose willingness to act as the principal supervisor at a later stage in this study's development was of critical importance. Dr. Rowan Williams' willingness to act as the external supervisor/assessor (*Zweitgutachter*) to the study has been a source of great joy, and I am grateful for the honor he has bestowed upon me in doing so, as well as for his very constructive critique.

Moreover, I am very thankful to Christos Yannaras for his ongoing valuable counsel and guidance, as well as for the initial inspiration for this work; it is to him that I owe my encounter with one of the most original and innovative thinkers that I have ever encountered, Maximus the Confessor. My special thanks are extended to Fr. Andrew Louth and to Fr. Maximos Constas, who have both repeatedly offered their expert counsel to me out of genuine kindness and interest, without having any obligation to do so by an official academic involvement in the development of this study. For this, I am indebted to them.

I wish to also thank scholars and friends Dionysios Skliris, Andrew Kaethler, Timothy Carroll, Travis Buchanan, Pui Him Ip, Chryssi Sidiropoulou, and Johannes Borjesson for their vigorous engagement in constructive conversations that helped the formation of this study both directly and indirectly, as well as Torstein Tollefsen and the group of scholars participating in the *Ambigua* reading groups he regularly convenes. It is difficult to thank each and every member of the vibrant community of Maximian scholars by name, but I am most indebted to them, since the discussions we engaged in during many international conferences have proven truly formative in the context of my Maximian apprenticeship.

My sincerest thanks are extended to Dr. Maria Trumpf-Lyritzaki for her generous support through the *DAAD-Maria Trumpf-Lyritzaki scholarship* during the first year of my doctoral studies, as well as to the German Academic Exchange Service (DAAD), whose research scholarship during the last two years of my studies made the research behind this book possible. Finally, I am grateful to the editors of Cascade's *Veritas* series, Conor Cunningham and Eric Austin Lee, for including this book in their series, as well as to the Athens-based artist Fikos, who kindly gave the permission for the use of his mural *We Feel the Sick Body* in the cover. It goes without saying that I am solely responsible for every omission, inadequacy, and error in the present work; the engagement with Maximus the Confessor's staggeringly fecund *corpus* cannot but be a never-ending process, and as such this book is far from being the definitive fruit of this continuing enquiry.

Abbreviations

THE FOLLOWING ABBREVIATIONS DENOTE my primary sources:

CCSG	*Corpus Christianorum Series Graeca*
PG	Jacques Paul Migne's *Patrologiae Cursus Completus — Series Graeca*
Cantarella	Raffaele Cantarella (ed.): *S. Massimo Confessore. La mistagogia ed altri scritti.* Florence: Testi Cristiani 1931.
Ceresa-Gastaldo	Aldo Ceresa-Gastaldo: *Massimo Confessore— Capitoli sulla caritá. Ed. criticamente con introd., versione e note.* Verba Seniorum, collana di testi e studi patristici, n.s. 3. Rome: Studium. 1963.
Constas Constas–DOML 28/29	Nicholas Constas (ed. & trans.): *Maximos the Confessor: On Difficulties in the Church Fathers— The Ambigua* (two volumes). Dumbarton Oaks Medieval Library 28 & 29. Cambridge: Harvard University Press, 2014.

Abbreviations of Maximus' Works

i. Q.Thal. I

Πρὸς Θαλάσσιον, περὶ διαφόρων ἀπόρων τῆς θείας Γραφῆς (Πρὸς Θαλάσσιον) Quaestiones ad Thalassium. CCSG 7.

ii. Q.Thal. II

Πρὸς Θαλάσσιον, περὶ διαφόρων ἀπόρων τῆς θείας Γραφῆς (Πρὸς Θαλάσσιον) Quaestiones ad Thalassium. CCSG 22.

iii. Q.Dub.

Πεύσεις καὶ Ἀποκρίσεις καὶ Ἐρωτήσεις καὶ Ἐκλογαὶ διαφόρων κεφαλαίων ἀπορουμένων (Πεύσεις καὶ Ἀποκρίσεις). Quaestiones et dubia. (PG90 785–856.) CCSG 10.

iv. Exp.Psalm.

Ἑρμηνεία εἰς τὸν νθ΄ Ψαλμόν. Expositio in Psalmum lix. (PG90 856–72.) CCSG 23, 3–22.

v. Or.Dom.

Εἰς τὴν προσευχὴν τοῦ Πάτερ ἡμῶν, πρὸς ἕνα φιλόχριστον ἑρμηνεία σύντομος (Εἰς τὴν προσευχὴν τοῦ Πάτερ ἡμῶν). Expositio orationis Dominicae. (PG90 872–909). CCSG 23, 27–73.

vi. Lib.Asc.

Λόγος ἀσκητικός. Liber asceticus. (PG90 912–57.) CCSG 40. Cantarella, 30–98.

vii. Car.

Κεφάλαια περὶ ἀγάπης. Capita de caritate quattuor centuriae. (PG90 960–1073.) Ceresa-Gastaldo.

viii. Th.oec.

Κεφάλαια Σ΄ περὶ θεολογίας καὶ τῆς ἐνσάρκου οἰκονομίας τοῦ Υἱοῦ Θεοῦ. Capitum theologicorum et oeconomicorum duae centuriae. PG90 1084–1176.

(Κεφάλαια διάφορα θεολογικά τε καὶ οἰκονομικὰ καὶ περὶ ἀρετῆς καὶ κακίας [Κεφάλαια διάφορα / Diversa capita]—Apart from l.1–15, this is not by Maximus as such, but is an anthology based mainly on Quaestiones ad Thalassium. PG90 1177–1392.)

ix. Q.Theop.

Πρὸς Θεόπεμπτον σχολαστικόν. Quaestiones ad Theopemptum. PG90 1393–1400.

x. Opusc.

Ἔργα θεολογικὰ καὶ πολεμικά. Opuscula theologica et polemica. PG91 9–286.

xi. D.Pyrrh.

Ζήτησις μετὰ Πύρρου. Disputatio cum Pyrrho. PG91 288–353.

xii. Anim.

Περὶ ψυχῆς. Opusculum de anima. (PG91 353–61.) Cantarella, 220–32.
It is to be noted that the attribution of *De Anima* to Maximus is an erroneous one; see Francesco Celia's article "Il λόγος κεφαλαιώδης dello ps.-Gregorio il Taumaturgo: uno status quaestionis e un primo approccio al problema delle fonti," *Adamantius* 17 (2011) 164–89.

xiii. Ep.

Ἐπιστολαί. Epistulae. PG91 364–649.

xiv. Myst.

Μυσταγωγία. Mystagogia. (PG91 657–717.) CCSG 69. Cantarella, 122–214.

xv. Ambigua / Ambiguorum Liber:

xvi. Amb.Th.

Πρὸς Θωμᾶν τὸν ἡγιασμένον. Ambigua ad Thomam. (PG91 1032–60.) CCSG 48, 3–34. (and Constas—DOML 28.)

xvii. Amb.Io.

Πρὸς Ἰωάννην ἀρχιεπίσκοπον Κυζίκου. Ambigua ad Ioannem. (PG91 1061–1424.) Constas—DOML 28 & 29.

Since Constas' critical edition (vol. I and II are Dumbarton Oaks Medieval Library 28 and 29 respectively) names Migne's PG column of each respective passage, while many scholars still depend on PG's Ambigua, I will simply cite Amb.Io. with PG91 columns for the readers' convenience, as PG91 columns can be easily traced back to Constas' pages, while the opposite is naturally not the case. I will cite CCSG 48 for the Ambigua ad Thomam, and CCT2 (Corpus Christianorum in Translation 2) for Joshua Lollar's English translation.

(Epistula secunda ad Thomam. CCSG 48, 37–49.)

The translations are the author's if not otherwise noted.[1] Where available, I will provide published English translations of Maximus' passages. Many translated passages have been slightly modified (in accordance with the Greek original) in order to retain a certain uniformity in terminology throughout my study, while the original translator is still cited: this is particularly the case with my translation of αἰὼν as Aeon in many instances, for reasons that will be adequately explained, and of λόγοι as λόγοι instead

---

1. With the exception of chapter 8, "The Fundamentals of Temporality, Spatiality, and Motion, Sections 35–40 from the Tenth 'Difficulty,'" where all translations derive from Andrew Louth's *Maximus the Confessor*.

of "principles," etc. When a Maximian quote's paraphrase is provided in the text, I will often cite the original Greek passage in the footnotes, depending on its importance and size. In cases of crucial terminology, both the English translation and the original text will be provided for reference. I will use the following abbreviations for translated passages:

Berthold   George C. Berthold (ed. and trans.): *Maximus the Confessor: Selected Writings*. New York: Paulist, 1985.

Blowers   Paul M. Blowers and Robert Louis Wilken (eds. and trans.): *On the Cosmic Mystery of Jesus Christ: Selected Writings from St. Maximus the Confessor*. Crestwood, NY: St. Vladimir's Seminary Press 2003.

Constas   Nicholas Constas (ed. and trans.): *Maximos the Confessor: On Difficulties in the Church Fathers—The Ambigua* (two volumes). Dumbarton Oaks Medieval Library 28 & 29. Cambridge: Harvard University Press, 2014.

Lollar   Joshua Lollar (trans.): *Maximus the Confessor: Ambigua to Thomas and Second Letter to Thomas*. Corpus Christianorum in Translation 2. Turnhout: Brepols, 2010.

Prassas   Despina Prassas (ed. and trans.): *St Maximus the Confessor's Questions and Doubts*. DeKalb, IL: Northern Illinois University Press 2009.

Louth   Andrew Louth: *Maximus the Confessor*. London: Routledge—Taylor & Francis e-Library 2005.

Introduction

THIS BOOK IS A study of Maximus the Confessor's philosophy, focusing on his understanding of time and claiming he possesses a *threefold theory of temporality* that merits a position of its own in the history of philosophy. I approach Maximus' works and thought through the perspective of three original thinkers in the world of contemporary Christian Orthodox thought: mainly Christos Yannaras with his *critical and relational ontology*, an exposition of which will be provided, but also John Zizioulas and Nicholas Loudovikos. Apart from this contemporary perspective of ours, I will also invoke the Aristotelian theory of time, a most obvious influence on Maximus,[1] as a historical starting point for my enquiry into Maximus' temporality, rather than focusing on late antiquity and Neoplatonism as the Confessor's intellectual context—thus continuing and evolving Betsakos' comparative study of Aristotelian and Maximian theories of motion.[2] A comparison with Maximus' Neoplatonic and late antique contemporaries is a most fecund scholarly path that, however, has been already traversed by most Maximian scholars, providing us with ample material in this direction, which need not be re-invented here; thus, I choose to take a different route.

Maximus has not written a treatise on time, nor has he composed a comprehensive theory of time like, for example, Aristotle. However, the definitions and formulations scattered in his work bear the marks of a

---

1. I must here note that the reception of Aristotle and Plato in Maximus' time, in the seventh century AD, was radically different from today's. Plato and Aristotle were considered as more or less complementary to each other, resulting in an "Aristotelian Plato" and a "Platonized Aristotle." According to this, one cannot speak of Maximus as *either* Aristotelian *or* Platonic, his education must have incorporated both philosophers, while "Aeon" as a notion in Maximus' work seems to have originated from Plato's *Timaeus*, among other influences. However, the *language* that Maximus uses, his way of articulating philosophical thought, is clearly primarily Aristotelian in nature. One can draw much more fruitful conclusions by approaching Maximus' understanding of time as a continuation and—most importantly—radical renewal of Aristotle's understanding and definition, while at the same time examining Plato's passages concerning the Aeon (cf. *Timaeus* 37, especially 37d).

2. Betsakos, Στάσις Ἀεικίνητος.

unique understanding of this pillar of ontology and cosmology that is time and temporality. Maximus is not merely influenced by Aristotle, but neither does he resume the Stagirite's philosophy or try to fit the Christian world-view into Aristotle's system. Even identical terminologies do not necessarily signify identical worldviews. Maximus' use of Aristotelian philosophy as *the language of philosophical thinking and expression*, as a potent tool to formu-late and express a radically different ontology from that of Aristotle's, leads us to examine his understanding of time, Aeon, and temporality in relation to Aristotle's theory of time. A philological and historical approach to these subjects would require that we also take into account other influences on Maximus, such as Plato and his notion of time and *Aeon* (αἰών) in *Timaeus*, or earlier notions of time in general. However, it is my conviction, as will be expounded in the relevant chapters, that Maximus consciously draws a parallel to Aristotle's theory of time in particular in his definitions and for-mulations concerning temporality. If that is the case, a comparison between Aristotle and Maximus rather than between Plato and Maximus would lead to a fuller hermeneutical efflorescence concerning Maximus' ontology, if one is to study this subject philosophically, rather than merely historically. Before proceeding to the examination of Maximus' hermeneutic approach to temporality, I will attempt to introduce the reader to his thought to his ontology, cosmology, and anthropology by referring to representative themes thereof, like his ontological λόγοι doctrine, his theory of motion, or the question of the body/soul relationship in the human person.

Aristotle was not the only major influence on Maximus. The Ar-eopagite writings[3] are crucial in understanding the Confessor, and a large part of his works is dedicated to explaining them (which also means: in

---

3. The fifth/sixth century author(s) of the *Corpus Areopagiticum* wrote under the pseudonym of Dionysius the Areopagite, the Athenian convert of St. Paul mentioned in Acts 17:34 and Athens' first bishop in the first century. His exact identity is still unknown, despite numerous hypotheses. The false attribution was not revealed until many centuries later, and one can safely suppose that his commentators, Maximus the Confessor and John of Scythopolis, as well as the most of the undivided Christian church, thought that the *Corpus Areopagiticum* was indeed Dionysius' work (despite the documented suspicions concerning the lack of citations in earlier church fathers). However, the *Corpus Areopagiticum'* unknown author has been elevated to the status of one of the most important church fathers due to the brilliance of the writings them-selves. (One's writings can never be the sole criterion for such an exalted status in the church, but this is the matter of another discussion.) Today, researchers refer to the author of the Areopagite corpus as "Pseudo-Dionysius the Areopagite" or "Pseudo-Denys" in their works. In my study, I will prefer the impersonal phrase "the Areopagite corpus" to refer to the *Corpus Areopagiticum* and its unknown author. (For a short introduction to the Areopagite corpus, consult Louth's *Origins of the Christian Mystical Tradition*, 154–73, and his *Denys the Areopagite*.)

dispelling accusations of "too much Neoplatonism" in them and in helping to incorporate them—or to keep them incorporated—in the tradition of the church fathers recognized by the undivided Christian church).

Part of this study's hypothesis is that Maximus' notions of time (χρόνος) and the *Aeon* (αἰών) play a crucial part in his teaching on deification (θέωσις), and that the seemingly contradictory concept of *ever-moving repose* (στάσις ἀεικίνητος) and *stationary movement* (στάσιμος ταυτοκινησία)[4] is a key concept for understanding θέωσις. Apart from examining Maximus' perspective on time as an attribute, a quality of the *cosmos*, I will also approach it as a key component of his anthropology, or rather his *ontological anthropology*, i.e., the participation of man in an event of primarily ontological importance, θέωσις—which, together with his eschatology, permeates the totality of his thought in a definitive manner. As such, deification becomes a key concept in expounding Maximus' thought on a number of subjects that may seem unrelated with this doctrine in particular.

Apart from Aristotle's theory of time and the Areopagite corpus itself, I will not focus on tracing the *influences* on Maximus' thought, but on implementing my hermeneutic tools in order to understand Maximus' ontology. I will examine Maximus' work from a philosophical standpoint, recognizing not merely the annotation of a given *doctrine* in his work, but an *original synthesis*, a philosophical interpretation of the nature of creation, existence, reality, being and becoming, meaning, cause, and purpose; an *ontology*.

As has already been said, a considerable aid in approaching Maximus' ecclesial language as a philosophical theory and an instrument for the realization of this undertaking will be the philosopher Christos Yannaras'[5] (but also John Zizioulas'[6] and Nicholas Loudovikos'[7]) work in philosophy and theology respectively, who undertook a task similar to that of Maximus,'

---

4. Maximus the Confessor, *Q. Thal. II*, 65.544–46.

5. I will use a great part of Yannaras' work, but will primarily rely on the approach expounded in his greatest work, *Person and Eros*. As my study will be saturated by the perspective found therein while focusing on Maximus' work, I will attempt to keep my explicit references to this monograph at a minimum, in order to minimize the reader's distraction. However, it must be clear that the basis of my *approach* to Maximus and the patristic thought in general is to be traced in *Person and Eros*. My illustration of *apophaticism* will also rely on Yannaras' monograph entitled *On the Absence and Unknowability of God*. His general philosophical approach will be studied through *Relational Ontology* and *Propositions for a Critical Ontology* (in Greek, Προτάσεις κριτικῆς ὀντολογίας).

6. I will rely on Zizioulas' *Being as Communion* and *Communion and Otherness*.

7. Loudovikos, *Eucharistic Ontology*, but also his recently (2016) published *Church in the Making*.

namely to express the testimony of the church fathers and of the ecclesial body in a consistently philosophical language. It is no coincidence their work draws heavily on Maximus the Confessor among the church fathers, and I maintain that their focus on Maximus played an important role in the kindling of the recent scholarly interest on Maximus, among other factors. As a consequence, the *perspective* of this study will be the *perspective* of a critical and relational ontology, of Yannaras' contribution to philosophy. In this work, I will implement Yannaras' approach more extensively than any other's in philosophy and Maximian scholarship. As such, this study is not only about Maximus the Confessor, but also about Christos Yannaras' philosophical approach.

This study is divided in two parts. In the first part, I introduce the reader to the framework of my contemporary reading, Christos Yannaras' philosophy, as well as to themes in Maximus' thought. This includes an introductory exposition of the Confessor's ontology and the importance of the created/uncreated distinction in it, as well as of elements of his philosophical anthropology. I examine key terms such as apophaticism, substance, hypostasis, otherness, and so on. The second part is concluded with an examination of Maximus' doctrine of the λόγοι, a key concept in his ontology and a prerequisite for approaching my main research question.

The second part of this study is dedicated to motion and temporality. First I introduce the reader to the Aristotelian theory of motion and time, in order to proceed to Maximus' radical innovation thereof. I examine Maximus' understanding of motion as either a motion according to nature (κατὰ φύσιν), a *returning* motion, or a deviation thereof. Subsequently, I examine the motion and motionlessness of the uncreated according to Maximus, as well as the world as the outcome of a perpetual creative motion and repose (στάσις) as the goal of the *returning* motion. In understanding Maximus' conception of time as χρόνος, we see that he speaks of the unity of spatiality and temporality in the sensible world, a kind of spatiotemporal continuum; as a consequence, spatiality and temporality are examined together on the basis of a number of passages from his *Ambigua*. Furthermore, and drawing from a number of Maximian primary sources, I proceed to the examination of the Confessor's *second* mode of temporality apart from time (χρόνος), *the Aeon* (αἰών), a "time without movement" and the temporality of the intelligible—but not quite what we today understand with the concept of eternity. After an examination of the notion of καιρός, I proceed to Maximus' *third* mode of temporality, the radical transformation of temporality and motion in the ever-moving repose (στάσις ἀεικίνητος) of deification. I expound Maximus' understanding of temporality in deification through the λόγος-τρόπος distinction and the notion of the *eighth day*.

With these three distinct modes of temporality, χρόνος, αἰὼν, and στάσις ἀεικίνητος, a unique Maximian theory of time can be reconstructed. In this, time is not merely measuring ontological motion, but rather a *relationship*, the consummation of which effects the transformation of time into a dimensionless present devoid of temporal, spatial and generally ontological *distance*—thereby manifesting a perfect communion-in-otherness. This Maximian understanding of temporality is far from being commonplace among his contemporaries (or Christian philosophy in general) and, in my opinion, demands more attention than it has received—both in the context of the history of philosophy and in today's ontological enquiry concerning the question of time.

PART I

Introducing Maximus the Confessor
—and Our Contemporary Perspective

CHAPTER ONE

Maximus the Confessor

Maximus' Life

THE PRESENCE OF MAXIMUS the Confessor in the history of the Christian church and of the Eastern Roman (Byzantine) Empire, and as such in the overall history of ideas, is truly unique. Living the life of a simple monk (not merely without the episcopal powers of a bishop or a prominent rank in the church, but probably even without the priesthood) and facing rejection, persecution, exile, and martyrdom, his name was restored in the consciousness of the empire and the doctrine of the church only after his death, and he changed both empire and church for ever. And now, at the dawn of the twenty-first century, his work and history are receiving an explosion of interest from scholars.

Currently, there is a heated scholarly debate concerning the details of Maximus' early life, and the state of the question is quite controversial[1]—as such, I will not enter into details. A tenth-century hagiographic Greek *Vita* (PG90, 58–109) and a seventh-century slanderous Syriac document (see Brock, "An Early Syriac Life," written by a certain George of Reshaina, a Monothelite and enemy of Maximus, and bearing the pronounced title "The history concerning the wicked Maximus of Palestine who blasphemed against his Creator, and whose tongue was cut out") are, among other lesser material, the main—and contradictory—sources on the Confessor's life. While it is true that currently, and in a rapidly changing and evolving scholarship, the pendulum swings more to the slanderous and earlier

---

1. Concerning latest scholarship on the subject, a timeline marking the main events of Maximus' life is offered in Allen, "Life and Times of Maximus," which strongly favors Maximus' alleged Palestinian origin as illustrated in the Syriac life (while Louth, in his recent "Maximus the Confessor," 250, claims that this part of the Syriac document is not to be trusted).

Syriac life (as Sebastian Brock has entitled this document, which is by no means a proper *vita*) rather than the later hagiographic Greek life, one can be rightly concerned with the relative enthusiasm with which the Syriac life is embraced, due to it allegedly providing solutions to problems that the Greek life cannot resolve. The Syriac document has its own considerable problems, paradoxes, contradictions, and inconsistencies, which may not merit a wholly unreserved enthusiasm for its basic premises[2]—the same, though, is true of the later Greek *Vita*.[3]

Maximus seems to have been born in 580 AD, either in Constantinople[4] or in Palestine. It is quite probable Maximus had studied the works of Plato and Aristotle in the course of his education, as well as the works of their commentators, either in the original or through Christian sources like, for example, *florilegia*. His extensive knowledge of Aristotle's works (in the form in which they were delivered to the society of Constantinople) and the profound influence that they exerted on him in articulating his philosophical and theological *language* is evident in his later works, as we will see, and decisively shaped the way in which he would raise and answer questions and attempt hermeneutic approaches concerning the universe, philosophy, and his ecclesial faith. While he was a monk—in a number of different monastic establishments; his life was one of extensive travelling—he gradually developed an intense anti-heresy activity, against Monoenergism at first

2. For example, in *Questiones et dubia* II, 8 (166–67 in CCSG 10, and 155 in Prassas' *Questions and Doubts* translation), Maximus seems to have no clue about the location of the Jordan river and must depend on other witnesses' accounts concerning it, which is inconceivable had he lived in Palestine, if we are to follow the Syriac life—I owe this observation to Vladimir Cvetkovic and Dionysios Skliris, who pointed out to me Bishop Atanasije Jevtic's repeated references to the passage. In the same book, the authorship of which has not been disputed, Maximus claims to know only secondhand about a shrine outside of Jerusalem, something which, among many other factors, raises doubts concerning the Syriac life.

3. This has considerable problems as well. As Andrew Louth puts it, "Michael [Exaboulites] pieced this Life together from diverse materials, and that, for Maximus' early years, he simply paraphrased the beginning of the Life of the eighth-century reformer of the Stoudios monastery, St. Theodore the Studite, omitting the proper names, from which we can infer that he had no direct evidence at all. The evidence about his service under the Emperor Heraclius is, however, more secure, since it appears to be dependent on earlier material and has some independent attestation" (Louth, *Maximus the Confessor*, 4). Andrew Louth has mentioned to me that Maximus' reference to his lack of even rhetorical learning in his preface to the Mystagogia is obviously a modesty *topos*, but not to be ignored because of that, I know no convincing evidence that Maximus' philosophical learning was not drawn from Christian sources (e.g., *florilegia*, etc.). His Greek style would confirm his professed lack of rhetorical training.

4. His subsequent familiarity with figures in the emperor's court indicates this as well.

and subsequently against Monothelitism.[5] His struggle against the heresies of Monothelitism and Monoenergism would last throughout his life and would be the cause of his exile and martyrdom,[6] while it would also be his primary contribution to the ecclesiastical history of the undivided Christian church.

The Fourth Ecumenical Council, the Council of Chalcedon in 451 had pronounced the "Chalcedonian Definition," the doctrine according to which Jesus Christ has a complete human nature/substance and a complete divine nature/substance (οὐσία/φύσις) realized in one single person/hypostasis (πρόσωπον/ὑπόστασις). According to this terminology, hypostasis (the person) is the specific, actually existing realization of the substance (i.e., nature), and in this case the singular person of Christ is the realization of his two natures. The Council of Chalcedon condemned Monophysitism (Miaphysitism), the notion of a single nature in Christ, either his divine nature or a synthesis of divine and human nature respectively, as heretical.

Large populations of Monophysites resided in the eastern boundaries of the Empire, and a new Christological dispute had begun to shake the Empire, different from Monophysitism as such. In an effort to bridge the Chalcedonian faith with Monophysite Christology, a new formulation started to surface according to which, whereas Christ's person realizes two natures, his will (θέλησις) and his activity (ἐνέργεια/"energy") are singular: Christ's person does not possess two wills and activities, a divine and a human one.[7] This dogmatic formulation was also attractive to the political leadership of the empire, since it offered the possibility to affiliate parts of the Monophysite populations or the populations with a "Monophysite substrate," thereby reducing the doctrinal and, as such, political friction within the Empire. Maximus would gradually recognize in these Monothelite and Monoenergist formulations a crucial distortion of his faith, of the ecclesial body's testimony and experience concerning the hypostasis of Christ, a confutation and annihilation of the Chalcedonian Definition "in the small print," an indirect enforcement of Monophysite Christology.

The patriarch of Constantinople, Sergius I (610–38), introduced Monoenergism officially in an attempt to support Emperor Heraclius in his war against the Persians and in his political decision to promote the union between the two sides of the doctrinal dispute. Sergius promoted the

---

5. Monothelitism: the doctrine that Jesus Christ possesses one will rather than two, a divine and a human will. Monoenergism: the doctrine that Jesus Christ possesses one activity (ἐνέργεια/energy) rather than two, a divine and a human activity.

6. See Thunberg, *Microcosm and Mediator*, 5.

7. A lucid exposition of these theological controversies is to be found in Louth, *Maximus the Confessor*, 7–15.

position that Jesus Christ had two natures, one divine and one human, but one activity (ἐνέργεια) which is to be ascribed to his singular hypostasis. This position could satisfy the moderate Anti-Chalcedonians, which in turn could lead to their union with the Orthodox Catholic Church, a burning political challenge of the time. In 633 in Alexandria the restoration of the communion between the Orthodox and the anti-Chalcedonians, their unification, took place.

Patriarch Sergius issued the *Psephos* (Ψῆφος), a text confirmed by the synod of Constantinople,[8] which prohibited any further discussion on Christ's one or two activities and the adoption of a language that attributes two activities to Christ.[9] Maximus did not express any objections at that point, but agreed cheerfully to the termination of a dispute that was the cause of much uproar in the life of the church.[10] When Sophronius was enthroned as patriarch of Jerusalem in 634, he sent, as was customary, an encyclical with his profession of orthodoxy addressed to all the patriarchs in which, without explicitly attributing two activities to the Christ's hypostasis, he essentially professed his Dyothelite faith and his serious objections to the Monoenergist stance towards Christology.[11] The friction concerning the one or two activities of Christ continued to be evident, and after Sophronius' death in 638 Emperor Heraclius issued an imperial decree, his *Ecthesis* (Ἔκθεσις), which is essentially an extension and repetition of Sergius' *Psephos* under imperial auspices.[12] Heraclius' *Ecthesis* explicitly prohibits any discussion concerning Christ's one or two activities while, instead of proclaiming one activity in Christ, one will is proclaimed (Monothelitism). The Ecthesis was supported by all five patriarchs (Pentarchy) of the time: Honorius of Rome, Sergius of Constantinople, Cyrus of Alexandria, Macedonius of Antioch, and Sergius, the new patriarch of Jerusalem. Sergius of Constantinople convened a synod to ecclesiastically validate the *Ecthesis* in the same year, while his successor and continuator, patriarch Pyrrhus (638–41, 654) repeated the same procedure soon after his enthronement.[13]

Maximus emerged as a strong opponent of the monothelite position. In 645, a public debate was organized in Carthage under the auspices of exarch Gregory between Maximus and Pyrrhus—the now-deposed, former

---

8. Hovorun, *Will, Action, and Freedom,* 70.

9. Sherwood, *An Annotated Date-list,* 11.

10. Hovorun, *Will, Action, and Freedom,* 76.

11. Ibid., 71.

12. Sherwood, *An Annotated Date-list,* 13.

13. Hovorun, *Will, Action, and Freedom,* 73–74.

patriarch of Constantinople—concerning the one or two wills of Christ.[14] Pyrrhus officially declared he was convinced by Maximus and renounced Monothelitism.[15] Maximus traveled in 646 to Rome, possibly together with Pyrrhus (who returned to his earlier beliefs next year, becoming a Monothelite again), in recourse to the Pope as the guarantor of orthodoxy in the church. He stayed for a number of years in Rome and played a key role in the realization and organization of the Lateran Council, which was convened by Pope Martin I in 649 and which condemned Monothelitism, with the Pope arising as a defender, protector, and guarantor of orthodoxy and Dyothelitism.[16]

The actions of Pope Martin and Maximus to counter Monothelitism were perceived by the Monothelite Emperor of the Eastern Roman Empire Constans II as an attack against him and in 653 he ordered the arrest of Pope Martin and the monk Maximus in Rome. Pope Martin was exiled and died in 655 in the Chersonesus region of the Crimean Peninsula. Maximus was condemned to exile in Thrace's Bizya.[17] In this trial, mainly political accusations such as treason were used against him, he was not accused as a heretic. He was sentenced again in the year 568 in Constantinople, as a heretic this time, with the Emperor of New Rome–Constantinople and the Patriarch supporting Monothelitism. Maximus refused to accept the Monothelite doctrine and was therefore sent back to exile for four years. In 662 he faced trial for the third time, he confessed his Dyothelite faith again and he was again named a heretic. After the trial he was subjected to torture: according to written tradition, his right hand was amputated, so that he could not write letters and treatises, and his tongue was cut off, so that he could not confess and defend his faith.[18] Subsequently he was exiled to the Lazica of Pontus, where he took his last breath on 13 August 662, physically exhausted from old age, from the torture inflicted on him for his faith, and from the conditions of his exile. Thus, he was later proclaimed a martyr.[19] During the last years of his life he was, together with his two disciples, the first Anastasius and Anastasius the *apocrisarius*, virtually the only proponent of Christ's two wills in the vast Eastern Roman Empire, and therefore

14. Ibid., 78. The proceedings of the debate are included in the PG's works of Maximus. *D.Pyrrh.,* PG91 288–353.

15. Balthasar, *Cosmic Liturgy,* 79.

16. Ibid., 79.

17. Thunberg, *Microcosm and Mediator,* 6, Sherwood, *An Annotated Date-list,* 21.

18. Ibid., 22; Balthasar, *Cosmic Liturgy,* 80. See also §17 of the *Dispute at Bizya* in Allen and Neil, *Maximus the Confessor and his companions,* 118–19.

19. See also Savvidis, *Die Lehre von der Vergöttlichung,* 13. Thunberg uses the expression that Maximus "died a martyr's death while in exile."

the only person who would confess the two wills of Christ as orthodoxy and Monothelitism as heresy.[20]

Almost twenty years after Maximus's death, in 680/81, the Sixth Ecumenical Council was held in Constantinople (the Third Council of Constantinople) on the subject on Monothelitism, on the wills of Christ. The Council acknowledged Jesus Christ as having two activities (ἐνέργειαι) and two wills (divine and human) and condemned Monoenergism and Monothelitism: Maximus' theological position was proclaimed as the doctrine of the undivided Christian church. And while Maximus' theological heritage was fully vindicated, his name is not mentioned in the Council's proceedings, as he was up until then a subject of controversy.[21] However, he would be soon thereafter recognized as a saint, a confessor, and a church father. Maximus the Confessor is one of the last historical figures to be recognized as a father of the church from both today's Orthodox and Roman Catholic Churches.

Maximus' Works and their Reception

Maximus' voluminous work[22] is to a large extent comprised of individual letters or treatises addressed to a specific person, either in answer to questions or difficulties of a dogmatic and Christological nature or concerning the ascetic life. His purpose is to elucidate on important subjects, to clarify confusions, to give explanations concerning obscure biblical passages, to articulate his position on controversial issues. The context of his writing is almost always his communication with specific persons or his participation in a broader theological debate, seldom are they in the form of an autonomous treatise independent from a specific dialogue or debate. He is particularly fond of the *Centuries*, comments of an apothegmatic character on a particular subject presented in groups of a hundred, a common genre of his time.

While Maximus' texts and passages usually deal with a specific subject or constitute an answer to a specific question, his need for the presence of the conditions that can provide accuracy to his answers and support his theological positions leads him to adopt a personal language of a philosophical nature. As a consequence, the whole of his work composes a

20. See Louth, *Maximus the Confessor*, 16, "Resistance to Monothelitism was virtually reduced to one man, Maximus."

21. Ibid., 17.

22. A new date-list of Maximus' corpus has been recently published: see Jankowiak and Booth, "Updated Date-List."

philosophical interpretation of existence and reality based on his experience of the ecclesial event,[23] his testimony of it, his philosophical education, and his unique genius.

Maximus does not consider his work to be original; he does not assume to construct a *new*, original philosophical or theological synthesis. It is clear from his work that he perceives it as an analysis, annotation, clarification, and restatement of truths that have already been articulated, of his faith's tradition and of the fathers of the undivided church's first centuries. By doing exactly this, he is led to construct the most complete, most consistent, and more markedly philosophical synthesis of the whole of the patristic *Weltanschauung*, from the time of the Cappadocian fathers up to that of Gregory Palamas in the fourteenth century at the very least, in a torrent of originality. This is a common mind-set during the centuries of the Byzantine Empire and is not only to be encountered in theological literature, but also in art (see, for example, the fusion of repetition and originality in the realm of hagiography), etc. It produces originality without consciously aiming at it, but rather in the context of a restatement that strives to be as faithful to the original as possible.

According to tradition, after cutting the right hand and tongue of the persecuted and exiled Maximus so that he would not be able to defend his theological positions, both his hand and tongue were miraculously regenerated by the action of divine providence. The explosion of interest among scholars in Maximus' work and the relevant publishing activity that we witness today, in the twenty-first century, indicate that the spreading of Maximus the Confessor' written work through the world does indeed continue and that his voice is indeed still being heard, long after his torture and death. Tradition's account is thus proven, in a certain way, accurate.

Maximus the Confessor "has been the subject of extensive examination in our time";[24] the relevant bibliography is becoming almost unmanageable in comparison to earlier scholarship concerning him. However, this was not always the case. For many centuries, Maximus the Confessor was considered an important figure in the West mainly for the history of the development of church doctrine, because of his role in the Christological controversy of

23. "Ecclesial event" is a phrase that is often used by Yannaras, among others, to denote the Christian church not as a conviction system or an institution but as a fact of life and of Eucharistic communion, the testimony of which is the experience of those that participate in it. Yannaras explains that the ecclesial event, due to its very nature, cannot but be the opposite of religion. See *Against Religion*, and particularly 21–48, "The Ecclesial Event." I will prefer this term throughout this study.

24. Zizioulas, "Person and Nature," 85. See also Knežević, *Maximus the Confessor (580–662): Bibliography*.

Dyothelitism versus Monothelitism. At best, he was also considered as a figure uniting East and West due to his Eastern background combined with his strong relationship with Rome and the Papacy, and at the very best the importance and implications of his Christological conception of the will for the notion of the human will in general would be acknowledged. His *Scholia* on the Dionysian corpus would also attract attention, although these have now proven to derive mostly from John of Scythopolis, not from Maximus' hand. We can witness more engagement with Maximus' thought in the East, in Orthodox countries from Georgia[25] to Ukraine and Russia—with special mention of Epifanovich's pioneering work[26]—and Greece's *Philokalia*.

Starting from the middle of the twentieth century, this situation has changed radically, and now Maximus the Confessor is widely acknowledged as a comprehensive thinker that achieved a most fecund and profound re-capitulation of Christian and early Byzantine thought with wide-ranging implications and in its complete philosophical and theological scope. And if that small revolution started with Hans Urs von Balthasar's seminal book *Cosmic Liturgy* (*Kosmische Liturgie. Das Weltbild Maximus des Bekenners*, in 1941 and substantially revised in 1961) and continued with Polycarp Sherwood's *The Earlier Ambigua of Saint Maximus the Confessor and His Refutation of Origenism* (1955) and Lars Thunberg's *Microcosm and Media-tor: The Theological Anthropology of Maximus the Confessor* (1965) as im-portant milestones of an ever-unfolding scholarship, it has recently reached a new level of collective scholarly engagement, as recent years have seen an intense publishing activity concerning St. Maximus the Confessor, span-ning from journal articles and chapters to theses, monographs and collec-tive volumes,[27] as well as many recent international conferences, symposia, and workshops analyzing his thought in Helsinki, Oxford, Berlin, Belgrade, Tbilisi, and Athens, to name but the most important.[28] To cite an example

25. See Khoperia, "Georgian Tradition."

26. See Benevich, "Maximus' Heritage in Russia and Ukraine."

27. For example, Vasiljević, ed., *Knowing the Purpose of Creation through the Res-urrection*; Lévy et al., eds. *The Architecture of the Cosmos;* and Mitralexis et al., eds, *Maximus the Confessor as a European Philosopher.*

28. In recent years, conferences include the "International Conference on St. Maxi-mus the Confessor, The Architecture of the Cosmos," University of Helsinki and Studi-um Catholicum, Helsinki, 2–4 September 2013. "International Symposium on Saint Maximus the Confessor," University of Belgrade and Fordham University, Belgrade, 18–21 October 2012. "A Saint for East and West, The Thought of Maximus Confessor in Eastern and Western Christian Theology," XVI International Conference on Patristic Studies, University of Oxford, Oxford, 9–11 August 2011. "Simpozionul Internaţional, Teologie şi spiritualitate în gândirea Sfântului Maxim Mărturisitorului," Univer-sity of Craiova, Craiova, 17–18 September 2008. "Neoplatonism and St. Maximus the

of most recent publications on Maximus of a larger scale, 2015 saw the publication of *The Oxford Handbook of Maximus the Confessor*, both signalling the heightened interest in the Confessor's thought and initiating further engagement with his legacy.

A most interesting fact is that this explosion of interest took place without the existence of English translations of Maximus' arguably most important (and certainly most lengthy) books, namely the *Ambigua* ("On Difficulties in the Church Fathers") and *Ad Thalassium*. One can speak of a *French school* in Maximian scholarship, not so much because of a consensus among French scholars but because of the vivid interest in Maximus in the francophone world. Jean-Claude Larchet, Irénée Henri Dalmais,[29] Alain Riou,[30] Jean-Miguel Garrigues,[31] and others formed and continued a tradition of approaching Maximus as one of the most important fathers of the church, while advancing Maximian research as a whole. The beginnings should be traced in the Dominican monk Marie-Joseph Le Guillou's legacy:[32] his pupils' books on Maximus (Riou, Garrigues, Lethel, and Piret) all carry his preface. The subject of most of their work was to illustrate Maximus as a precursor to Thomas Aquinas. More recently Antoine Lévy, also a Dominican, has also compared Maximus the Confessor to Thomas Aquinas, although in a more elaborate and qualified way.[33] It is not coincidental that French translations of Maximus' above-mentioned most important works became available relatively recently, along with French translations of a number of Maximus' other works. However, the fact remains that the English-speaking world is now the main epicenter for

Confessor," Norwegian Institute at Athens, University of Liverpool and the Academy of Finland. Athens, 11–13 December 2008. "The 2nd International Theological Scientific Conference dedicated to St. Maximus the Confessor," St. Maximus the Confessor's International Theological Scientific Centre, Tbilisi, 9–15 October 2007, etc. Apart from these, in September 26–28, 2014 an international colloquium entitled "Maximus the Confessor as a European Philosopher" took place in Berlin. This multitude of conferences specifically dedicated to Maximus the Confessor is a new phenomenon, the last major conference before the new millennium was also the first one, the 1980 Fribourg Symposium ("Symposium sur Maxime le Confesseur," Fribourg, 2–5 September 1980). It is also interesting to note that the newly established (2010) Amsterdam Centre for Eastern Orthodox Theology, associated with the VU University of Amsterdam, is dedicated to Maximus, naming him the Father of Byzantine Theology (http,//www.aceot.nl/pages/sub/35476/_St_Maximos_the_Confessor.html, retrieved 7 April 2013).

29. Dalmais, *Théologie de l'église* and many individual articles.

30. Riou, *Le monde et l'Eglise selon Maxime le Confesseur*.

31. Garrigues, *Maxime le Confesseur*.

32. Le Guillou, *Le Christ et l'Église*.

33. Lévy, *Le Cree Et L'incree*.

Maximian scholarship—in spite of the fact that English translations of the Confessor's most important books were simply not available.

Consequently, books on Maximus were written by and for scholars that could read the original Greek text. A notable exception is Andrew Louth's *Maximus the Confessor,* published in Routledge's The Early Church Fathers series in the 1990s, which, apart from being a very good general introduction to Maximus by one of the pioneers in Maximian studies, contains valuable English translations of selected passages from the *Ambigua.* This was the first time some of the Confessor's most obscure *Ambigua* passages became available in English, and Louth's *Maximus the Confessor* has certainly played an important role in the dissemination and popularization of Maximus' thought. A number of anthologies containing translations of Maximian material, among them also passages from the *Ambigua,* have been published in the past; but no complete translation of the lengthy *Ambigua,* which covers about 400 columns in PG 91, appeared until 2014.

While critical editions of most of Maximus' works have been published, until recently there was neither a critical edition of the complete *Ambigua*[34] nor an English translation thereof. Thankfully, Fr. Maximos (Nicholas) Constas recently filled that gap.[35] Maximus the Confessor is notorious for his use of delicate philosophical distinctions leading to a difficult language that is open to more than one possible translations. Constas' translation is in my opinion a very good translation of Maximus' obscure text and syntax: clear and accessible, the translation pays attention to the subtle hues of Maximus' use of words and terminology and ends up with a text that is both close and faithful to the original as well as thoroughly readable—a combination that is not to be taken for granted in any attempt to translate a text such as the *Ambigua.* The approach employed in this translation is particularly useful for my endeavor,[36] for one could say that there are roughly two ways

---

34. We know that, from very early on, two collections of Difficulties have been treated as one book, the *Ambigua* or *Ambigorum liber.* However, there has been a debate as to whether the inclusion of these two distinct books (written at different periods of Maximus' life) in a "complete" *Ambigua* goes back to Maximus himself or is a later development, see Janssens's article "Does the combination of Maximus' *Ambigua ad Thomam* and *Ambigua ad Iohannem* go back to the Confessor himself?" as well as in his introduction to CCSG 48. Andrew Louth remarks that "this arrangement of the two collections appears to go back to Maximus himself, as in the first of the opuscula (645–6), he retracts an unfortunate monenergist phrase from what he calls "the seventh chapter of the Difficulties in the great Gregory" (Opusc. 1:33A, this is the reading of all the Greek manuscripts)" (Louth, *Maximus the Confessor,* 78).

35. Constas, *Maximos the Confessor: On Difficulties in the Church Fathers.*

36. I will, however, rely on both Constas' and Louth's translations, noting the source. If there is no such note, usually in shorter passages, then the translation is the author's.

of translating this text: the first would result from engaging with it as a difficult and very demanding (but also very rewarding) piece of philosophy and theology, the second would see it as a "spiritually useful" text, it would attempt to translate a Greek "religious text" into an English "religious text." Thankfully, Constas has taken the first route; his thorough immersion in Maximian theology (cosmology, ontology, anthropology) is of added value for the task I have undertaken.

While the foundations of modern Maximian studies were built by von Balthasar, Sherwood, Thunberg, and later Louth, this field has since then flourished extensively. The first major American study on Maximus the Confessor was Paul M. Blowers' *Exegesis and Spiritual Pedagogy in Maximus the Confessor* in 1991, in which Blowers examines the pedagogical and exegetical models used by the Confessor in his *Questions to Thalassius*. In the first decade of the new millennium, four monographs on Maximus the Confessor have been published by Oxford University Press' Early Christian Studies series. Demetrios Bathrellos' *The Byzantine Christ: Person, Nature, and Will in the Christology of Saint Maximus the Confessor* focuses on the Monothelite controversy and on Christ's human will; Adam G. Cooper raises in *The Body in St. Maximus the Confessor—Holy Flesh, Wholly Deified* the question of the body's state in deification; Melchisedec Törönen in his *Union and Distinction in the Thought of St. Maximus the Confessor* explores the titular subject with a philosophical perspective; and Torstein Tollefsen published *The Christocentric Cosmology of St. Maximus the Confessor*. It should be noted Tollefsen, today a Professor of Philosophy at the University of Oslo, considered his study on Maximus to be a philosophical one, submitted it in the University of Oslo's Faculty of Philosophy and maintains that Maximus' *Weltanschauung* is a purely cosmological one, albeit "Christocentrically" cosmological. As such, his monograph is of crucial importance in my attempt to approach Maximus as a *philosopher*. Tollefsen elaborated this philosophical approach in his later monograph *Activity and Participation in Late Antique and Early Christian Thought*, a study of Gregory of Nyssa, Dionysius the Areopagite, Maximus the Confessor, and Gregory Palamas, in which he highlights the philosophical importance of the notion of *activities* (ἐνέργειαι).

Before turning to studies that stand in proximity to my particular endeavor concerning temporality, I ought to mention Vasilios Karayiannis' exposition of the importance of the substance-activities (οὐσία-ἐνέργεια, commonly translated as essence-energies) distinction in Maximus' ontology in his *Maxime le confesseur: Essence et énergies de Dieu*; a distinction that is crucial for this study. Pascal Mueller-Jourdan's 2005 monograph *Typologie Spatio-Temporelle de l'Ecclesia Byzantine: La Mystagogie de*

Maxime le Confesseur examines space and time in the context of the liturgy as expounded by Maximus in his Μυσταγωγία. While this monograph isn't quite an exposition of Maximus' hermeneutic approach to time *per se* (due to its specific focus on liturgical spatio-temporality), it is certainly the work that stands nearest to my endeavor. Another doctoral thesis in close proximity to my study is Vasileios Betsakos' Στάσις Ἀεικίνητος, which approaches Maximus' theory of motion as a thorough and radical renewal of Aristotle's theory in an ecclesial context. An account of the Greek fathers' understanding of temporality in general and a comparison to theories of time developed in the Christian West (with a special mention of Augustine and Boethius) is to be found in David Bradshaw's article "Time and Eternity in the Greek Fathers."[37] Paul Plass has published a noteworthy article treating Maximus the Confessor's approach to transcendent time,[38] while Edward Epsen's article "Eternity Is a Present, Time Is Its Unwrapping"[39] makes a number of references to Maximus.

This is a merely indicative survey of secondary literature, and a number of most noteworthy Maximian scholars (like Georgi Kapriev,[40] Vladimir

37. Bradshaw mentions Maximus' contribution on pp. 346–52 and is one of the first to elaborate on it, providing illuminating comments. However, he has focused on the *Scholia* to the Dionysian corpus, and as a consequence I have been led in the present dedicated study of Maximus' understanding of temporality to partly (but substantially) different conclusions. For example, Bradshaw speaks of "eternity" and does not differentiate between the Aeon and the third mode of temporality in deification (the στάσις ἀεικίνητος), assuming on p. 351 that the Aeon is the "eternity" of deification as well (i.e., that the "seventh day" is identical to the "eighth day," etc.). However, as I hope to show, Maximus speaks of two substantially different "eternities," he starkly differentiates between the eternity of the Aeon, which "has had a beginning" and belongs to (intelligible) creation and the different eternity of the uncreated and of the participation in the uncreated, being beyond time and timelessness and beyond motion and fixity (which is the primary reason that I have avoided consistently translating any one of Maximus' terms as "eternity"). To understand Maximus' αἰὼν simply as eternity, as the etymological ἀεὶ ὢν ("the one that always is") can be misleading, due to the many different shades of meaning found in Maximus. However, I must note that, in general, Bradshaw's comparison between Western and Eastern Christian conceptions of temporality is a truly valuable one, underlining important but often neglected differences between the two.

38. Plass, "Transcendent Time in Maximus the Confessor." See also his article, "Transcendent Time and Eternity in Gregory of Nyssa," as well as his account of Maximus' στάσις ἀεικίνητος, "'Moving Rest' in Maximus the Confessor."

39. Apart from these, Andrew Louth had presented a paper entitled "Time and Space in Maximos the Confessor" at the "Neoplatonism and St. Maximus the Confessor" conference in 2008 in Athens, but this paper hasn't yet been published. It contains valuable remarks on διάστημα as distance, a notion that will play a key role in my analysis.

40. Georgi T. Kapriev's monograph *Philosophie in Byzanz* constitutes an interesting

Cvetkovic, Dionysios Skliris, and many others) have not been included for the sake of brevity. Maximian scholarship is currently in a state of extreme fecundity, and consequently even the most extensive survey of secondary literature would soon become obsolete—a fact in which the Maximian scholar can rejoice.

As I have already clarified I will not focus on extensively comparing Maximus to his late antique and Neoplatonic intellectual environment, opting for a contemporary reading instead.[41] However, the reader interested in this environment would do well to study Antonio Vargas' "Proclus and the Metaphysics of Time," which incorporates the latest scholarship concerning Neoplatonic conception(s) of temporality and Proclus in particular. In this, the reader will recognize themes and topics seemingly comparable with Maximus' ideas—even precursors to Maximus' "ever-moving repose." However, I hope to demonstrate the uniqueness of Maximus' contribution beyond this similarity in appearances and themes. What follows now is an exposition of the framework I will employ in my contemporary reading of Maximus—Christos Yannaras' philosophy and theology.

---

attempt to compose an overview of Byzantine philosophy through four major points of synthesis, namely Maximus the Confessor, John Damascene, Patriarch Photius of Constantinople, and Gregory Palamas. Maximus the Confessor has a fair share in it and the summary of his thought by Kapriev is an accurate and balanced one. Kapriev's understanding of *what Byzantine philosophy is* differs from his predecessors' in that it productively transcends the philosophy-theology divide, which, in the case of the Byzantine Empire, is an anachronistic construct imposed upon a society that thought, discussed, wrote, and acted in quite different terms, as Kapriev expounds. The reception of Byzantine philosophy through the philosophy-theology divide as it has been developed in Western Europe has effected an unbalanced focus on lesser Byzantine thinkers, which however had the advantage of not being "theologians." This tendency is gradually being corrected in academia, and the relevance of a given thinker to philosophical enquiry is becoming the criterion of what Byzantine philosophy is—as it should have been.

41. For all intents and purposes, the former comparison on questions concerning temporality has already been done by Mueller-Jourdan in his *Typologie Spatio-Temporelle*.

CHAPTER TWO

Hermeneutic Tools in Approaching Maximus: Christos Yannaras' Ontology

YANNARAS' CRITICAL AND RELATIONAL ontology can be approached as an ontology implicitly based on Maximus' vocabulary and thought, as well as on his elaboration of the λόγος-τρόπος distinction, which is crucial for understanding the Confessor. With the hermeneutic aid of Yannaras' ontological proposal, his "toolbox" as it were, which I will present in the following sections, I will attempt to expound Maximus' theory of time as an alternative *paradigm* for understanding temporality. In doing this, I hope to present Maximus the Confessor as a thinker who is not merely of historical/philological interest, but as a philosopher who has a relevance reaching far beyond late antiquity and into modern times.

Christos Yannaras as a Maximian Commentator

The "new era" in Greek theological and philosophical thought expressed through Christos Yannaras and John Zizioulas (continued by a new generation of Orthodox theologians like Nicholas Loudovikos) bears the mark of Maximus the Confessor's thought most distinctively. Christos Yannaras' work is both explicitly and implicitly in constant dialogue with Maximus the Confessor's writings, as can be clearly seen in his magnum opus *Person and Eros*,[1] the German edition of which bears a subtitle that describes it

---

1. As an example of Yannaras' dependence on Maximus' thought, see *Person and Eros*, 194–99. His exposition of the iconizing principle ("iconic disclosure") for the whole of patristic thought is almost entirely based on Maximus' formulations, with the exception of a quote from the Areopagite writings. Yannaras finds in Maximus a most skilful recapitulator of the whole of the Greek patristic tradition in a language and thought consistently rich in philosophical value and fertility, and it is in this mind-set

most abundantly: *A Comparison of the Ontology of the Greek Fathers and the Existential Philosophy of the West.*[2] Indeed, it is no coincidence that both Christos Yannaras' philosophy and John Zizioulas' theology are heavily influenced by the Confessor: with the exception of the Cappadocians, no other church father's thought is so densely present and so often mentioned in their books as is Maximus'.[3] One could maintain it is exactly Maximus' excellence in the philosophical recapitulation of Greek patristic thought up to his time and his aptness in formulating lucid definitions of most obscure and complicated notions that made this "new era" possible and gave a solid patristic grounding to it.[4] In that sense, and from a point of view focusing on the Christian theological side of Yannaras' work, one could read Yannaras and Zizioulas as a commentary on Maximus' work and an elucidation thereof, as has been recognized by many.[5]

For the purposes of this study, I will take the reverse route: instead of studying Maximus to understand Yannaras better, I will choose to study Yannaras in order to shed light on Maximus the Confessor's ontology, not as an artefact merely pertaining to the history of philosophy, to the "Museum of Philosophy," but as a proposed answer to the ontological problem and the question of philosophical cosmology.[6] The hermeneutic tools provided by the study of an ontology that is articulated in contemporary philosophical language while based on Maximus' thought itself (i.e., Yannaras' ontology)

that I am approaching Maximus as well.

2. Yannaras, *Person und Eros: eine Gegenüberstellung der Ontologie der griechischen Kirchenväter und der Existenzphilosophie des Westens.*

3. Cf. Russell, "Modern Greek Theologians and the Greek Fathers," 88: "Maximus was also one of the most philosophically informed of the church's ascetical teachers, who has contributed much to the expositions of relation and personhood by both Zizioulas and Yannaras."

4. In addressing the subject of patristic grounding, see Pui Him Ip's illuminating paper, "On the Patristic grounding of Yannaras' 'Prosopocentric Ontology', A Philosophical Argument," presented at the "Conference in Honour of Christos Yannaras, Philosophy, Theology, Culture," 2–5 September 2013, St. Edmund's Hall, Oxford; forthcoming.

5. Among others, see for Dionysios Skliris' paper, where he seems to have adopted a similar position, "The Use of the Term 'tropos' ('mode') by Christos Yannaras," presented at the "Conference in Honour of Christos Yannaras, Philosophy, Theology, Culture," 2–5 September 2013, St. Edmund's Hall, Oxford; forthcoming. There, Skliris attempts to shed light on Yannaras' use of the term "mode" through Maximus the Confessor's use of the same term, attesting the proximity of both philosophers' use of a certain terminology.

6. It is not the first time that such an approach is attempted at a scholarly level, as Kapsimalakou's above-mentioned thesis, "Ελευθερία καὶ ἀναγκαιότητα," follows the same path, attesting the historical-philological and methodological legitimacy of such an approach, apart from its purely philosophical value.

will give me the opportunity to engage with the Confessor's ontology not in the philological manner of the history of philosophy, but with the mind-set, method, and goals of systematic philosophy.

An Introduction to Christos Yannaras' Philosophy

Christos Yannaras, Professor Emeritus of Philosophy at the Panteion University of Social and Political Sciences in Athens, Greece, has written extensively on ontology, epistemology, ethics, theology, and politics. He is considered to be "Greece's greatest contemporary thinker" (Olivier Clément) and "one of the most significant Christian philosophers in Europe" (Rowan Williams),[7] whereas Andrew Louth describes him as "without doubt the most important living Greek Orthodox theologian,"[8] albeit being quite controversial in Greece. Until recently,[9] the English-speaking reader could unfortunately acquire only a fragmentary view of Yannaras' work, as most English translations of his works have only been published in the last few years. And a number of Yannaras' books, covering important aspects of his thought or crucial elaborations, have not been translated as yet (for example, *The Effable and the Ineffable: The Linguistic Limits of Metaphysics*[10] and *Propositions for a Critical Ontology*). Fortunately, Norman Russell's arduous work in translating the main bulk of Yannaras' work has brought a significant number of his monographs to print, including his magnum opus *Person and Eros* and his comprehensive overview of philosophy in *The Schism in Philosophy*.

A second difficulty for the English-speaking researcher relates to the fact that most European and American academics who have studied Yannaras' work to date have been theologians and have tended to focus on its theological aspects, considering him exclusively a theologian rather than a philosopher as well. This has not allowed for his work to be judged as a *philosophical* proposal, even in a strictly academic sense and classification.

For the above reasons, I consider it useful to attempt a summary of his work from a primarily philosophical point of view. A simple categorization would be to classify his main works according to the branches of philosophy

7. See Rowan Williams' endorsement on the back cover of Yannaras' Holy Cross Press translations.

8. In his introduction to Yannaras' *On the Absence and Unknowability of God*, 1.

9. This is still the case now, but when this introduction was first written to be published as Mitralexis, "Person, Eros, Critical Ontology" (on which it is based), fewer English translations of Yannaras' works had already been published (cf. my bibliography).

10. Yannaras, *Tὸ ῥητὸ καὶ τὸ ἄρρητο.*

to which they pertain. Thus, one may classify the works *Person and Eros, Relational Ontology, Propositions for a Critical Ontology,* et al. under ontology/metaphysics, the works *On the Absence and Unknowability of God: Heidegger and the Areopagite, The Effable and the Ineffable: The Linguistic Limits of Metaphysics* under epistemology, and finally *The Freedom of Morality* under ethics. Other notable contributions include treatises on social philosophy (*Rationality and Social Practice*),[11] political economy (*The Real and the Imaginary in Political Economy*),[12] the relation between contemporary physics and philosophy (*Postmodern Metaphysics*), philosophy of religion,[13] and the historical background of the clash of civilizations.[14]

Yet, Yannaras himself has provided us with a much better approach than such a categorization. In his latest book in Greek under the title *Six Philosophical Paintings*[15]—which I would describe as a "philosophical autobiography"—he introduces us to his thought in a manner that reflects the whole spectrum of his contribution to philosophy. I shall attempt to present such a prioritization here by primarily referring to that particular book as encapsulating Yannaras' most mature and recapitulatory thought, while considering other areas of his research—such as his political philosophy or his purely ecclesial writings—as a corollary of this main body of ideas.

Apophaticism as the Epistemological Stance of the Greek Tradition

To approach Yannaras' work we must first consider the importance and scope of the term "apophaticism" for him, which is exhaustively grounded in the Greek patristic corpus in both *On the Absence and Unknowability of God: Heidegger and the Areopagite* and *Person and Eros.* It is the Areopagite corpus and Maximus the Confessor's works that provide Yannaras with the primary sources of the most explicit elucidations of apophaticism in the patristic tradition.

The term "apophaticism" is usually understood as a method to speak about God in theology, as the "via negativa," that is to say by defining God not through the characteristics that God has, but through the characteristics that God *does not* have (*ineffable*, etc.). Yannaras, however, saw in apophaticism something immensely wider in importance, namely an epistemological

11. Yannaras, Ὀρθὸς λόγος.
12. Yannaras, Πραγματικὸ καὶ φαντασιῶδες.
13. Yannaras, *Against Religion.*
14. Yannaras, *Orthodoxy and the West.*
15. Yannaras, Ἕξι φιλοσοφικὲς ζωγραφιές.

tendency of the whole of the Hellenic/Greek civilization from the time of Heraclitus (with his famous quote, "for if we are in communion with each other, we are in truth, but if we exist privately, we are in error")[16] to that of Gregory Palamas. As an overall *stance* and *attitude* towards the question of the nature of knowledge and truth, towards epistemology, and not as a *theory* on epistemology, explicit formulations concerning this apophatic *stance* can only be found in fragmentary form in the corpus of Greek texts and seldom as a systematic exposition. As is almost always the case with the epistemological attitude of a civilization, this attitude cannot but be *implicit*, as it is taken for granted in the context of that civilization itself.

According to Yannaras, apophaticism is the stance towards the verification of knowledge that underlies every facet of this civilization and can be defined as "the refusal to exhaust truth in its formulations, the refusal to identify the understanding of the signifier with the knowledge of the signified."[17] Formulations of truth can only *refer* to the signified truth or knowledge, not exhaust it. By coming to know the formulations that refer to truth, one does not *know* truth—truth can only be lived, experienced, and as such it is not static. There is a gap of crucial cognitive importance between the signifier and its signified reality, as Maximus the Confessor asserts.[18]

In an apophatic epistemology, the individual cannot conceive truth individually as a finite formulation. Truth lies in the field of experience, and more specifically shared experience because "there is no relation that does not constitute an experience and there is no experience . . . not arising from a relation or establishing a relation. Moreover, relation is the foundational mode of the human logical subject: the way in which Man exists, knows, and is *known*."[19]

Truth can only be attained through shared experience, communed experience, life in communion, and cannot be confined in finite formulations.[20] This excludes the possibility of *a priori* truths, prescribed doctrines and axiomatic theories.[21] Yannaras writes: "Prerequisite and criterion for

---

16. Diels-Kranz, *Fragmente der Vorsokratiker*, Band I, 148, 28–30.

17. Yannaras, Ἔξι φιλοσοφικὲς ζωγραφιές, 32.

18. In speaking about truth, Maximus the Confessor stresses the need to understand—and apply—the difference between the signifiers (τῶν λεγομένων) and their signified realities (τὰ σημαινόμενα), or else confusion will emerge, *D. Pyrrh.*, PG91 292BC: δεῖ, τὸν περὶ ἀληθείας λόγον ποιούμενον διαστέλλεσθαι τῶν λεγομένων τὰ σημαινόμενα, διὰ τὴν ἐκ τῆς ὁμωνυμίας πλάνην.

19. Ἔξι φιλοσοφικὲς ζωγραφιές, σ. 58.

20. Yannaras often reminds us Democritus' example about the "bitter honey," Diels-Kranz, II, 119, 22–26.

21. Ἔξι φιλοσοφικὲς ζωγραφιές, 26.

critical thinking (that is, thinking that strives to discern right from wrong, truth from falsehood) was the communal verification of knowledge."[22] According to him, "communed experience and not the accuracy of the individual's intellectual faculty verifies knowledge, even if proper communion of experience presupposes the accuracy of intellectual faculties."[23] The signifiers allow us "to share our common reference to reality and experience, but cannot replace the cognitive experience itself. This obvious difference can only then be understood when the criterion of the critical function is the communal verification of knowledge."[24]

I must here note that Yannaras' apophatic epistemology and the usual understanding of apophaticism (in the context of the study of religion and theology) as the *via negativa* that banishes knowledge to the realm of mysticism are not merely different, but can be seen as polar opposites of each other. The cataphatic approach (either to the understanding of God in theology or of *anything else* in general) would be to attribute characteristics to something and attest that these characteristics truly reflect the nature of their object or phenomenon. *Via negativa* is the choice of negative attributes or of non-attributes in our attempt to encircle reality and knowledge with our intellect. The *via negativa* consists in the attempt to progressively claim the knowledge of an object or phenomenon by *rejecting* certain characteristics or attributes, by defining it in terms of what it is *not*, in order to arrive at a closer intellectual understanding that excludes certain errors and misconceptions. In this context, true knowledge—and above all transcendental knowledge—can only be achieved in the realm of radical subjectivity, in the realm of "mysticism," without any possibility of sharing it effectively through language and without any vital reference to the community that would exclude the transmutation of radical subjectivity into radical individualism. However, apophatic epistemology, i.e., the refusal to exhaust truth in its formulations and the refusal to identify the understanding of the signifier with the knowledge of its signified reality, lies beyond this polarization between cataphaticism and *via negativa* and beyond a choice of negations rather than affirmations: it is based on the symbolic character of every epistemic expression. Apophaticism sees language as *referring to* truth and reality, *signifying* reality and *iconizing* it,[25] while not exhausting it. It is not *negation*, but the *signifying/semantic function* that characterizes the relationship between language and reality. As such, language is not an obstacle

22. Ibid., 25.
23. Ibid., 25.
24. Ibid., 27.
25. On the iconizing function, cf. Yannaras, *Person and Eros*, 184–87.

hindering us from achieving an individualistic "mystical" knowledge, but a medium to share, to commune knowledge and truth, and an attempt at a communal participation to it. This elevates the communal verification of knowledge to a criterion of knowledge itself.

So, whereas the *via negativa* is usually understood as *anti-realism*, apophaticism for Yannaras is the prerequisite for realism and realism is the goal of apophaticism. Or rather realism is the *stance and attitude* that is guaranteed by a consistent apophaticism.

Knowledge emerges from participating in experience, not from the understanding of a linguistic formulation. "And the experience is not exhausted in what is affirmed by the senses," writes Yannaras. "Nor is it simply an intellectual fact—a coincidence of meaning with the object of thought. Nor is it even an escape into a nebulous 'mysticism,' into individual existential 'experiences' beyond any social verification. By the word *experience* I mean here the totality of the multifaceted fact of *relation* of the subject with other subjects, as also the relation of the subject with the objective givens of the reality surrounding us."[26]

For Yannaras, every ontological system or statement presupposes and is based on the epistemology on which it is built, i.e., the criteria through which knowledge is considered as valid or invalid.

That is why, he remarks, "we conclude from history that common epistemology (incorporated in the everyday life of the people) and not common ontology constitute a common civilization, i.e., the otherness of common way of life: it is not the content we attribute to truth, but it is the way in which cognitive validity is confirmed that confers otherness in shaping public life, identity of civilization, and ensures the historical continuity of that cultural otherness."[27] Therefore, the criterion of the communal validation of knowledge is a crucial prerequisite for the understanding of the ancient Greek ontology and the early Christian ontology as well.

This apophatic epistemology, this communal epistemology, refers the possibility of "existence in truth" not in the individual level, but in the field of the relations between logical "othernesses," relations that manifest the "other" in these "othernesses." The most suitable term for the will-to-relate, not as a quality of the individual but as a way of being, a mode of existence, is ἔρως. "For Plato, the fullest knowledge is love, ἔρως: a relationship that attains freedom from all selfishness, that attains the offering of the self to the other."[28] If valid knowledge and truth can only be attained through a

---

26. Yannaras, *Person and Eros*, xiii–xiv.

27. Yannaras, Ἔξι φιλοσοφικὲς ζωγραφιές, 45.

28. Ibid., 26.

self-transcendent relation with existence, then the mode of truly existing is the transcendental relation, ἔρως according to the Greek language and the Platonic and Areopagite writings.

ἔρως and πρόσωπον: Eros and Person

With the word ἔρως, we are introduced to the first of the two elements that constitute Yannaras' ontology of the person (or more precisely, *prosopocentric ontology*, as it is termed in proposition 12.3.2 of *Relational Ontology*; I use this term in order to discern it from personalism),[29] the "person" (πρόσωπον) being the second.[30] "The replies given to the ontological question, as I have identified them in the particular philosophical tradition that I have studied, may be summarized under two basic terms: person and ἔρως," Yannaras writes. "In the Greek philosophical literature of the early Christian and medieval periods, the starting-point for approaching the fact of existence in itself is the reality of the *person*. And the mode of this approach which makes the person accessible to knowledge is ἔρως."[31]

Ἔρως here means exactly what it means for the Areopagite writings or for Maximus the Confessor, i.e., self-transcendence, the offering of the self

29. Cf. Zizioulas' distinction between personalism and the ontology of personhood (*prosopocentric ontology*) in his *One and Many*, 19–24. Zizioulas regards their comparison as a "superficial association in terminology" (p. 20), noting that no substantial similarities exist between these two approaches, as the term "person" bears a different semantic content in each case. As such, references to an "Orthodox personalism" remain unsubstantiated. I would say that Zizioulas' explanation is wholly applicable to Yannaras' works as well; the ontology of personhood (*prosopocentric ontology*) is not to be regarded as a stream of thought within (or parallel to) personalism in which the term "person" denotes an individual—instead of a being of relations and otherness.

30. After the publication of Yannaras' breakthrough studies on the importance of the notion of πρόσωπον for philosophy through patristic thought in 1970, Zizioulas' "Personhood and Being" (first published in 1977 in Greek and subsequently in English in *Being as Communion*, 27–65) offered a comprehensive analysis of the development, content, and importance of the term from ancient Greek philosophy to patristic thought and came to be recognized as a landmark publication on this ontological proposal in the English-speaking world. Confusingly enough, this contains a long footnote (in 44–46) downgrading Yannaras' 1970 dissertation, i.e., the very source of this prosopocentric understanding of theology and philosophy of which "Personhood and Being" is such a fine specimen, as wholly subjecting patristic thought to Heidegger's ontology, thereby alienating it from its source. In my opinion, the cited arguments bear little or no relevance to Yannaras' actual text, and Zizioulas' account of an ontology of personhood is in no way different from Yannaras'. In general, the attempt to find such substantial differences in Yannaras' and Zizioulas' thought, especially in theological matters, would be a true challenge.

31. Yannaras, *Person and Eros*, xiii.

to the other.³² If we define the subject merely as an individual, as ἄτομον, as an undifferentiated unit of a whole that cannot be further divided,³³ then by definition it cannot manifest ἔρως.

In this semantic frame, only the person (πρόσωπον) can manifest ἔρως, and πρόσωπον is a word with an absolutely unique semantic content. It is constituted of the words πρὸς (towards, with direction to) and ὢψ/ ὠπὸς (face, eye), so that it defines someone whose face looks at, or rather is directed towards, someone or something.³⁴ Someone who exists in-relation-to, only in relation and in reference to other beings, someone who refers his existence to the other, coming out of his existential individuality; someone who exists only by participating in relations and relationships.³⁵ So, πρόσωπον is not merely defined as reference and relation, but it defines a reference and relation itself.³⁶ This entails that personhood is the only possible relationship with beings, as beings are "things-set-opposite," ἀντι-κείμενα in Greek, Gegen-stände in German, etc. Being is manifested only in relation to the person, and as such beings emerge as phenomena, they appear/are disclosed in the horizon of personal relation.³⁷ Yannaras adds in a Heideggerian tone "beings are (εἶναι) only as phenomena, only insofar as they become accessible to a referential relation or disclosure. We cannot speak of the *being-in-itself* of beings; we can speak only of being-there or being present (παρ-εῖναι), of co-existence with the possibility of

---

32. Zizioulas makes an interesting remark that applies to Yannaras' approach as well, "For *eros* to be a true expression of otherness in a personal sense, it must be not simply *ekstatic* [sic] but also and above all *hypostatic*, it must be caused by the free movement of a particular being and have as its ultimate destination another particular being. This cannot be the case either in the [purely] sexual or in the 'platonic' form of *eros*. In the case of [purely] sexual *eros*, the erotic movement stems from the self and is dictated by the laws of nature. It is neither caused by the Other nor is it directed ultimately towards the Other. Equally, in the case of *eros* as presented by Plato, love is attracted irresistibly by the good and the beautiful; the concrete particular is used as a means to an end, and finally sacrificed for the sake of the idea" (Zizioulas, *Communion and Otherness*). Zizioulas previously mentions that "[Yannaras' exposition of the ecstatic character of eros in *Person and Eros* is] different from my own approach in many ways" (ibid., 70, fn. 160). Having studied both Yannaras and Zizioulas, I have failed to trace substantial differences in their approaches in regard to this particular subject. I could add that the very nature of *eros* as a whole is to be *hypostatic* and *personal* in character; a failure to be thus realized leaves *eros* as a mere *possibility* or *ability*, essentially deprived of its τέλος.

33. See Yannaras, Ἔξι φιλοσοφικὲς ζωγραφιές, 61.

34. Ibid., 63.

35. Ibid., 103.

36. Yannaras, *Person and Eros*, 5.

37. Ibid., 6.

their disclosure. We know beings as presence (παρ-ουσία), not as substance (οὐσία)."[38]

From early Christian times the word person, πρόσωπον, was very wisely identified with the word ὑπόστασις, meaning actual existence. "The fact that the identification of the terms person and hypostasis was originally used to logically clarify meta-physical references of the ecclesial experience does not restrict this identification from being used in the field of anthropology. However, a prerequisite for that would be to retain the communed experience of relations as the criterion of the formulations in language."[39] These pairs of terms, person/hypostasis (πρόσωπον/ὑπόστασις) and substance/nature (οὐσία/φύσις) were first defined and at some point agreed upon and elaborated (as there were many different schools of terminology before the Cappadocians) in relation to God and Christology. This, however, only reflects the way in which the philosophers and church fathers articulated their understanding of the world in language: these terms cannot be reserved exclusively for Christology, the terms reflect their approach to ontology as well.

Yannaras observes "self-transcendent love, ἔρως, was recognized in the philosophical language of the Christianized Hellenic and Byzantine civilization as the highest existential attainment (or fullness and causal principle) of freedom."[40] Freedom, because self-transcendence is really self-transcendence when the subject can be freed even from the necessities and prerequisites of his own substance (οὐσία). This can only happen if the hypostasis of the subject, the actual and specific manifestation of its substance, has an ontological priority over its substance and is not restricted to the constraintments and prerequisites of its substance.

According to the patristic corpus, the testimony of the ecclesial experience identifies such a priority in the case of God, a Trinity of persons/hypostases with common substance. It is being testified in the case of Jesus Christ, who transcends the necessities/prerequisites of his divine substance/nature ("logical" necessities of being outside the boundaries of time, space, the cycle of life and death) without losing it or impairing it by being incarnated as a human being, a crying baby in the manger, in a very specific time and place, and by dying on the cross. And he transcends the necessities/prerequisites of his acquired human substance/nature through the resurrection. Ecclesial experience testifies to man as being made "in the image of

---

38. Ibid., This first chapter of *Person and Eros* provides a thorough analysis of the signifier πρόσωπον and its implications for philosophy.

39. Yannaras, Ἕξι φιλοσοφικὲς ζωγραφιές, 104.

40. Ibid., 60.

God" and in the image of this triune existence-as-πρόσωπον, establishing man's capability to transcend by grace the necessities/prerequisites of his substance and nature through its hypostatic manifestation.[41]

With the coordinates of person, ἔρως, and otherness, Yannaras builds a "relational ontology." He states "otherness is realized and known in-rela-tion-to-the-other, always relationally. It is an outcome and an experience of relation and relationship. Through this perspective, we can speak (with logical consistency) of a relational ontology."[42] Relation and relationship is never granted or finite, but a dynamic event that is continually found or lost, a fact that can be traced in our human experience. Given the apophatic nature of the epistemology on which we base "propositions for an ontologi-cal interpretation of existence and reality that are subject to critical verifica-tion or refutation,"[43] Yannaras concludes a relational ontology can only be a "critical ontology."[44] He defines "critical ontology" as follows:

> We term onto-logy the theoretical investigation of existence (τὸν λόγον περὶ τοῦ ὄντος), the logical propositions for the interpretation of reality. We try, with our rational faculties, to interpret reality and existence as to the fact that it is real and that it exists. We try to interpret the meaning of existence, the cause and purpose of existence.
>
> With the word "critical" we term the process of evaluat-ing ontological propositions, evaluating the logical accuracy of these propositions on the grounds of κοινὸς λόγος (i.e., com-mon sense, word, rationality, language and understanding), evaluating the capability of the ontological propositions to be empirically verified through shared, communed experience accessible to all.[45]

Propositions of a critical ontology are never finite, granted, or "closed": they are always subject to communal verification or refutation, to the communal criterion of truth, due to the fact that there is no way of individually "secur-ing the truth" of said propositions.

According to Yannaras, every attempt to continue the philosophical tradition of the ancient Greek or Christianized Hellenic and Byzantine

41. See ibid., 74.

42. Ibid., 58.

43. Ibid., 54.

44. As such, I will use these terms interchangeably, as synonyms. However, to be precise, a relational ontology is the outcome of a consistently critical stance towards ontology.

45. Yannaras, Ἔξι φιλοσοφικὲς ζωγραφιές, 51.

civilization without the fundamental prerequisite of apophaticism is inherently dysfunctional. He writes "despite the post-roman West's boasting of inheriting and continuing the ancient Greek tradition of philosophy and science, the refutation of the fundamental characteristics of Hellenism, i.e., apophaticism and the communal criterion, leaves no room for the validity of such a claim."[46] Based on this, Yannaras argues that the reception of classical and Christian thought in the West was crucially undermined by the reversal of its epistemological preconditions and their replacement with epistemological criteria that are entirely based on the individual's capacity to think rationally (*facultas rationis*), a criterion that the West ascribes to the philosophical legacy of Aristotle.

I will come to the philosophical importance of the activities[47] (ἐνέργειαι) and their relation to the hypostatic manifestation of the substance in the following chapter. But I must stress here that Yannaras regards the activities as absolutely important for a coherent ontological terminology. He remarks "an ontology which (out of conviction or ignorance) denies to discern the substance/nature and the hypostasis from the activities of substance/nature, which are hypostatically manifested is condemned to an irreversible deficit of realism; it is trapped in the separation and dissociation of thinking (νοεῖν) and existence (εἶναι)."[48]

46. Ibid., 35.

47. I have chosen to translate ἐνέργειαι as "activities" throughout this study for a variety of reasons. The obvious translation of the patristic term ἐνέργεια as "energy" leads the English-speaking researcher to misunderstand its meaning, as the word loses its crucially important polysemy and it is often understood as some sort of "magical agent" (i.e., in the same way that some theologians understand χάρις, grace). For example, in the context of the Monothelite controversy, Maximus speaks of the two "energies" of Jesus Christ, but the meaning of this is better conveyed in English with the word "activities." Andrew Louth, Tollefsen, Melchisedek Törönen, and others have preferred "activities" over "energies" as the translation of "ἐνέργειαι," and I will here follow their example. However, the word "activity" has certain disadvantages of its own. For this reason and to prevent further misunderstanding due to the use of the improved translation of ἐνέργεια as activity, I will attempt to mention the Greek original word ἐνέργεια side by side with its translation as "activity" as often as possible in this book. However, I explicitly state that "activity" is still an incomplete translation of ἐνέργεια with inherent semantic problems and that we are still in search for a better translation.

48. Yannaras, Ἕξι φιλοσοφικὲς ζωγραφιές, 101.

Studying Yannaras' Philosophical Terminology
through His Critical (and Relational) Ontology

It is interesting to note *Propositions for a Critical Ontology*[49] is one of the few philosophical books by Yannaras that does not mention the church, the Trinity, the person of Christ, or the Eucharist *at all*—it seems to emphasize that "critical ontology" is meant as a *philosophical proposition* in the most strict sense, bearing no resemblance to what we term and categorize under "theology"—for it is certain that Yannaras does not believe in the exclusion of the ecclesial body's ontological testimony from the field of philosophy. One could perhaps try to explain this omission by saying that the book is also directed towards people who *do* believe in such a contrast between theology and philosophy, but I would have to disagree: *Propositions for a Critical Ontology* attempts to trace the *preconditions* for an ontological enquiry that would be free from philosophical dead ends and contradictions arising from traditions of thought that are, in Yannaras' view, characterized by arbitrary apriorisms and axiomatic certainties (which would be the case of not only, e.g., idealism or monism, but also of empiricism or materialism)—to "clear the ontological path," so to speak. His proposal for the *content*, not merely the preconditions, of an ontology freed from problematic starting points, of a truly *critical* ontology, is to be found in the book's sister volume published twenty years later, Yannaras' *Relational Ontology*—or, for that matter, in *Person and Eros*,[50] where the patristic literature is studied and employed much more extensively.

This later book, *Relational Ontology*, opens with a phrase from Ludwig Wittgenstein's *Vermischte Bemerkungen* (1930): "Every proposition that I write always means the whole, and is thus the same thing over and over again. It is as if they are only views of a single object seen from various angles."[51] The same could be said of *Propositions for a Critical Ontology*: Yannaras applies here certain very specific criteria to a multitude of categories (ontology, epistemology, even society) and arrives at an ontological proposition that calls for communal empirical verification and validation.

---

49. Yannaras, *Προτάσεις κριτικῆς ὀντολογίας*. A form of this introduction to Yannaras' critical and relational ontology will soon be published as Mitralexis, "Relation, Activity and Otherness."

50. Yannaras, *Person and Eros*.

51. The phrase is here taken from Yannaras' *Relational Ontology*, v. The Greek original, *Ὀντολογία τῆς σχέσης*, has been published in 2004 in Athens by Ikaros Publishing.

Preconditions for a Critical and Relational Ontology:
λόγος, Relation, Consciousness

According to Yannaras, we can name *critical ontology* the answer to the ontological question that is subject to critical evaluation and verification, subject to the principle of the falsifiability of knowledge (2nd proposition).[52] Answers to the ontological question can only then be subject to critical and empirical verification or refutation "if we affirm the cognitive access to the existential event as an experience of *relation*." "A *critical* ontology is possible, if we affirm the experience of the subject's consciousness of self as a starting point for the interpretation of the existential event" (7.3).

This experience of the self's consciousness of self is the only cognitive event that is truly, universally verified by all human persons—and "this experience is only constituted through *relation*, which means that the experience of relation and its *referential widening* (i.e., the communal verification of the relation) constitutes the prerequisite for the cognitive access to the existential event." Knowledge is the experiencing of relation, and the nexus of shared experiences validates and verifies knowledge (7.3). The criterion thereof is the communal verification of knowledge, which can never be finite or taken for granted. This verification is an "attainment" (κατόρθωμα), and by "attainment" I mean it is always open to a fuller, a more complete communal verification, excluding the possibility of certainties or apriorisms (2.1). Linguistic and semantic formulations "signify the experience of relation without being able to exhaust it, as a relation is actualized [ἐνεργεῖται] as the manifestation and unveiling of the subject's existential otherness" (2.11).

Consciousness of self is a prerequisite for this. The subject's consciousness, the consciousness of the fact that it exists, is the first and only certainty. The reality of consciousness precedes every assertion concerning reality (1.41). The existence of consciousness, of the self, can be the only constant of a critical epistemology and ontology, as it is a cognitive event that precedes any epistemological stance, method, or assertion, even a *critical* stance. Consciousness of the self, the consciousness of one's existence and otherness, cannot but be *the only certainty* of a critical ontology (1.42). However, this does not lead us to forms of solipsism, as it is the relation to other realities that reveals our consciousness of self.

---

52. For practical reasons, in this chapter I will not cite the book's pages in footnotes, but its propositions in brackets, which are hierarchically numbered statements in the style of Wittgenstein's *Tractatus*. An elaboration of each point I make can be found in the book's cited proposition, which is also the case with the quotes mentioned.

The semantic function, not only in its linguistic meaning, but in every relation of signifier and signified, is a cornerstone of the actuality of relations. The word Yannaras uses to denote all facets of the semantic function is the word λόγος, with all of its multiple meanings (and, sadly, any translation of the word in English would annihilate this polysemy). This use of λόγος is the manifestation of a signifier, which in turn signifies a presence. To be signified is to be manifested as a presence, and this referential function of λόγος turns it into the first precondition and manifestation of *relation*. A relation is *logical* as it pertains to λόγος (1.3). Each manifestation of something in the horizon of consciousness is a λόγος, a revealing of the other to the subject, to the subject's consciousness. It is a referential revealing; a relational revealing (1.31). For Yannaras, "λόγος is the subject's ability to *relate*, to manifest a perceptual relation to existence. The subject perceives existence as a revealing, as a manifestation which signifies the *otherness* of each phenomenon" (1.33).

I am not referring to abstract conceptions of relation. The physical impression constitutes a relation, as it functions as a signifier representing something for someone. The term we use for each and every semantic function is λόγος: it effects the distinction between the two constituents of the relation, and in doing so constitutes the relation (1.332).

To perceive a λόγος (whether visual or auditory, sensible or intelligible, etc.) and to experience a relation to and connection with something or someone is to become conscious of one's individuality, as one perceives the other part of the relation as an otherness. Consciousness of the self is the consciousness of a difference, of an otherness, which is revealed in the relation. But the *fact* of consciousness precedes this: the *event* of consciousness is the prerequisite for every relation, it is manifested through relation, but it precedes it, thus making it possible (1.341).

Yannaras maintains the word λόγος signifies every referential activity that manifests the subject's otherness. (A similar definition of λόγος that he often employs is that λόγος is the mode in which everything that *exists* is *manifested*, becomes *known*.[53]) In different contexts, λόγος can mean a word, a meaning, "an image, a sound, a visual representation, form, shape, a musical melody, a painting, etc. The polysemy of λόγος allows us to say that the mode in which λόγος informs us of the subject's otherness is the mode of λόγος (ὁ τρόπος τοῦ λόγου)—that the subject itself is actualized (ἐνεργεῖται) as λόγος." This would mean that λόγος is the *mode of relation*. "The *mode of relation* in the subject's ability to make the participation in its

---

53. Cf. Yannaras, Σχεδίασμα εἰσαγωγῆς, 20: "τὸν λόγο τοῦ κόσμου, τὸν *τρόπο* μὲ τὸν ὁποῖο ὅ,τι *εἶναι* γίνεται φανερό, *φαίνεται.*"

otherness possible, as well as the *mode of relation* in the subject's ability to participate in the activities that manifest the other subjects' othernesses" (6.13).

Ontological Categories: Substance, Particulars, Activities

What would be the meaning of *truth* in a critical ontology? The notion of truth as a static and finite formulation, either known or unknown, would surely be excluded, together with the notion of truth as stemming solely from the individual's rational faculty. For a critical ontology, truth is not an *object*, but an event in which we participate: truth is *the mode of reality*. For Yannaras, it is the fullness of the subject's participation in existence that is the criterion of truth (2.3). It is an empirical truth, the knowledge of which can never be finite and consists of the nurturing of the subject's relationship with reality. However, the subjective experience of the individual is not enough: the cognitive event of individual experience is to be validated inter-subjectively. The fullness of this communal verification is also a criterion of truth (2.31). For Yannaras, if truth is the mode of reality, then every true knowledge has a sound ontological starting point: he excludes the possibility of relativism or skepticism concerning the existence of truth itself (2.32).

It is in recognizing truth as the mode of reality and reality as manifested through relation that we are led to an anti-essentialist notion of substance (οὐσία). Yannaras traces in the Greek *word* οὐσία, in its etymological implications, a relational conception thereof. Stemming from the feminine participle of the verb *to be* (εἰμὶ—οὖσα),[54] it signifies the event of *participating in being*. It defines existence *as the mode of participating in being*, which is even more the case when the word οὐσία is used to specify a specific substance, the qualities that manifest something as different from something else. Something is different from something else (in this context, a stone from a horse, not this horse from that horse), because it has a different *mode of participating in being*, and this is what defines its substance. In this, the *substance* (οὐσία) is the *mode of participating in being*—the substance not as a *what*, but as a *how* (4.13).[55]

---

54. Cf. *Scholia in De Divinis Nominibus*, CD4.1 313C, "ἀπὸ γὰρ τοῦ εἶναι τὸ ὄνομα παρῆκται τῆς οὐσίας."

55. Yannaras also illustrates notions such as the body and soul as *modes* and not as *entities*, *modes* that are revealed and manifested as relations through the activities. To conceive of these sums of actualized relations in a perpetual becoming as *things*, as some sort of material or immaterial *objects*, would be a grave misunderstanding, he writes (2.372—3.1).

This understanding of substance (οὐσία) as the mode of existence dictates a corresponding understanding of a *particular existence*. Excluding an understanding of substance as an entity in itself, we have cognitive access to the substance only through its particular actualizations and manifestations—through the mode in which they are different, through the mode in which they manifest otherness. "Every particular actualization of the substance recapitulates the substance in its universality without exhausting it. A piece of stone embodies the universal truth of 'stone,' by coming to know this particular piece we come to know *what stone is*, but the reality of 'stone' is not limited to that particular piece. That piece of stone manifests the totality of the mode in which something is a stone, it manifests the *substance* (οὐσία) of stone. However, this mode has also other, possibly infinite, manifestations." We can only know the substance through its particular manifestations (4.131).

The Greek word for "mode" (τρόπος, from the verb τρέπω, i.e., to turn, to turn in a certain direction, to alter, to change) does also have a dynamic meaning: it presupposes action/activity (ἐνέργεια) and an actualized relation. Substance (οὐσία), *the mode of participating in being*, is an event of perpetual becoming (it is interesting to note the patristic identification of οὐσία with φύσις, nature, which stems from φύεσθαι, to grow, to become). And it is known to us through the subject's perceptive activity (ἐνέργεια). The substance as the mode of participating in being *is* and *is manifested* as a whole of activities and realized relations (4.133).[56]

The Activities (ἐνέργειαι) as a Primary Ontological Category

According to Yannaras, the activities (ἐνέργειαι) are to be ascribed to the substance, to the mode of existence—they constitute each hypostasis, each particular existence, and manifest its substance. For him, "the activities constitute an *ontological category*—the third ontological category together with the *substance* and the particular existence (καθέκαστον)," what one more commonly terms as the *hypostasis* (4.2).[57]

56. On a comparison with some of Maximus the Confessor's definitions, see *Opusc.*, PG91 149B, 152A, 260Df., *Car.*, 4.9.2–3, "Πᾶσα δὲ ἡ κτίσις σύνθετος ὑπάρχει ἐξ οὐσίας καὶ συμβεβηκότος."—"Every creature is a composite of substance and accident" (trans. Berthold).

57. On an account of the philosophical importance of the *activities* (ἐνέργειαι) in patristic thought and related matters, see also *Person and Eros*, 43–70 (in which ἐνέργειαι is rendered as *energies*). The reader would do well to consult this chapter in relation to Maximus' understanding of the activities as well.

The notion of *activities* (ἐνέργειαι) emerges as a key term in Yannaras' propositions for a critical ontology, a criterion for the existential realism of said propositions. For Yannaras, the *activities* are not just a "third term," an elucidation of previous terminology, but another way of perceiving and analyzing reality. By approaching the existential event through the relations of (a) substance and activities, (b) substance and the particular (the hypostasis), and (c) the particular and the activities, our terminology acquires the prerequisites for a realism that is not to be found in the common distinction of substance and hypostasis.[58] As Yannaras writes,

a. We acquire cognitive access to the *substance* through its *activities* as its common mode of participating in being, as the sameness of the particulars' nature.

b. We come to know each *particular*, each hypostasis, as a manifestation of its *substance*, while the substance itself is known through its particular existential realizations.

c. We come to know the *activities* as the *modes* that signify the *substance*, but also as the othernesses which constitute the particular as particular (4.21).

"The *substance* is distinct from both the activities *and* the particular, as it is *through the activities* that the substance's sameness of nature and the otherness of the particular is manifested, and as it is *through the particular* that the substance is recapitulated and manifested but not exhausted." To mention an example, *smiling, to smile*, or *laughing, to laugh*, is an activity of the human substance and nature, it is to be found in every human being, in every particular manifestation of "humanity."[59] But *each human person* manifests smiling or laughing, *smiles and laughs*, in a completely unique

58. As Maximus the Confessor is accounted with noting in Ἐξήγησις τῆς κινήσεως, *Documents from Exile* 62–63, "No being exists without natural activity.... It is impossible for any nature at all to exist or be recognized apart from its essential activity."—"οὐδὲν γὰρ τῶν ὄντων χωρὶς ἐνεργείας φυσικῆς ὑφέστηκεν . . . μήτε εἶναι μήτε γινώσκεσθαι χωρὶς τῆς οὐσιώδους αὐτῆς ἐνεργείας τὴν οἱανδήποτε φύσιν."

59. Note, in comparison, how Maximus the Confessor names various human activities in order to stress Jesus Christ's incarnation and his human nature in *Amb.Th.*, 5.85–92, "For the Λόγος beyond being came into the realm of being as human once and for all, and possessed as his own undiminished property, along with the things characteristic of human being, the movement of being which properly characterizes him as human. This was formally constituted by everything that he did [ἐνήργει φυσικῶς, which stems from ἐνέργεια] naturally as human, since indeed he truly became human, breathing, talking, walking, moving his hands, naturally making use of the senses for the apprehension of sensible realities, hungering, thirsting, eating, sleeping, growing weary, weeping, struggling" (trans. Lollar).

way, in a way that actualizes (not merely *reveals*, but *actualizes*) his substance as a hypostasis, in a way that *actualizes complete otherness*. The activities, being distinct from both the substance itself *and* the hypostasis itself, *belong to the substance but actualize the hypostasis*. The activities (ἐνέργειαι) are *hypostatically manifested activities of the substance* (4.211).

These *signifiers*, together with their signified realities, cannot function as apriorisms, as axiomatic statements and certainties, because their definitions emerge from their intertwined relations, relations that "signify the realized manifestation of the existential event." That is why the notion of activities as an ontological category is a precondition and a necessity for the articulation of a critical ontology, if it is to be truly critical (4.212).

It is the interference of the notion of *activities* that subjects this ontology to the critical (intersubjective and communal) validation or rejection of its empirical testimony. For it is the notion of *activities* that demonstrates the contradictory character of a perception of either the substance or of the particular as existences-in-themselves, thereby transcending ontological categories such as the *phenomena* or the *noumena,* materialism and idealism, etc. (4.213).

Otherness (ἑτερότητα) and Artistic Expression

The absolute otherness of each human person and its indeterminacy in language is not an abstract concept. Even the physical form of each particular person is impossible to be exhaustively described by language—and by physical form I am referring to "the way (τρόπος) in which [each person's] bodily otherness is actualized (ἐνεργεῖται)—from the fingerprints and the exact shape of the body to his gaze, his smile, his hand gestures." Even an exhaustive description of a person cannot but correspond to more than one human hypostases, as the function of each separate specification is to objectify the specified for it to be understood by more people—whereas shared, common experience affirms that each human being constitutes a whole of absolutely unique and unprecedented mental and physical activities and actualizations (ἐνέργειαι), "an absolute existential otherness" (6.11).

We come to *know* this otherness, we have cognitive access to it, but we cannot *define* it, exhaust its reality in formulations of language. And we come to know each otherness through the manifestation of its activities (ἐνέργειαι), of the mode in which they are actualized. To directly experience a personal otherness is to participate in the activities and actualizations (ἐνέργειαι) that manifest it, in the way in which this otherness becomes *known.* "And that is why the recognition of another subject's otherness is a *relational* event, a *relational experience*" (6.12). *Descriptions*, however exhaustive, cannot contain, manifest, or reveal a person's otherness. However, the participation (μετοχὴ-μέθεξη) in the λόγος of a person's creations can and does reveal it. A painting, a musical symphony, a poem, or a sculpture *can* and *do* reveal the otherness of their creators[60]—"only the creation's λόγος can 'signify' the reality of the subject, its otherness" (6.321).

It is in artistic creations we can more clearly discern this reality, but every act, creative activity, and creation (πρᾶγμα, πεπραγμένο) has the subject's otherness imprinted in it and is manifesting it—however evidently or subtly.[61] Human *action* is not merely contrasted to *theory*, but it manifests and preserves the personal otherness' λόγος, the personal otherness' reality. And as such, "every human action is a relational event, a communal event" (6.322). Yannaras mentions the example of man's ability to discern the otherness of the poet in his poetry, or of the musician in his music—to be able to recognize Baudelaire's poetry and to distinguish it from Eliot's poetry, to be able to recognize the otherness of Mozart in his music and to be able to discern it from Bach's music. The fact that man is led from the information gathered by the senses to the "empirical recognition of the otherness of the artist's creative λόγος is a cognitive event that is valid and true while annulling the 'objectivity' of perceptible information," as it cannot really be demonstrated scientifically or formulated linguistically in its fullness. It can be only experienced and never defined, only inadequately signified through language, science, or by other means. In the communal validation

60. Applied to creation and its relationship with its Creator, Maximus follows a similar train of thought in order to describe the path from contemplating the λόγοι of beings to knowing (the otherness of) God, their Creator, as follows, *Amb.Io.* 15, 1216AB, "Who, through the mediating power of λόγος, conducts the forms and figures perceived by the senses toward their manifold inner λόγοι, and concentrates the manifold diversity of the λόγοι that are in beings (discovered through the power of λόγος) into a uniform, simple, and undifferentiated intuition, in which that knowledge, which is called indivisible, nonquantitative, and unitary, consists—such a person, I say, through the medium of visible things and their good order, has acquired a true impression (as much as is humanly possible) of their Creator, sustainer, and originator, and has come to know God, not in His substance and subsistence (for this is impossible and beyond our grasp), but only with respect to the simple fact that He exists" (trans. Constas).

61. Cf. Maximus the Confessor's *Amb.Io.* 26, 1265D–1268B, "They say that among beings there exist two general kinds of activities. The first of these enables beings naturally to bring forth from themselves other beings identical in form and substance and absolutely identical to them. . . . The second kind of activity is said to produce things that are external to the essence, as when a person actively engages something extrinsic and substantially different, and from it produces something foreign to his own substance, having constructed it from some other source of already existing matter. They say that this kind of activity is a scientific characteristic of the arts" (trans. Constas).

of experience, experiences of different persons *do* overlap, but this does *not* constitute "objectivity," "as the affirmation of the difference between Bach's music and Mozart's music is not adequate to transmit the knowledge of this difference" (7.2201).[62]

Axiomatic Dichotomies and Problematic Ontologies

A critical ontology is an attempt to transcend philosophical apriorisms and dichotomies of the past, which were based on a lack of realism. Philosophical contemplation has at times identified the *abstract* with the *non-existent*, or the *abstract* with the *truly existing*. However, both theses overlook the fact that every abstract formulation functions as a signifier and every signifier constitutes a relation. This relation is an empirical reality in cases of both sensible signified realities and abstract/intelligible notions. For Yannaras, the question is not whether the signified is sensible or abstract/intelligible, but if the relation between the subject and the signified is genuine or false, real or imaginary—and this is to be verified communally, not individually, it is to be judged from the wholeness of relations (2.35). To equate the abstract with the non-existent or with the truly existing is to impose apriorisms and axiomatic certainties to reality, giving birth to dichotomies such as materialism and idealism, whereas the basis of a critical ontology would be the realism of relation (2.351).

In a critical ontology, both the reality of sensible and abstract/mental signifiers and manifestations are subject to intersubjective, communal experience, to the "cognitive widening" of experience (2.36). "Knowledge can neither be solely objective (independent of the subject) nor solely subjective (irrelevant of the object). The contradistinction of objectivity and subjectivity divorces and contrasts the object from the subject, it ceases to accept them as partners and constituents of a cognitive relation" (2.361).

---

62. Art, usually not a subject directly pertaining to ontology, gives me the opportunity to comment on ontology's relation to *society*. There are ontological preconditions, whether clearly articulated and widely known or not, behind each collective approach to the *meaning* of reality, each approach to organizing society, each choice in living collectively. A particular interpretation or reality, a particular ontological approach is to be discerned even in facets of life or in disciplines where one would not suspect the direct presence of ontology—perhaps due to the absence of articulated ontological reasoning (8.11). Yannaras discusses Karl Marx's insights on several occasions in his *Propositions for a Critical Ontology* (mostly in 6.2–6.613). In these pages, Yannaras not only demonstrates Marx's vital and radically new ideas concerning the core of Western philosophy's dead ends, but also the inner contradictions of Marx's own system—contradictions that pertain to its implied or explicit ontological basis.

It is not only philosophy as an isolated "discipline" that gives birth to the need for a critical ontology. Yannaras maintains that the profound changes in the scientific worldview during the twentieth century and up to the present cannot but change the way we see philosophy. Our perception of reality cannot be the same as the one offered to us by Newtonian physics, Euclidian geometry, and the Cartesian "cogito." Yannaras discerns in science's recent developments that our perception of reality as a sum of separate entities of a given structure cannot but be substituted with a perception of reality as a sum of relations and relationships that cannot be understood and explained in a singular and given way. "Relation emerges as both the *mode* of reality and the *mode* of *knowing* reality," of having cognitive access to it (4). In this it is *physics* that trace new paths for *metaphysics*.

For Yannaras, the sharp distinction between physics and metaphysics that is taken for granted and self-evident in mainstream philosophy seems to be the corollary of a specific understanding of λόγος as individual *ratio*, as *facultas rationis*. The cognitive access to reality is thus limited, as he analyses, to the formulations stemming from method, ideology, and proof, giving birth to dualisms such as matter and spirit, dualism and monism, physics and metaphysics, science and ontology (7–7.023). However, the antithetical distinction between physics and metaphysics (ontology) seems to exclude the possibility of a *critical* access to the ontological question, the possibility of a critical ontology. For this contradistinction to exist "every anti-thesis presupposes a definitive thesis, a thesis not subject to critical evaluation. In terms of the distinction between physics and metaphysics, the position (thesis) that is not critically examined and evaluated is the assumed axiom of either matter, or mind, or both. Because of that, the contrast between physics and metaphysics is always subjecting ontological reflection to the dogmatic apriorism of either dualism or monism" (7.1).

The focus of critical ontology on experience and consciousness does not lead to empiricism or mysticism. The experience of (self-)consciousness transcends the information gathered by the senses. Consciousness of the self "is not the only cognitive event that arises from experience without being limited to the information that is gathered by the senses." Yannaras maintains that "every relational experience, every experience of relation is a cognitive event which may arise from the information of the senses, but the relation as a cognitive event is not limited to this information" and transcends it (7.22).

Different Accesses to Reality:
A Personal Causal Principle and the Fullness of Participation

Every subject is participating in reality, the question is to what extent one participates in the fullness of reality.[63] Yannaras illustrates how a different stance towards reality produces seemingly equally valid conclusions in their inner logic, which are however radically different from one another. For example, while contemplating a painting by Van Gogh, a strict positivist would acknowledge the reality of it as a sum of canvas and oil paint. A different access to the reality of the painting would be to recognize the image it depicts. A third possibility would be to define the painting by its subjective aesthetic integrity, mastery of technique, etc. A fourth and different type of access to the reality of the painting would be "to recognize in the painting the visual λόγος of the person that created it, the otherness of the creative activity (ἐνέργεια) of this particular artist, whom we today have never met as a tangible presence, but the existential otherness of whom is 'defined' by the reality of his painting. Neither of these four interpretations is false concerning the description of the painting's reality, but the description and definition of reality differs according to the fullness of the subject's relation to it," which is actualized by the degree of the subject's participation in the observed reality (7.4101).[64]

Yannaras applies the same approach to the subject's perception of reality as a whole. There are approaches to reality as a whole that only recognize the constituents of reality, matter and energy, or even the beauty of the cosmos. However, another approach to accessing reality—an approach signified by the fullness of one's personal participation in the world, to reality as a whole—would be "to recognize in cosmic reality the otherness of a personal creative activity (ἐνέργεια), the 'bearer' of which we have never encountered as a sensible presence, but whose personal existence is signified by the world's reality." The fullness of one's personal participation in the aforementioned painting or to reality as a whole is that which distinguishes these different paths to accessing reality, none of which is false in itself, even

---

63. Maximus the Confessor makes a similar distinction in Q.Thal. I, 49.311–14.

64. According to Maximus the Confessor, this participation in reality that becomes a participation in the personal otherness of its Creator, a relationship with him, is the very purpose of creation. For him, creation has not been brought into existence out of any necessity, but with the purpose of the creatures' participation in their Creator, Car., 3.46.1–2, "God who is beyond fullness did not bring creatures into being out of any need of his, but that he might enjoy their proportionate participation in him" (trans. Berthold). And, in Car., 4.11.1, "God is participated only; creation both participates and communicates" (trans. Berthold).

if they represent different degrees of personal participation in the fullness of reality (7.411).[65]

If it is the experience of relation that constitutes the cognitive event, if reality is known and is manifested and revealed through relation and the dynamics of relation, the question about its fullness (7.42), then "the hermeneutic access to the [philosophical] problem of the *causal principle* of reality can be freed from the dualism and contrast between physics and metaphysics," between science and ontology (7.43). The dynamics of each person's (and humanity's) relation to reality is an actual event, "which can be subjugated to neither the natural 'objectivity' of the sensible," to the natural sciences, "nor to the abstract (mental, reductive) nature of metaphysical enquiry" (7.4202). This is in no way to be understood as a "proof of God's existence" or even "proof of God's inexistence" or anything of the sort: the very notion of a critical ontology is constituted against "proofs" as compulsorily convincing constructs of the logical faculty. However, it recognizes the communal affirmation of the presence of the relationship's Other—of the wholly Other of each person's relationship with reality, God. The personal discovery of a personal creative activity (ἐνέργεια) beyond physical reality, which constitutes physical reality, "is a hermeneutic access to reality that cannot be confined or subjugated to the 'extra-subjective' (objective) certainties of science and metaphysics. It remains a hermeneutic proposal that differs from other hermeneutic proposals in the fullness of the personal relation to [and participation in] the cosmic reality that it actualizes" (7.43). The fullness and realism of the subjective, personal, cognitive participation in reality is to be judged by "the wide referentiality of relation, its *communal validation*" (7.44). The *meaning* that each person's participation in reality grants to his life, the meaning that each society's or community's collective participation in reality grants to each facet of human coexistence, makes a very real and tangible difference in the mode of that participation (7.45).

The recognition of a personal causal principle of the world in the field of ontology has direct implications for our human coexistence. If the universe in its infinite complexity and vastness is not a product of randomness but the outcome of a personal activity (ἐνέργεια), if the world is a manifestation of God's activity (ἐνέργεια), then "the principle of conscious experience (consciousness), freedom, and creativity is not an inexplicable exception pertaining only to the human subject, but the causal principle

---

65. Cf. Maximus the Confessor, *Q.Dub.*, 44.9–15, "For to those who recognize the Creator from the beauty of the created things and through these are led up to their cause, there is knowledge of good; but to those who remain in the sense-perception alone and, being tricked by the superficiality of perceptible things, have turned every appetite of the soul toward matter, there is the knowledge of evil" (trans. Prassas).

of existence"—the causal principle of existence as the existential otherness arising from consciousness and freedom. If that is the case, freedom and otherness must be recognized as "real (and not evaluative, i.e., arbitrary) criteria for the genuineness of history and society: dependence, subjugation, and oppression are to be recognized as very real forms of existential corruption," not merely as the corruption of social relations (5.22).

Ultimately, the question of a critical ontology is a question of meaning, a question of truth. And this question is not limited to the world of philosophy, but extends to the world of human coexistence, of civilization and history.

> Philosophical *ontology* is a proposal concerning the *meaning* of man's existence and its relations—a proposal of meaning concerning the mode of existence. And *critical* ontology builds its proposal on the subject's existential self-awareness as an experience of freedom and otherness. Freedom and otherness become accessible to us as a cognitive and empirical event through relation and the dynamic indeterminacy of relation. The criterion of reality is the experience of relation to reality and the verification of the relation's genuineness through its collective widening—i.e., the equally indeterminable dynamics of the social event that constitutes history and civilisation. (8.21)

Yannaras completes his *Propositions for a Critical Ontology* with proposition number 9: "For a critical ontology, truth is relation. And relation—i.e., truth—is never taken for granted. It is an attainment" (9). If Ludwig Wittgenstein has completed his *Tractatus Logico-Philosophicus* with the famous phrase "Whereof one cannot speak, thereof one must be silent," I could say that Yannaras' answer would be: *Whereof one cannot speak, therein one must participate.*

Employing Yannaras' Thought as a Hermeneutic Tool

I have attempted to expound Christos Yannaras' philosophical terminology through perhaps his most densely philosophical book, i.e., *Propositions for a Critical Ontology*, without presenting those monographs of his that explicitly reflect on ecclesial ontology, history, and practice; that is, by consciously overlooking the fact that in many of his other works he engages directly with the ecclesial event's history, the patristic tradition, and the thought of church fathers such as the Cappadocians or Maximus the Confessor. I have chosen to do so in order to first present Yannaras as a philosopher and not as a commentator or exegete, which would be a grave misunderstanding of the nature of his philosophical work and would deprive me of *hermeneutic tools*, supplying me with *helpful comments* instead. (The same misunderstanding would be effected if I were to approach Maximus the Confessor merely as a commentator or exegete—regardless of the fact that he might very well have considered himself as one.) I aimed at studying Yannaras' primary contributions to philosophy and, specifically, ontology. However, it is exactly his scholarly engagement (and the monographs that are its fruits) with Maximus the Confessor, the church fathers, and the ecclesial tradition, history, and practice that makes Yannaras' work so valuable in shedding light on Maximus the Confessor's dense and difficult—while at the same time immensely illuminating—formulations and definitions, Maximus' comprehensive *Weltanschauung*.

The definitions of a great many Greek terms provided in the previous pages will prove valuable in the course of the present study. Yannaras provides us with definitions and elucidations of key notions for the Greek fathers and Maximus the Confessor—such as λόγος, substance (οὐσία), hypostasis (ὑπόστασις), nature (φύσις), person (πρόσωπον), activity (ἐνέργεια), etc.—in a manner that is not lacking in patristic grounding and in a way that is more illuminating than a significant number of philological treatises and articles on the historical development of these terms' meaning, at least in the context of my systematic endeavor.

The same can be said of John Zizioulas' work, which, however, is dedicatedly theological in nature and, like Yannaras', markedly Maximian in perspective and approach. I will not present John Zizioulas' work in a dedicated chapter, as this has been already done by many.[66] However, the approach, perspective, and terminology of Christos Yannaras and John Zizioulas will be cited and implemented throughout my study, both in chapters dealing with the early Christian/patristic context of Maximus' philosophy, as in the previous one, and in chapters expounding the basic tenets of Maximus the Confessor's unique ontology. It is this perspective of Yannaras that I will refer to as "relational."

With this perspective in mind, I can now proceed to a contemporary reading of a number of patristic Christian and Maximian themes in ontology, cosmology, and anthropology, before embarking on the study of his understanding of motion and temporality and his notion of time, as this preliminary study is a prerequisite for the latter one.

---

66. See e.g. Knight, *Theology of John Zizioulas*, which also includes a comprehensive bibliography up to 2007. Apart from this particular book, a great number of doctoral and master's theses on Zizioulas' work have been written and published worldwide.

CHAPTER THREE

Ontological, Epistemological, Anthropological Themes in Maximus

IN THIS CHAPTER, I will attempt to provide the reader with the minimum prerequisites for approaching Maximus the Confessor's thought and the patristic or Byzantine *Weltanschauung* from a contemporary perspective, focusing on fundamental tenets of Maximian and Byzantine ontology, cosmology, and anthropology. My introduction to (a) the philosophical articulation of the ecclesial testimony and its emergence, (b) the fundamental ontological and cosmological division, the created-uncreated distinction and the *modal* nature of its constitutive categories, and (c) Christology and its corresponding anthropology, as well as related matters, should serve as a necessary "toolbox" in further examining Maximus' ontology and cosmology. The study of Maximus' more distinct contributions, such as the λόγοι doctrine[1] or his unique understanding of motion, space, and temporality, will then follow.

---

1. The analysis of which is, in turn, crucial and indispensable for the exposition of Maximus' theory of motion, space, and time. The reasons for this will become apparent as the analysis of Maximian motion and time unfolds. I could safely say that the λόγοι doctrine acts as both the essence of and the prerequisite for all other aspects of Maximus' ontology. The widespread erroneous tendency to understand this theory in Platonic or Neo-platonic terms (i.e., as a Christianized form of Platonic *ideas*) is an oversimplification that, in my opinion, has effectively clouded numerous attempts to understand Maximus' thinking. I will argue against this reception of the λόγοι doctrine in the relevant chapter.

Ontotheology?

Despite their distinction in two separate disciplines, the relationship and interaction between philosophy and theology was always very strong. In acknowledging this in the deepest level, Heidegger criticizes the whole of Western metaphysics as *ontotheology*.[2] This interrelation of ontology and theology is usually seen as problematic, as a problem that philosophy must overcome. However, a vital part of Christian ontology is the created-uncreated distinction[3] and the subsequent implications of *creation ex nihilo*,[4] which differs fundamentally from Greek philosophy and which forbids ontotheology in the literal sense.

2. In essence, ontotheology means considering God as a being i.e., as one of the beings, even though a very exalted one (and not, for example, as residing *beyond* the category of beings). This term has suffered much; it originated with Immanuel Kant and became widely known through its use (with a different content) by Heidegger. Today it is usually used in a much wider sense, denoting the hardly avoidable inclusion of philosophical theology in philosophy through metaphysics (Aristotle's "first philosophy"), where a sharp distinction between the philosophical and theological aspects of it is extremely difficult. The problem is that by including God in the ontological enquiry, God is reified, he is made an object within existence—albeit the highest, the most perfect, etc., but nonetheless one *object* within *being*. For an account of Heidegger's meaning of the term, consult Thomson, "Ontotheology?" According to p. 323, Kant's original definition of ontotheology is "that kind of transcendental theology which (like Anselm's famous 'ontological argument' for the existence of God) 'believes it can know the existence of an [original being, *Urwesen*] through mere concepts, without the help of any experience whatsoever,'" in contrast to the empirically-oriented cosmotheology. In my opinion, the philosopher Jean-Luc Marion successfully attempts in his now-classic monograph *God without Being* to *radically transcend ontotheology* when philosophically engaging with the subject of God, thereby achieving a truly crucial contribution to philosophy.

3. See, e.g., Maximus the Confessor's *Amb.Io.* 15, 1221A: "the Creator and creation are not the same, as if what is attributed to the one must by necessity be attributed likewise to the other, for if this were the case the natural differences between them would no longer be evident" (trans. Constas). Ibid., 1168B: "Since the uncreated is not naturally contained by creation, nor is the unlimited comprehended by what is limited" (trans. Louth). There can be no middle ground between the uncreated and the created, *D.Pyrrh.*, PG91 341A, ἢ κτιστήν, ἢ ἄκτιστον λέγειν ταύτην ἀναγκασθήσεσθε· ἐπειδὴ μέσον κτιστῆς καὶ ἀκτίστου οὐδεμία ὑπάρχει τὸ σύνολον. See also Maximus' list of cosmological divisions, influenced by Gregory of Nyssa—the first of them is the created-uncreated distinction, *Amb.Io.* 41, 1304D: "They say that the substance of everything that has come into being is divided into five divisions. The first of these divides from the uncreated nature the universal created nature, which receives its being from becoming" (trans. Louth).

4. Cf. Maximus the Confessor, *Car.*, 4.1.3, ἐκ τοῦ μηδενὸς τῆς τῶν ὄντων εἰς τὸ εἶναι παρήγαγεν ὕπαρξιν [ὁ Θεός].—"From nothing he has brought into existence everything that is" (trans. Berthold).

The ontotheological position is that one can know the first cause of existence (or God or existence's meaning and sense) through concepts (through philosophy)—as it is a being, one of the beings. This is perfectly compatible with an ontology that traces the first cause of existence, or God, or existence's meaning and sense, *in the world, within* existence. If it is one of the components of the world then its truth can be accurately thought of, spoken of, articulated, defined (within the means of language's realism). Aristotle's prime unmoved mover does not reside *outside* of the world, he is *within* the world. However, and in contrast with Greek ontology before Christianity, the religion of the Hebrews and the testimony of the Christians speak of a creation *ex nihilo*, of a distinction between created reality and the uncreated God, of a first cause that resides *outside* of the cosmos, i.e., the *ktisis* (κτίσις), *outside* of the created world (of course, without the spatio-temporality that "outside" seems to imply).

The genius of Ludwig Wittgenstein has provided us with another *language* to express this from another perspective: according to him, "the sense of the world must lie outside the world."[5] Wittgenstein explains: "In the world everything is as it is, and everything happens as it does happen: in it no value exists—and if it did exist, it would have no value. If there is any value that does have value, it must lie outside the whole sphere of what happens and is the case. For all that happens and is the case is accidental. What makes it non-accidental cannot lie within the world, since if it did it would itself be accidental. It must lie outside the world."[6] The question of the *sense* of the world is the question of its *cause,* the question about God. However, "the limits of my language signify the limits of my world."[7] To signify in language what lies *beyond* the limits of my world, the extremities of which are the limitations of createdness, would be impossible, it would be *non-sense.* One cannot truly philosophize about what lies beyond the limits of createdness, and as such of language. "Whereof one cannot speak, thereof one must be silent."[8] If one *has* to speak, then a truly *apophatic* stance towards knowledge and language is necessary.

Thus, the primary affirmation of ontotheology cannot be accepted by the ecclesial testimony under any circumstances. For the fathers of the church, philosophy was certainly not a means to *know* God, as this would

---

5. Wittgenstein, *Tractatus,* §6.41.

6. Ibid.

7. Ibid., §5.6.

8. Ibid., §7.

not be possible, and to deem it possible would be to deny basic tenets of the ecclesial testimony.[9]

Maximus' Apophaticism: "God Does Not Exist"

Maximus the Confessor anticipated Wittgenstein's advice: he does not speak of what cannot be said. Maximus speaks of God (and of everything) "according to the measure of our language (for it is not possible for us to transcend it)."[10] In an utter respect for the realism of language, Maximus declares that God does not exist, for his existence is completely beyond everything that we call "being" and "existence."[11] For the Confessor, this is not a mere rhetorical device: he explicitly writes "nonbeing is properly meant with regard to [God], since he is not among beings."[12] Every designation concerning God and the sense of the world cannot but be incorrect, as it emerges from within the limits of our world. The mode of existence (τρόπος ὑπάρξεως) of creatures cannot be the same or comparable to the mode of existence of their source of being, to the mode of existence of the uncreated, and nothing at all can be said about it, as it resides beyond the limits of createdness. Language cannot even circumscribe truth when trying to signify the uncreated: "for since it is necessary that we understand correctly the difference between God and creatures, then the affirmation of being beyond

9. On this subject, cf. Tollefsen, *Activity and Participation*, 33–46. On a side note, let me remark that in an attempt to be able to know God through concepts and to bridge the gap between the Christian God and ancient Greek conceptions of a first cause, the principle of the *analogia entis* was employed in the Christian West; however, as this cannot be traced in Maximus the Confessor or in the Eastern church both prior to Maximus and thereafter, I will not deal with it here.

10. *Scholia in De Divinis Nominibus*, CD4.1 189B (p. 122, fn.), "τῷ μέτρῳ τῆς ἡμετέρας γλώσσης ἀκολουθῶν, (οὐ γὰρ ὑπερβῆναι ταύτην δυνατὸν ἡμῖν)."

11. *Myst.*, proem.109, "καὶ διὰ τοῦτο τὸ μὴ εἶναι μᾶλλον, διὰ τὸ ὑπερεῖναι, ὡς οἰκειότερον ἐπ᾽ αὐτοῦ λεγόμενον προσιέμενος."—". . . because of his being beyond being, [God] is more fittingly referred to as nonbeing."

12. *Q.Dub.*, 2.14.4–6: "Κυρίως γὰρ ἐπ᾽ αὐτοῦ λέγεται τὸ μὴ ὄν, ἐπειδὴ οὐδέν ἐστι τῶν ὄντων" (trans. Prassas). In an attempt to find contemporary approaches (besides Yannaras and Zizioulas) showing a profound *understanding* of what Maximus strives to articulate, even if not explicitly basing this understanding on Maximus and his texts, I am once again led to Jean-Luc Marion's *God without Being*. It seems to me that Marion, in describing a God that *exists* but is *without* being, i.e., *beyond* being, has achieved to express in contemporary philosophical language the patristic era's apophatic testimony of a God that is ὑπερούσιος, i.e., *beyond* being (cf. *Scholia in De Divinis Nominibus*, CD4.1 313C, CD4.1 188A and CD4.1 204D). In that sense, Jean-Luc Marion's *God without Being* constitutes the answer to the question of *what apophaticism is*, if it is not merely the *via negativa* or negative theology (i.e., a delimitation through negations), but a much more crucial *stance* towards metaphysics and theology.

being [ὑπερεῖναι, ὑπερούσιος] must be the negation of beings and the affirmation of beings must be the negation of being beyond being. In fact, both names, being and nonbeing, are to be reverently applied to [God] although not at all properly."[13]

We have seen that for Yannaras apophaticism is not the *via negativa*, for it denies even negation itself as a way of true knowledge. Rather, for him, apophaticism is "the refusal to exhaust truth in its formulation and to identify the understanding of the signifier with the knowledge of its signified reality."[14] In accordance with this, Maximus stresses the need to understand God transcends "all affirmation and negation":

> For nothing whatsoever, whether being or nonbeing, is linked to him as a cause, no being or what is called being, no nonbeing, or what is called nonbeing, is properly close to him. He has in fact a simple existence, unknowable and inaccessible to all and altogether beyond understanding, which transcends all affirmation and negation.[15]

Of course, the same honesty towards knowledge and language, either explicit or implicit, is to be expected from Maximus throughout the totality of his work, not only when he speaks of the uncreated. This *stance* towards knowledge and language permeates his *Lebensanschauung* and marks his work, an epistemological realism "beyond affirmation and negation." In highlighting my point, I can only refer to the fifth chapter of *Mystical Theology* from the Areopagite corpus, the writings that exerted so profound an influence on Maximus. This passage is very well known, but I will nonetheless quote it to stress the importance of (i) apophaticism and (ii) the created-uncreated distinction to this study.

> Once more, ascending yet higher we maintain that It is not soul, or mind, or endowed with the faculty of imagination, conjecture, reason, or understanding; nor is It any act of reason or

13. Maximus the Confessor, *Myst.*, proem.110–15, "Δεῖ γάρ, εἴπερ ὡς ἀληθῶς τὸ γνῶναι διαφορὰν Θεοῦ καὶ κτισμάτων ἐστὶν ἀναγκαῖον ἡμῖν, θέσιν εἶναι τοῦ ὑπερόντος τὴν τῶν ὄντων ἀφαίρεσιν, καὶ τὴν τῶν ὄντων θέσιν εἶναι τοῦ ὑπερόντος ἀφαίρεσιν, καὶ ἄμφω περὶ τὸν αὐτὸν κυρίως θεωρεῖσθαι τὰς προσηγορίας, καὶ μηδεμίαν κυρίως δύνασθαι· τὸ εἶναι, φημί, καὶ <τὸ> μὴ εἶναι" (trans. Berthold).

14. Yannaras, Ἔξι φιλοσοφικές ζωγραφιές, 32.

15. *Myst.*, proem.120–25, "Ὅτι γὰρ μηδὲν τὸ σύνολον φυσικῶς κατ᾽ αἰτίαν συνέζευκται, ἢ ὂν ἢ μὴ ὄν, τούτῳ οὐδὲν τῶν ὄντων καὶ λεγομένων, οὐδὲ τῶν μὴ ὄντων καὶ μὴ λεγομένων, εἰκότως ἐστὶν ἐγγύς. Ἁπλῆν γὰρ καὶ ἄγνωστον καὶ πᾶσιν ἄβατον ἔχει τὴν ὕπαρξιν καὶ παντελῶς ἀνερμήνευτον, καὶ πάσης καταφάσεώς τε καὶ ἀποφάσεως οὖσαν ἐπέκεινα" (trans. Berthold). Cf. *Amb.Io.* 17, 1128B, 1129C, and *Th.oec.*, 1141Df.—2.39.

understanding; nor can It be described by the reason or perceived by the understanding, since It is not number, or order, or
greatness, or littleness, or equality, or inequality, and since It is
not immovable nor in motion, or at rest, and has no power, and
is not power or light, and does not live, and is not life; nor is It
personal essence, or eternity, or time; nor can It be grasped by
the understanding since It is not knowledge or truth; nor is It
kingship or wisdom; nor is It one, nor is It unity, nor is It Godhead or Goodness; nor is It a Spirit, as we understand the term,
since It is not Sonship or Fatherhood; nor is It any other thing
such as we or any other being can have knowledge of; nor does
It belong to the category of non-existence or to that of existence;
nor do existent beings know It as it actually is, nor does It know
them as they actually are; nor can the reason attain to It to name
It or to know It; nor is it darkness, nor is It light, or error, or
truth; nor can any affirmation or negation apply to it; for while
applying affirmations or negations to those orders of being that
come next to It, we apply not unto It either affirmation or negation, inasmuch as It transcends all affirmation by being the perfect and unique Cause of all things, and transcends all negation
by the pre-eminence of Its simple and absolute nature-free from
every limitation and beyond them all.[16]

At first, philosophical discourse and a sincerely apophatic stance seem
to be wholly incompatible. Philosophical analysis tries to articulate definitions that reflect the true state of this as closely as possible, while apophaticism denies that these definitions reflect the true state of things. However,
the key to an apophatic philosophy is the awareness that definitions in
language reflect reality *as closely as possible* ("according to our measure" as
Maximus would say)[17] and that this may not be very close at all, but it pro-

16. Corpus Areopagiticum, *De Mystica Theologia*, CD II, 149f. (Trans. Rolt, *Dionysius the Areopagite*, 201f.)

17. Maximus' and the ecclesial tradition's uncompromising apophatic approach
prevents a clash between ecclesial cosmology and the cosmology of each age's scientific
worldview. The *symbolic* character of expressions in language, their struggle to articulate the *meaning* of reality and to answer the "why" of the world, guarantees that they
are not claiming to provide an answer to the "what" of the world, the questions of
scientific cosmology. The language employed in order to articulate answers to ontological questions "according to our measure" (e.g., the fall, the creation of the world, man's
creation out of clay and the breath of God et al.) cannot claim a historicity pertaining to branches of knowledge substantially foreign to ontological enquiry, branches of
knowledge employing a radically different kind of language (e.g., "conjectured eleven-
dimensional space," etc.) in order to articulate answers to different questions. Of course,
it is utterly fascinating and truly thought-provoking when formulations arising from
the ontological enquiry bear a resemblance to formulations arising from the scientific

motes the knowledge of reality insofar as it makes a fuller participation in it possible. Thus are language and philosophy very far from useless; the key is in being fully aware of their limits/limitations and of their capability to *signify* truth, but not to *exhaust* it. Maximus seems very conscious of this *caveat* in his work. Philosophy is one of the languages employed to articulate and communicate the ecclesial testimony (another one is, for example, art; a third, architecture). However, for the church fathers, it does not *substitute* the ecclesial testimony; Maximus uses the word *symbol* (σύμβολον),[18] which means much more than what we understand today with the same word, but nevertheless retains a vital difference from what is symbolized. In following this example, every affirmation or negation that I will articulate, especially concerning a territory by definition outside "the limits of our world" (i.e., concerning the uncreated) will be only articulated for the convenience of philosophical analysis, never with bolder claims.

Basic Terminology: Person, Substance, Hypostasis

During the centuries-long attempt to articulate the ecclesial testimony in precise philosophical language, Greek philosophical terminology was not always employed in a uniform manner. Different local churches gave different meanings to a variety of terms; e.g., the churches of Antioch and Alexandria did not attribute the same meanings to terms such as hypostasis (ὑπόστασις) or substance (οὐσία).[19] Terminology has more or less solidified

---

enquiry and vice-versa. However, to claim the *validity* of the one's answers for the questions of the other, to claim the validity of formulations testing the measures and the limits of our language(s) for both of these radically different branches of human enquiry, would be non-sense—in the Wittgensteinian use of the word.

18. Q.*Thal. II,* 65.159–60, "ὅτι μηδὲν πέφυκε ταὐτὸν εἶναι τῇ φύσει τὰ σύμβολα." Note an extreme example of an apophatic formulation in *Car.,* 3.99.1–2, containing the thrice contradictory phrase "τὸν ὑπεράγνωστον ὑπεραγνώστως ὑπερεγνωκώς," "The perfect mind is the one that through genuine faith supremely knows (ὑπερεγνωκώς) in supreme ignorance (ὑπεραγνώστως) the supremely unknowable (τὸν ὑπεράγνωστον)" (trans. Berthold). For the notion of symbol in the Corpus Areopagiticum, see Perl, "Symbol, Sacrament, and Hierarchy."

19. The rendering of these key terms into Latin and, subsequently, into the languages that stem from Latin has also been problematic. The Greek word οὐσία has been translated as both *essentia* and *substantia* in various contexts (English, essence and substance, German, *Essenz* and *Substanz*, etc.). And while *essentia* bears a clear etymological resemblance to οὐσία, *substantia* bears an equally clear etymological resemblance to ὑπόστασις, causing much confusion concerning the translation of the οὐσία-ὑπόστασις pair, which is so fundamental for Christian doctrine. Apart from that, the English word *substance* in certain cases tends to imply some form of materiality, of which οὐσία is devoid (the particular is material, the hypostasis). I have chosen to render οὐσία as

due to the crucial contribution of the Cappadocians in the fourth century and the imprinting of it in the creeds of the Ecumenical Councils. However, problems continued to emerge: even the schism with the Anti-Chalcedonians at the Council of Chalcedon in 451 can be safely read as a problem of Christological terminology—and, as such, as equally important and crucial—rather than a problem of Christology itself, of a substantially different Christology (and the later Monothelite controversy itself can be seen as a political play with the subtleties of terminology on the part of the Roman Emperor in Constantinople, in order to keep both the Orthodox and the Monophysite-inclined populations content). And again, the problem is not terminology itself, the difference of formulations, but the philosophical (or Christological or doctrinal) implications of these different uses of terms: the content and complexity of Maximus' struggle against Monothelitism bears witness to this. Seemingly small differences and a lack of preciseness in these doctrinal formulations can lead to substantially different ontologies, with the most famous example being to previously mentioned iota controversy between ὁμοούσιος and ὁμοιούσιος in the context of Arianism.

According to the common terminology after the Cappadocians and the first Ecumenical Councils, οὐσία and ὑπόστασις roughly bear the meaning of Aristotle's secondary substance (οὐσία δευτέρα) and primary substance (οὐσία πρώτη) respectively. The word "nature" (φύσις) is used interchangeably with the word "substance,"[20] and in the case of human beings and God the word "person" (πρόσωπον) is used interchangeably with the word "hypostasis."[21]

Substance, οὐσία, is the homogeneity of the particulars, the "what" of something, the reason that it is what it is. "Substance" denotes the way in which something participates in existence. "Cat," "human," "horse" are substances; however, these cannot be encountered isolated, as pure substances/natures, but only is particular existences, in hypostases.

Hypostasis, ὑπόστασις, is the particular existence, the specific way in which it is what it is.[22] This *particular* human being, this *particular* horse,

---

substance in this study, as it is the most common translation in contemporary discourse. However, this translation of the terms is even today a cause of significant confusion concerning their exact meaning, as it often leads the English speaking reader to inaccurate presuppositions.

20. See, e.g., Maximus the Confessor, *Ep.*, PG91 485D, "οὐσίας γὰρ ἤτοι φύσεως." *Opusc.*, PG91 149B, "Οὐσία καὶ φύσις, ταυτόν." (Authorship is disputed.)

21. Maximus' account of οὐσία, ὑπόστασις and related subjects can be found, among many other passages, in his first letter to the deacon Cosmas (*Ep.*, PG 544D–576B). Cf. *Opusc.*, PG91 152A, "ὑπόστασις καὶ πρόσωπον, ταυτόν."

22. Cf. Maximus the Confessor, *Car.*, 4.9.2–3, "Πᾶσα δὲ ἡ κτίσις σύνθετος ὑπάρχει ἐξ οὐσίας καὶ συμβεβηκότος."—"Every creature is a composite of substance and

and this *particular* table are hypostases actualizing the substances "human," "horse," "table"—they *hypostasize* (actualize) *the substance*.[23]

It is a patristic *topos* that there is no substance or nature not actualized in one or more hypostases, there is no "naked" nature, there is no οὐσία ἀνυπόστατος: Maximus the Confessor is clear on that as well.[24] Maximus is in line with the common patristic terminology: "Substance, and nature, is the common, the universal, the general. The hypostasis, and the person, is the particular and the partial."[25] I mentioned that of all created beings, only the human being is endowed with the tendency of becoming a person, of existing in-relation-to. (Man *is* a person, as his otherness is manifested and actualized in relations and communion, but simultaneously *can become* a person in the fullest sense of the world: this simultaneous co-existence without division and without confusion—the Chalcedonian συναμφότερον—of a future state wished for and of the present state that is already a reality is also a *topos* of patristic thought, due to the atemporal character of the uncreated.) A more precise formulation would be that, compared to other creatures, man is a person *par excellence* due to his creation "in the image and likeness" of the Triune prototype.[26] It is under this light that we must

accident" (trans. Berthold).

23. Maximus the Confessor, *Opusc.*, PG91 260Df., "Ὅτι οὐσία μὲν αὐτὸ τὸ εἶδος καὶ τὴν φύσιν, ὅπερ ἐστὶ καθ᾽ ἑαυτήν, δηλοῖ, ὑπόστασις δέ, τόν τινα τῆς οὐσίας ἐμφαίνει." Yannaras, *Elements of Faith*, 26–28. For a fuller identification of person and hypostasis, there is a tendency among certain church fathers to speak of hypostases only in the case of human beings and God, i.e., only in the case of persons, not generally in the sense of particulars. However, Maximus applies the term *hypostasis* to everything that exists (*Ep.*, PG91 549BC).

24. E.g., in *Opusc.*, 149B. A thorough examination of the use of these terms by Maximus is to be found in Metropolitan John (Zizioulas) of Pergamon's article "Person and Nature."

25. *Ep.*, PG91 545A. Cf. 549B. For a comprehensive analysis of Maximus' notion of a human hypostasis, see Tollefsen, "St. Maximus' Concept of a Human Hypostasis." Concerning the inexistence (and non-preexistence) of unhypostasized substances, of substances that are not to be encountered as particular actualizations and instances, it must be noted here that, in examining Maximus' thought, we are not to confuse the existence of an οὐσία with the (pre)existence of its λόγος. The (pre)existence and imperishability of a λόγος (i.e., a divine intention) residing beyond createdness does not necessarily entail the existence of the unhypostasized (unactualized) substance to which it would correspond were this substance hypostasized (actualized) in specific and particular realizations. This would be particularly the case if all hypostases of a given substance were to perish, the substance would perish as well, but not its λόγος, λόγοι being uncreated wills and utterances of God and substances being created and intelligible.

26. Nikolaos Loudovikos offers a more precise formulation, "Man becomes a person, then, inasmuch as he in turn is formed into the likeness of Christ, the locus and mode of communion among entities—that is to say, a personal being. . . . Thus man

understand Maximus' explicit assertion that *"person and hypostasis* are one and the same."[27] Nature is nature, and the tendency of the created (the cause of which is outside of itself) towards individual onticity (non-relation; corruption; death) is *non-prosopic*, it does not describe personhood. However, there is also the tendency towards relation, the tendency and motion towards the return to the uncreated source of createdness and towards the full communion with it, i.e., the hope for the *redemption* of creation. In this we see that the *possibility* of personhood, of existing relationally and in communion, is to be found in all created beings; all created beings are characterized by the tendency to personhood according to the uncreated λόγος of their nature (κατὰ τὸν λόγον τῆς φύσεως), and all the λόγοι are recapitulated in the one person of the Λόγος (an exposition on the subject of Λόγος and λόγοι will follow later in this study). However, this *personalization* of nature (i.e., the redemption of creation) cannot be achieved by nature alone, it is the task of the human being, the priest and mediator of creation, it is the task of *mediation*.[28] In that sense, and without losing the relative and apophatic character of formulations in language, I could say with Maximus that each hypostasis is also a person(-in-waiting).

The ecclesial body attempted to address the philosophical problems that seem to arise from its testimony with the use of this terminology. Do Christians have one or three Gods? The limits of createdness signify the limits of language, any "definition" of the uncreated God cannot but be an *apophatic* formulation, and this formulation is that the divine substance is one, but it is hypostasized (actualized) in three persons.[29] This is denoted with a language that does not define God through individual onticity, but through relation, self-transcendence, radical referentiality: God is the *Father*, a being whose definition refers to another being, the *Son*, a name that

participates by grace in the personal mode of existence of God the Word" (*Eucharistic Ontology*, 152).

27. Maximus the Confessor, *Opusc.*, PG91 152A, ὑπόστασις καὶ πρόσωπον, ταυτόν.

28. Masterly expounded by Thunberg in his *Microcosm and Mediator*, particularly in the chapter "Performing the Task of Mediation," 331–432 (and especially 404–32). The goal of man's mediating task is the "union of everything," the transcendence of division, *Amb.Io.* 41, 1305BC, "For this reason the human person was introduced last among beings, as a kind of natural bond mediating between the universal poles through their proper parts, and leading into unity in itself those things that are naturally set apart from one another by a great interval. In order to bring about the union of everything with God as its cause, the human person begins first of all with its own division, and then, ascending through the intermediate steps by order and rank, it reaches the end of its high ascent, which passes through all things in search of unity, to God, in whom there is no division" (trans. Louth).

29. *Caveat*: this actualization does not entail temporal progression, which would be a trait of createdness.

does not define atomicity, but relation.[30] God is not *God*, self-sufficient and existing as a monad, subsequently having the attribute of fatherhood. What God *is*, is that God is the *Father*; what God *is*, is that God is the *Son*; God is *Breath*, the breath of the *Father* (πνεῦμα ἅγιον). This illustrates the meaning of the word πρόσωπον, the etymological beings-towards-someone, existence-as-relation. Three persons sharing the same activity (ἐνέργεια) and will (θέλημα).[31]

An even more difficult challenge for the articulation of the ecclesial testimony was its claim God has been incarnated, both preserving his divinity in full and assuming humanity in full.[32] The preciseness of the articulation of this was of paramount importance, as the very notion of existential redemption for the human beings and victory over death presupposed a real bridging of the gap between the created and the uncreated through the incarnation and resurrection of Christ. In Christ, the unbridgeable chasm between creation and the uncreated is transcended: both the nature and mode of the uncreated and the nature and mode of createdness coexist in a single person, transcending the limitations of both complete othernesses. The incarnation marks the transcendence of the limitations of the uncreated, the resurrection the transcendence of the limitations of createdness; both open the way for the human person to be able to participate in the uncreated, to be able to acquire its mode of existence, as the uncreated God acquired created humanity's mode of existence. In Christ, according to the ecclesial testimony, the unbridgeable chasm between creation and

30. Maximus the Confessor, *Amb.Io.* 26, 1265D, "The name of 'Father' is neither the name of an essence [οὐσίας] nor an activity [ἐνεργείας], but rather of a relation, and of the manner in which the Father is related to the Son, or the Son to the Father" (trans. Constas).

31. Yannaras, *Relational Ontology*, 10.3.2–6 (52–55). Cf. Maximus the Confessor, *Car.*, 2.29.1–3, "Ὅταν λέγῃ ὁ Κύριος· Ἐγὼ καὶ ὁ Πατὴρ ἕν ἐσμεν, τὸ ταὐτὸν τῆς οὐσίας σημαίνει. Ὅταν δὲ πάλιν λέγῃ· Ἐγὼ ἐν τῷ Πατρὶ καὶ ὁ Πατὴρ ἐν ἐμοί, τὸ ἀχώριστον δηλοῖ τῶν ὑποστάσεων."—"When the Lord says, 'The Father and I are one', he is signifying identity of substance. And when he says again, 'I am in the Father and the Father is in me', he indicates the inseparability of the persons" (trans. Berthold). And *Car.*, 2.29.10–12, "Καὶ γὰρ «διαιρεῖται» μέν, ἀλλ᾽ «ἀδιαιρέτως», κατὰ τὸν αὐτόν, καὶ «συνάπτεται» μέν, «διῃρημένως» δέ."—"God is 'divided' and yet 'without division', and 'united' yet 'with distinction'" (trans. Berthold).

32. Maximus the Confessor, *Amb.Th.*, 2.6–13, "The Λόγος of God exists as a full, complete essence (for he is God), and as an undiminished hypostasis (for he is Son). But, when he emptied himself, he became the seed of his own flesh, and when he was composed in an ineffable conception, he became the hypostasis of the very flesh that was assumed. Having truly become a whole human being, without change, in this new mystery, he was himself the hypostasis of two natures, of the uncreated and the created, of the impassible and the passible, receiving without fail all of the natural λόγοι of which he is a hypostasis" (trans. Lollar).

the uncreated is bridged through the hypostatic union of a created and an uncreated nature,[33] *renewing* existence and enabling it to transcend its limitations.[34] Philosophical consistency would not allow for such a union of natures in Christ to be understood in the sense of "mixture," "synthesis," blending; thus the four famous adverbs of the Chalcedonian creed. One could safely say that the undivided church saw in all the deviations from the formulations of her testimony concerning the nature of Christ this single threat: the danger of losing this "Christological bridge" from createdness to the uncreated, of rendering it incomprehensible, of closing the way to it. From the controversies that led to the Nicaean Creed and up to the great Christological definition of the Councils of Ephesus and Chalcedon and to the conciliar adoption of Maximus' struggle against Monothelitism in the seventh century (and beyond), what was at stake was the reality and realism of the possibility of victory over death, which for the Christians presupposed the real and true unity of divinity and humanity in Christ, i.e., a unity in which the human person can truly participate. Teachings entailing (i) an absence of true divinity in Christ (Arianism et al.), (ii) an absence of true humanity in Christ (Monophysitism), (iii) Christ's divinity consuming his humanity (Eutychianism et al.), (iv) an imperfect union of the divine and human nature in Christ (Nestorianism), or (v) the absence of a true and full humanity in Christ (Monothelitism) were gradually recognized by the church as annulling the existential hope of the ecclesial body.

33. Maximus, *Q. Thal. II*, 60.10–26. "He is of course referring to Christ the whole mystery of Christ, which is, manifestly, the ineffable and incomprehensible hypostatic union between Christ's divinity and humanity. This union draws his humanity into perfect identity, in every way, with his divinity, through the λόγος of the hypostasis; it is a union that realizes one person composite of both natures, inasmuch as it in no way diminishes the essential difference between those two natures. And so, to repeat, there is one hypostasis realized from the two natures and the difference between the natures remains immutable. In view of this difference, moreover, the natures remain undiminished, and the quantity of each of the united natures is preserved, even after the union. For, whereas by the union no change or alteration at all was suffered by either of the natures, the essential λόγος of each of the united natures endured without being compromised. Indeed, that essential λόγος remained inviolate even after the union, as the divine and human natures retained their integrity in every respect. Neither of the natures was denied anything at all because of the union" (trans. Blowers).

34. Maximus explains Christ's incarnation in a great number of passages throughout his work; a short but thorough exposition on that and related matters can be found in his letter to Julian (*Ep.*, PG 579C–584D). Cf. *Opusc.*, PG91 146A–149A, as well as *Amb.Th.*, 3.35–13.36, "The teacher says, 'He has become one' (Εἷς δέ γέγονεν); he did not say, 'one thing' (ἀλλ᾽ οὐχ ἕν), showing that, even in the identity of the one hypostasis, the natural otherness of those natures that are united remains unconfused, since the word 'one' (εἷς) is indicative of hypostasis, while the words 'one thing' (ἕν) would indicate nature" (trans. Lollar).

At the Council of Chalcedon, Christ was acknowledged as one single hypostasis, one single person, one single particular being, in which two natures are present, "inconfusedly, unchangeably, indivisibly and inseparably": divine, uncreated nature and human nature. This is commonly termed the *hypostatic union* of the natures.[35]

The challenge of articulating the ecclesial testimony concerning the person of Christ in precise philosophical language was a Herculean achievement with numerous philosophically fascinating implications that cannot be properly dealt with in a mere subsection; however, I must proceed to my next subject, namely the exposition of some aspects of Maximus' anthropology.

Concerning the Body/Soul Distinction in Maximus the Confessor's Thought

A unique system of philosophical anthropology is to be discerned in Maximus's works,[36] an anthropology that elaborates extensively on the subjects of human will and freedom, like no other thinker before him. Due to his ex-

---

35. Maximus the Confessor, *Amb.Io.* 42, 1320C, "Neither did He fulfill the plan of salvation in an imaginary form or simulated appearance of the flesh (as if He had simply appropriated the accidents of a substrate without the actual substrate itself), but to the contrary He made human nature His very own—literally, really, and truly—uniting it to Himself according to hypostasis without change, alteration, diminishment, or division [καθ᾽ ὑπόστασιν ἀτρέπτως καί ἀναλλοιώτως καί ἀμειώτως καί ἀδιαιρέτως], and maintaining it unaltered in accordance with its essential principle and definition" (trans. Constas). And *Amb.Th.*, 4.74–90, "For in the exchange of the divine and the fleshly he clearly confirmed the natures of which he himself was the hypostasis, along with their essential activities, i.e., their movements, of which he himself was the unconfused unity, a unity which admits of no division with respect to the two natures of which he was a hypostasis, since they naturally belong to him. This is because he acts monadically, that is, in a unified form, and by means of each of the things that are predicated of him, he shows forth the power of his own divinity and the activity of his flesh at one and the same time, without separation. For he is one, and there is nothing more unified and nothing more unifying and able to save than him, or than what is proper to him. Because of this, even when suffering, he was truly God, and even while working wonders, the same one was truly man, since he was the true hypostasis of true natures according to ineffable union. Acting in them both reciprocally and naturally, he was shown truly to preserve them, preserving them unconfused for himself, since he remained both dispassionate by nature and passible, immortal and mortal, visible and intelligible, the same one being both God [by nature] and man by nature" (trans. Lollar). See also, Maximus' definition of hypostatic union in *Opusc.*, PG91 152B.

36. The best account of which, so far, can be found in Thunberg's *Microcosm and Mediator*, 95–168 (and 195–230 as well, with important elucidations concerning Maximus' understanding of the *gnomic will*).

tended involvement in the Monothelite controversy, Maximus developed an elaborate anthropology in order to base his Christological insights[37] upon the careful examination of faculties pertaining to the human person, such as the natural and gnomic will, the activities/operations (ἐνέργειαι), etc. This anthropology was implemented by him in his battle against Monothelitism. The distinction between body and soul does indeed have a prominent position in the Confessor's anthropology. However, Maximus sees this distinction in a unique and truly illuminating way, the understanding of which presupposes a firm grasp of his ontological terminology. I will not focus here on the subject of human will, but on the concept of the soul in the light of the writings of Maximus the Confessor and in the light of a distinction between substance and hypostasis rather than between body and soul.[38]

The soul was not always considered as "something" that "exists somewhere" or "does not exist," in the sense that it is understood today in order to be rejected or confirmed. As is common knowledge, the Greek words for soul and spirit (ψυχή and πνεῦμα, both etymologically related to breath) were used to denote and signify the difference between a living, breathing human person and his or her dead body, bereft of life.[39] This difference was deductively located in the presence or absence of the breath, i.e., the soul or spirit. Philosophical theories entailing a strict duality or even a dichotomy between body and soul, such as in Platonic philosophy, are not a necessary corollary of speaking about the presence of a soul. But what is Maximus the Confessor's stance on this subject?

The first thing to note is Maximus uses the philosophical language of his time,[40] what we call today "Neoplatonism." However, this does not *make* him a Neoplatonist: the question is not which philosophical language he uses, but which philosophical and theological testimony he is trying to articulate and to whom it is directed. As Torstein Tollefsen puts it, "[Maximus] received a Christian intellectual heritage that could freely express itself in this kind of vocabulary, and, strictly speaking, these are not 'Neoplatonic

---

37. Maximus' intention is to articulate a sound Christology, not an anthropology *as such*. However, in analyzing the aspects of Christology pertaining to Christ's human nature, Maximus is developing a thorough anthropology in the process.

38. See also Yannaras' account in *Person and Eros*, 46–48. First drafts of the approached proposed here have been published as Mitralexis, "Transcending the Body/ Soul Distinction," and Mitralexis, "Aspekte der Philosophischen Anthropologie."

39. Yannaras, *Elements of Faith*, 55.

40. On recent accounts of Maximus' philosophical language in general, see Guiu's paper, "Christology and Philosophical Culture" and Chvátal's, "Maxime le Confesseur et la tradition philosophique."

terms,' rather they are Greek words, used by the Fathers."[41] For example, one of his primary concerns is not to contemplate about the soul[42] in general, but to counter the Origenist theory of the pre-existence of the soul,[43] using the same language used by the Origenists. This makes it very easy for someone to conclude from the study of texts that have been erroneously attributed to Maximus for centuries[44] that he proposes a strict dichotomy of body and soul: for example, these texts speak of the soul as a bodiless, simple, intelligible, incorruptible, and immortal substance: οὐσία ἀσώματος, νοερά, ἐν σώματι πολιτευομένη, ζωῆς παραίτια,[45] ἀσύνθετος, ἀδιάλυτος, ἄφθαρτος, ἀθάνατος.[46]

However, Maximus' concern is to guard the oneness and wholeness of the human person, of the human hypostasis.[47] In understanding this, one must keep in mind that, as I have said, in the common patristic terminology there is no οὐσία ἀνυπόστατος, we cannot speak of any substance insofar as it is not to be encountered as a hypostasis, a specific realization and manifestation. As I have noted previously, Maximus follows the common patristic terminology of his time, in which οὐσία (substance) is synonymous with φύσις (nature), and the specific realization of the substance (ὑπόστασις) is

---

41. Tollefsen, *Christocentric Cosmology*, 11.

42. On a side note, Maximus writes both about a distinction of body and soul *and* about a distinction of mind, body and soul (νοῦς, σῶμα, ψυχή). Here I will focus on the contrast of body and soul, not attempting to analyze the latter distinction, which is treated in Thunberg's *Microcosm and Mediator*, 107–13.

43. See for example *Amb.Io.* 42, 1325D, "οὔτε προὔπαρξιν οὔτε μεθύπαρξιν ψυχῆς ἢ σώματος, συνύπαρξιν δὲ μᾶλλόν φαμεν"— "We are not speaking of an existence of the soul either before or after the existence of the body, but of their co-existence [their concurrent emergence]." See also Polycarp Sherwood's *Earlier Ambigua*.

44. *De Anima* has not been penned by Maximus; see Celia, "Il λόγος κεφαλαιώδης dello ps.-Gregorio il Taumaturgo." The definition of the soul found therein has caused quite some confusion to Maximian scholars not aware of its erroneous attribution to the Confessor.

45. ps.-Gregory Taumaturgus, *Anim.*, Cantarella 8.1–2.

46. *Anim.* 4–6.

47. I must repeat here Maximus is concerned with the question of human nature and hypostasis only in relation to Christology and the Trinity—he does not *consciously* develop an anthropology *as such*. However, in treating the subjects of the hypostatic union of human and divine nature in Christ, his wills and his activities, he is indeed developing a detailed anthropology. We cannot treat his analyses concerning human nature, will, and activity in their presence in Christ as distinct and different from his perception of human nature in the case of ordinary persons, the human nature of humanity and the human nature in Christ is one and the same (the latter, however, being fully "according to nature" and, as such, perfect in the case of Christ). As such, while Maximus does not refer to the human hypostasis in the way that we might have today, he is developing a unique anthropology, albeit in order to apply it to the question of Christ's human and divine natures.

in the case of man and God synonymous with πρόσωπον (the person).[48] He defines the relation between the body and the soul in two radically different ways. Maximus uses the substance-hypostasis distinction with utmost versatility in order to shed light to the soul-body problem. In this, it will become apparent that Maximus thinks of the "substance" and the "hypostasis" as *modes*, not as *things*; otherwise, we would have to consider him as gravely inconsistent, which is not the case.

The Confessor makes *two seemingly contradicting statements* when he speaks about the soul and the body and when he constructs his anthropology parallel to his Christology.[49] He states that (1) man, in contrast to Christ, has a "composite nature"[50] (φύσις σύνθετος, whereas in Christ we can only speak of a composite hypostasis), and in another text that (2) man constitutes a hypostatic union of two different substances,[51] the body (as substance) and the soul (as substance), in an analogy to Christ's hypostatic union of the divine and human nature.[52] In (1), the body and the soul are two natures-substances that merge into one composite nature-substance, the "human" nature-substance. Whereas in (2) the substance "body" and the substance "soul" co-exist in one single hypostasis, in one actual realization, retaining their distinct nature in a way similar to Christ's hypostatic union. "Composite nature" and "union of two natures in one hypostasis" are two diametrically opposed formulations (and the essence of the Chalcedonian controversies, as the Monophysites argued in favor of Christ's

48. See for example, *Ep.,* PG91 485D, "οὐσίας γὰρ ἤτοι φύσεως—Ibid., 545A, Κοινὸν μὲν οὖν ἐστι καὶ καθολικόν, ἤγουν γενικόν, κατὰ τοὺς πατέρας, ἡ οὐσία καὶ ἡ φύσις· ταυτὸν γὰρ ἀλλήλαις ταύτας ὑπάρχειν φασίν.Ἴδιον δὲ καὶ μερικόν, ἡ ὑπόστασις καὶ τὸ πρόσωπον· ταυτὸν γὰρ ἀλλήλοις κατ' αὐτοὺς τυγχάνουσιν—Ibid., 545AB, [τάδε γράφων ὁ μέγας Βασίλειος] ὅτι ὃν ἔχει λόγον τὸ κοινὸν πρὸς τὸ ἴδιον, τοῦτον ἔχει ἡ οὐσία πρὸς τὴν ὑπόστασιν.. . . Οὐσία δὲ καὶ ὑπόστασις ταύτην ἔχει τὴν διαφοράν, ἣν ἔχει τὸ κοινὸν πρὸς τὸ καθέκαστον.—Ibid., 549B, Εἰ δὲ ταὐτὸν μὲν οὐσία καὶ φύσις· ταυτὸν δὲ πρόσωπον καὶ ὑπόστασις, δῆλον ὡς τὰ ἀλλήλοις ὁμοφυῆ καὶ ὁμοούσια, πάντως ἀλλήλοις ἑτεροϋπόστατα."—Ibid., 552A, "τῷ λόγῳ τῆς οὐσίας ἤτοι φύσεως διαφέρουσι· ὡς ἐπὶ ψυχῆς ἀνθρωπίνης ἔχει καὶ σώματος,, καὶ τῶν ὅσα καθ' ὑπόυ ιασιν ἐυχήκασι τὴν πρὸς ἄλληλα σύνοδον. Οὐ γὰρ ἀλλήλοις ὁμοούσια ταῦτα τυγχάνουσιν."

49. It must be noted that this contradiction is traditional by Maximus' time; he did not invent it.

50. E.g., *Ep.,* PG91 488D, "ὡς ἐπί τε τοῦ ἀνθρώπου ἔχει, καὶ τῶν ἄλλων ὅσα συνθέτου εἶναι ἔλαχον φύσεως."

51. Ibid., 552D, *Opusc.,* PG91 152A.

52. On the analogy between the unity of body and soul in man and the unity of divine and human nature in Christ, on the "hypostatic union" of soul and body in man, see, e.g., Thunberg, *Microcosm and Mediator,* 101–4, as well as Uthemann's mention of Maximus' understanding of the unity of soul and body as both a hypostatic union and a natural synthesis ("Der Mensch als Einigung von Seele und Leib ist also hypostatische Union und natürliche Synthese zugleich"—230 in "Das anthropologische Modell").

"composite nature").[53] If we accept Maximus *consciously* employs both to denote the body-soul relationship, then we need to abandon the dualistic understanding of the notions "body," "soul," "substance," and "hypostasis" in order to understand him and see his seemingly contradictory references as different languages in order to signify the totality and wholeness of the human person.

Polycarp Sherwood regards this as an inconsistency on Maximus' part, as Thunberg remarks,[54] but I maintain it is perfectly consistent not only with Maximus' logic, but also with the *inner logic* of the terminology he uses. His (1) first exposition—that the substance of man is one composite nature, a φύσις σύνθετος—is a natural corollary of the philosophical language that Maximus uses: each human person, each human hypostasis, partakes in the common nature of being human, the common substance of all human beings, that which makes a human being human. This human nature, each specific manifestation of which is every human being, has most certainly a dual character in the Confessor's eyes: "each one of us is of a dual nature, both from a soul and from a body."[55] Human nature is characterized by materiality, which is a nature in itself, a distinct way of partaking in existence (it is the *mode* of materiality and in a sense the λόγος of its being) but at the same time possesses qualities that are to be ascribed to an intelligible nature, beyond pure materiality, a way of partaking in existence different than that of pure materiality: a soul, a distinct λόγος of being, a distinct mode (τρόπος) of existence: "the λόγος and mode of the soul is different from that of the body."[56] These two natures, these two substances,[57] coexist in human nature, in the common substance of all human beings.

However, (2) Maximus also approaches the subject from a seemingly radically different perspective (even incompatibly so), understanding man not as one composite nature and hypostasis, but as one hypostasis in two distinct natures, as a "hypostatic union" of some sort. He makes it clear:

53. However, the acceptance of this paradox is characteristic of sixth-century dyophysite Neo-Chalcedonism (e.g., Nephalios, John of Caesarea, Leontios of Jerusalem), which, in order to find a middle ground with moderate monophysites, spoke of the *synthesis* of natures in Christ—employing a word favored by moderate monophysites— and the *hypostatic* union of the natures as opposed to their natural union in one nature.

54. Thunberg, *Microcosm and Mediator*, 101, fn. 49.

55. *Amb.Io.* 53, 1373C, "ἕκαστος ἡμῶν διπλοῦς ἐστι τὴν φύσιν, ἐκ ψυχῆς καὶ σώματος συνεστώς."

56. *Amb.Io.* 42, 1321C, "ἄλλος ὁ λόγος καὶ ὁ τρόπος τῆς ψυχῆς, ἄλλος τῷ σώματι."

57. *Ep.*, 488A, "Οὐχ ὁ αὐτὸς γὰρ θεότητος καὶ ἀνθρωπότητος λόγος· ὥσπερ οὐδὲ ψυχῆς καὶ σώματος, ὡς πᾶσιν εὔδηλον."

"Man is not of one nature which is constituted of body and soul,"[58] rejecting the definition on which I just elaborated above. Maximus compares Christ's union of two natures in one hypostasis with man's union of body and soul in one hypostasis, but not in one (composite) nature: as he writes, "the one and single Christ is known by the natures from which and in which he is constituted, just as each one and single human being is known by the natures [i.e., body and soul] from which he has been constituted and in which he exists."[59] In speaking about a *hypostatic union* of soul and body in the human being, Maximus changes perspective and chooses to focus on the two natures and substances that constitute every specific human being and not on the qualities of man's general nature, which in the former exposition make it a composite nature. However, this is not to suggest a dichotomy, but quite the contrary: Maximus proposes it to underline the oneness and wholeness of the human person, a oneness and wholeness similar but not identical to the coexistence of Christ's two natures in his person *"without confusion, without change, without division and without separation."*[60]

And here I come to my point: in both of Maximus' definitions on the relationship of soul and body, the hypostasis, the specific manifestation of the general substance "soul" is *the particular human person as a whole.*

(1) In Maximus' view of the composite human nature and substance, composed of the substance "body" and the substance "soul," its specific manifestation and actual existence, the realization of this composite nature, is the human person as a whole.

(2) In the Confessor's view of a hypostatic union of these two natures and substances in man, there is again one actual specific existence, one hypostasis: this specific human person—one could say, following Chalcedon, *without confusion of the two natures, without change in them, without division and without separation.*

Maximus does speak of a soul, of the soul as an immortal, bodiless, intelligible, and simple substance.[61] However, in the field of *actual existences*, the whole human person is that which actually exists: the soul in itself would be an οὐσία ἀνυπόστατος. There is no hypostasis of the substance "soul," apart from the human hypostasis as an undivided whole, the

---

58. Ibid., "Ἀλλ᾽ οὐδὲ τὸν ἄνθρωπον μίαν φύσιν τὴν ἐκ ψυχῆς καὶ σώματος."

59. Ibid., "ὡς ἑνὸς πυρός, αἱ περὶ αὐτὸ ποιότητες καὶ ἰδιότητες, καὶ ἑνὸς Χριστοῦ, αἱ φύσεις ἐξ ὧν καὶ ἐν αἷς συνεστὼς γνωρίζεται· καὶ ἑνὸς ἀνθρώπου, τὰ ἐξ ὧν συνετέθη καὶ ἐν οἷς ὑπάρχων γινώσκεται."

60. ἀσυγχύτως, ἀτρέπτως, ἀδιαιρέτως, ἀχωρίστως, as the creed of the Chalcedonian Council would put it.

61. *Ep.*, 357C–361A.

whole of the human person.[62] In thus defining the soul-body relationship, Maximus makes a critically important contribution to the subject, given the usual Christian understanding thereof.

I mentioned a union "without division" and "without separation." But is not the soul separated from the body after death? An examination of Maximus' writings would suggest his answer would be "yes *and no*": for him, the dead body and the intelligible soul are only the parts of a whole,[63] they are the body *of this* human person and the soul *of that* human person, they are not to be thought of in themselves, as separated from the one human person that they constitute, i.e., that they constitut*ed* and, in Maximus' view, do still constitute, and will constitute again. "The soul is not simply called 'soul' after death," Maximus writes, "but this specific person's soul. And the body is not simply called 'body' after death, but this specific person's body, even if that body is subject to decay. Thus, one cannot speak of body or soul separately, as if they were irrelevant to one another."[64] "One cannot conceive of a soul without body or of a body without soul,"[65] he testifies. Even after death, the hypostasis, the specific manifestation and realization, continues to be the whole human person. This shifts the ontological and soteriological

---

62. See also, *Amb.Io.* 42, 1336A, Ἡνώθη δὲ τῷ Θεῷ Λόγῳ μετὰ τῆς ψυχῆς καὶ τὸ σῶμα. Ἄρα μετὰ τῆς ψυχῆς καὶ τὸ σῶμα σωθήσεται. ("The body as well as the soul have joined the God Logos. That is, the body will also be saved along with the soul.")— PG91 1336A, σαρκοῦται ὁ τοῦ Θεοῦ Λόγος ἵνα καὶ τὴν εἰκόνα σώσῃ καὶ τὴν σάρκα ἀθανατίσῃ. ("The Logos of God has been incarnated both in order to save the image/icon and to immortalize the flesh.")

63. Cf *Amb.Io.* 7, 1100C–1101A.

64. Ibid., 1101BC: "For after the death of the body, the soul is not called 'soul' in an unqualified way, but the soul of a man, indeed the soul of a particular human being, for even after the body, it possesses, as its own form, the whole human being, which is predicated of it by virtue of its relation as a part to the whole. The same holds in the case of the body, which is corruptible by nature, but has a particular relation on account of its origin. For the body, after its separation from the soul, is not simply called 'body', even though it will decompose and be dissolved into the elements from which it was constituted, but the body of a man, indeed of a particular man. For like the soul it possesses the form of the whole human being predicated of it, by virtue of its relation as a part to the whole. Thus the relation of the two, by which I mean soul and body, as the whole human form whose parts can be separated only in thought, reveals that both come into being simultaneously, and demonstrates their essential difference from each other, without violating in any way whatsoever the principles of their respective substances. For this reason it is inconceivable to speak of (and impossible to find) the soul and body except in relation to each other, since each one introduces together with itself the idea of the other to which it belongs. Thus, if either were to exist before the other, it would have to be understood as the soul or the body of the other to which it belongs, for the relation between them is immutable" (trans. Constas).

65. *Amb.Io.* 42, 1324B: "Καὶ τούτῳ τῷ λόγῳ οὔτε σώματος χωρὶς ἡ ψυχή, οὔτε ψυχῆς σῶμά ποτε νοηθήσεται."

focus from a notion of the soul as a bodiless human to that of the whole human person, of the human person *as we know it*.

An "Immortal" Soul? Hell and the Possibility of Inexistence

Furthermore, as Maximus speaks of the *immortal* nature of the human soul, I come to my second question, which is integrally connected to the first one: if the human person truly possesses a free will as an ontological fact,[66] could his soul or his hypostasis be *inevitably* eternal? Is the answer to God's creative call, which creates us "from non-being into being"[67] or into eternal being, *inevitably* affirmative? And if so, is the freedom of the person true freedom, or does God force the person to accept an existence that this person could otherwise deny?

Speaking about the answer to God's creative call, I am not referring to an event *before our birth* or *after our death*, but to a continuous event, or to be more precise an event *outside of time* as we know and experience it. If freedom and free will allow us to prepare during our life a receptiveness to the possibility of being given existence beyond the constraints of natural life, beyond the grave, then freedom would also allow us to deny such a possibility. However, the price of such a choice would not be an eternal punishment imposed by a God, who is only defined as love, but, simply, inexistence; the denial to participate in his love, which calls us "from non-being into being."[68] The inability to revisit such a choice, as "there is no repentance after death," would be, truly, hell.

---

66. As Maximus' chief theological battle was against Monotheletism, there is ample bibliography on his treatment of the human will's freedom, a subject to which Maximus' contribution was and is crucial on both a theological and philosophical level. I would suggest Bathrellos' monograph *Byzantine Christ*, which examines both the historical development and the philosophical/theological importance of Maximus' contribution, both the historical and systematic aspect, in a way that explains in depth many related subjects as well (person/hypostasis, nature etc).

67. Maximus Confessor, *Amb.Io.* 35, 1288D: "τὰ ὄντα ἐκ τοῦ μὴ ὄντος παραγαγεῖν τε καὶ ὑποστήσασθαι." Cf. *Myst.*, 5.75, "God, from whom I received being." See also *Car.*, 3.28.9–11.

68. Maximus Confessor, *Myst.*, 1.70–72, καὶ κινδυνεύσῃ αὐτοῖς καὶ αὐτὸ τὸ εἶναι εἰς τὸ μὴ ὂν μεταπεσεῖν τοῦ Θεοῦ χωριζόμενον. "So that . . . they will not run the risk of having their being separated from God to dissolve into nonbeing" (trans. Berthold). Eschatologically, the "works of sin" will either way return to inexistence, ἀνυπαρξία, *Q.Dub.*, 159.19–20, "ἐν τῷ μέλλοντι αἰῶνι τὰ ἔργα τῆς ἁμαρτίας εἰς ἀνυπαρξίαν χωροῦσιν"—"But, also, in the future age, the works of sin give way to nothingness [inexistence]" (trans. Prassas).

Christos Yannaras, commenting on Maximus the Confessor's passages on "our hopes hereafter,"[69] has analyzed the possibility that "what we term in our language as 'hell' could refer to man's free choice not to exist. If the foundation of existing is the relationship with God, and the 'logical'-personal relationship (which, to be logical-personal, must be free) constitutes the logical-personal existence, then this relationship-existence can be either accepted or even rejected, leading to nonexistence."[70] Yannaras considers this view well founded in the texts of church fathers like the Confessor: "Hell, says Maximus, is the negation to participate in being, in well-being and in ever being: the free self-exclusion from existence, from relation-participation in being, the negation of the relationship and as such the negation of existing, of existence. And this voluntary nonexistence as a deprivation and loss of the gift of deification can perhaps only be signified symbolically in language with the image of endless torture, of the suffering and weeping. Thereby is the unbearable scandal dispelled, that a God who is love preserves his deniers eternally in existence only to see them suffer hopelessly."[71] Maximus' relevant passage is revealing: according to him, the participation or the refusal to participate in being, well-being, and ever being is a punishment for those who cannot participate and a bliss and delight for those who can participate.[72] Of course, Maximus does not explicitly write that hell is inexistence, that the negative answer to God's call would result in inexistence—this would be contrary to his assertion that the soul (i.e., the human person) is immortal.[73] However, Maximus denotes the totality of existence with his three categories of being (εἶναι), well-being (εὖ εἶναι), and ever being (ἀεὶ εἶναι): the refusal or inability to participate in *any of them* cannot but mean the refusal or inability to participate *in existence, in reality*, if we follow Maximus' language precisely—who also mentions the possibility of φεῦ εἶναι, i.e., ill-being or being in vain. And he is right in writing that we cannot but perceive this conscious choice of inexistence (whether this inexistence will be granted to us or not) as "punishment."

69. Yannaras, "Ontological Realism."

70. Ibid., 385.

71. Ibid.

72. *Amb.Io.* 42, 1329B, "and for those who participate or do not participate proportionately in Him who, in the truest sense, is and is well, and is forever, there is an intensification and increase of punishment for those who cannot participate, and of enjoyment for those who can participate" (trans. Constas).

73. Does patristic thought affirm that the human being or the human has as immortal *nature*? This would annul the created-uncreated distinction, as something created would be beyond the constraints of createdness *per se*, due to its very nature. On these and other relevant matters, cf. Zizioulas, *Communion and Otherness*, 259–69.

It is interesting to note Maximus speaks in another context of the "irrational and absolute and substanceless *inexistence*"[74] that results from a life in sin, i.e., a life contrary to our real nature (παρὰ φύσιν). Judging from the Confessor's general precise use of philosophical and theological signifiers, I think his reference to the "irrational and absolute and substanceless *inexistence*" that results from a life that embodies a conscious refusal of God's creative and relational call is not merely a literary or rhetorical *topos*. In such a case, hell would be a signifier (and not merely a "symbol") of *inexistence*, the result of a life consistently "contrary to nature." However, the question arises: is it possible at all for the human being's answer to God's creative call to be *wholly negative and rejective* (or wholly affirmative, for that matter)? Can man's life be constituted as a continuous and absolute choice of non-relation, death, non-communion, and inexistence (or of communion, relation, and life)? Or are these absolute choices extremities that cannot be truly attained in their wholeness, thereby annulling the possibility of a human person's life truly resulting in "absolute and substanceless inexistence"? In such a case, "irrational and absolute and substanceless inexistence" would remain a potentiality/possibility (a signifier of the will's true freedom) that cannot be truly actualized in its wholeness. The possibility a person's life has been a chosen rejection God's creative call, relation, communion, and life, but has not "achieved" the completeness of rejection that would result in inexistence (thereby being granted a participation in existence that cannot but be incomplete due to the person's overwhelming rejection of it) illustrates an existential drama; an eternal hell.

Certain passages of the Confessor's could lead to this conclusion. In *Πρὸς Θαλάσσιον II*, CCSG 22, 59.159–70, Maximus mentions the delight (ἡδονή) of those that will be united with God by his nature and grace[75] and the pain and anguish (ὀδύνη) of those that "will be united with God by his nature but contrary to grace."[76] The criterion is each human person's own "quality of disposition,"[77] each human person's preparedness for this union, i.e., the full and absolute union of God with each and every one at the "end

---

74. *Scholia in De Divinis Nominibus*, CD4.1 305B (fn. 309), "Τῆς κατὰ φύσιν κινήσεως ἤτοι τάξεως ἀποτυγχάνοντες, φερόμεθα εἰς τὴν παρὰ φύσιν ἄλογον, καὶ παντελῆ καὶ ἀνούσιον ἀνυπαρξίαν."

75. *Q.Thal. II*, 59.160–63, "ὑπὲρ φύσιν δὲ λέγω τὴν θείαν καὶ ἀνεννόητον ἡδονήν, ἣν ποιεῖν πέφυκεν ὁ θεὸς φύσει κατὰ τὴν χάριν τοῖς ἀξίοις ἑνούμενος."

76. Ibid., 59.163–65, "παρὰ φύσιν δὲ τὴν κατὰ στέρησιν ταύτης συνισταμένην ἀνεκλάλητον ὀδύνην, ἣν ποιεῖν εἴωθεν ὁ θεός, φύσει παρὰ τὴν χάριν τοῖς ἀναξίοις ἑνούμενος."

77. Ibid., 59.165–66, "κατὰ γὰρ τὴν ὑποκειμένην ἑκάστῳ ποιότητα τῆς διαθέσεως."

of the ages."[78] According to the Confessor, this union with the uncreated, a union effecting the continuation of existence through life-giving relation and communion, will take place in any case due to God's own nature. The ones whose answer to God's continuous creative call from nonbeing into being is a negative one are bound to experience this union as pain and anguish, for it is a union contrary to their preparedness for receptiveness and communion, contrary to their quality of disposition. This reading of Maximus', contrary to his passage concerning the "irrational and absolute and substanceless inexistence,"[79] accounts for a *tendency* of the disposition towards inexistence that, regrettably, cannot be truly actualized; an existential hell.[80]

Essentially, this is not a question of philological and exegetical preciseness but of ontological consistency, much in the vein of Maximus the Confessor's own primary concern as a church father. The affirmation of both a truly free will and immortality of the soul in the context of the ecclesial testimony remains, in my opinion, an unresolved philosophical *problem* in need of bold attempts at consistently addressing it.

Createdness and the Uncreated[81]

Following this short examination of aspects of Maximus' anthropology and in order to understand his ontology and cosmology, I need to elaborate on the created-uncreated distinction and on its difference from ancient Greek ontology and cosmology.[82] According to Greek philosophy,[83] to the almost

---

78. Ibid., 59.168–70, "ἕκαστος ὑφ' ἑαυτοῦ διαπεπλασμένος πρὸς ὑποδοχὴν τοῦ πάντως πᾶσιν ἐνωθησομένου κατὰ τὸ πέρας τῶν αἰώνων."

79. *Scholia in De Divinis Nominibus*, CD4.1 305B (fn. 309).

80. The reader is here reminded of Maximus the Confessor's aforementioned explicit reference to "the *risk* of dissolving into nonbeing" in *Myst.*, 1.70–72.

81. On Maximus' account of *creatio ex nihilo* as "the basic gulf" between creation and the uncreated and an accurate and comprehensive overview of Maximus' cosmology and ontology in general, see Thunberg's *Microcosm and Mediator*, 49–93.

82. On the importance of this distinction, cf. Zizioulas, *Communion and Otherness*, 250–69; "'Created' and 'Uncreated', the Existential Significance of Chalcedonian Christology."

83. However, the differences between the ancient Greek and the Hellenized early Christian and Byzantine ontology and cosmology do not entail a discontinuity in Greek philosophical thought, but an evolution thereof. See Oehler, *Antike Philosophie und Byzantinisches Mittelalter*, and particularly the chapter entitled "Die Kontinuität der Philosophie der Griechen bis zum Untergang des byzantinisches Reiches," 15–37. As the notion of πρόσωπον is of particular importance in this study, please note Oehler's comments on it in the context of the continuity of Greek philosophical thought.

unanimous view of Greek philosophers, nothing can come out of nothing;[84] a *creatio ex nihilo* would be absurd, and matter is pre-existing and eternal (even if not in its present form and order).[85] A direct consequence of this is that the prime characteristic of existence is *necessity* (albeit a mostly harmonious and orderly necessity, as a number of philosophers would have it): existence *is what it is*, it could not have been something else. This is illustrated even in these fragments of Greek philosophical thought according to which the world has been intentionally created by a God. In Plato's *Timaeus*, the Demiurge created the world according to his free will (θελήσει).[86] However, even this cannot escape the principle of necessity, it cannot accomplish freedom: God the Creator (i) *had* to create out of pre-existing matter, (ii) *had* to conform with the ideas of Beauty and Goodness, and (iii) *had* to be limited to a pre-existing space (χώρα). As such, his creation according to his free will was, actually, an unfree act, an ontologically constrained act.[87] The notion of *creatio ex nihilo* is absent in Greek thought, for which matter is essentially eternal,[88] while necessity dictates even the attributes of Aristotle's prime unmoved mover.

The Judaeo-Christian notion of *creatio ex nihilo* by a personal uncreated Creator, and especially its elaboration and refinement during the patristic era, replaces the ontological precedence of necessity[89] with *otherness* and *freedom*. Otherness and freedom become primary ontological characteristics of existence.

Otherness, because the absolute difference of the created and the uncreated (Maximus speaks of it as the first division)[90] constitutes an absolute

---

84. See, e.g., Aristotle, *Physics*, 191a, 23.

85. Zizioulas, *Communion and Otherness*, 15.

86. Plato, *Timaeus*, 29.

87. Zizioulas, *Communion and Otherness*, 16.

88. Cf. Maximus the Confessor, *Car.*, 3.28.1–2, "When the Greek philosophers affirm that the substance of beings coexisted eternally with God and that they received only their individual qualities from him, they say that there is nothing contrary to substance" (trans. Berthold).

89. According to Maximus the Confessor, it is an "utter blasphemy" to speak of *necessity* in the case of God, even of the necessity of him being good or creative, *D.Pyrrh.*, PG91 293C, "Εἰ γὰρ κατ᾽ αὐτὴν τὸ φυσικὸν πάντως καὶ ἠναγκασμένον· φύσει δὲ ὁ Θεὸς Θεός, φύσει ἀγαθός, φύσει δημιουργός· ἀνάγκη ἔσται ὁ Θεὸς Θεός, καὶ ἀγαθὸς καὶ δημιουργός· ὅπερ καὶ ἐννοεῖν, μήτι γε λέγειν, ἐσχάτης ἐστὶ βλασφημίας." Cf. *Amb. Io.* 42, 1332A.

90. Maximus the Confessor, *Amb.Io.* 41, 1304D, "ὧν πρώτην μέν φασιν εἶναι τὴν διαιροῦσαν τῆς ἀκτίστου φύσεως τὴν κτιστὴν καθόλου φύσιν, καὶ διὰ γενέσεως τὸ εἶναι λαβοῦσαν."—"The first of these divides from the uncreated nature the universal created nature, which receives its being from becoming" (trans. Louth).

otherness of these two, an otherness that proves to be constitutive of being and existence, an otherness on an ontological level.[91] However, otherness is known as difference, difference is manifested through comparison, and comparison presupposes relation; otherness emerges, becomes manifest through relation, "communion does not threaten otherness; it generates it."[92] The fact that the Judaeo-Christian tradition speaks not of a creative *principle* or *power* but of a creative *person* makes *personal* otherness, *hypostatic* otherness, a primary ontological principle of existence.

And *freedom*, because the very fact that creation emerged out of nothing means that it could have also *not* emerged at all; the fact that *existence exists* is not a prescribed necessity, but the actualization of a possibility that is not devoid of alternatives. As such, creation is a *free* act, an act devoid of necessity, a *choice*, an act that transcends predeterminations and necessities.[93] If we take into account that, apart from creation, God also actualizes *his own existence* through the distinction of his hypostases "atemporally and out of love" (κινηθεὶς ἀχρόνως καὶ ἀγαπητικῶς),[94] this manifests freedom as nothing less than the *causal mode of creation*: creation is a result of freedom.[95] However, there is also another side to a creation *ex nihilo*: the fact that existence emerged out of nothing means that it could also return to nothing (τὸ μὴ ὄν). Total, absolute inexistence (either of something, someone, or the totality of existence) becomes possible, whereas in Greek philosophy it would be impossible. In actuality, a creation out of nothing is bound to perish, for if this was not the case, it would have emerged out of an imperishable something, thus not having absolute otherness and freedom.[96] Atemporality and endlessness can be attained only if the participation in the mode of the uncreated were possible.

This difference between the ancient Greek and Christian thought, the created-uncreated distinction, is the very frame and foundation of their ontologies: to compare secondary characteristics of these ontologies without taking into account the profound implications of this difference would not lead to sound philosophical conclusions. If the uncreated existence signifies the possibility of existence without decay, death, time, constraints, and

---

91. *Amb.Io.* 10, 1077A, Ἐπὶ Θεοῦ δὲ καὶ πλέον, ὅσον ἀκτίστου καὶ κτιστῶν ἄπειρον τὸ μέσον ἐστὶ καὶ διάφορον.

92. Zizioulas, *Communion and Otherness*, 5.

93. On the correlation of the created-uncreated dialectic and existential freedom, see Zizioulas, *Communion and Otherness*, 255–56. Also note Zizioulas' comments on death as an existential event emerging from the created-uncreated dialectic in 257–59.

94. *Scholia in De Divinis Nominibus*, CD4.1 221A.

95. Yannaras, *Relational Ontology*, 10–10.3.6 (49–55).

96. Zizioulas, *Communion and Otherness*, 18f.

limits, then the only hope of creatures is to participate in its *mode of exis-tence* (τρόπος ὑπάρξεως),[97] as they cannot participate in its nature.

The Mode of the Uncreated

The very distinction between substance, hypostasis, and the activities that hypostasize (actualize) the substance, the very mention of the *difference* be-tween the λόγος of nature-substance and the *mode* of its existence (λόγος φύσεως—τρόπος ὑπάρξεως) implies that creatures need not be mechanisti-cally actualized (hypostasized), but that their actual existence can manifest a certain freedom from the predeterminations of their substance, lest all hypostases be identical. "The difference of natures, the difference of uncre-ated and created, can be transcended at the level of the common mode of existence, the mode of personal existence."[98] An extreme case is the incarna-tion of the Son, whose divine nature seems incompatible with his human presence. The boundless freedom of God (even the freedom to become that which he is not) is iconized in human beings, each "unique, dissimilar, and unrepeatable"[99] human hypostasis is constituted as a person (i.e., as an existence-in-relation that can determine its reality beyond its substance), "in the image and in the likeness" of the One who can adopt a wholly other mode of existence, of God—whose nature or substance *as such* is totally unapproachable.[100]

The mode (τρόπος) of a being "is an inseparable aspect of being, as primary ontologically as substance or nature."[101] The question of *how* a

97. On an account of Maximus' use of the term τρόπος, as well as of πρόσωπον and ὑπόστασις, cf. Skliris' article "'Hypostasis', 'Person', 'Individual', A Comparison between the Terms that Denote Concrete Being in St. Maximus' Theology."

98. Yannaras, *Elements of Faith*, 59.

99. Yannaras, *Relational Ontology*, 10.3.2 (p. 52).

100. *Amb.Io.* 34, 1288B, "Ἐκ τῶν κατὰ τὴν οὐσίαν, τουτέστι ἐκ τῆς οὐσίας αὐτῆς, ὁ Θεὸς οὐδέποτέ τι ὑπάρχων γινώσκεται. Ἀμήχανος γὰρ καὶ παντελῶς ἄβατος πάσῃ τῇ κτίσει. . . . . Πάντα δὲ τὰ περὶ τὴν οὐσίαν οὐ τὸ τί ἐστιν, ἀλλὰ τί οὐκ ἔστιν ὑποδηλοῖ, οἷον τὸ ἀγέννητον, τὸ ἄναρχον, τὸ ἄπειρον, τὸ ἀσώματον, καὶ ὅσα τοιαῦτα περὶ τὴν οὐσίαν εἰσί, καὶ τό τι μὴ εἶναι, οὐχ ὅτι δὲ τό τι εἶναι αὐτὴν παριστῶσιν."—"From those things that pertain to God's substance, that is, from the substance itself, it has never at any time been known what God is. For to have even an idea of what God might be is impossible and completely beyond the reach of all creation. . . . But all the things that are 'around' the substance do not disclose what the substance itself is, but what it is not, such as not being created, not having a beginning, not being finite, not being corporeal, and any other such things that are around the substance, and which indicate what it is not, but not what it is" (trans. Constas).

101. Zizioulas, *Communion and Otherness*, 24–25.

thing exists is as important as is the question of *what* it is; the particulars' existence cannot be downgraded when compared to their substances, as this would constitute an ontology that divorces ontological models from the world that they claim to represent.

It is not natural creation by itself, but God's *incarnation* that bridges the abyss between the creatures and the uncreated.[102] In Maximus' understanding, Christ's incarnation, birth, death, and resurrection *renews* the very foundations of creation and nature, as it bridges the absolute gap between creation and the uncreated.[103] By taking on human nature, God has fulfilled the preconditions for man to receive divine properties and qualities, to partake in divine, uncreated reality, for man to be *deified*, saved, and completed.[104] As the connecting link between the created world and the uncreated, as the *sense* of the created world and the hope of its completion in full communion with the uncreated, the person of Jesus Christ is the center of Christian ontology and cosmology: Torstein Tollefsen speaks of the *Christocentric* cosmology of Maximus the Confessor, and very accurately indeed.[105] Maximus asserts the human person can be deified in every sense "except of the identity of substance":[106] the human person cannot take on the divine *substance* in place of his human substance, but is able to partake in every other way in God's divinity, by iconizing and actualizing the existential *mode* of the uncreated, the mode of relation, self-transcendence, and

102. Their main and definitive difference is that creation does not contain its cause within itself—as well as its purpose. See *Amb.Io.* 7, 1072BC, οὐδὲν γὰρ τῶν γενητῶν ἑαυτοῦ τέλος ἐστίν, ἐπειδὴ οὔτε αὐταίτιον, ἐπεὶ καὶ ἀγένητον καὶ ἄναρχον καὶ ἀκίνητον. "No created being is the end and purpose of itself, as it is not the cause of itself, or else it would be unoriginated and beginningless and motionless." A sentence later, Maximus clarifies, "τέλος ἐστὶν οὗ ἕνεκεν τὰ πάντα, αὐτὸ δὲ οὐδενὸς ἕνεκεν"—"Purpose and end is that due to which everything exists, but that which does not owe its existence to something else," i.e., God. τὸ αὐτοτελὲς γάρ πως καὶ ἀναίτιον—"For that which contains its purpose and end contains also its cause."

103. For example, cf. *Amb.Th.*, 5.73–74, 5.143–46.

104. Cf. *Amb.Th.*, 5.152–55, *Amb.Io.* 31, 1273D–1276D, 1280C, *Amb.Io.* 36, 1289D, and *Q.Thal. I*, 22.8–13: "The plan was for him to mingle, without change on his part, with human nature by true hypostatic union, to unite human nature to himself while remaining immutable, so that he might become a man, as he alone knew how, and so that he might deify humanity in union with himself" (trans. Blowers).

105. Tollefsen, *Christocentric Cosmology*.

106. *Ep.*, PG91 376AB, "ὅλοι δι' ὅλου γινόμεθα θεοὶ χωρὶς τῆς κατ' οὐσίαν ταυτότητος." And *Q.Thal. I*, 22.40–44, "πάντως καὶ τῆς ἐπὶ τῷ θεωθῆναι τὸν ἄνθρωπον μυστικῆς ἐνεργείας λήψεται πέρας, κατὰ πάντα τρόπον, χωρὶς μόνης δηλονότι τῆς πρὸς αὐτὸν κατ' οὐσίαν ταυτότητος, ὁμοιώσας ἑαυτῷ τὸν ἄνθρωπον"—"Then God will also completely fulfill the goal of his mystical work of deifying humanity in every respect, of course, short of an identity of substance with God; and he will assimilate humanity to himself" (trans. Blowers).

love, for love[107] is the identity of God, not merely one of his attributes: "God is love."[108] However, the human person cannot attain deification by himself, it is not in his nature: it can only be granted to him, given to him as a present (χάρις, χάρισμα) by the Other of the relationship.

According to the ecclesial testimony, only the human person can attain deification, for only the human being is truly a *person*, i.e., a creature in the image and likeness of the Creator; the *return* of creation to the full communion with God, the *redemption* of creation, can only take place *through* man's deification; this is the task of mediation.[109] As such, man is responsible not only for his individual completion-salvation-deification, but constitutes the hope for the salvation of the whole of creation, he is the priest and mediator of creation, man is truly a *microcosm and mediator*.[110]

God's nature and substance remains absolutely unapproachable, but man can partake in God through God's *activities* (ἐνέργειαι).[111] The presence of God in all of creation through his *activities*[112] can be described as

107. There is a surprisingly extended tendency to understand the word love (ἀγάπη) when applied to God or Christians in a moral, ethical sense, pertaining to *behavior* (to associate it with kindness, altruism, etc.). However, such a use of the word is devoid of ontological content; and the ontological content of both ἀγάπη and ἔρως is that of radical referentiality and existential self-transcendence instead of individual onticity and atomicity. Interestingly, the author of the Areopagite corpus remarks that even as early as his time, theologians tended to treat the name of love as kindness (ἀγάπη) as equivalent to that of love as ἔρως; and he prefers to attribute true ἔρως to things divine because of the "misplaced prejudice" of the theologians, who misunderstand the meaning of ἀγάπη. Corpus Dionysiacum, *De Divinis Nominibus*, CD I, 157, "Ἐμοὶ γὰρ δοκοῦσιν οἱ θεολόγοι κοινὸν μὲν ἡγεῖσθαι τὸ τῆς ἀγάπης καὶ τοῦ ἔρωτος ὄνομα, διὰ τοῦτο δὲ τοῖς θείοις μᾶλλον ἀναθεῖναι τὸν ὄντως ἔρωτα διὰ τὴν ἄτοπον τῶν τοιούτων ἀνδρῶν πρόληψιν."

108. 1 John 4:8, "ὁ θεὸς ἀγάπη ἐστίν."

109. A shorter account by Thunberg on the "fivefold mediation of man as a perfect realization of the theandric dimension of the universe," i.e., on the transcendence of all five major ontological, cosmological, and anthropological divisions/distinctions within creation, can be found in 80–91 of his *Man and the Cosmos*.

110. *Microcosm and Mediator* is the title of Thunberg's book on Maximus, as I mentioned earlier. It should be noted again that Thunberg's understanding of Maximus is most profound, making his monograph one of the best studies on Maximus; among the studies of Maximus' anthropology, it stands out as without doubt the most illuminating treatise on the subject. A different account of Maximus' ontology and cosmology *through* his anthropology, and particularly through the notion of *sin*, can be found in Völker's *Maximus Confessor als Meister*, and particularly in 23–101, i.e., up to Völker's treatment of the subject of sin as such.

111. There is an ever-increasing bibliography on the substance/activities distinction in Maximus the Confessor, well before Gregory Palamas, but the only monograph dedicated to the subject remains Karayiannis' *Maxime le Confesseur: Essence et energies*.

112. Cf. Maximus the Confessor, *Amb.Io.* 7, 1080B, "For all things, in that they came

in a way similar to the presence of the painter in his painting or of the poet in his poem—and yet more real, as it can lead to an encounter in all immediacy. The presence of God within creation through his *activities* refers to the *indirect* presence of God's otherness through and within his creatures, in roughly the same way that any artist's person and otherness is, indirectly, present in his creations. (Maximus would say God is present within creation through the λόγοι of beings, which in turn are divine activities, as we will see.) This is substantially different from theologies stating that God, exactly due to his absolute otherness, is *wholly absent* from creation. However, the abyss between Creator and creation is only bridged by the incarnation, for it is only then that God has a full and *hypostatic* presence within creation, i.e., not merely through the outcomes of his creative otherness (outcomes that possess their own, distinct otherness), but through the concrete presence of this otherness itself.

It is the incarnation and resurrection that make deification possible. According to the Confessor, the participation in the uncreated radically transforms the created, it *deifies* the created, as it fully restores the communion with its source of existence. Maximus describes this participation in the uncreated as follows:

> Participation in supranatural divine [realities] is the assimilation of those who participate to that in which they participate. The assimilation of those who participate to that in which they participate is their identity with it, actively achieved through assimilation. The identity of those who participate with that in which they participate, which can be actively achieved through assimilation, is the deification of those accounted worthy to be deified. And deification is the encompassing and ultimate end of everything that exists in time and eternity, according to the general description of all times and ages. The inclusion and ultimate end of the times and ages and everything that exists within them is the inseparable unity within those who are being saved between the absolute very beginning of things and their absolute and literal end.[113]

---

to be from God, participate proportionally in God, whether by intellect, by λόγος, by sense-perception, by vital motion, or by some habitual fitness" (trans. Blowers). And *Myst.*, 23.8–10, "Among us they [i.e., the Greeks] would never have been called wise because they could not or would not recognize God from his works" (trans. Berthold).

113. *Q.Thal. II*, 59.134–49, "Μέθεξις δὲ τῶν ὑπὲρ φύσιν θείων ἐστὶν ἡ πρὸς τὸ μετεχόμενον τῶν μετεχόντων ὁμοίωσις· ἡ δὲ πρὸς τὸ μετεχόμενον τῶν μετεχόντων ὁμοίωσίς ἐστιν ἡ κατ᾽ ἐνέργειαν πρὸς αὐτὸ τὸ μετεχόμενον τῶν μετεχόντων δι᾽ ὁμοιότητος ἐνδεχομένη ταυτότης· ἡ δὲ τῶν μετεχόντων ἐνδεχομένη κατ᾽ ἐνέργειαν δι᾽ ὁμοιότητος πρὸς τὸ μετεχόμενον ταυτότης ἐστὶν ἡ θέωσις τῶν ἀξιουμένων θεώσεως· ἡ

An Ontological Ecclesiology?

I stated earlier that for the consciousness of the undivided Christian church, the person of Jesus Christ as the hypostatic union of human and divine, of created and uncreated nature, is the model for transcending the abysmal gap between the finite, decaying, temporal creation, and the fullness of freedom, the uncreated—the hope of humanity, creatures, and creation itself for the overcoming of limitations, distance, decay, and death.

However, this is not to be understood as the following of an example or as an object of imitation, as these would constitute moral/behavioral terms, not existential/ontological ones. A *reproduction* of Christ's mode of existence without his real presence is unanimously excluded as a possibility. Only the *participation* in Christ and in Christ's mode of existence can actualize this change in the mode of existence—a participation in what the ecclesial testimony attests as the *body* of Christ, the church. The root of the ontological and anthropological significance of the church for Christians is precisely the fact that they recognize it as the real *body* of Christ, the realism of the possibility of participation in his mode of existence, the realism of accepting the iconizing of this mode of existence (existence-as-relation, love, ἔρως) as a path towards the fullness of his likeness, the fullness of communion-in-otherness. The fullness of communion is, simultaneously, the disclosure of absolute otherness, as we have seen. The church professes to be the body of a person, and the personal character of both the church and one's participation in it is of paramount importance, as "only a person can manifest communion and otherness simultaneously, thanks to it being a *mode* of being, that is, an identity which, unlike substance or energy [i.e., activity], is capable of 'modifying' its being without losing its ontological uniqueness and otherness."[114] According to Zizioulas' analysis, other ways of explaining the communion of creation and the uncreated are either non-ontological attempts (ethics, psychology, natural religiosity) or an undermining of the reality of the hypostatic union between created and uncreated being in a single person, i.e., the incarnation.[115] If such was the case, the ecclesial event would have no place in a discussion pertaining to ontology

---

δὲ θέωσίς ἐστι καθ' ὑπογραφῆς λόγον πάντων τῶν χρόνων καὶ τῶν αἰώνων καὶ τῶν ἐν χρόνῳ καὶ αἰῶνι περιοχὴ καὶ πέρας· περιοχὴ δὲ καὶ πέρας τῶν χρόνων καὶ τῶν αἰώνων ἐστὶ καὶ πάντων τῶν ἐν αὐτοῖς ἡ τῆς ἀκραιφνοῦς καὶ κυρίως ἀρχῆς πρὸς τὸ κυρίως τέλος καὶ ἀκραιφνὲς ἐν τοῖς σῳζομένοις ἀδιάστατος ἑνότης· ἀδιάστατος δὲ τῆς ἀκραιφνοῦς ἀρχῆς τε καὶ τέλους ἑνότης ἐν τοῖς σῳζομένοις ἐστὶν ἡ κρείττων τῶν οὐσιωδῶς ἀρχῇ τε καὶ τέλει μεμετρημένων τῶν κατὰ φύσιν ἔκβασις." Trans. by Theokritoff, in Loudovikos, *Eucharistic Ontology*, 17.

114. Zizioulas, *Communion and Otherness*, 29.

115. Ibid.

(the basics of existence, its limitations, and the possibility to be freed from these limitations)—no ontological content or significance at all—but merely a behavioral, "moral" role, perhaps transmuting man's *behavior*, but without any hope of changing man's *being*, man's *existence*.

The hope of the church is to change the *"howness"* of creatures, their mode of existence. As there is no "naked" nature, no οὐσία ἀνυπόστατος, the hope of men, creatures, and creation is that their relationship with the uncreated, with God, through Christ's person can allow for a true and full communion of othernesses, communion with each other's being and existence, without a change of natures, of substances, of the *"whatness"* of beings. For this reason, "the relation of God to the world is not 'ethical' or 'psychological' or anything other than *ontological*."[116] One could say that believers see the body of Christ as "applied ontology." In being *members* of this body, the partakers of the ecclesial event do not hear a teaching or shape a way of behavior, but they iconize the transmutation of the mode of the world's existence. They use bread and wine,[117] not to nourish their individual beings, not for their individual subsistence and survival, but to share life as communion—and they trust the promise that this is not mere symbolism, but that it constitutes the answer to a call that is perpetually formulated, the uncreated God's call to enter a direct relationship with him. In order to do this, they do not encounter the world as an aggregation of objects, but as *creation*, the outcome of a person's creative activity and his free present to them—to which they respond with gratitude, thanksgiving, εὐχαριστία, the Eucharist. As such, the Eucharistic stance towards reality is not a behavior, but a distinct mode of contemplating/receiving the world, a distinct mode of relating with reality, a mode that is not the goal (a set behavioral objective), but the *outcome* of the transmutation of one's way of existing, a person's τρόπος ὑπάρξεως, by experiencing life as communion and not in its fragmented ("fallen") state.

To achieve such a transmutation of one's mode of existence by being a member of the body of the person that is the hypostatic union of created and uncreated nature and by gradually adopting the *mode of existence* of that person, Christ, is to be *sanctified*. To *actualize* the mode of existence of the uncreated is to become *deified,* to *become God* without, of course, being able to adopt its nature or substance, as Maximus asserts.[118] The way

---

116. Ibid., 25.

117. Which are no mere consumable goods, but recapitulate a year's toil in the context of the agrarian society, a year's toil to provide subsistence to oneself and to one's family.

118. *Ep.*, PG91 376AB, "ὅλοι δι᾽ ὅλου γινόμεθα θεοὶ χωρὶς τῆς κατ᾽ οὐσίαν ταυτότητος."

to this is one of *adoption*, of iconizing the internal relations of the Trinity by recognizing the uncreated person of the Father as the father of your created person.

I would say, following John Zizioulas, that as the created-uncreated distinction is one of the foundations of existence for the ecclesial community, *the church is a primary ontological category*, for it embodies Christ's union of createdness and the uncreated, the possibility and practice of a transformative communion of two wholly other modes of existence: the mode of createdness and the mode of the uncreated, the mode of decay and the mode of freedom.[119] As such, it constitutes a *third* reality or possibility along createdness and the uncreated—or, more precisely, a *mode* distinct from the modes of these two. The language to portray this mode is the language of *communion* and *otherness*. According to Zizioulas' reading of Maximus, this is a "Maximian ontology, which . . . is philosophically the best and most satisfying way of working out an ontology of communion and otherness,"[120] "an ontology which permits communion and otherness to coincide thanks to the intervention of personhood between God and creation."[121]

Gregory of Nyssa's Influence

In this chapter, I have attempted to provide an overview of the ecclesial *Weltanschauung* in which Maximus thinks, operates, and writes, including fragments of his own contributions to the rich texture of this *Weltanschauung*. While I have repeatedly stressed that I will not focus on his late antique context, the influence of Gregory of Nyssa on Maximus' thought must at least be explicitly noted here.

This is especially the case concerning a concept that will prove to be pivotal for Maximus' spatio-temporal philosophy, i.e., Gregory of Nyssa's appropriation of the notion of διάστημα and its reception by Maximus.

---

119. The fact that limitations, spatio-temporality, and decay are primary characteristics of created reality as we know it does not mean the world is *bad*; on the contrary, creation is asserted as *truly good* (καλὰ λίαν, Gen 1:31). Maximus asserts in *Q.Thal. I*, 27.56–64 that the contemplation of the beings' λόγοι leads one to acknowledge that there is nothing impure within creation, it is corruption that provides us with the illusion that there is impurity and conflict within creation. However, the *difference* of the uncreated from creation *as we know it*, the actualization of a mode of atomicity, existential individuality and death (death as non-relation) manifests these characteristics. In ecclesial language, this is termed *the fall*.

120. Zizioulas, *Communion and Otherness*, 26.

121. Ibid., 26.

Space/place and διάστημα, as well as ontological "distance" *in general,* is a nexus of ideas indispensable for Maximus' thought, which goes back to Gregory. Note Hans Urs von Balthasar's remarks: "Maximus took up Gregory of Nyssa's axiom that finite being is essentially characterized by *spatial intervals* (διάστημα) and, therefore, by *motion*";[122] "Time and space are, for Maximus and Gregory of Nyssa, the expression of finitude itself; they are pure limitation. Space is not fundamentally a physical or astronomical reality but an ontological category, 'the limitation of the world through itself.'"[123] All this is integrally related to the notion of motion: "the ontology of created being is a study of motion. More precisely, it is the study of the relationship between rest and motion, whose balance is what defines the essence of finite being"[124]

I must here once more stress, while Maximus draws from diverse sources in order to achieve his unique synthesis and considers himself a natural continuator of the patristic tradition, Gregory of Nyssa must have been a particularly strong influence on his thought, especially on matters concerning motion and time. Maximus' explicit and implicit use of the notion of spatial, temporal, and generally ontological *distance* (διάστημα, often translated as interval or extension), which among other things is a key difference between creation (which possesses it and which is defined by it) and the uncreated (where there is no *distance*), is based on Gregory of Nyssa's conception thereof. And it is on this notion that a great number of interconnected Maximian concepts depend, as we will see in the next chapters.

While there are a number of paradoxical phrases concerning motion prior to Maximus' στάσις ἀεικίνητος,[125] it is also on this matter that Gregory's influence (to which Maximus was subject) must have been most decisive. Gregory of Nyssa's eschatological identification of eternal movement with fixity[126] must have served as a predecessor and influence for Maximus' "ever-moving repose."[127]

---

122. Von Balthasar, *Cosmic Liturgy,* 138.

123. Ibid., 139.

124. Ibid., 154.

125. Such as Proclus' κίνησις ἀκίνητος, cf. Gersh, *Κίνησις Ἀκίνητος.*

126. "This is the most marvelous thing of all, how the same thing is both a standing still (στάσις) and a moving (κίνησις)": Gregory of Nyssa, *Vit. Mos.,* 2.243.

127. On this, see Blowers' article "Maximus the Confessor, Gregory of Nyssa, and the Concept of 'Perpetual Progress,'" 157–65, where this is demonstrated. On Gregory of Nyssa's thought on distance, time and the Aeon, see also Plass' "Transcendent Time and Eternity in Gregory of Nyssa" and his "Transcendent Time in Maximus the Confessor," as well as Bradshaw's "Time and Eternity in the Greek Fathers," 335–42. See also

It is precisely due to the fact that a comparative approach to Gregory and Maximus on motion, time, space, and most importantly *distance* would merit at least a book-length monograph of its own that such an approach would be outside the scope of this study. However, before embarking on Maximus' λόγοι doctrine, I must nevertheless note that Gregory's influence on Maximus on these matters is much, much more discernible than that of other church fathers prior to the Confessor.

Plass' account of the Maximian στάσις ἀεικίνητος in his "'Moving Rest' in Maximus the Confessor." On the evolution of the notion of διάστημα up to Gregory of Nyssa, see Cvetkovic's "St Gregory's Argument," 369–73, and for Gregory's contribution see 373–82. Tollefsen's analysis of Gregory of Nyssa in *Activity and Participation* are also of interest here, even if not directly focusing on διάστημα.

CHAPTER FOUR

Maximus' "Logical" Ontology: The λόγοι of Beings

THE NOTION OF THE λόγοι is of fundamental importance in understanding St. Maximus the Confessor's thought—his ontology in particular—and, quite naturally, there is ample bibliography on the subject.[1] However, it is quite often the case that parts of the relevant secondary literature can be misleading in some points. Some scholars attempt a partial and fragmentary approach to the λόγοι doctrine as it has been modified, formulated, and elaborated by Maximus, focusing only on a limited part of the theory's spectrum, while others approach Maximus' λόγοι from an exclusively comparative or historical/philological perspective (i.e., "from the outside," not from the study of Maximus' thought in itself), nearly equating them with versions of the Platonic doctrine of ideas circulating among Maximus' Neoplatonic contemporaries. More often than not, this approach results in missing St. Maximus' point, for his understanding of the λόγοι is much more intriguing than being a mere Christian appropriation of the Platonic doctrine of ideas, to the point of being nearly non-comparable once one moves beyond the level of mere appearances.

In this chapter, I will attempt to provide the reader with a brief introduction to understanding Maximus' λόγοι doctrine from a philosophical and at times contemporary (i.e., deliberately anachronistic)

---

1. An interesting introduction is to be found in the λόγοι chapters of Tollefsen's monographs, *Activity and Participation* and *Christocentric Cosmology*, as well as in Louth's "St Maximos' Doctrine of the *logoi* of Creation." Apart from these, an account of the λόγος doctrine in Maximus and up to Maximus, as well as of the λόγος φύσεως-τρόπος ὑπάρξεως (λόγος of nature-mode of existence) distinction, is located in Sherwood's *Earlier Ambigua*, 155–80.

perspective.[2] My aim will be to address (or rather merely hint at) the numerous aspects that together comprise Maximus' vision of the λόγοι: (a) the uncreated λόγοι as links between creation and the uncreated, (b) the relationship between the λόγοι and the Λόγος as well as the recapitulation of the many in the one Λόγος, (c) the importance of the λόγος of nature for the "according to nature"-"contrary to nature" distinction, (d) the λόγοι as the basis for a dialogical reciprocity between Creator and creatures/humanity, (e) the accomplishment of the contemplation of the λόγοι within asceticism, of the ability to clearly see God's uncreated wills, utterances, and intentions behind and within created beings, (f) the λόγοι as signifying a divine creative act of *freedom*, not of necessity or predetermination, etc. As Maximus' works are not comprised of systematic expositions of his terminology, but of a terminology that is quite chaotically scattered in his voluminous and dense work, in this brief introduction I will prefer to provide an overall overview through my hermeneutic perspective and through my secondary sources and not a textual analysis of certain passages. Two issues that will *not* be hinted at at this point in my study—because they require a deeper overview of the λόγος φύσεως τρόπος ὑπάρξεως distinction than this introduction can achieve and a focus on the notion of the *mode* (τρόπος)—are (i) the prevalence of the τρόποι over the λόγοι in the context of the historical reality that leads to the ἔσχατα, which has its roots in the fact that (ii) while substances/natures are actualized in hypostases in accordance with their λόγοι, the human/created and divine/uncreated natures do not share a common λόγος of nature. This means the hypostatic union in Christ is achieved on the level of the τρόπος of a hypostasis, not on the level of the λόγοι of nature(s), that it is reflected only in the τρόπος and not in the λόγοι, thus stressing the importance of the transcendence of some of the λόγοι's "predeterminations" through the τρόπος in an eschatological and soteriological perspective.[3]

In order to introduce the reader to the λόγοι, I will first present the semantic polysemy of λόγος *as a word*. Ensuing some remarks on Λόγος as God and as the person of the Son in particular, I will subsequently proceed to a discussion of the relationship between the λόγος, the nature/substance and the motion "according to nature," as well as of the recapitulation of the many λόγοι in the one Λόγος. Concluding, I will remark on how the λόγοι cause reality to be actualized as a dialogical reciprocity of humanity and

2. A version of this introduction to Maximus' "logical ontology" has been published as Mitralexis, "Maximus' 'Logical' Ontology" in the journal *Sobornost*.

3. See also Lévy, *Le Créé et l'Incréé*, 327. It is to Dr. Dionysios Skliris that I owe this observation, which has been kindly shared with me.

the Creator in the context of humanity's *mediating* cosmological function.[4] Of great use to me will be Metropolitan John Zizioulas' insights on the one Λόγος as the many λόγοι, Christos Yannaras' fundamental definition of the notion of λόγος as "the *mode* in which what *is* becomes manifest, is disclosed, becomes known"[5] and Nikolaos Loudovikos' understanding of the λόγοι as a Eucharistic ontology of dialogical reciprocity.[6]

The Semantic Frame of the Philosophical Notion of λόγος

A comprehensive overview of the philosophical use of the term λόγος (plural: λόγοι) up to Maximus the Confessor's time, both in the context of ancient Greek thought, the early church, and Neoplatonism, would be outside the scope of this study.[7] I will shortly examine what λόγος means *as a word* and subsequently turn to Maximus' unique contribution: his modification of the notion of the λόγοι is one of the most distinct characteristics of his philosophical thought.[8]

The polysemy of the word λόγος in the Greek language is vertiginously staggering.[9] As such, we cannot attempt to grasp its meaning by merely fo-

4. For humanity's cosmic mediating function (and the redemption of creation) in Maximus' thought, see Thunberg's magnum opus, *Microcosm and Mediator*.

5. Yannaras, Σχεδίασμα εἰσαγωγῆς, 20.

6. Loudovikos, *Eucharistic Ontology*.

7. There is ample bibliography on the matter, but a good introduction (for our intends and purposes) is to be found in the relevant chapters of Tollefsen's monographs, *Activity and Participation*, 64–137. An account of the λόγος doctrine in Maximus and up to Maximus, as well as of the λόγος φύσεως-τρόπος ὑπάρξεως (λόγος of nature-mode of existence) distinction, is to be found in Sherwood's *Earlier Ambigua*, 155–80, as well as in Louth's paper "St Maximos' Doctrine of the *logoi* of Creation."

8. On Thunberg's approach to Maximus' λόγοι cosmology and ontology, see *Microcosm and Mediator*, 72–79.

9. According to the Liddell-Scott-Jones *Greek-English Lexicon* and Geoffrey Lampe's *Patristic Lexicon*, the word λόγος can bear the following meanings, among others: relation, correspondence, proportion, ratio, analogy, rule, explanation, plea, pretext, ground, case, statement of a theory, argument, law, thesis, hypothesis, reason, definition, inward debate of the soul, reflection, deliberation, creative reason, speech, verbal expression, common talk, report, tradition, rumor, mention, notice, description, good report, praise, honor, discussion, debate, section, branch, oracle, proverb, maxim, saying, assertion, word of command, behest, intelligent utterance, sentence, spoken expression, word, statement, command, promise, conversation, discourse, report, tale, treatise, sermon, passage of Scripture, form of words, manner of speaking, substance of what is said, teaching, opinion, knowledge, language, immanent rationality, understanding, motive, principle, ground of cosmic order, formative and regulative law of being, principle or rule embodying the result of λογισμός, reckoning, computation, account, account of money handled, banking account, public accounts, measure, tale,

cusing on a number of its particular uses; we have to approach its general meaning, or more precisely the principle behind its polysemy, in a deductive manner. I have noted in previous chapters that Yannaras has formulated a definition of λόγος that succeeds in capturing the principle behind the polysemy of λόγος, a definition which I will repeat here: "λόγος is the mode by which everything that *is* becomes *manifest*, becomes *known*."[10] The word λόγος signifies every referential activity that manifests an otherness: as such, a primary meaning of λόγος is *disclosure*.[11]

This applies to almost all meanings of λόγος:

(a) Speech, word, language, is the *manifestation* and *disclosure* of a person's thought. Without this disclosure and manifestation, thought would not *be known* by any other person.

(b) In mathematical relations, λόγος as mathematical ratio and proportion discloses the truth of the relation of the given two terms. When we state that the number 2 is the λόγος or ratio of the division of 6 by 3, we mean that 2 is the *disclosure* of the relation of 6 to 3 in that division, we mean that 2 *manifests* and *discloses* the truth of that division. This applies to all meanings of λόγος as proportion.

(c) According to Christian theology, the uncreated God *speaks* (λέγει, aor. εἶπεν) and thereby *creates*: his λόγοι, his utterances, manifest and disclose his will to create, thereby creating. Creatures, as λόγοι, are the disclosure and manifestation of God's will and activity.[12] In the case of God, λόγος and ἔργον are identical, the λόγοι in God are God's activities (ἐνέργειαι).[13]

(d) God the Son is the *disclosure* of God the Father: it is through God the Son that the Father *is known*. It would be erroneous to understand this

sum, total of expenditure, consideration, value, matter, fact, regard, esteem, concern, interest, cause, manner, arrangement, condition, limitation, function, the second person of the Trinity, the Word or Wisdom of God, the source of man's rationality and of his communion with God *et alia*. The verb λέγω, of which λόγος is the verbal noun, initially meant both to pick up, to gather for oneself, to choose for oneself, to pick out, and to say, to tell, to speak, to mean, to count. See Liddell, Scott & Jones, *A Greek-English Lexicon* and Lampe, *A Patristic Greek Lexicon*.

10. Yannaras, Σχεδίασμα εἰσαγωγῆς στὴ φιλοσοφία, 20.

11. Cf. Yannaras, *Person and Eros*, 159–72, "The Logos as Disclosure of the Person," on both the etymological and semantic content of λόγος and its meaning as disclosure.

12. In the first chapter of *Genesis*, God's utterance is a creative action in itself, God creates everything in the world by speaking—with the sole exception of the human person, which is crafted by God "in God's image."

13. Gregory of Nyssa, *Hexaemeron*, PG44, 73A: Ἐπὶ γὰρ τοῦ Θεοῦ . . . τὸ ἔργον λόγος ἐστί.

under a Sabellianist light, annulling the reality of the difference of the hypostases: the mere fact that the Son is testified as being the Λόγος of the Father means that the Son is also the disclosure of the Father, the *signifier* of the Father, the revelation of the Father—while being a distinct hypostasis, a distinct actualization of God's being.[14]

"Logical" Existence and the God as Λόγος

Λόγος is also an inherently relational concept: the λόγος of an object *speaks* to us (λέγω), i.e., informs us of its identity, of its *what*-it-is, of its substance or nature (and of its *how*-it-is as well, of its particular actualization, of its hypostasis). The λόγος of something is its *mode* of communicating its existence and nature to us, the *mode* of its disclosure. Existence manifests itself as "logical" when its identity becomes a personal disclosure to a subject bearing the consciousness and personhood needed to actualize the relationality of this disclosure.

In this sense, the Λόγος of God,[15] the person of Christ, is the disclosure of God and the mode of God's disclosure, one of God's hypostases, i.e., actual realizations. The Λόγος of God informs us about God's identity as a Trinity of radical relationality and opens up the possibility of direct *participation* in the uncreated God's mode of existence.

Maximus states the λόγοι of beings are uncreated, preexistent in God:

> From all eternity, He [the Λόγος] contained within Himself the preexisting λόγοι of created beings. When, in His goodwill, He formed out of nothing the substance of the visible and invisible worlds, He did so on the basis of these λόγοι. *By His word (λόγος) and His wisdom He created* and continues to create *all things*—universals as well as particulars—at the appropriate time.[16]

The λόγοι of beings *define* the beings to which they correspond.[17] The λόγοι are not "things" or "thoughts": they can be seen as God's wills, *inten-*

14. John 14:7–9, "If you had known me, you should have known my Father also, and from henceforth you know him, and have seen him. . . . [H]e that has seen me has seen the Father."

15. John 1:1–3, "In the beginning was the Λόγος, and the Λόγος was with God, and the Λόγος was God. He was with God in the beginning. Through him all things were made; without him nothing was made that has been made."

16. Maximus the Confessor, *Amb.Io.* 7, 1080A—trans. Constas.

17. Cf. *Amb.Io.* 7, 1081B, "For in their substance and formation all created things are positively defined by their own λόγοι, and by the λόγοι that exist around them and

tions, intentions to create any given creature and being in the way that it would be created. The difference between *wills/intentions* of God and *ideas* of God is crucial, as to locate the blueprint of the cosmos in the *free will and choices* of God and not in his "ideas" is to cite freedom and not necessity as the foundational mode of existence's creation. Thus, the Platonic *Ideas* and their Neoplatonic echoes bear resemblances to the Maximian λόγοι only on the surface of the matter; they circumscribe substantially different concepts. Apart from that, the λόγοι are in no way to be identified with the καθόλου of Greek philosophy, for, according to Maximus, both the universals and the particulars (τὰ καθόλου τε καὶ τὰ καθ' ἕκαστον) have been created, and are being created, "at the right moment" (κατὰ τὸν δέοντα χρόνον) accord-ing to their λόγοι.[18] The λόγοι are "the personal destiny of every created thing, the plan of God and in God for each thing created."[19] The λόγοι τῶν ὄντων are responsible "for the substance, nature, form, shape, composition, and power of things, for their activity and what they undergo, as well as for their differentiation as individuals in terms of quantity, quality, relationship, place, time, position, movement and habitual state."[20] The λόγοι also incor-porate the end and purpose (τέλος) of beings: "they are responsible for the beginning, middle, and end of things, that is to say, for the λόγος or prin-ciple that makes the connection between the beginning of each thing and its end point, by way of its intermediate term."[21] As *intentions*, they are not created (an intention is not a creative action, it exists "in the mind" of God, however relative that phrase may be) and they are (pre)existent in God; as they reside in the uncreated, they are not subject to temporality, they are not only *in* God, but *preexistent in* God (more precisely: they are preexistent in God *because* they are in God). As uncreated, God's intentions do not emerge

---

which constitute their defining limits" (trans. Constas), and *Amb.Io.* 10, 1136A, "just as from the beginning the fashioner determined and established that it was to be, what it was to be, and how and how much it was to be" (trans. Louth). See also *Amb.Io.* 42, 1329AB, "The λόγοι of all the beings that exist essentially—whether they exist now or will exist in the future, whether they have come to be or will come to be, or have appeared or will appear—preexist and are immovably fixed in God, and it is according to these that all things are, and have come to be, and remain always drawing closer to their own predetermined λόγοι through natural motion, and ever more closely ap-proximated to being by their particular kinds and degrees of motion and inclination of choice" (trans. Constas). The λόγοι disclose the divine *purpose* of every creature (*Q.Thal. I*, 13.6–13).

18. *Amb.Io.* 7, 1080A.

19. Riou, *Le monde et l'Eglise*, 56. Cited and translated in Loudovikos, *Eucharistic Ontology*, 55.

20. Loudovikos, *Eucharistic Ontology*, 57.

21. Ibid., Cf. *Amb.Io.* 17, 1228A-D.

in time, in temporality. Therefore, while substances and natures are attested as most certainly created, their λόγοι, God's intention for their creation, are to be recognized as uncreated, without any conflict emerging between these two realities: God's intentions for creating a creature, the λόγοι, are not identical with the mode with which creatures participate in being, the substances or natures. Maximus is clear in his distinction between (a) the λόγοι, (b) the Λόγος of God, and (c) the things that God created "in accordance with the λόγοι."[22] Both the λόγοι and the outcomes of God's creative action can be seen as activities (ἐνέργειαι): the former as uncreated activities, the latter as "created activities," or more precisely as outcomes of activities (ἐνέργημα), i.e., creations, creatures.[23] The question remains: are the uncreated λόγοι to be traced in creation and traced back to the uncreated God? Are the λόγοι a pathway for the participation of the human person in the uncreated and in the communion with God?

The λόγοι are also a disclosure of the uncreated God in creation. Any piece of art is a λόγος of its artist and the contemplation of this λόγος can reveal this artist's otherness and manifest the piece of art as the presence of its artist (a presence *in absence*), as a relationship with him. To contemplate the λόγος of a painting—not as a piece of canvas, but as the artist's creation—is to trace the artist in the painting, to trace his person in the outcome of his ἐνέργεια, in the outcome of his activity encapsulating his otherness. In the case of God, the various λόγοι are also God's ἐνέργειαι, as God is described by the ecclesial testimony as creating by speaking. As such, the λόγος of everything in creation can disclose God if it is contemplated as such (a distinct type of *pan-en-theism*), the λόγος of anything can be a starting point for a relationship with God, as it is God's creation. Maximus states that "everything that has its being from God participates in God proportionately."[24]

"λόγος of Nature," Nature-as-such and "According to Nature"

As such, the λόγοι of everything in creation are not merely their own λόγοι, the disclosure of their own identity. The λόγοι are also the λόγοι proceeding

22. Loudovikos, *Eucharistic Ontology*, 59f.

23. Cf. *Amb.Io.* 26, 1265D–1268B. On the relationship of the (uncreated) λόγοι and the uncreated activities in God, cf. Loudovikos, *Eucharistic Ontology*, 97–101, "The Place of the Theology of the logoi in Interpreting the Uncreated Energies of God." Tollefsen's earlier account of the divine activities in Maximus can be found in 160–89 of *Christocentric Cosmology*.

24. *Amb.Io.* 7, 1080AB: "πάντα γὰρ μετέχει διὰ τὸ ἐκ Θεοῦ γεγενῆσθαι."

from God, the outcome of *God's* creative utterance—an idea that goes back to the first chapter of Genesis. The attempt to contemplate the λόγος of something is the attempt to discover it not as an *object*, but as *God's creation*, and, as such, as the actualization or disclosure of one's own relationship with God.

But creatures in themselves (nature and human nature considered apart from its capability to be deified) are finite and bound to perish due to their createdness; they cannot exist forever, they cannot participate in ever-being (ἀεὶ εἶναι) by themselves.[25] How real is the disclosure of the uncreated through the λόγοι of created beings, that is, beings subject to the constraints and limitations of createdness? According to Maximus the Confessor, due to the relation of the λόγοι to God who spoke/created them, the λόγοι of nature correspond to the state of nature as seen from the perspective of the uncreated, "before the fall" as the ecclesial language would formulate it. When speaking of λόγος φύσεως, Maximus refers to the state of nature *as it should be*, in full communion with the uncreated. That is why "Maximus speaks of being "according to nature" (κατὰ φύσιν) as the highest form of existence, and of deviation from nature (παρὰ φύσιν) as synonymous with the Fall."[26] In Maximus' writings, λόγος of nature refers not to nature as it is and as we know and experience it, but to nature "according to its aim (σκοπὸς) or end (τέλος), that is, to nature as it exists in the hypostasis of the divine Λόγος."[27] As such, the κατὰ φύσιν (according to nature) does not mean according to nature *as we know it,* according to "fallen" nature, but "according to the λόγος of nature (κατὰ τὸν λόγον τῆς φύσεως), and this in turn means to exist in the way that God *intended* nature to be incorporated in the hypostasis of the Λόγος."[28]

The Many, the One, and the Contemplation of the λόγοι

Here we come to a very important point, the recapitulation of all the λόγοι in the person of the Λόγος (which is also the reason for the *preexistence* of the λόγοι in God, as they belong to the Λόγος of God).[29] Maximus writes:

25. E.g. *Q.Thal. I*, 47.70–71.

26. Zizioulas, *Communion and Otherness*, 64.

27. Ibid., Zizioulas cites Maximus' *Amb.Io.* 7, 1080B-C and 1084B.

28. Zizioulas, *Communion and Otherness*, 64.

29. *Amb.Io.* 7, 1081B, "When, however, we exclude the highest form of negative theology concerning the Λόγος—according to which the Λόγος is neither called, nor considered, nor is, in His entirety, anything that can be attributed to anything else, since He is beyond all being, and is not participated in by any being whatsoever—when, I say, we set this way of thinking aside, the one Λόγος is many λόγοι and the many are One"

Who—knowing that it was *with reason* and wisdom that God brought beings *into existence* out of nothing—if he were carefully to direct the contemplative power of the soul to their infinite natural differences and variety, and, with the analytical power of reason, were (together with these) to distinguish in his mind the λόγος according to which they were created, would not, I ask, fail to know the one Λόγος as many λόγοι, indivisibly distinguished amid the differences of created things, owing to their specific individuality, which remains unconfused both in themselves and with respect to one another? Moreover, would he not also know that the many λόγοι are the one Λόγος, seeing that all things are related to Him without being confused with Him, who is the essential and personally distinct Λόγος of God the Father, the origin and cause of all things . . .?[30]

Shortly thereafter, the Confessor adds:

the one Λόγος is many λόγοι and the many are One. According to the creative and sustaining procession of the One to individual beings, which is befitting of divine goodness, the One is many. According to the revertive, inductive, and providential return of the many to the One . . . insofar as the One gathers everything together, the many are One.[31]

According to Maximus' approach, in the sum of the λόγοι of everything, the Λόγος himself is to be seen, as God intended that the whole of his creation be recapitulated in the person of his Son, in the *disclosure* of God to the world, in God's hypostasis of the Son.[32] In the course of the creative procession, Maximus discerns the origin of the many λόγοι in the one Λόγος, and in the returning motion of the creation to God Maximus discerns the gathering of the many λόγοι in the one Λόγος: Loudovikos remarks that Maximus "provides the primary ontological basis for the λόγοι: their multiplicity constantly evokes the one Word [Λόγος] to whom they owe their distribution."[33] This recapitulation of all the λόγοι in the person of

---

(trans. Constas).

30. *Amb.Io.* 7, 1077C, trans. Constas.

31. *Amb.Io.* 7, 1081C, trans. Constas. Again, note also John 1:3: "Through him [the Λόγος] all things were made; without him nothing was made that has been made."

32. Cf. *Amb.Io.* 7, 1084D, "For the Λόγος of God (who is God) wills always and in all things to accomplish the mystery of His embodiment" (trans. Constas).

33. Loudovikos, *Eucharistic Ontology*, 58. Cf. *Amb.Io.* 7, 1077C–1080A: "Who—knowing that it was *with reason* and wisdom that God brought beings *into existence* out of nothing—if he were carefully to direct the contemplative power of his soul to their infinite natural differences and variety, and, with the analytical power of reason, were

Christ can be seen as both an existing reality and an ongoing process (as is the case with many, many elements of the ecclesial testimony): the process of redemption as the incorporation and recapitulation of the various λόγοι in the one Λόγος, in the person of Christ, can be seen as a process of "personalizing" existence, thereby redeeming it. For the ecclesial testimony, life is relation and communion while death is the absence of relations: to restore the radical relationality of the created world, to fully restore its relation to and communion with the uncreated God, to make it a *person* out of an *object*, is to *redeem* the world, the totality of created existence. Redemption is the "restoration of [nature's] very being as personal dialogue."[34] And this *authentic* existence, existence in communion with God through God the Λόγος, is the κατὰ φύσιν, as I mentioned earlier. For the ecclesial testimony, to exist authentically is to exist "in Christ," in the person of Christ, "to exist in the hypostasis of the Λόγος. There is no escape from personhood in Christian cosmology."[35] Maximus describes the conjunction of the Λόγος and the λόγοι and the realism of participation in both the λόγοι and the Λόγος as follows:

> When the superessential Λόγος and creator of all existent things wanted to enter into being [as we know it], he brought with him [in his incarnation] the natural λόγοι of all that is, all things sensible and intelligible as well as the incomprehensible concepts of his own divinity. Of these, we say that the λόγοι of things intelligible are the blood of the Λόγος; those of things sensible are the visible flesh of the Λόγος. Therefore because the Λόγος is the teacher of the spiritual λόγοι in both sensible and intelligible things, it is fitting and reasonable that he should give those who are worthy the knowledge contained in things visible to eat, as flesh, and the knowledge contained in things intelligible to drink, as blood. It is these that Wisdom mystically prepared long ago with her cup and her victims, speaking of this

---

(together with these) to distinguish in his mind the λόγος according to which they were created, would not, I ask, fail to know the one Λόγος as many λόγοι, indivisibly distinguished amid the differences of created things, owing to their specific individuality, which remains unconfused both in themselves and with respect to one another? Moreover, would he not also know that the many λόγοι are one Λόγος, seeing that all things are related to Him without being confused with Him, who is the essential and personally distinct Λόγος of God the father, the origin and cause of all things, *in whom all things were created, in the heavens and on earth, visible and invisible, whether thrones or dominions or principalities or authorities: all thing were created from Him, through Him, and return unto Him?* [Col 1:16; see Rom 11:36]" (trans. Constas).

34. Loudovikos, *Eucharistic Ontology*, 58.

35. Zizioulas, *Communion and Otherness*, 66.

in Proverbs. But the bones, which are the λόγοι concerning the deity and surpass understanding, he does not give, as they are infinitely beyond every created nature in the same measure. For the nature of beings lacks the power to have any relationship with those λόγοι. . . . Again, perhaps the flesh of the Λόγος is the complete return and restoration of our nature to itself through virtue and knowledge; the blood is the deification which will direct our nature, by grace, to eternal well-being; and the bones are the unknown power which draws our nature to eternal well-being through deification.[36]

The return to God is a question of the "restoration of nature," not of transcending it: the ἀποκατάστασις of nature refers to its original state, as God intended it to be, not to "fallen" nature, nature according to its tendency towards individual onticity, non-relation to its source of existence, death. Note, according to Maximus, the sum of all the λόγοι as we can know and experience them do not *constitute* the one Λόγος, they do not suffice for that. In Maximus' allegory, there are also the bones, "the λόγοι concerning the deity," which "surpass understanding," as they are completely beyond createdness, "as they are infinitely beyond every created nature in the same measure. For the nature of beings lacks the power to have any relationship with those λόγοι."[37] So, even the totality of the uncreated λόγοι of created existence are not enough to circumscribe the uncreated Creator.

If the λόγοι φύσεως of everything are a doorway to direct communion with God, why isn't this communion perceived as the everyday experience of all human persons, why is it an *attainment* and a *gift*? One of Maximus' famous triads[38] is the triad of the human person's attainment and asceticism: practical philosophy (πρακτικὴ φιλοσοφία), natural contemplation (φυσικὴ θεωρία), and theological mystagogy (θεολογικὴ μυσταγωγία),[39] corresponding to being (εἶναι), well-being (εὖ εἶναι), and ever-being (ἀεὶ εἶναι), respectively. Practical philosophy is the first step, the preparation, the purification, and the overcoming of the "carnal mind." The next step, natural contemplation, consists in achieving to discern the λόγοι of the be-

36. *Ad Thalassium*, CCSG 7, 35.7–44 (trans. Theokritoff from Loudovikos, *Eucharistic Ontology*, 42–44).

37. Ibid.

38. For an overview of them, see Loudovikos, *Eucharistic Ontology*, 76–84. Loudovikos lists eleven triads.

39. On this triad and especially φυσικὴ θεωρία, cf. Betsakos, *Στάσις Ἀεικίνητος*, 152–76. In *Q.Dub.*, 58.6–7, Maximus mentions this triad as a philosophical triad, "κατορθώσῃ δεόντως πρακτικὴν καὶ φυσικὴν καὶ θεολογικὴν φιλοσοφίαν."—". . . he might accomplish successfully the practical, natural and theological philosophy" (trans. Prassas).

ings' natures, the inner principles of beings.[40] And theological mystagogy is identified with deification and στάσις ἀεικίνητος, which is the communion of man with God,[41] becoming "similar and equal to God." According to Maximus, as we can see, it is possible to discern the λόγοι of beings and their relationship with God as part of the φυσικὴ θεωρία, i.e., as part of a certain level of attainment.[42] This needs training, ἄσκησις, asceticism and can be *granted* to a person, in the context of the person's relationship with God, not individually achieved. The discernment of the λόγοι comes after a certain step on the path to deification: our addiction to death, our addiction to non-relation, does not allow us to discern the λόγοι freely. We still perceive the world as an aggregate of objects, not as a manifestation of God's will to create and as a relationship with him.

An Ontology of Dialogical Reciprocity

There is also another aspect when taking into account the usual meaning of λόγος as speech, articulation, discourse in examining the λόγοι doctrine. According to that, the fact that everything is permeated and actualized through the λόγοι of God means creation is a dialogue: God does not engage in a monologue through these λόγοι; God's creative action through λόγοι means that God converses with the human person and, as such, the interaction and participation in this dialogue is a primary characteristic of existence, an ontological category. The fact that God's λόγοι do not constitute a monologue but call for a dialogue discloses existence as a *dialogical reciprocity*[43] between creation and the uncreated God through the human person. And man's (and through man, creation's) participation in this dia-

---

40. Which has its prototype in the experience of Christ's disciples during his transfiguration at Mount Tabor, *Amb.Io.* 10, 1128A, "Then, having both their bodily and the spiritual senses purified, they [Peter, John, and Jacob/James] were taught the spiritual meanings [λόγοι] of the mysteries that were shown to them" (trans. Louth). The contemplation of the λόγοι leads to the knowledge of their divine cause (*Q.Thal. I,* 13.32–35), the λόγοι *declare* their Creator, so that man can find and meet him (*Q.Thal. I,* 51.7–17).

41. Cf. Loudovikos, *Eucharistic Ontology,* 79f.

42. Maximus sums it up as follows, *Amb.Io.* 20, 1241C, "The task of practical philosophy is to purge the intellect of all impassioned images, while that of natural contemplation is to show forth the intellect as understanding the science of beings in light of the cause that created them, while the aim of theological mystagogy is to establish one by grace in a state of being like God and equal to God, as much as this is possible, so that by virtue of this transcendence he will no longer give any thought to anything after God" (trans. Constas).

43. Cf. Loudovikos, *Eucharistic Ontology,* especially 201–6.

logical reciprocity can either be a positive answer, an affirmation of God's creative love, or a negative answer, a refutation of existence-as-dialogue with the uncreated source of creation (a choice of individual onticity), a continuous refutation of God's creative call from non-being into being (or a total indifference for this dialogue).

But which would be man's affirmative answer? To receive the world not as something that necessarily exists and can be taken for granted, but as a gift by a person that creates it out of love is to have a stance of gratitude towards existence, to perceive the world in a *Eucharistic* manner, to answer to the uncreated God's continuous creative call with continuous thanksgiving—that is, to iconize the divine mode of existence, the mode of the One who extends the creative call. For man, this Eucharistic stance is a motion towards the uncreated, an "ek-static" motion: "just as God, who is by nature unmovable, goes outside himself in creating a personal relationship of love with his creature, so man's movement is in its ultimate essence a response of ἔρως to the ek-stasis of God in his goodness and love, as a 'sober madness' of personal ek-stasis of nature in favour of this dialogue between man and God."[44] As I have remarked before, this is not one of the *accidents* of reality or a matter of *behavior*; it is a question of how existence *as such* and being *as such* are understood, it is a primary *ontological* question. Therefore, Nikolaos Loudovikos' denotion of Maximian ontology as a *Eucharistic ontology* is a fitting one—as is his remark that a Eucharistic ontology is an ontology of dialogical reciprocity that places its consummation in an eschatological future:[45]

> This Eucharistic ontology takes as its starting point Maximus' idea that being is not only fulfilled in well-being, but even exists "eschatologically," i.e., for the sake of well-being, for the boundless divine vitality which as "fixed motion-in-sameness" is offered to personal beings and through them to the entire created order; and it reveals to us that every movement of things and every action of persons is ontologically justified inasmuch as it is directed towards the ἔσχατον, the eternal well-being which is perfect incorporation into the risen Body of Christ. Here we have a revealed ontology outside-the-created, the only true ontology of the personal mode of being.[46]

44. Ibid., 202.

45. The fact that Maximus gives an ontological content to the notion of τρόπος (*mode*, which entails a becoming, which in turn entails temporality) and that he positions the true, κατὰ φύσιν state of beings in an eschatological *future* effects the inclusion of eschatology into ontology proper in the context of his thought.

46. Loudovikos, *Eucharistic Ontology*, 204.

As a stance towards the question of existence and being *as such*, the Eucharist—i.e., existential gratitude as the communion with the uncreated source of an existence that need not have necessarily been—constitutes an ontology of dialogical reciprocity and a distinct ontological category. The λόγοι are the key concept for this dialogical reciprocity, as they in themselves are uncreated, (pre)existent in the uncreated God and the initiative of God for the call to relation and communion—and most of them can be participated in through creation, through the beings of which these λόγοι are λόγοι φύσεως. The fact that the λόγοι (through the Λόγος) open up a pathway of communion between creation and the uncreated is what grants them their ontological importance. Another aspect of this possibility of communion is Maximus' understanding of *motion* (κίνησις). Before embarking on its examination, I will first introduce the reader to Aristotle's theory of *motion* and *time*. As we will see, understanding Aristotle's theory of motion and time is a prerequisite for approaching Maximus' *renewal* thereof.

PART II

*Maximus the Confessor's Understanding
of Motion and Temporality*

CHAPTER FIVE

Motion and Time in Aristotle's *Physics* as a Precursor to Maximus' Definition of Time

Aristotle's Theory of Motion (κίνησις)

ARISTOTLE'S THEORY OF *MOTION* (κίνησις) is mainly expounded in the *Physics*, and more specifically in books III–VIII. References regarding the theory of motion, which is a central theory of Aristotle pertaining to the examination of nature,[1] are also to be found in other works by the philosopher (for example, in the Μετὰ τὰ Φυσικά), but I will rely mainly on the Φυσικά, where the main body of the exposition of his theory of motion is to be found.[2]

In some instances, Aristotle differentiates[3] between *motion* and *change*, κίνησις and μεταβολή, but in other instances and earlier in the Φυσικά he

---

1. See also, Bostock, *Space, Time*, 2.

2. I have previously worked on Aristotle's understanding of time and motion in Mitralexis, "Temporality in Aristotle's Philosophy," on which the present chapter is based.

3. See also, as an example, *Physics*, 225a 34-b2, "ἐπεὶ δὲ πᾶσα κίνησις μεταβολή τις, μεταβολαὶ δὲ τρεῖς αἱ εἰρημέναι, τούτων δὲ αἱ κατὰ γένεσιν καὶ φθορὰν οὐ κινήσεις, αὗται δ᾽ εἰσὶν αἱ κατ᾽ ἀντίφασιν, ἀνάγκη τὴν ἐξ ὑποκειμένου εἰς ὑποκείμενον μεταβολὴν κίνησιν εἶναι μόνην"—"Since, then, every movement is a transition, and two of the three forms of transition, viz. genesis and perishing (which are transits to and from contradictory opposites) are not movements, it remains that the only transition that is a movement is that from positive to positive." As well as *Metaphysics*, 991a11, "οὔτε γὰρ κινήσεως οὔτε μεταβολῆς οὐδεμιᾶς ἐστιν αἴτια αὐτοῖς."—"For they are not the cause of any motion or change in them." The translation of all quotes from the Μετὰ τὰ Φυσικὰ used in these chapters is derived from Aristotle, *Physics, Books I–IV, with an English translation by Philip H. Wicksteed and Francis M. Cornford*, volume I and II, unless otherwise noted.

identifies them,[4] so following the example of other scholars, and given the succinct character of this presentation, I will not insist on differentiating them.

For Aristotle, *motion* is one of the fundamental principles of nature, one of the basic attributes of the world: "nature is (the cause and) the beginning of motion and change."[5] With the term motion[6] (κίνησις) and change (μεταβολή) he signifies every kind of change, transformation, transition, and motion (not only physical motion or some limited understanding of the term) and in it he sees the *manifestation* of nature and the world. He notes:

> Since nature is a source (ἀρχή) of motion (κίνησις) and change (μεταβολή), and the source of our enquiry concerns nature, we must not neglect the question of what motion (or change) is, since if we are ignorant about what this is so too are we ignorant about nature. Once we have determined what motion is, we must endeavour to tackle in like manner what follows in its appropriate order. Change seems to be continuous, and the first thing manifested in the continuous is the infinite. This is why it so often falls to those defining the continuous to attempt an account of the infinite: being continuous is being divisible into infinity. In addition to these matters, change is impossible without place, void, and time. It is clear, then, because of these relations, and also because of their being common and universal to all, that we must inquire into each of these, arranging them in advance, since a study of more specific topics is posterior to a study of the more common topics. But first, as we have said, our enquiry is into motion.[7]

---

4. See for example *Physics*, 218b 20, "μηδὲν δὲ διαφερέτω λέγειν ἡμῖν ἐν τῷ παρόντι κίνησιν ἢ μεταβολήν."—"At the moment, we do not need to distinguish between movement and other kinds of change." While Aristotle identifies the two in the third book of his *Physics*, he proceeds to clearly differentiate between them in the fifth chapter.

5. *Physics*, 200b 12: "ἡ φύσις μέν ἐστιν ἀρχὴ κινήσεως καὶ μεταβολῆς."

6. The classic definition of motion derives from the third book of the *Φυσικά* (201a 10f): "ἡ τοῦ δυνάμει ὄντος ἐντελέχεια, ἧ τοιοῦτον, κίνησίς ἐστιν"—"motion is the actuality of what exists potentially, as such." On Aristotle's notion of κίνησις and its problems, see Kosman's article "Aristotle's Definition of Motion," Graham's "Aristotle's Definition of Motion," Brague's "Aristotle's Definition of Motion" and Friedrich Kaulbach's monograph *Der philosophische Begriff der Bewegung*, 1–29. See also the habilitation thesis by Aichele, *Ontologie des Nicht-Seienden* and the analysis of the definition itself in chapter B.II.2., "Die Definition der Bewegung," 191–222.

7. *Physics*, 200b 12–25 (trans. Shields, *Aristotle*, 198).

In Aristotle's stressing of the importance of the concept of motion as constitutive of the understanding of reality, he does not omit to mention the realities that are directly related to the motion, i.e., space (τόπος), void (κενόν), infinite (ἄπειρον), and time (χρόνος).[8] It is crucial for us to understand that motion does not exist by itself, independently from the existing beings and things, but is a trait of the existing beings and is manifested through them. Motion does not exist without specific manifestations, but only when it is realized in its specific manifestations:

> Apart from things being changed, there is no change. For what changes always changes either in substance or quantity or quality or in place and we claim that it is not possible to identify anything common to these, which is neither a particular thing nor a quantity nor a quality nor any of the other things categorized. Consequently, there is no motion or change apart from the things mentioned, since there is in fact nothing beyond the things mentioned. In each of these cases everything is in one of two ways. So, for example, in the case of a particular thing, it has either a form or a privation; in the case of quality, the light or the dark; in the case of quantity, the complete or the incomplete. Similarly, in the case of local motion we have up or down, or light or heavy. Consequently, the kinds of motion and change are as many as the kinds of being.[9]

To underline the breadth of the philosophical category of motion, I quote the basic definition of it by Aristotle and the types of movement he recognizes in principle:

> The fulfilment of what exists potentially (ἡ τοῦ δυνάμει ὄντος ἐντελέχεια), in so far as it exists potentially, is motion; namely, of what is alterable in so far as it is alterable, alteration; of what can be increased and in opposition of what can be decreased (for there is no common name for both), increase and decrease; of what can be created and what can deteriorate, creation and corruption: of what can be carried along, locomotion.[10]

We detect in these definitive assertions a much broader perception and understanding of motion than the current sense of the word, i.e.,

8. See also, Ibid., 200b20–21: ἄνευ τόπου καὶ κενοῦ καὶ χρόνου κίνησιν ἀδύνατον εἶναι—"Movement cannot occur except in relation to place, void, and time." On the relation between time and space in Aristotle, see the doctoral thesis by Sattler, "Emergence of the Concept of Motion," and especially the chapter "The Homogeneous Measure of Movement, The Relation of Time and Space," 121–30.

9. Ibid., 200b 32–201a 9 (trans. Shields, *Aristotle*, 199).

10. Ibid., 201a 10–15 (trans. Hardie and Gaye).

spatial movement, which is here restricted to the subcategory of locomotion (φορά)—that is why the Aristotelian concept of motion is often translated simply as change, which in turn is the accurate translation of μεταβολή, creating much confusion. "There are as many kinds of change as there are categories of existence."[11] For Aristotle, apart from spatial movement, "the term includes also change in quality, alteration (ἀλλοίωσις), quantitative change (αὔξησις-φθίσις), and substantial change or transition from inexistence to existence and vice versa (γένεσις-φθορά)"[12]—although Aristotle does not recognize a complete transition from inexistence to existence, from non-being to being. Ultimately and by definition, motion is the general transition from what exists potentially (δυνάμει ὄν) to the fulfillment and realization thereof (ἐντελέχεια), from that which is not fully realized to its realization and perfection, and any such motion-movement-change constitutes the *motion* that manifests *nature*.[13] Aristotle explains: "Motion is the fulfilment of what is potential, when it is already fulfilled and operates not as itself but as something movable."[14]

The Prime Unmoved Mover (πρῶτον κινοῦν ἀκίνητον)

I will refrain from expanding further on these introductory remarks concerning Aristotle's notion of motion. However, before I proceed to his theory of time, I should refer to his prime unmoved mover[15] (πρῶτον κινοῦν ἀκίνητον), the first cause of motion and, as a consequence, of the world according to the philosopher.

---

11. Ibid., 201a 8–9. In *Metaphysics* (1068a 9–10), Aristotle defines three categories of κίνησις: "There must be three kinds of motion, in respect to quality (*ποιοῦ*), quantity (*ποσοῦ*), and place (*τόπου*)."

12. Betsakos, *Στάσις Ἀεικίνητος*, 39. (I will refer Betsakos' analysis extensively, as he attempted a systematic study of the relation of the Aristotelian κίνησις with similar notions in Maximus the Confessor's work). See also Roark's *Aristotle on time*, 63–64.

13. Let it be noted that φύσις in Greek, otherwise a blank term, does not etymologically denote a static, unchanging reality, but a dynamic event, the eternal becoming of a φύεσθαι, φύσις "acquires a dynamic meaning, manifests not primarily a *being*, but a *becoming*" (Betsakos, *Στάσις ἀεικίνητος*, 36 fn. 29, where also Heidegger's similar perspective is noted).

14. *Physics*, 201a 27–29: "ἡ δὲ τοῦ δυνάμει ὄντος ἐντελέχεια, ὅταν ἐντελεχείᾳ ὂν ἐνεργῇ οὐχ ᾗ αὐτὸ ἀλλ' ᾗ κινητόν, κίνησίς ἐστιν."

15. This subject has been extensively researched. For example, see Oehler's *Der Unbewegte Beweger des Aristoteles*, as well as Manuwald, *Studien zum Unbewegten Beweger*. The reader would do well to consult Bradshaw's *Aristotle East and West*, 24–44, as well.

For Aristotle, every motion (in all its forms and aspects, as stressed) is a part of the general, overall sequence of motions, of the totality of motion: everything that is "in motion" is moved by something else (another factor causes its motion, the setting of it in motion), which in turn is moved by something else, etc.: "Everything that is in motion must be moved by something."[16] Aristotle's logical inference is that, if such is the case, the whole sequence of motion needs to begin from something that *moves*, causes the motion, *without being moved*, i.e., without being preceded by other factors causing motion. "Tracing back the sequence of *moved* and *mover thereof* leads us to the necessity of a first principle of motion, of a prime unmoved mover. The motion that exists in the world is caused by a first source of activity which must be unmoved in itself, in stillness and repose. The prime unmoved mover must be one and eternal, outside of any change."[17] Is this unmoved mover Aristotle's "God"? Several elements of Aristotle's philosophy—and essentially his "first philosophy," i.e., ontology (a much later word)—have been accurately characterized as "theology" (a word that Aristotle himself uses), especially Book Λ of the "Metaphysics." According to the study of Leo Elders, "The central doctrine of the Book is the conception of an unmoved mover, who is unchangeable and eternal; his being is subsistent thinking; he is the final cause of all movement and the God desired by the cosmos."[18] Elders goes on to mention Paul Natorp's view that for Aristotle "God is part of the subject of the πρώτη φιλοσοφία."[19] There seems to be a consensus that, referring to Aristotle's prime unmoved mover, one can legitimately speak about Aristotle's "God."

---

16. *Physics,* 256a 13–14: "ἀνάγκη πᾶν τὸ κινούμενον ὑπό τινός τε κινεῖσθαι." See also *Metaphysics* 1073a 23–28, 32–34, "The first principle and primary reality is immovable, both essentially and accidentally, but it excites the primary form of motion, which is one and eternal. Now since that which is moved must be moved by something and the prime mover must be essentially immovable, and eternal motion must be excited by something eternal, and one motion by some one thing; . . . then each of these spatial motions must also be excited by a substance which is essentially immovable and eternal."

17. Betsakos, *Στάσις ἀεικίνητος,* 64. See also *Physics,* 258a 5–258b 9.

18. Elders, *Aristotle's Theology,* 1: "The central doctrine of the Book is the conception of an unmoved mover, who is unchangeable and eternal; his being is subsistent thinking; he is the final cause of all movement and the God desired by the cosmos." See also Elser's *Die Lehre des Aristoteles über das Wirken Gottes.* On whether this "Aristotelian God" is monotheistic, see the chapter "Λ8 and the Problem of Aristotle's Monotheism" in Elders, *Aristotle's Theology,* 57–68, whereby it is concluded that we can speak of an "Aristotelian monotheism." Other researchers like Jaeger or Gigon have underlined the "theological" nature of earlier Greek philosophers (in Jaeger, *Theology of Early Greek Philosophers,* and Gigon, "*Theologie der Vorsokratiker*").

19. Elders, *Aristotle's Theology,* 1.

However, such a conception of God is, as I hope to show later in this study, radically different from Maximus the Confessor's perspective: in the Aristotelian theology of the "prime unmoved mover," the first cause and principle of existence is ultimately *subject to existence and subject to the cycle of motion*, it is a part of it,[20] it is subjugated to its conditions of functionality. Betsakos observes:

> [Aristotle] treats his prime unmoved mover as one of the be-
> ings that, like all the others, "serves" from a supreme position
> the necessity of a motion that precedes everything existentially.
> It is notable that Aristotle's highest proof of the Prime Mover's
> existence resides in the principle of necessity, in the fact that "it
> is necessary" (ἀνάγκη δὴ στῆναι) [Cf. Μετὰ τὰ Φυσικά, 1070a
> 4 and Φυσικά, 242b 71–72]. The Aristotelian (cosmological,
> ontological) proof of the Prime Unmoved Mover's existence is
> ultimately reduced to a logical necessity: the Prime Mover is
> presented as a necessary concept, a logical principle to explain
> the notion of motion.[21]

For Aristotle, the prime unmoved mover is seen as a final cause that explains motion, a priority that is necessary for the understanding of the overall motion—without it being understood as a relative notion. In this sense, the *logical need* that dictates the existence of a prime unmoved mover, so that motion as a cosmological and ontological principle can function, *seems to have a priority over the prime unmoved mover himself*. If we con-sider the prime unmoved mover as the Aristotelian "God," then his *neces-sity in existing* as well as the cycle of motion itself is, in a sense, *a power and principle superior to God*, which constraints him to its necessities and preconditions. Maximus the Confessor's perspective is, as I have argued, radically different.

The Aristotelian Theory of Time

For Aristotle, time is rooted in motion.[22] He defines time through the idea of motion as follows: "time is a number of motion with respect to the before

20. Quite naturally, as there is no created-uncreated distinction.

21. Betsakos, Στάσις ἀεικίνητος, 65–66.

22. Breidert, *Das aristotelische Kontinuum in der Scholastik*, 20. The Aristotelian theory of time has also been extensively researched, here I will attempt a very short summary. Apart from Paul F. Conen's classic doctoral thesis, "Die Zeittheorie des Ar-istoteles," I note here the following studies: Coope, *Time for Aristotle*; Leiss, *Die aristo-telische Lehre von der Zeit*; Marquardt, *Die Einheit der Zeit bei Aristoteles*; Rudolph, *Zeit,*

and after."[23] For him, time is not motion in itself, but *a number, a measurement* of motion in respect to the before and after, to the transition from past to future.[24] He explicitly states while with the term "number" (ἀριθμός) two realities could be understood, both the object that is numbered/measured and the measuring tool or unit itself, time is what is numbered/measured—not the measuring tool or merely the unit.[25] In the same way that Aristotle excludes the identification of time with movement itself, he also excludes the possibility of the existence of time or of any sort of temporality without motion, movement, change: he finds that this is obvious (φανερόν), self-evident.[26] The perception of motion is inevitably linked to the perception of time: the one implies the other.[27]

However, before pondering the nature of time, Aristotle wonders if time exists, whether it is to be counted among the existing realities or not[28]—and warns us about his unusual conclusions.[29] The parts of time, of

---

Bewegung, Handlung; Bostock, *Space, Time, Matter, and Form,* chapter on "Aristotle's account of time (1980)," 135–57; Roark, *Aristotle on Time*; Shields, *Aristotle,* chapter on "Time," 206–15; Wagner, *Enigmatic Reality of Time,* see "Part II. Aristotle's Real Account of Time," 149–271.

23. *Physics,* 219b 1–2: "τοῦτο γάρ ἐστιν ὁ χρόνος, ἀριθμὸς κινήσεως κατὰ τὸ πρότερον καὶ ὕστερον"—"For this is just what time is, the number (calculable measure or dimension) of motion with respect to before-and-afterness." Aristotle analyses his understanding of time mainly in *Physics,* 217b–224a. More on the Aristotelian definition of time itself in Conen, *Zeittheorie des Aristoteles,* 30–61.

24. See also Bostock, *Space, Time, Matter and Form,* 137, "Time is defined as a quantity of motion either (i) in respect of the before and after *in time* (i.e., in respect of temporal instants), or (ii) in respect of the before and after *in movement* (i.e., in respect of the momentary status of moving bodies), or finally (iii) in respect of the before and after *in place.*"

25. *Physics,* 219b 5–8, "But now, since 'number' has two meanings (for we speak of the 'numbers' that are counted in the things in question, and also of the 'numbers' by which we count them and in which we calculate), we are to note that time is the countable thing that we are counting, not the numbers we count in—which two things are different."

26. Ibid., 219a 1–2: "Ὅτι μὲν οὖν οὔτε κίνησις οὔτ' ἄνευ κινήσεως ὁ χρόνος ἐστί, φανερόν." Ibid., 218b 33–219a 1: "φανερὸν ὅτι οὐκ ἔστιν ἄνευ κινήσεως καὶ μεταβολῆς χρόνος."—"Plainly, then, time is neither identical with movement nor capable of being separated from it."

27. Ibid., 219a 3–4: "ἅμα γὰρ κινήσεως αἰσθανόμεθα καὶ χρόνου"—"For when we are aware of movement we are thereby aware of time."

28. Ibid., 217b 29: "πότερον τῶν ὄντων ἐστὶν ἢ τῶν μὴ ὄντων, εἶτα τίς ἡ φύσις αὐτοῦ."—"First, is time among the things which exist or not? Then, what is its nature?" (trans. Shields, *Aristotle,* 207). The Aristotelian "aporias" on time are analyzed in Conen, *Die Zeittheorie des Aristoteles,* 17–21.

29. *Physics,* 217b 32–34, "ὅτι μὲν οὖν ἢ ὅλως οὐκ ἔστιν ἢ μόλις καὶ ἀμυδρῶς, ἐκ τῶνδέ τις ἂν ὑποπτεύσειεν"—"The following considerations might incline one to

any sort of temporality according to Aristotle, are the "before" (πρότερον) and the "after" (ὕστερον), past and future. The boundary between them, the "now" (νῦν) is not a part of time, as I will explain. The past (the "before," the πρότερον) and the future (the "after," the ὕστερον) do not exist now, they do not exist in the present—the past has ceased to exist, and the future does not exist yet. So, when something is constituted by parts that do not exist,[30] can we really claim that it exists, that it is part of the existing realities? Does time exist?

No part of time exists. The moment of transition from "before" to "after," the νῦν, cannot be considered a part of time itself: the parts of something are added or multiplied to constitute its totality, but a sum of "many nows," if such an expression can be used,[31] does not constitute an interval of time.[32] We cannot accurately speak of "many nows," of a multitude of νῦν,

---

suspect that time does not exist, or that it exists faintly and obscurely" (trans. Shields, *Aristotle*, 207).

30. Ibid., 217b 33–218a 3: "τὸ μὲν γὰρ αὐτοῦ γέγονε καὶ οὐκ ἔστιν, τὸ δὲ μέλλει καὶ οὔπω ἔστιν. ἐκ δὲ τούτων καὶ ὁ ἄπειρος καὶ ὁ ἀεὶ λαμβανόμενος χρόνος σύγκειται. τὸ δ' ἐκ μὴ ὄντων συγκείμενον ἀδύνατον ἂν εἶναι δόξειε μετέχειν οὐσίας"—"Part of time has been and is not, while another is going to be and is not yet. But time regarded either as infinite or in terms of any segment selected is composed of these. Yet it would seem impossible for something composed of what is not to have any share of being" (trans. Shields, *Aristotle*, 207–8).

31. Aristotle uses it, in *Physics*, 231b 9–10 ("στιγμῶν δ' ἀεὶ τὸ μεταξὺ γραμμή, καὶ τῶν νῦν χρόνος"), he notes that between two points there is a line, as between two "nows" there is time. (See also Leiss, *Die aristotelische Lehre von der Zeit*, 145, "Wie bereits erwähnt, ist das Jetzt für Aristoteles nicht ausschließlich der gegenwärtige Zeitpunkt, der dem mathematischen Punkt strukturell und funktionell entspricht.") However, the notion of two or more "nows" is problematic and slightly abusing language, as for a "now" to really be a "now," a point that manifests the present time in an absolute and explicit way, it must be dimensionless. A calculable "now" would imply a "motion in respect to the before and after," a dimension in time, and as such would not really be a "now." This constrains the dimensionless "now" in being each time unique, and as far as it literally is a "now," one in number.

32. *Physics*, 218a 3–8: "πρὸς δὲ τούτοις παντὸς μεριστοῦ, ἄνπερ ᾖ, ἀνάγκη, ὅτε ἔστιν, ἤτοι πάντα τὰ μέρη εἶναι ἢ ἔνια· τοῦ δὲ χρόνου τὰ μὲν γέγονε τὰ δὲ μέλλει, ἔστι δ' οὐδέν, ὄντος μεριστοῦ. τὸ δὲ νῦν οὐ μέρος· μετρεῖ τε γὰρ τὸ μέρος, καὶ συγκεῖσθαι δεῖ τὸ ὅλον ἐκ τῶν μερῶν· ὁ δὲ χρόνος οὐ δοκεῖ συγκεῖσθαι ἐκ τῶν νῦν."—"Moreover, if something has parts, then whenever it is, so too must its parts be, presumably all of them or at least some of them. Yet time has parts, *and some have been and others are going to be, but none is*. For the now is not a part, for the part is a measure of the whole, which must be composed of parts; and time does not seem to be composed of nows" (trans. Shields, *Aristotle*, 208). However, exactly as the "sum of many 'nows'" does not constitute time, so can there be no existence of time without the "now." See also Marquardt, *Die Einheit der Zeit bei Aristoteles*, 41–43. A synopsis of the "aporias" is articulated by Hussey, *Aristoteles: Aristotle's physics*, 138: "(1) (217b33–218a3) and (2) (218a3–8) present the same idea in different forms and may be taken together:

as this would require the "nows" to have a duration that would either place them in the past (which does not exist anymore) or in the future (which does not exist yet), nullifying the nature of now as a dimensionless present, without any duration at all. Dimensionless, because any understanding of the νῦν as having duration would place it either in the future or in the past, in the "before" or in the "after" thereby forming an interval in time, while the νῦν is precisely the boundary between them. Any perception of it as having a duration would presuppose a transition from the "before" to the "after," from past to future. It is exactly the dimensionless nature of νῦν, of the present, that constitutes it as an existing reality, as it has neither passed to the past nor is it not existing yet, but *is now, exists now*. However, this existence of it does not realize time as a whole by including it in the existing realities, as the νῦν cannot be considered as one of time's parts.[33]

Aristotle wonders about the dimensionless present, about the νῦν, if it always remains the same or if is differentiated each time. He notes the difficulty of this question precisely because it requires to conceive a "multitude of nows," as if the "presents" were more than one, namely this specific and particular one that denotes the present now, without turning into past or future. Both possibilities, that the νῦν is different each time or that it is one and the same each time, arrive at a dead end, while the philosopher

---

(1) claims that time is made up of past time and future time, neither of which exists; (2) fills the gap by claiming that there can be no present part of time, whatever the present is, it is not a part of time."

33. See also, Kuhlmann, "'Jetzt'? Zur Konzeption des νῦν in der Zeitabhandlung des Aristoteles (Physik IV 10–14)," in Rudolph, *Zeit, Bewegung, Handlung,* 63–96. In 95, he notes, "Das νῦν ändert in seiner scheinbaren 'Jetzt'-Funktion als ὅρος von Vergangenheit und Zukunft seinen Charakter als operative Phasenbegrenzung nicht. Vergangenheit, Zukunft und Gegenwart—sofern sie überhaupt thematisiert werden—erscheinen ausschließlich als Präzisionen der relationalen πρότερον-ὕστερον-Struktur der Zeit als ἀριθμὸς κινήσεως." See also "Kapitel III, Das Jetzt" in Conen, *Die Zeittheorie des Aristoteles,* 62–116, and Strobach, "Jetzt—Stationen einer Geschichte" in Müller, *Philosophie der Zeit,* 50–54 (i.e., the chapter "Aristoteles, zum Jetzt und zu Zeitpunkten"). This seems to be the standard understanding of these passages. For an overview of Heidegger's similar account of the Aristotelian "now," see McLure, *Philosophy of Time,* 182–89. Apart from that, cf. Mainzer, *Zeit,* 22–23: "Die Zeit, so sagt [Aristoteles], hängt im Jetzt stetig zusammen. Der Zeit kommt aber kein eigenes Dasein zu. Wirklich sind nur die Bewegungen der Natur. Das Jetzt eines Augenblicks ist ein Schnitt im Kontinuum der Bewegung. Da man potentiell unbegrenzt viele Schnitte im Kontinuum vornehmen kann, ergeben sich abzählbar viele Augenblicke, ohne das Kontinuum je ausschöpfen zu können." This book by Mainzer is noteworthy, as it compares the time theories of the philosophical tradition with the insights on temporality provided to use by modern physics, Quantum mechanics, biology etc. A similarly interesting contribution can be found in Ray's *Time, Space and Philosophy.* A more philosophical account can be found in Hörz's *Philosophie der Zeit.*

highlights the nature of νῦν as a boundary (between past and future) and not as a unit: that is, as a dimensionless present.[34]

All of this makes the assertion that time exists a very difficult assertion to make, if not an impossible one. Aristotle does not theorize further on the existence or non-existence of time, does not revise or repeat his assessment that time "either does not exist at all or barely exists."[35] I would say that *for Aristotle, time is the measurement of an existing reality, i.e., motion, and therefore as real as the reality that it measures—albeit not having an existence of its own.*[36] It *counts*,[37] it *measures* something real, something existing, but it is not real in itself, in the full sense of the word.

However, as I have stated, it is not time that counts and measures motion: the subject, the observer, is the one who counts, numbers, and measures the continuous motion and transition from the "before" to the "after" as time.

For Aristotle, time and the subject that measures it, the consciousness that ascertains its passing, that experiences motion as a transition

34. *Physics*, 218a 8–30: "Further, regarding the now, it seems to divide the past and future and yet it is difficult to see whether it (i) remains always one and the same, or (ii) is on one occasion one thing and on another occasion something else. For (ii) if we have different nows on different occasions, and one part of time is never simultaneous with another (unless one includes one time surrounding another which is surrounded, as a shorter time is surrounded by a longer), and if what is not now though previously was must have perished at some point, then the nows will not be simultaneous with one another and it will always be the case that the previous nows have perished. Yet the prior now could not have perished in its own instant, since it was then; nor could a previous now perish in a later now. Let it further be agreed that nows cannot be next to one another, just as one point cannot be next to another point. If, then, a previous now has not perished in the next now but in some later now, it will be simultaneous with those nows in between, which are infinite in number; but that is impossible. Yet (i) nor can the now remain always the same. For it is not the case that there is just one limit for whatever is divided and finite, whether it is continuous in one dimension or more than one. But the now is a limit, and one can grasp the notion of a limited segment of time. Further, if being simultaneous in time means being neither before nor after, but rather being in one and the same now, and earlier and later things are in some one now [since all nows are the same], then what happened ten thousand years ago is simultaneous with what is happening today and nothing is ever before or after anything else" (trans. Shields, *Aristotle*, 208–9). It would be outside the limits of the present study to analyze the reception of the Aristotelian νῦν as *nunc stans* in the Western European Middle Ages.

35. *Physics*, 217b 32–33, "ἢ ὅλως οὐκ ἔστιν ἢ μόλις καὶ ἀμυδρῶς."

36. See also Sarnowsky, *Die aristotelisch-scholastische Theorie der Bewegung*, 235: "Die Existenz der Zeit folgt aber auf jeden Fall aus der auch subjektiv erfahrbaren Existens des *presens*, und ihre Realität folgt—obwohl sie als *numerus* nur in der Seele existieren kann—aus der Realität der Bewegung."

37. I.e., it is the *soul* that counts, as Aristotle notes.

and numbers it, are clearly connected: "For it is when we are aware of the measuring of motion by a prior and posterior limit that we may say time has passed."[38] Not just when there *is* a motion with respect to the before and after, but when the subject realizes this transition: "when we are aware." This perception, this awareness includes what we would term today subconscious or unconscious awareness (but in any case, awareness): even if one does not see or feel, writes Aristotle, but the motion takes place "in his soul," then time is numbered and measured.[39]

For Aristotle, time and the subject that measures it, the consciousness that ascertains its passing, are clearly connected: he does not articulate a definitive formulation or clarification on the matter of time that is independent of the observer. However, one must not conclude that the existence of time, the measuring or time—the measuring of motion, is *subjective* in a sense that could be misinterpreted as meaning *unreal* or *solipsistic*. Aristotle's perspective, thought, and writings do not form a basis for such an understanding of it.[40]

The following judgment by Aristotle is crucial for its comparison with Maximus' understanding of time, as Maximus differs greatly: Aristotle makes clear that if we perceive and experience νῦν simply as present and as one, without any conception of motion or transition with respect to the before and after, then we cannot speak of either time or movement.[41] Aristotle excludes the possibility of our experiencing time as a dimensionless present, for he thinks of it as merely a mistake that shows that there is no motion or time. For even if man, the subject, is the one who measures and numbers motion as time, man is wholly subject to the sequence of the "before" and "after" and to the corresponding motion: if the perception of said sequence, transition, and motion ceases, this can only indicate the absence of mo-

38. *Physics*, 219a 23–25, "καὶ τότε φαμὲν γεγονέναι χρόνον, ὅταν τοῦ προτέρου καὶ ὑστέρου ἐν τῇ κινήσει αἴσθησιν λάβωμεν."

39. Ibid., 219a 4–6: "καὶ γὰρ ἐὰν ᾖ σκότος καὶ μηδὲν διὰ τοῦ σώματος πάσχωμεν, κίνησις δέ τις ἐν τῇ ψυχῇ ἐνῇ, εὐθὺς ἅμα δοκεῖ τις γεγονέναι καὶ χρόνος."—"If it were dark and we were conscious of no bodily sensations, but something were 'going on' in our minds, we should, from that very experience, recognize the passage of time."

40. On the relation between the measuring subject and the measuring of the motion as time, see the chapter "Time and the Soul" in Coope, *Time for Aristotle*, 159–72.

41. *Physics*, 219a 30–33: "ὅταν μὲν οὖν ὡς ἓν τὸ νῦν αἰσθανώμεθα, καὶ μὴ ἤτοι ὡς πρότερον καὶ ὕστερον ἐν τῇ κινήσει ἢ ὡς τὸ αὐτὸ μὲν προτέρου δὲ καὶ ὑστέρου τινός, οὐ δοκεῖ χρόνος γεγονέναι οὐδείς, ὅτι οὐδὲ κίνησις. ὅταν δὲ τὸ πρότερον καὶ τὸ ὕστερον, τότε λέγομεν χρόνον"—"Accordingly, when we perceive a 'now' in isolation, that is to say not as one of two, an initial and a final one in the motion, nor yet as being a final 'now' of one period and at the same time the initial 'now' of a succeeding period, then no time seems to have elapsed, for neither has there been any corresponding motion. But when we perceive a distinct before and after, then we speak of time."

tion—and, as a result, the absence of time. The very perception of νῦν on behalf of the subject turns νῦν into past, as it follows νῦν in time, making it essentially inexperienceable. By trying to reach out and grasp the νῦν, we are already in the future-"after" while νῦν has hidden in the past-"before." Maximus the Confessor's perspective on the subject of time and νῦν differs greatly from that of Aristotle, as we will see.

Time and Corruption

Having just examined what it means for someone or something to be "in time,"[42] Aristotle remarks (or, to be more precise, consents to the general assertion) that time is directly related to "φθορά," that is decay, corruption of life, and the path to inexistence; that time is the cause of corruption, and as such that time *measures* corruption. "Everything grows old under the power of time and is forgotten through the lapse of time. . . . Time is the cause of corruption."[43] Every transition from the "before" to the "after," every present that passes into inexistence by becoming past, measures our corruption, the decay of our lives, old age and our march towards death and nothingness. Time *consumes* everything, and the truth of that matter is revealed, Aristotle remarks, in the fact that no one ever claims the opposite, i.e., that time makes persons or objects younger or more beautiful. Our course in time is, for Aristotle, a path towards nothingness and, in the case of mortal human beings, death; a course that is measured through old age, corruption, and oblivion.

---

42. *Physics*, 221a 26–30: "ἐπεὶ δ᾽ ἐστὶν ὡς ἐν ἀριθμῷ τὸ ἐν χρόνῳ, ληφθήσεταί τις πλείων χρόνος παντὸς τοῦ ἐν χρόνῳ ὄντος· διὸ ἀνάγκη πάντα τὰ ἐν χρόνῳ ὄντα περιέχεσθαι ὑπὸ χρόνου, ὥσπερ καὶ τἆλλα ὅσα ἔν τινί ἐστιν, οἷον τὰ ἐν τόπῳ ὑπὸ τοῦ τόπου"—"And since what exists in time exists in it as number (that is to say, as countable), you can take a time longer than anything that exists in time. So we must add that for things to exist in time they must be embraced by time, just as with other cases of being 'in' something; for instance, things that are in places are embraced by place."

43. Ibid., 221a 30–221b 3: "καὶ πάσχει δή τι ὑπὸ τοῦ χρόνου, καθάπερ καὶ λέγειν εἰώθαμεν ὅτι κατατήκει ὁ χρόνος, καὶ γηράσκει πάνθ᾽ ὑπὸ τοῦ χρόνου, καὶ ἐπιλανθάνεται διὰ τὸν χρόνον, ἀλλ᾽ οὐ μεμάθηκεν, οὐδὲ νέον γέγονεν οὐδὲ καλόν· φθορᾶς γὰρ αἴτιος καθ᾽ ἑαυτὸν μᾶλλον ὁ χρόνος· ἀριθμὸς γὰρ κινήσεως, ἡ δὲ κίνησις ἐξίστησιν τὸ ὑπάρχον."—"And it will follow that they are in some respect affected by time, just as we are wont to say that time crumbles things, and that everything grows old under the power of time and is forgotten through the lapse of time. But we do not say that we have learnt, or that anything is made new or beautiful, by the mere lapse of time; for we regard time in itself as destroying rather than producing, for what is counted in time is movement, and movement dislodges whatever it affects from its present state."

A path to nothingness, because for Aristotle everything that has a beginning (like human beings and lives) has inevitably an end, a finite duration. Time measures the increasing approach of this end, and it measures it as corruption. The only alternative is the eternal existence without beginning and end; if there is a starting point in one's existence, there is no way in which this existence may have no end.[44] However, eternal existences are excluded from decay, corruption, and old age. As a consequence of the above, Aristotle expels and excludes eternal existences from time and temporality. Everything that exists eternally, and due to the fact that it exists eternally, does not reside *in time*, is outside of any temporality.[45] With the reversal of this position by Maximus through the implementation of his conception of the *Aeon* (αἰών), the Confessor introduces a fruitful objection, as I will examine.

The interdependence of the existence (or the measuring) of time by the subject and of the subject's corruption by time constitutes an interesting nexus that naturally occurs from Aristotle's thought, which is particularly tragic in nature. The subject measures motion as time, and thus in a sense gives time its existence; however, the subject being *in time*, measured time relentlessly measures the decay and corruption of the measuring subject, which is subjugated to time, and ultimately its inevitable path to nothingness and inexistence.[46]

44. Coope, *Time for Aristotle*, 154, fn. 26: "Aristotle's discussion of being in time assumes that anything that exists must either have a finite duration or last forever without beginning or end. He is assuming, then, that it is impossible for anything to have come to be but never cease to be, or conversely, to cease to be without ever having come to be."

45. *Physics*, 221b 3–8: "ὥστε φανερὸν ὅτι τὰ ἀεὶ ὄντα, ᾗ ἀεὶ ὄντα, οὐκ ἔστιν ἐν χρόνῳ· οὐ γὰρ περιέχεται ὑπὸ χρόνου, οὐδὲ μετρεῖται τὸ εἶναι αὐτῶν ὑπὸ τοῦ χρόνου· σημεῖον δὲ τούτου ὅτι οὐδὲ πάσχει οὐδὲν ὑπὸ τοῦ χρόνου ὡς οὐκ ὄντα ἐν χρόνῳ."— "From all this it is clear that things which exist eternally, as such, are not in time; for they are not embraced by time, nor is their duration measured by time. This is indicated by their not suffering anything under the action of time as though they were within its scope." See also Coope, *Time for Aristotle*, 143–45, 150–53.

46. Coope writes that Aristotle sees the relation between time and corruption as causal, i.e., that time is *the cause* of corruption (chapter "Time as a cause" in Coope, *Time for Aristotle*, 154–58), *Physics*, 221b: "φθορᾶς γὰρ αἴτιος καθ᾽ ἑαυτὸν μᾶλλον ὁ χρόνος." However, I will prefer to also state that time *measures* corruption, or even that the numbering of time discloses existence as a gradual corruption, for the purposes of contrasting it with Maximus the Confessor's perspective. For it is the *motion* that primarily causes decay, that "dislodges whatever it affects from its present state" (ibid., 221b, "ἡ δὲ κίνησις ἐξίστησιν τὸ ὑπάρχον"), and it is *time* that is the numbering of this motion that ultimately causes decay (ibid.: ἀριθμὸς γὰρ κινήσεως). As such, time is both the cause of corruption and the numbering of the motion that causes the changes that result in corruption, apart from *causing* decay, time *measures* decay as well.

Of course, Aristotle's theory of time is a much broader subject, served by a vast philological and philosophical secondary literature, which my brief presentation cannot do justice to. I have merely attempted to summarize and underline the main points that will prove useful in my examination of Maximus the Confessor's approach to the subject of time and temporality. However, before we get to that, the reader must also acquire a brief overview of Plato's concept of *Aeon* as it appears in *Timaeus*.

The Aeon in Plato's *Timaeus:*
Time as a "Moving Image of Eternity"

As I mentioned earlier, my main point of reference in this study of Maximus' notion of temporality will be Aristotle's theory of time. However, it is also necessary to mention Plato's concept of Aeon as it appears in his dialogue *Timaeus*[47] (and especially *Tim.* 37d), yet without embarking on the exposition of further details concerning Platonic ontology and cosmology. It is highly probable that Maximus had this concept of Aeon in mind when forming his own definition, but his modifications and overall context result in a substantially different approach, as is to be expected, given their radically different ontologies and cosmologies. A similarity in certain formulations or an influence in their articulation does not necessarily entail a substantial similarity in philosophical and ontological content.

Plato's theory of time has been extensively studied[48] and as such I will not advance beyond the examination of the passage in *Timaeus* concerning the Aeon. In discussing the creation of the universe by the Demiurge—"the father"—and the temporality of eternity, the following is remarked in Plato's text:

> Now so it was that the nature of the ideal was eternal. But to bestow this attribute altogether upon a created thing was

47. Here I would like to once more remind the reader of the fact that today's sharp distinction between Plato and Aristotle was not present in Maximus' time. Maximus the Confessor, as one would expect from a philosopher in late antiquity, seems to regard Aristotle's theory, language, and terminology as refinements of a fundamentally Platonic understanding of time and eternity. However, this does not mean that his approach is, in the end, more Platonic than Aristotelian; Maximus' own theory, language, and terminology bears witness to that.

48. As a minimum example of the rich bibliography, see Schmidt, *Platons Zeittheorie;* "Platon über Zeit als Abbild der Ewigkeit" in Mesch, *Reflektierte Gegenwart,* 133–94; "Platons Zeitlehre im Timaios," in Böhme, *Zeit und Zahl,* 17–158; Sattler, *Emergence of the concept of motion,* 56–84; Taylor, *Commentary on Plato's Timaeus,* 186–87; Cornford, *Plato's Cosmology,* 97–104.

impossible; so he bethought him to make a moving image of
eternity [αἰών], and while he was ordering the universe he made
of eternity that abides in unity an eternal image moving according to number, even that which we have named time.[49]

In Plato's cosmology, eternity and eternal life cannot be the mode of
temporality of created beings (γεννητά). So God, the Demiurge,[50] devised
another mode of temporality besides the already existing Aeon: *a moving
image of the Aeon*, an *eternal image moving according to number*, which *we
have named time*. That is to say that time, as it is perceived by us humans,
is merely an image, an icon and reflection, of an eternal temporality that is
not "moving," that is not characterized by motion.[51] Eternity, the Aeon, is
motionless; time is in accordance with motion, and as such it is merely an
image of its eternal condition. The need for (the creation of) time appears
due to the emergence of motion and is actualized at the emergence of motion, not being able to be identified with the Aeon, but still *iconizing* the
Aeon, constituting "a moving image" thereof. The relationship between time
and Aeon is one pertaining at the same time to motion and the iconizing
function (εἰκών).

It is interesting to note that the word αἰών did not explicitly mean "eternity" before Plato. Its primary meanings were lifetime, life, a long time, age,
generation, etc.;[52] αἰώνιος was not synonymous with ἀΐδιος. Here, however,
Plato defines the Aeon not as *prolonged time* or even as *time without ending*,
but introduces a mode of temporality beyond duration, of which normal
temporality, time, is but an "image," an incomplete reflection in motion.[53]

49. Translation, Archer-Hind, *Timaeus of Plato*, 119–21.

50. The reader should be aware that I am here using the word "God" in the Platonic
context of the Creator-God, i.e., the Demiurge, not in the Christian context, and it is
used without further elucidations in order to preserve the brevity of this summary.

51. Cf. Taylor, *Commentary on Plato's Timaeus*, 187, "Time, which is *measured* duration, may be said to be, in virtue of its character as measurable, an image of eternity.
It is to eternity as the series of integers (the ἀριθμοὶ) are, on the *Pythagorean theory of
number*, to the unit or number 1."

52. See Sattler, *Emergence of the Concept of Motion*, 64, where more sources on these
multiple meanings are cited.

53 As Wolfgang Scheffel remarks, an eternity without any kind of temporality, an
eternity deprived of temporality, is conceivable in the context of Plato's *Timaeus*, "Der
vorkosmische Zustand einer chaotischen Chora umschreibt eine Art Ewigkeit, in der es
kein Früher und Später gab, da irreguläre richtunglose Bewegungen keine Zeit definie-
ren können, Zeit ist immer meßbare Zeit. Wenn es aber keine meßbaren Bewegungen
gibt, die sich kontinuierlich wiederholen, gibt es auch keine Zeit" (Scheffel, *Aspekte
der platonischen Kosmologie*, 141). Cf. Ibid., 41: "Da aber die Zeit ein 'ewiges Bild' ist,
so muß man hier einen modifizierten Begriff von ewig (αἰώνιος) annehmen, während
ἀΐδιος auf den absoluten Aion zugewandt ist. . . . Während ἀΐδιος also im strengen Sinn

The importance of this Platonic concept of αἰὼν for Maximus' own distinct ontology and cosmology will be apparent as soon as we arrive at the analysis of the Confessor's "double" and interconnected definition of Aeon and time and the role of motion in it; there is an interesting similarity of specific formulations in the context of two irreconcilably different ontologies and cosmologies, meaning that the semantic content of similar terms is different as well.

'ewig' heißt, beschreibt das Prädikat αἰώνιος eine Partizipation am αἰὼν im Sinne eines Bildes der Ewigkeit." The reader is asked to keep these remarks in mind when we will approach Maximus' understanding of ἀϊδιότης.

CHAPTER SIX

Maximus' Philosophy of Motion

Origination—Motion—Fixity

THE *THEORY OF MOTION* is very prominent in Maximus the Confessor's thought.[1] Following Aristotle,[2] Maximus interprets existence as a perpetual becoming (γίγνεσθαι), an aggregate of continuous changes that are recapitulated in the word "motion" (κίνησις). Following Aristotle, Maximus discerns several different type of motion: locomotion (φορά, μετάστασις ἐκ τόπου εἰς τόπον), change and alteration (ἀλλοίωσις), corruption/decay (φθορά), origination (γένεσις), return (ἐπιστροφή), change into something else (ἑτεροίωσις); growth, increase (αὔξησις), decrease (φθίσις), spiral

1. On various aspects of Maximus' theory of motion, see Tollefsen's paper "Causality and Movement in St. Maximus' *Ambiguum 7*," in *Studia Patristica* 48, 85–93, and Vladimir Cvetkovic's "St. Maximus on Πάθος and Κίνησις in *Ambiguum 7*," *Studia Patristica* 48, 95–104. This introduction to Maximus' theory of motion has also been published as Mitralexis, "Maximus' Theory of Motion."

2. I must once again remark here that Maximus does not see himself as a commentator of Aristotle or Plato or anything similar; Maximus does not write *about* the Aristotelian philosophical language, but his writings *echo* this language—without necessarily repeating its original contents. Betsakos, in his comparative study of Aristotle and Maximus, writes that Maximus is integrated into the Aristotelian tradition of thought (into the Aristotelian philosophical language) in the way that native speakers are integrated into their mother tongue, they appropriate it, without it belonging to them; they are speaking it, not *about* it; they use it to articulate formulations concerning truth, but truth always remains beyond language; they use language as a means for their expression, not as an agent imposing limitations in content. Maximus uses the Aristotelian *language* in order to denote a truth other than that of Aristotle's (cf. Betsakos, Στάσις Ἀεικίνητος, 261f.). As I have remarked previously, we cannot know for certain if Maximus has studied the writings of Aristotle and the ancient Greek philosophers in their original form or if his thorough familiarization with them is a result of the study of *florilegia* and, generally, channels of transmission of the ancient Greek thought incorporated into Christian education.

movement (ἑλικοειδής), cyclical movement (κυκλική),[3] etc.—in short, every conceivable type of change or movement.

For Maximus' philosophy of motion,[4] to exist *is* to be in motion: "according to Maximus, the created character of things entails their being in motion."[5] Everything in creation is in motion, nothing can be described as motionless, beyond movement, change, and alteration: "nothing that has come into being is motionless, not even something inanimate and tangible."[6] For Maximus, this motion "does not have to do with the mutability or change or corruption of things, but is an ontological property belonging to them."[7] This motion is not opposing the true nature of things, it is not to be interpreted as a "consequence of the fall," as the ecclesial language would formulate it. The source and cause of this motion resides beyond createdness.[8] "Everything that comes from God and is subsequent to him undergoes motion, inasmuch as these things are not in themselves motion or power. So they do not move in opposition [to their nature], as it has been said, but through the λόγος creatively placed within them by the cause which framed the universe."[9]

Motion, an ontological property of beings, is a result of *relation*. "All beings are absolutely stable and motionless according to the λόγος by which they were given subsistence and by which they exist."[10] However, it is from the beings' *relation* to one another that their motion emerges—which, in turn, signifies the presence of God's dispensation (οἰκονομία) for the universe: "by virtue of the λόγος of what is contemplated around them, they [the beings] are all in motion and unstable, and it is on this level that God's dispensation of the universe wisely unfolds and is played out to the end."[11] The *relationality* of beings is a prerequisite for the emergence of motion, this most fundamental ontological property of theirs: without this relationality, they are "stable" and "motionless," they do not participate in being. Motion is the signifier of a being's existence, and this signifier emerges in the beings' relationship to other beings, to "the λόγος of what is contemplated around

---

3. E.g., *Scholia in De Divinis Nominibus*, CD4.1 257A-D, 381B-D.

4. The phrase is Sherwood's, *Ascetic Life*, 49.

5. Loudovikos, *Eucharistic Ontology*, 165.

6. *Amb.Io.* 7, 1072B: "οὐδὲν γὰρ τῶν γενομένων ἐστὶ . . . ἀκίνητον, οὐδ' αὐτῶν τῶν ἀψύχων καὶ αἰσθητῶν."

7. Loudovikos, *Eucharistic Ontology*, 166.

8. *Amb.Io.* 15, 1217C.

9. *D.Pyrrh.*, PG91 352AB, trans. Theokritoff in Loudovikos, *Eucharistic Ontology*, 165.

10. *Amb.Io.* 15, 1217AB, trans. Constas.

11. *Amb.Io.* 15, 1217AB, trans. Constas.

them," as has been actively willed by God. As we have examined, the very notion of λόγος contains this relationality.

Maximus reverses the order of the Origenist triad of *fixity-motion-generation* (στάσις-κίνησις-γένεσις) into *origination-motion-fixity* (γένεσις—κίνησις—στάσις), which he sees as the "uniquely possible order."[12] The Confessor explains this by stating, "If, then, motion naturally presupposes origin, and rest presupposes motion, it is obvious that origin and rest cannot possibly be among those things which are simultaneous in existence, since between them stands a natural obstacle that separates them: motion."[13] According to this substantial revision, which changes the Origenist triad completely, (a) birth and origination also mean the setting-in-motion, the beginning of motion, (b) the whole of existence and life, as well as each particular existence, is characterized by motion from the moment it exists up to its definitive end, and (c) everything moves towards an end, the motion of everything aspires towards its end and repose. I must here note that the Greek word τέλος denotes both the temporal end and the causal end, the purpose and consummation—while ἀρχὴ can mean both temporal beginning and source as well as origin and cause.[14] (With this semantic frame, God cannot but be described as both the cause, the purpose, the beginning, the end, and the middle ground of all). Motion is an ontological property that "applies to all created beings without exception and not only to rational beings."[15]

12. See Sherwood, *Ascetic Life*, 47ff., where this particular subject is treated. However, Sherwood has erroneously cited the Origenist triad as having the following order, generation–fixity–motion (γένεσις-στάσις-κίνησης), something which also seems to be the case in Andrew Louth's treatment of the subject in *Maximus the Confessor*, 64. Andrew Louth has recently pointed out to me that the Origenist position is an explanation of γένεσις, according to which the λογικοὶ originally existed eternally in a state of rest (στάσις)—their "beginning" is not to be traced in their becoming, but in them being at contemplative rest. In *moving from* this state of rest (i.e., in proceeding from στάσις to κίνησις) and initiating the realm of becoming, which they came to occupy, they initiate γένεσις. As such, the correct Origenist triad is *fixity-motion-generation* (στάσις-κίνησις-γένεσις), the order of which is reversed by Maximus.

13. *Amb.Io.* 15, 1217D, trans. Constas.

14. As well as principle, power, authority, element, sovereignty, empire, realm etc., according to the LSJ and Lampe's Patristic Lexicon.

15. Loudovikos, *Eucharistic Ontology*, 165.

Motion κατὰ φύσιν, Returning Motion, Motion παρὰ φύσιν

However, motion is not only and always of the aforementioned type. Motion has two "directions" or "tendencies,"[16] one "according to nature" (κατὰ φύσιν) and, secondly, its deviation and failure, i.e., motion "contrary to nature" (παρὰ φύσιν).[17] Note the word "nature" is here used with the meaning it bears in the context of the λόγοι τῶν ὄντων: "according to nature" means according to the end and purpose (τέλος) of nature and in God, according to "pre-fallen" nature, and "contrary to nature" means contrary to this end and purpose, according to the mode of existence of nature in its "fallen" state.[18] Motion "according to nature" is motion towards the fuller communion with the uncreated person of God, the *returning motion*[19] to the

16. I am not referring here to the three motions of the soul in *Amb.Io.* 10, 1112D–1117A, but to a distinction of a different type.

17. Cf. *Amb.Io.* 8, 1104A: on the movement towards passions, corruption, and death—1112AB: "Every human mind has gone astray and lost its natural motion, so that its motion is determined by passion and sense and things perceived by the senses, and it cannot be moved anywhere else as its natural motion towards God has completely atrophied"—*Amb.Io.* 10, 1112C: "the soul, when it is moved contrary to nature through the means of flesh towards matter, is clothed in an earthly form, but when, in contrast, it is moved naturally by means of the soul towards God . . ." (trans. Louth). Note that these two tendencies/directions of motion correspond to man's two wills, his natural will (θέλημα φυσικὸν) towards motion according to nature and his gnomic will (θέλημα γνωμικὸν) towards motion contrary to nature, *Opusc.*, PG91 153A: "Θέλημα φυσικόν ἐστιν, οὐσιώδης τῶν κατὰ φύσιν συστατικῶν ἔφεσις. Θέλημα γνωμικόν ἐστιν ἡ ἐφ᾽ ἑκάτερα τοῦ λογισμοῦ αὐθαίρετος ὁρμή τε καὶ κίνησις." Cf. *Opusc.*, PG91 192BC.

18. I.e., "according to nature" means "according to the λόγος of nature," according to God's *intention* for his creature. See *Amb.Io.* 42, 1329AB: "It is according to these [the λόγοι] that all things are, and have come to be, and remain always drawing closer to their own predetermined λόγοι through natural motion, and ever more closely approximated to being by their particular kinds and degrees of motion and inclination of choice. They receive well-being through virtue and through their direct progress toward the λόγος according to which they exist; or they receive ill-being through vice and their movement contrary to the λόγος by which they exist. To put it concisely, they move in accordance with their possession or privation of the potential they have naturally to participate in Him who is by nature absolutely imparticipable, and who offers Himself wholly and simply to all—worthy and unworthy—by grace through His infinite goodness, and who endows each with the permanence of eternal being, corresponding to the way that each disposes himself and is. And for those who participate or do not participate proportionately in Him who, in the truest sense, is and is well, and is forever, there is an intensification and increase of punishment for those who cannot participate, and of enjoyment for those who can participate" (trans. Constas).

19. *Amb.Io.* 10, 1188C, "εἰς αὐτὸν τὰ πάντα ἐπιστρέφεσθαι, καθάπερ εἰς οἰκεῖον ἕκαστα πέρας"—"Everything will return to [God], as each to its own goal" (trans. Louth). Note that the Neoplatonic notion of return/conversion (ἐπιστροφὴ) is substantially different to Maximus' ἐπιστρεπτικὴ ἀναφορά, cf. Vladimir Cvetkovic's "St. Maximus on Πάθος and Κίνησις in *Ambiguum 7*," 99f.

Creator and the source of creation: "for the whole world [the] cause is God, in relation to whom it naturally moves."[20] Motion has the tendency to "be directed toward the unmoved, uncreated God, who is unmoved in the sense that he is not subject to precisely the passivity characteristic of creature-hood's motion, because there is nothing higher than himself toward which he could move."[21] This *returning motion* is not described as an automatically actualized tendency, but as an intense longing for communion with the Creator, as an ἔρως for him that must be affirmed freely and willingly—an ἔρως that constitutes the answer to God's ἔρως for the world, the answer to God's call for communion.[22] For Maximus, to *know* God is to be *in communion* with God and vice versa; knowledge signifies a personal encounter, not a transmission of information; knowledge equals participation[23]—and relationship and communion grants and constitutes the *knowledge* of the Other's otherness. This *returning motion* to God is described as the fullness of hope and the created beings' driving force for striving forward.[24] Fragmented reality, the many, are summoned back to the one, and this union with the one, this communion-in-otherness, this participation in the cause, constitutes the true and primary knowledge.

The deviation from "motion according to nature" is the tendency of created beings to exist for themselves and in themselves, without the communion with the source of their existence that gives them life and being, without the communion with the absolute otherness that manifests and actualizes them as othernesses and hypostases. It is a motion that aspires to actualize non-relation as a mode of existence, and as such it is a motion towards death. This tendency of creation and created beings towards individual onticity, non-relation, corruption, decay, and death is a motion "contrary to nature";[25] it does not reflect the true nature of createdness. In the

20. Von Balthasar, *Cosmic Liturgy*, 138.

21. Loudovikos, *Eucharistic Ontology*, 167.

22. *Myst.*, 11.2–4, "τὴν ἐμφαντικὴν δηλοῦν ἔφασκε τῶν θείων ἡδονὴν ἀγαθῶν, πρὸς μὲν τὸν ἀκήρατον τοῦ Θεοῦ καὶ μακάριον ἀνακινοῦσαν ἔρωτα"—"The delight (ἡδονὴ) that discloses the divine blessings moves [the souls] towards the clear and blessed ἔρως of God." Cf. *Q.Thal. I,* 54.154–63.

23. This knowledge-through-participation is a standard theme in Maximus' mentions of a cognitive becoming. E.g., *Amb.Io. 7,* 1077B: "γνώσεως . . . μόνης καὶ μετεχομένης"—"knowledge . . . singular and subject to participation". Cf. Loudovikos, *Eucharistic Ontology*, 176.

24. *Q.Thal. I,* 49.48–51: "ἑρμηνεύεται ἐπιστροφή, σαφῶς μηνύουσα δι' ἑαυτῆς τὸν πληρέστατον τῆς θείας ἐλπίδος λόγον, οὗ χωρὶς οὐδαμῶς οὐδενὶ καθοτιοῦν πρὸς θεὸν ἐπιστροφὴ γίνεσθαι πέφυκεν."

25. As this motion "contrary to nature" is, according to Maximus, a result of man's *fall*, of man's inability to exist in communion with his Creator; God's incarnation—and

case of the human person, motion contrary to nature is manifested through the "passions"[26] and, eventually, evil.[27]

To conceive of evil and of the "passions" in such a way is to transfer these concerns from the moral level (the level of ethical *behavior* or lack thereof) to the ontological level, the level of the question concerning the existence (and, by extension, man's existence) *as such*. For Maximus, it is not a matter of *behavior*, but a matter of *motion*, a matter of one of the primary ontological properties, paving the way for an "ontological ethics," not one based on authority or convention.[28] As Nikolaos Loudovikos remarks regarding these two types of motion,

> Maximus distinguishes sharply between the "irrational impetus towards non-being" which he calls "unstable behaviour and a terrible disordering of soul and body" and again "deliberate inclination towards the worse" [*Amb.Io.* 7, 1084 D]; and on the other hand "positive movement" as a property of the inner principle of the creature's nature. The latter is the creature's "ascent and restoration" (due precisely to the natural operation and

as such, the renewal of nature through the bridging of the gap between createdness and the uncreated—has been necessary in order to remedy this and to enable man's return to the motion "according to nature." Cf. *Amb.Io.* 41, 1308CD, "Since then [since the fall] the human person is not moved naturally, as it was fashioned to do, around the unmoved, that is its own beginning (I mean God), but contrary to nature is voluntarily moved in ignorance around those things that are beneath it, to which it has been divinely subjected, and since it has abused the natural power of uniting what is divided, that was given to it at its generation, so as to separate what is united, therefore 'natures have been instituted afresh,' and in a paradoxical way beyond nature that which is completely unmoved by nature is moved immovably around that which by nature is moved, and God becomes a human being, in order to save lost humanity. Through himself he has, in accordance with nature, united the fragments of the universal nature of the all, manifesting the universal λόγοι that have come forth for the particulars, by which the union of the divided naturally comes about, and thus he fulfils the great purpose of God the Father, to recapitulate everything both in heaven and earth in himself (Eph. 1:10), in whom everything has been created (Col. 1:16)" (trans. Louth). The focal point of this *renewal* is, of course, corruption, *Q.Thal. I*, 42.18–20, "Therefore our Lord and God, rectifying this reciprocal corruption and alteration of our human nature by taking on the whole of our nature" (trans. Blowers).

26. *Car.*, 2.16.1, Πάθος ἐστὶ κίνησις ψυχῆς παρὰ φύσιν.—"Passion is a movement of the soul contrary to nature."

27. Cf. Betsakos, Στάσις Ἀεικίνητος, 177–86. *Car.*, 4.14, "Οὐ περὶ τὴν οὐσίαν τῶν γεγονότων τὸ κακὸν θεωρεῖται, ἀλλὰ περὶ τὴν ἐσφαλμένην καὶ ἀλόγιστον κίνησιν."—"Evil is not to be regarded as in the substance of creatures but in its mistaken and irrational movement" (trans. Berthold). According to Maximus, evil is the result of motion contrary to nature, and more precisely an ἀλόγιστος κίνησις (*Q.Thal. I*, epist.220–23).

28. On a discussion concerning this matter in relation to the whole of the patristic era and not exclusively to Maximus, cf. Yannaras' *Freedom of Morality*.

power of things consequent upon their essential principle) to its "divine goal" [Amb.Io. 7, 1080 C]. And precisely by reason of the supreme goal of this movement, "nothing originate has ever halted in its motion, nor has it attained the lot appointed to it according to the divine purpose." [Amb.Io. 7, 1089 A][29]

As a consequence, man's striving is an ontological one: it is not only to restore his motion as *motion according to nature*, but to freely answer God's call to himself and to the whole of creation. It is not to be content with the returning motion of createdness (next to its deviation, motion-as-corruption) but to actualize this return and strive for the repose[30] (στάσις) and the ever-moving repose in God (στάσις ἀεικίνητος) that is the "ever well-being" (ἀεὶ εὖ εἶναι), the fullness of the communion with the wholly Other.

The Motion of the Uncreated

Maximus' uncompromisingly apophatic stance is apparent when he is treating the subject of God's motion. According to Maximus, God is (a) motionless/immovable[31] *and* (b) moving *and* (c) beyond movement and fixity (διὰ τὸ κατὰ φύσιν ὑπὲρ πᾶσαν εἶναι κίνησίν τε καὶ στάσιν).[32] Locomotion

---

29. Loudovikos, *Eucharistic Ontology*, 166.

30. *Amb.Io.* 7, 1069B: "οὐδὲν ἄρα κινούμενον ἔστη, ὡς τοῦ ἐσχάτου μήπω τυχὸν ὀρεκτοῦ."—"Nothing that is in motion has stopped before arriving at its object of desire."

31. Everything that is created has a cause and is in motion, but God has not been created and has no cause but is himself the cause of everything; as a consequence, God is motionless. *Amb.Io.* 23, 1260A, "Now if every being which is moved (which also means that it has been created) exists and is in motion and has been created in consequence of a cause, then whatever does not exist in consequence of a cause is obviously neither created nor moved. For that which does not have a cause of being is not moved at all. If, then, the uncaused is necessarily also unmoved, it follows that the Divine is unmoved, insofar as it does not owe its being to a cause, being itself the cause of all beings. How, then, someone perhaps might ask, does this marvelous teacher, in the passage cited above, introduce a Divinity in motion?" (trans. Constas).

32. *Amb.Io.* 15, 1221AB: "And if someone should ask, 'How can rest be attributed to God without it having been preceded by motion?', I would answer first by saying that the Creator and creation are not the same, as if what is attributed to the one must by necessity be attributed likewise to the other, for if this were the case the natural differences between them would no longer be evident. I would, in the second place, state the principal objection, strictly speaking, God neither moves nor is stationary (for these are properties of naturally finite beings, which have a beginning and an end); He effects absolutely nothing, nor does He suffer any of those things which are conceived or said of Him among ourselves, since by virtue of His nature He is beyond all motion and rest, and in no way is subject to our modes of existence" (trans. Constas).

requires space and change manifests in time, and, as a consequence, to speak of motion in the case of the uncreated God would be illogical: the uncreated is by definition beyond categories entailing spatio-temporality. However, under different perspectives and contexts we can describe God as both motionless and being in motion, if we remain conscious of language's unavoidably relative and apophatic character—especially in signifying the uncreated (which, residing "beyond the limits of our world," is "beyond the limits of our language"). Even if we do employ concepts such as motion or fixity in relation to God, Maximus warns us we cannot think of them in terms of the motion of created beings.[33]

To ask whether God *is moved*, whether he *suffers* motion or change, would be irrational. God is motionless and infinite, he is by definition beyond change and beyond motion,[34] beyond beginning and end, beyond substance, activity, or potency.[35] As God's intentions (pre)existing in him, the λόγοι of beings are motionless as well, in contrast to the beings of which they are the λόγοι.[36] Therefore, the *potentiality* and *capability* to arrive at a repose and to attain fixity is innate in the λόγος of each being and manifests itself as a tendency and longing to achieve this fixity, to arrive at this repose. This is clearly stated by Maximus: God attracts his creations and moves them towards a spiritual union of ἔρως with him in order to be longed for and loved by them; he is the cause of motion in that he moves his creations through their λόγος in order to return to him.[37] Our tendency towards the divine person(s) is primarily a tendency of radical self-transcendence and full communion, an erotic motion (ἐρωτικὴ κίνησις) without beginning or end.[38] It is this ἐρωτικὴ κίνησις that can restore the human person's full communion with the divine persons: "love is the ek-stasis which makes the rational creature a person," i.e., deifies it, according to Maximus, identifying

33. *Scholia in De Divinis Nominibus*, CD4.1 381B, Ἀκούων κινεῖσθαι τὸν Θεόν, μηδέποτε νοήσῃς κίνησιν τὴν ἐπὶ τῶν κτιστῶν νοουμένην καὶ μάλιστα τῶν αἰσθητῶν.

34. *Amb.Io.* 7, 1069B, *Scholia in De Divinis Nominibus*, CD4.1 252CD, *Th.oec.*, 1084A: 1.2.

35. *Th.oec.*, 1084BC–1.4.

36. *Amb.Io.* 15, 1217AB.

37. *Scholia in De Divinis Nominibus*, CD4.1 265D (fn. 253): "Προσαγωγικὸν καὶ κινητικὸν πρὸς ἐρωτικὴν συνάφειαν τὴν ἐν πνεύματι τὸν Θεὸν εἶναί μοι νόει, τουτέστι μεσίτην ταύτης, καὶ πρὸς ἑαυτὸν συναρμοστὴν τοῦ ἐρᾶσθαι αὐτὸν ὑπὸ τῶν αὐτοῦ ποιημάτων καὶ ἀγαπᾶσθαι. Κινητικὸν δέ φησιν ὡς κινοῦντα ἕκαστα κατὰ τὸν οἰκεῖον λόγον πρὸς αὐτὸν ἐπιστρέφεσθαι."

38. *Scholia in De Divinis Nominibus*, CD4.1 268B (fn. 253): "Ἡ ἐρωτικὴ κίνησις, τοῦ ἀγαθοῦ προϋπάρχουσα, ἐν τῷ ἀγαθῷ ἁπλῆ καὶ ἀκίνητος οὖσα καὶ ἐκ τοῦ ἀγαθοῦ προϊοῦσα αὖθις ἐπὶ τὸ αὐτὸ ἐπιστρέφει ἀτελεύτητος καὶ ἄναρχος οὖσα, ὅπερ δηλοῖ τὴν ἡμῶν ἔφεσιν πρὸς τὸ θεῖον."

it in the perfection of its movement with the "divinely perfect λόγος according to which it is and has come into being" [*Amb.Io.* 21, 1249B]."[39] God is the prototype, projector, and generator of ἀγάπη and ἔρως; these permeate existence and constitute its link to its cause, making God also the *object* of ἀγάπη and ἔρως, to whom the motion is directed—according to each human person's access to reality and longing for ever well-being.

While God is by his "substance" motionless, Maximus testifies to him as being in motion: "the Divine by essence and nature is completely unmoved, insofar as it is boundless, unconditioned, and infinite, but not unlike a scientific principle that exists within the substances of beings, it is said to be moved, since it providentially moves each and every being (in accordance with the principle by which each one is naturally moved)."[40] One could claim that, as God's relationship with creation and created beings is a relationship of activity (ἐνέργεια) and not of substance (οὐσία), God's motion is merely acknowledged from our perspective, not in actual reality. However, Maximus' texts would not encourage such a purely relativistic approach: God's existence as a Trinity of persons and hypostases is testified as a motion, as a perpetual movement; Maximus writes that God "has moved atemporally and out of love in order to arrive at the distinction of hypostases."[41] While the "substance" of God is described as motionless, the Trinity of his hypostases (actual existences) is described as being in perpetual interpenetration.[42]

If we are to employ the concept of motion to denote God's relationship with creation, we can only say that he *moves*, not that he *is moved* (not that he "receives the motion").[43] To say that God is moved would only make sense in the context that he is thirsty for being the object of thirst, that he longs to be the object of longing, that he loves being the recipient of love: "Being love and ἔρως, the divine is in motion, while being the object of love and longing it draws towards itself everything that is receptive to love and ἔρως."[44] According to Maximus, *we*, and not God, receive the motion (πάθος κινήσεως, πάσχειν τὴν κίνησιν). And the motion of God is his disclosure to us (or, vice versa: God's disclosure to us is his motion). We are moved in order to know

39. Loudovikos, *Eucharistic Ontology*, 175f.

40. *Amb.Io.* 23, 1260B. Trans. Constas.

41. *Scholia in De Divinis Nominibus*, CD4.1 221A: "ὁ Θεὸς καὶ Πατήρ, κινηθεὶς ἀχρόνως καὶ ἀγαθοπρεπῶς καὶ ἀγαπητικῶς προῆλθεν εἰς διάκρισιν ὑποστάσεων."

42. *Scholia in De Mystica Theologia*, PG4 425A: "Φησὶν οὖν ὅτι καὶ ἐν μονῇ ἀκινήτῳ ἀεὶ οὖσα ἡ θεία φύσις, δοκεῖ κινεῖσθαι ἐν τῇ ἀλλήλοις χωρήσει."

43. *Amb.Io.* 58, 1381CD. (Note that the generation and motion of beings emerges from the will, βούλησιν, and activity of God, not from his "substance.")

44. *Amb.Io.* 23, 1260C. Cf. Betsakos, 97.

God:[45] God's motion constitutes the knowledge of God's existence and God's mode of existence (τὸν τοῦ πῶς αὐτὴν ὑφεστάναι τρόπον) *for those that are receptive to this knowledge.*[46] To discern God's personal activity (ἐνέργεια) in creation, to acknowledge creation as a motion originating from God, is a *choice*. One must be *receptive* to encountering existence as the mediation of a personal relationship—as it is a *choice* to acknowledge a painting as a λόγος of its artist that founds a relationship with his otherness and not as mere sum of paint and canvas, as I have noted in my exposition of the prerequisites for a critical ontology. As a consequence, the human person's motion back to God is also a matter of *choice* and *freedom*, a motion according to man's free will: "man's movement toward spiritual communion with God is the expression of this freedom and consciousness of his: as Maximus says, it is a 'movement of free will,' and the capacity of free will [αὐτεξούσιον] is identified in his writings with man's will."[47]

Ever-moving Repose, Stationary Movement

In using the language of *motion* and *fixity* to describe God, the reader must bear in mind that what is described is a relation and communion *par excellence*, as the divine hypostases exist as *persons*, i.e., insofar as they are in communion with each other: the person of the *Father* is an existential and ontological reference to the person of the *Son*, not an individual onticity, the person of the *Breath/Spirit of God* is the breath of the *Father*, etc.: "The name of 'Father' is neither the name of an essence nor an activity, but rather of a

45. *Q.Dub.*, 105.12–19: "τῆς ἁγίας θεότητος κινούσης ἡμᾶς εἰς ἐπίγνωσιν ἑαυτῆς. ... Λέγεται οὖν κινεῖσθαι ἢ δι' ἡμᾶς τοὺς ἐπ' αὐτὴν κινουμένους ἢ ὡς αἰτία τῆς ἡμῶν πρὸς τὴν γνῶσιν αὐτῆς κινήσεως. Ἐκίνησεν οὖν ἑαυτὴν ἐν ἡμῖν πρὸς τὸ γνῶναι ὅτι ἔστιν τις αἰτία τῶν ὅλων· ὅπερ ἐστὶν *μονάδος κινηθείσης*."—"The holy divinity itself moves us into an acknowledgement of itself. ... And so, it is said to be set in motion either because of us, who are set in motion towards it [the Trinity], or as the cause of our movement toward the knowledge of it. It moved itself in us toward the knowledge that some cause of all things exists. That is "the Monad having been moved" (trans. Prassas).

46. *Amb.Th.*, 1.32–38: "But if, having heard the word 'movement', you wonder how the divinity that is beyond eternity is moved, understand that the passivity belongs not to the divinity, but to us, who first are illuminated with respect to the λόγος of its being, and thus are enlightened with respect to the mode of its existence, for it is obvious that being is observed before the mode of being. And so, movement of divinity, which comes about through the elucidation concerning its being and its mode of existence, is established, for those who are able to receive it, as knowledge" (trans. Lollar). Cf. Betsakos, Στάσις Ἀεικίνητος, 95.

47. Loudovikos, *Eucharistic Ontology*, 168. Cf. *D.Pyrrh.*, PG91 301A-C.

relation, and of the manner in which the Father is related to the Son, or the Son to the Father."[48]

So, the question arises: is *motion* or *fixity* a more accurate term in order to describe such an existence-in-communion? The fact that relation is a dynamic event, not a static one, the fact that it constitutes a perpetual becoming and not a coordinated given, would advocate for the word *motion* as a more accurate term. However, *motion* implies *distance*, a *distance* that has not been covered as of yet. (Once again: these words suggest a spatio-temporality that is not characteristic of the uncreated; but they are the only *words* we have, for they emerge from the only *world* we have—and they are to be understood apophatically.) And *distance* implies that a *fuller* relation and communion would be possible, for it measures *nonrelation*: distance measures the degree and extent to which the immediacy of relation has not yet been achieved, it measures how *far away* you are from something or someone. The fullness of communion and of existing-in-communion (of which the Trinity is the prototype) would not allow for any distance to be covered (through motion), as the existence of that distance would indicate that the fullness of relation and communion has not yet been achieved. This makes *motion* an unfit word.

However, *fixity* or *repose* is an equally unfit word to denote the "state" of God. A God whose hypostases, whose uncreated actualizations are described as being in perpetual interpenetration cannot be accurately de-scribed as a being in fixity and repose. The notion of a constant dynamic communion and an actualization in relation and radical referentiality is contrary to the notion of fixity, of repose, of being static and motionless. Interestingly, Maximus employs the notion of the absence of *distance* in order to declare motion as never-ending, not as inexistent: "For God is the truth toward which the mind moves continuously and enduringly, and it can never cease its motion: since it cannot find any distance (διάστημα) there, no cessation of motion can take place."[49]

Maximus transcends these limitations of language by writing about the "ever-moving repose" (στάσις ἀεικίνητος) and the "stationary movement" (στάσιμος ταυτοκινησία) that characterizes the communion with God.[50] It

48. *Amb.Io.* 26, 1265D: "οὔτε οὐσίας εἶναι τό πατήρ ὄνομα, οὔτε ἐνεργείας, ἀλλά σχέσεως, καί τοῦ πῶς ἔχει πρός τόν Υἱόν ὁ Πατήρ, ἤ ὁ Υἱός πρός τόν Πατέρα" (trans. Constas).

49. *Myst.*, 5.100–102.

50. According to Maximus, nature restored in its full communion with God will arrive at an "ever-moving repose," in perpetual motion around God; *Q.Thal. II*, 65.544–47: "ἐν δὲ τῷ θεῷ γινομένη ... στάσιν ἀεικίνητον ἕξει καὶ στάσιμον ταυτοκινησίαν, περὶ τὸ ταὐτὸν καὶ ἓν καὶ μόνον ἀϊδίως γινομένην." This notion will be analyzed in depth

is to be noted these paradoxical phrases are not merely rhetorical or standard phrases denoting apophaticism: they are attempts at a *most accurate* use of language. If we are to speak about *motion* or *fixity* concerning God, concerning the "motionless" God and the "perpetually interpenetrating" Trinity of divine persons, we have to acknowledge that it is both *the fullness of motion* and *the fullness of fixity*, an understanding that transcends even the designation of being "beyond motion." Maximus' genius formulates this in language by speaking of the "ever-moving repose" and the "stationary movement" of those that have restored the fullness of the communion with God.

Creative Motion

As I have noted, the existence of creatures denotes simultaneously their being in motion and the fact that their birth and origination is the beginning of this motion. Apart from God's "internal motion" (i.e., the interpenetration of the divine hypostases), God's creative activity is his "external motion": the creation of the world can be described as God's motion, and it is this motion that grants life and existence. Maximus does not describe this as a movement that occurs once, at the generation of the world or of each being: God's motion to the world is a continuous one, and to be separated from this motion, from this perpetual becoming, is to risk return to the state of non-being, to risk perfect inexistence.[51] Beings exist insofar as they are moved by God;[52] nothing moves on its own, everything receives the movement from God.[53] *Being* and *being in motion* are identical; the cause of being is also the cause of motion. Everything that exists and is in motion has a cause for moving and existing, a cause that is inherent in its origination and which is also its purpose and end:[54] God is the beginning and end,

---

later, in the chapters concerning temporality.

51. *Myst.*, 1.67–72.

52. And this motion constitutes a relation, meaning that beings exist insofar as they are in relation with God. To say that God is the source of motion (that the origin of motion lies beyond createdness) and that everything that exists is in motion (and, of course, that everything that is in motion *exists*, participates in being) is to define existing as being in some sort of relation, either a fuller relation or an inadequate one, with God, with the person(s) that is the uncreated source of being. Therefore, to sever this relationship completely is to cease to exist.

53. *Amb.Io.* 7, 1073B.

54. Ibid., 1257CD: "Everything which is moved according to nature is necessarily moved in consequence of a cause, and everything moved in consequence of a cause necessarily also exists in consequence of a cause; and everything that exists and is moved in consequence of a cause necessarily has as the beginning of its being the cause

origination and motion of created beings;[55] they are in motion due to him and thanks to him, and it is in him that they will be in repose. "The end and purpose of the activities according to nature is the repose at the cause of the created beings' motion."[56]

Fixity and Repose: στάσις

The fact that the beginning and cause of created beings is their origination in motion entails that their end and purpose is their repose and fixity. Maximus elucidates this by stating that nothing is in motion without a reason and a cause; the beginning of natural motion (κίνησις φυσική) is generation (γένεσις), and the beginning and cause of the generation of beings in motion is God. The end and purpose is also God; and this end and purpose entails the attainment of fixity and repose (στάσις), the annihilation of "any spatial or temporal distance"[57] (διάστημα)—i.e., the immediacy of relation

---

in consequence of which it exists and from which it was initially brought into being; likewise, the end of its being moved is the same cause in consequence of which it is moved and toward which it hastens. Now everything which exists and is moved in consequence of a cause is necessarily also created, and if the end of whatever is moved is the cause in consequence of which it is in motion, this cause is necessarily the same cause in consequence of which it was created and exists. From this it follows that the cause of whatever exists and is moved, in any way at all according to nature, is one single cause encompassing both the beginning and the end, to which everything that exists and is moved owes its existence and motion" (trans. Constas).

55. For example, see the interrelationship of cause, end, motion, repose, and God in *Amb.Io.* 15, 1217B-D: "For no being is completely self-actualized, since it is not self-caused, and whatever is not self-caused is necessarily moved by a cause, which is to say that it is actualized by being naturally set in motion by its cause, for which and to which it continues in motion. For nothing that moves does so in any way independently of a cause. But the beginning of every natural motion is the origin (γένεσις) of the things that are moved, and the beginning of the origin of whatever has been originated is God, for He is the author of origination" (trans. Constas).

56. *Amb.Io.* 15, 1220A: "For it was for activity that created things were brought into being, and every activity exists in relation to a particular goal, otherwise it is incomplete. For whatever does not have a goal of its natural activities is not complete, but the goal of natural activities is the repose of creaturely motion in relation to its cause. So that from one example we might understand the form of motion that obtains among all beings, take, for instance, the soul, which is an intellectual and rational substance, which thinks and reasons. Its potentiality is the intellect, its motion is the process of thinking, and its actuality is thought" (trans. Constas). See also *Amb.Io.* 7, 1073C: "Τέλος γὰρ τῆς τῶν κινουμένων κινήσεως αὐτὸ τὸ ἐν τῷ ἀεὶ εὖ ἐστίν."

57. *Amb.Io.* 15, 1217C: "The end of the natural motion of whatever has been originated is rest (στάσις), which, after the passage beyond finite things, is produced completely by infinity, for in the absence of any spatial or temporal interval [*distance*, διάστημα], every motion of whatever is naturally moved ceases, henceforth having

and communion. According to nature, generation precedes motion and motion precedes repose. However, repose is not a natural activity of beings in motion, stemming from the fact that they have been generated; it is their purpose and end, which remains a mere potentiality until it is finally achieved.[58] I gather that there are two different ways of understanding fixity: (a) when motion (i.e., being) consummates in repose (i.e., ever being) in man's approach to God (and in ever-moving repose, i.e., ever well-being, in the full communion with God), and (b) its deviation, when a creature is separated from God's life-giving motion and risks slipping into non-being. Instead of coming to be κατὰ φύσιν, repose is achieved only κατὰ γνώμην, only as a free choice; the striving towards ever being (εὖ εἶναι) and ever well-being (ἀεὶ εὖ εἶναι), towards God, can only be a deliberate path, an act of freedom.[59]

Deification is the consummation of motion in repose, but this repose is described as an "ever-moving repose" (στάσις ἀεικίνητος), as we have seen and as I will further examine. In deification, the divine state of motion is iconized, as man's and God's activity (ἐνέργεια) are united as one: "so that through all there is only one sole energy [activity], that of God and of those worthy of God, or rather of God alone, who in a manner befitting His goodness wholly inrerpenetrates all who are worthy."[60] Deification circumscribes an eradication of the differentiation between human and divine activity, as man is "acting in accordance with the λόγοι."[61] However, this

nowhere, and no means whereby, and nothing to which it could be moved, since it has attained its goal and cause, which is God, who is Himself the limit of the infinite horizon that limits all motion" (trans. Constas).

58. Ibid.: "Thus the beginning and end of every origin and motion of beings is God, for it is from Him that they have come into being, and by Him that they are moved, and it is in Him that they will achieve rest. But every natural motion of beings logically presupposes their origin, just as every condition of rest logically presupposes natural motion. . . . For rest is not a natural activity inherent within the origin of creatures, but is rather the end of their potentiality or activity, or whatever one might wish to call it" (trans. Constas).

59. *Amb.Io.* 7, 1073C: "If, then, rational creatures are created beings, then surely they are subject to motion, since they are moved from their natural beginning in being (εἶναι), toward a voluntary end in well-being (εὖ εἶναι). For the end of the motion of things that are moved is to rest within eternal well-being (ἀεὶ εὖ εἶναι) itself, just as their beginning was being itself, which is God, who is the giver of being and the bestower of the grace of well-being, for He is the *beginning and the end*. For from God come both our general power of motion (for He is our beginning), and the particular way that we move toward Him (for He is our end)" (trans. Constas).

60. *Amb.Io.* 7, 1076C: "ὥστε εἶναι μίαν καὶ μόνην διὰ πάντων ἐνέργειαν, τοῦ Θεοῦ καὶ τῶν ἀξίων Θεοῦ, μᾶλλον δὲ μόνου Θεοῦ, ὡς ὅλον ὅλοις τοῖς ἀξίοις ἀγαθοπρεπῶς περιχωρήσαντος" (trans. Constas).

61. *Amb.Io.* 7, 1084C.

eradication of the activities' differentiation does not entail an eradication of man's (or existence's) otherness, quite the contrary: in perfect communion, the perfect otherness of the beings-in-communion emerge. *Inconfusedly*, as they remain distinct othernesses and partners in communion and are not "swallowed up" by the divine. *Unchangeably*, as deification is not a change in nature or substance, but in mode of existence: man is deified in every sense "except of the identity of substance,"[62] as has been remarked. *Indivisibly* and *inseparably*: once attained, this new mode of existence is not to be abandoned and this fullness of communion is not to be ceased; the "ever-moving repose" will not lapse into ordinary motion any more.

Motion in Maximus and Aristotle

According to Betsakos, the philosophy of motion is, for both Maximus the Confessor and Aristotle, a potent tool for examining reality: both philosophers discern a comprehensive overview of existence in it, as motion is seen as one of the definitive components of the world, one of the modes of its existence. For both Aristotle and Maximus alike, φύσις denotes a *becoming*, not a static reality: this applies not only to φύσις as a whole, but also to the particular being's nature as well, which is led to its end and purpose (τέλος), to its consummation. Both philosophers distinguish *potentialities* from *actualities*, the δυνάμει from the ἐνεργείᾳ, and thoroughly employ this distinction in order to interpret reality.[63] Beings exist *in relation* to other beings, and the categories of time and space are components of motion; the existence of motion is seen as their *precondition*, while they act as the *dimensions* of that motion.

To recapitulate the crucial difference of Maximus' theory of motion to that of Aristotle's would be to highlight the fact that motion, according to Maximus, is primarily a *returning* motion,[64] a motion of creation and created beings back to their Creator, back to their source. Elements of the *returning* character of motion (albeit of a mechanistic, automatic, and inanimate nature) can be found in Aristotle as well, but in Maximus the returning motion is the dimension (the "horizon") of a relationship be-

62. *Ep.*, PG91 376AB—*Q.Thal. I*, 22.40–44.

63. As Betsakos remarks (Στάσις Ἀεικίνητος, 105), the Aristotelian distinction of potentiality and actuality (δυνάμει-ἐνεργείᾳ) is also employed by Maximus, the κατὰ δύναμιν motion is included in the substance of beings, but it is the πρὸς ἐνέργειαν κίνησις that gives actuality to this potential motion. Cf. *Th.oec.*, 1084B.

64. A thorough overview of the *returning* motion with a focus on its anthropological side is to be found in Betsakos, 143–209, "Η ἀνθρωπολογικὴ-γνωστικὴ κίνησις τῆς ἐπιστροφῆς."

tween persons, a longing for communion, an ἔρως for the annulling of the distance (διάστημα) between the persons. Man's returning motion to God circumscribes the consummation of this relationship, and through the human person as a cosmic mediator, the whole of createdness, the whole of the κτίσις aspires to full communion with the divine person(s) in the manner of personhood, in the manner of existence-as-relation. Maximus' substantial difference from Aristotle is that, according to his writings, motion itself has an end and purpose (τέλος) beyond createdness: creation's returning motion towards its uncreated Creator (himself beyond motion and motionlessness) transcends the cycle of motion and is the end and purpose (τέλος) of motion itself, not only of beings-in-motion. Motion not only leads beings towards their consummation, towards their end and purpose (τέλος), but motion *itself* has an end and purpose to be attained, namely the full communion of creation and Creator.[65]

As such, motion is a central aspect of Maximus the Confessor's cosmology, as it circumscribes the mode in which existence has been generated and exists. And the *end* and *purpose* of motion and beings-in-motion is a central aspect of the church father's ontology, as it discloses the meaning and true nature of beings and reality. The fact that the ontological integrity of being and beings is disclosed through their origin and cause but is consummated at their end and purpose frames the subject in question in a context of temporality, as the ontological integrity of being and beings seemingly resides in their *future*, not in their past or present. To articulate it more precisely, the atemporality of the fullness of repose for both being and beings is *to come*, integrating the element of eschatology into ontology itself.

---

65. See Betsakos, Στάσις Ἀεικίνητος, 282–83.

CHAPTER SEVEN

Introducing Maximus' Conception of Time

In STUDYING THE MAXIMIAN *corpus*, I will prefer to discern three "levels" of temporality, three distinct types of time: time as χρόνος, time as αἰὼν (the Aeon), and the implicit temporality of στάσις ἀεικίνητος. These are roughly analogous to Maximus' triad of "being" (εἶναι), "ever being" (ἀεὶ εἶναι), and "ever well-being" (ἀεὶ εὖ εἶναι)—however, an oversimplification of these notions would be misleading. I will examine each of these in detail, but before embarking on these individual analyses I will provide the reader with an introduction to these terms and a summary of Maximus' understanding of them, a "preview" of these three levels of temporality.

Time for Maximus the Confessor and Aristotle

Maximus defines time, χρόνος, as the numbering of motion: "time, measuring the motion, is circumscribed by number."[1] Time is nothing more and nothing less than numbered, "described" motion.[2] Maximus' primary definition of time is essentially identical to Aristotle's definition: "time is a number of motion in respect of the before and after."[3] The Confessor is surely conscious of that and initiates a dialogical relation between his own conception of temporality and the classic definition of Aristotle, a dialogical relation that does not aim at repeating or continuing Aristotle's theory, but at renewing it fundamentally, as we will see.[4] Maximus adopts Aristotle's

1. *Th.oec.*, 1085A, 1.5: "ὁ μὲν γὰρ χρόνος, μετρουμένην ἔχων τὴν κίνησιν, ἀριθμῷ περιγράφεται."

2. *Q.Thal. II*, 65.533–34: "ὁ δὲ χρόνος, περιγραφομένη καθέστηκε κίνησις."

3. Aristotle, *Physics*, 219b 1: "τοῦτο γάρ ἐστιν ὁ χρόνος, ἀριθμὸς κινήσεως κατὰ τὸ πρότερον καὶ ὕστερον."

4. On the transition from Aristotle to Maximus and the Greek fathers in general

definition as a starting point, but the philosophy of time that emerges from the overview of his writings (e.g., the nature of fixity, the reality of Aeon and its participable nature, the temporality of στάσις ἀεικίνητος, etc.) differs substantially, constituting a *renewal* of Aristotle's theory in the context of the ecclesial event's ontology. It could be said that the Confessor is asking the same questions Aristotle asks,[5] but goes on to provide substantially different answers.

Space-Time Continuum

For Maximus, time and space are completely interconnected, one cannot conceive of the one without including the other. Time and space form a space-time continuum, a coherent spatio-temporality.[6] In the Confessor's words, "space cannot be thought of, separate from and deprived of time (for they go together and one cannot be without the other)."[7] Nothing that is not in space and in time, that has not a "where" (τὸ ποῦ) and also a "when" (τὸ πότε), that does not possess "whereness" and "whenness," can exist at all: "neither substance, nor quantity, nor quality, nor relation, nor action, nor passion, nor motion, nor habit."[8] Each created being, be it sensible or intelligible, is necessarily located in a place/position and time/temporality, "in a concomitant way."[9] Even the substances of beings (οὐσίαι), being created

---

concerning the subjects of motion, space and time/Aeon, cf. Yannaras' *Σχεδίασμα εἰσαγωγῆς*, 322–27 and 350–55. On time and the Aeon, see also his *Person and Eros*, 131–38.

5. It is truly interesting to witness how the subtleties of Aristotle's definition(s) are present in Byzantine analyses. For example, in *Scholia in De Divinis Nominibus* CD4.1 316AB (be it a comment by Maximus or John of Scythopolis), the commentator hastens to clarify that time is not *motion itself*, but merely the *measurement* of motion—as would Aristotle do. And that the measuring instrument is not identical to the measured reality.

6. It would be most tempting and truly fascinating to compare these assertions of Maximus' with the worldview of contemporary physics. However, such a comparison would be a major undertaking by itself and resides outside the scope of the present study. Recent attempts at systematically comparing the patristic worldview to the modern scientific worldview in general include Nesteruk's *Universe as Communion*, as well as Yannaras' *Postmodern Metaphysics*. On contemporary views of temporality from the viewpoint of both physics and philosophy in general, see Maudlin's *Philosophy of Physics* and Callender's *Oxford Handbook of Philosophy of Time*, which, however, requires an education in physics and mathematics in order to be studied.

7. *Amb.Io.* 10, 1180B (trans. Louth).

8. Ibid., 1181B.

9. Mueller-Jourdan, "Where and When as Metaphysical Prerequisites." My use of the terms "whereness" and "whenness" as translations of τὸ ποῦ and τὸ πότε respectively

and having been originated, possess a spatio-temporal status—in contrast to God's uncreated intentions and wills, the being's λόγοι. Pascal Mueller-Jourdan asserts, "such a status conferred on 'being-when' and 'being-where' is extremely rare in the Judeo-Christian tradition."[10]

"Whereness" and "Whenness"

Everything created that is in motion has a beginning: this is the first element of the *generation–motion–fixity* triad (γένεσις–κίνησις–στάσις). And everything that has a beginning has also an end:[11] after its origination and before its end or its repose,[12] a being's primary ontological characteristic is that it is in motion. Beginning, middle, and end are characteristics of beings in time[13]—and, as such, of beings in space. As everything created has a beginning and is in motion, everything created is also in time and space,[14] possesses "whereness" and "whenness"—intelligible beings as well (for example: *substances*), not just sensible creatures.[15] In strong contrast to the Neoplatonists, Maximus ascribes a principle/beginning/generation to intelligible realities;[16] they are generated, they are in motion and they are in

derives from Jourdan's article.

10. Ibid.

11. However, according to Maximus this may not be the case for the intelligible creation and the human soul, which are at times referred to as imperishable "according to nature" and at times as imperishable "by grace." We have examined the question of the soul's imperishability, on the question concerning the imperishability of intelligible creation, earlier in this study.

12. As can be discerned in the totality of Maximus' writings, the end of motion in fixity can either mean the exit from existence, death, or the return to non-being, or the freedom from the cycle of motion in full communion with God, if the στάσις is to culminate into στάσις ἀεικίνητος.

13. *Th.oec.*, 1085A–1.5: "Beginning, middle, and end are characteristics of beings distinguished by time and it can be truly stated that they are also characteristics of beings comprehended in the Aeon. And if time and the Aeon are not without beginning, so much less are those things which are contained in them" (trans. Berthold).

14. The *mode* of spatiality in Maximus' intelligible creation is a more complex subject, as we will examine.

15. However, as we will see, time (χρόνος) has also a radically different actualization, the Aeon (αἰών); as such, there is indeed a difference in the spatio-temporality of sensible and intelligible beings. Even the Aeon, commonly translated as "eternity," has a beginning—and, as such, an end. (*Th.oec.*, 1085A–1.5: "Indeed time, which is measuring movement, is circumscribed by number, and the Aeon, which includes in its existence the category of when, admits of a separation [πάσχει διάστασιν] insofar as it began to be").

16. Cf. Mueller-Jourdan, "Where and When as Metaphysical Prerequisites," 293.

time—or, to be more precise, in some sort of temporality that is not wholly comparable to our own.

Motion "gives birth" to time and space by the fact that it exists. *Space is*, essentially, the assertion of the spatial distance that is generated by motion, the assertion of the διάστημα[17] that has come into being due to the totality of motion(s).[18] And, as we have seen, time is but the measuring and numbering of motion,[19] motion circumscribed by number. Being a *measurement* of something existing, motion, and not something existing in itself, Aristotle concludes that time does not exist, or that it exists faintly and obscurely.[20] It would not be arbitrary to suggest that Maximus follows Aristotle also concerning this specific consequence of their shared definition of time. If motion exists and time is its measurement, its number, then time exists insofar motion exists and only in relation to motion; it does not exist as an independent reality, it does not exist *in itself*.[21] It is interesting that while Maximus relates the position and spatiality of beings with the "natural limit of their λόγοι," their temporality is simply determined by their origination and beginning: "beings possess being in a certain way, and not simply, so that where they are is determined by their position and the natural limit of the λόγοι that are in them, and when they are [is determined] from their beginning."[22]

This interrelation of motion, space, and time applies not only to motion in our given reality and beings in general, but also to the coming to-be of this reality as well, to the creation of existence, of being itself.[23] It could

17. Thunberg offers a concise and short account of the Maximian understanding of διάστημα and διάστασις in *Microcosm and Mediator*, 57–60. Von Balthasar explains the relationship between διάστημα, motion, and ontological identity in speaking of "a fundamental nonidentity of the existing thing within its own being, in an extension [διάστημα, διάστασις] that finds its expression in momentum [φορά], and more specifically in the triad of coming to be, movement and coming to rest [γένεσις, κίνησις, στάσις]" (Balthasar, *Cosmic Liturgy*, 137).

18. Note Gregory of Nyssa's remark that creation is to be viewed in an extension of distances, τῆς δὲ κτίσεως ἐν παρατάσει τινὶ διαστηματικῇ θεωρουμένης (*Contra Eunomium*, I.1.361)—Cf., ὥστε πάντως ἢ ἐν διαστηματικῇ τινι παρατάσει θεωρεῖσθαι τὰ ὄντα ἢ τοπικοῦ χωρήματος παρέχειν τὴν ἔννοιαν (*Contra Eunomium*, 2.1.578)

19. *Q.Thal. II*, 65.533–34—*Th.oec.*, 1085A–1.5.

20. Cf. *Physics*, 217b 32–34.

21. However, there are uncreated λόγοι of time, *Amb.Io.* 10, 1164B: οἱ λόγοι τοῦ χρόνου ἐν τῷ Θεῷ διαμένωσιν.

22. *Amb.Io.* 10, 1180D-1181A, trans. Louth.

23. In Maximus' terminology, "being" does not include God, for he is beyond being. God exists, but is not part of being, as he is not one of the beings, "being is derived from him but he is not being. For he is beyond being itself, and beyond anything that is said or conceived of him, whether simply or in a certain way"—*Amb.Io.* 10, 1180D (trans.

be said that, in creating the world, God generates motion (as the creative motion is the first motion), which in turn discloses time and space as its dimensions and coordinates; not vice versa. Creative motion does not *take place in a space*; it is the motion that reveals space as a reality, it is motion that actualizes distance, which is the "unit" of space. Creative motion has not *a duration in time*; it is the motion that generates "temporal distance," the difference of the "before" from the "after," and this distance/difference is measured and numbered as time. Time and space emerge as coordinates of motion, which has an ontological priority over them.

Of course, space and time *preexist* (προεπινοεῖται) each particular being; "Every kind of being whatever, apart from the divine and unique being, which properly speaking exists beyond being itself, is already thought of as being somewhere, and that, together with this, it is necessarily thought of as certainly existing at some time."[24] The fact that beings are integrated in time and space does not mean that spatio-temporality has an ontological priority over beings, that it acts as an *a priori* transcendental reality. Rather, it is "the hypostases of beings that offer the existential basis for time and space to preexist them,"[25] as time and space cannot be thought of as independent from the beings and their motion. For Maximus, it is not nature that is integrated in spatio-temporality; instead, it is the beings that are integrated into a continuum of nature, time, and space[26]—"everything [i.e., every created thing] exists in space and time."[27]

The Definition of αἰών, the Aeon

Maximus is not content with the temporality of χρόνος, i.e., time as the number of motion: his ontology and cosmology require another form of temporality as well, the Aeon (αἰών). The Confessor's definitive formulation for both χρόνος and αἰών is one and the same, a joint definition for both terms: "Aeon is time, when its motion ceases, and time is the Aeon, when it is measured in its motion. So the Aeon, to formulate a definition, is time deprived of motion, and time is the Aeon when it is measured while in motion."[28]

Louth).

24. *Amb.Io.* 10, 1180B. (trans. Louth).

25. Betsakos, 109.

26. Ibid..

27. *Amb.Io.* 10, 1180B.

28. *Amb.Io.* 10, 1164BC. Note the similarity especially with Plato's *Timaeus* 37d, i.e., time as a "moving image of eternity."

Continuing Aristotle, Maximus relates time (and Aeon) with motion: however, in contrast with the Stagirite, time in Maximus is not merely the measuring of a given motion ("a number of motion, a measuring of movement") but "the Aeon, when it is measured in its motion" (while Aeon has no motion, as it is "time without motion"). *The Aeon*, a reality that is otherwise foreign to the sequence of the "before" and "after," constitutes *time* when it is integrated in these constrains, when it is "dislocated by motion" in the world that we know. Time is "the Aeon, when it is measured in its motion"—it is the Aeon when it unfolds in the sequence of motion. The Aeon is Maximus' understanding of the eternity, but an understanding of it as infinite linear time is completely excluded by him.

Maximus reiterates Aristotle's assertions that time is the numbering/delimiting/"circumscribing" of motion, as well as that time measures deterioration, alteration, and corruption:[29] "Time is circumscribed motion, and as a consequence the motion through one's life is altering everything in it."[30]

Conversely, the Aeon is not defined and described separately, as an aspect of time or timelessness of a world that differs from the one we know: it is time itself when "time's motion ceases," when the sequence of the "before" and "after" and the transition from the past to the future ceases. The Aeon is "time deprived of motion."

Unlike Aristotle, Maximus does not seem to question the very existence of time and the Aeon nor to deny it, in order to rule that it is invalid: he confirms the existence of both realities, reminding through the interconnectedness and interdependence of their definitions that they exist, to quote the Council of Chalcedon's formulations on Christological matters, *inconfusedly, unchangeably, indivisibly, and inseparably* from each other.

Beyond Time: The "Temporality" of στάσις ἀεικίνητος

The formulation of seemingly contradictory definitions in the aforementioned excerpt *Amb.Io.* 10, 1164BC, and essentially the absence of independent definitions (since the premises of each definition refer to the other and depend on it, thereby creating a relational cycle of semi-definitions) echoes

---

29. The measuring of ἀλλοίωσις within creation is also the measuring of corruption and decay. Cf. Völker, *Maximus Confessor*, 29: "Das Charakteristikum der Welt ist die gegenseitige Vernichtung ihrer Wesen, überall herrschen φθορὰ und ἀλλοίωσις, und es gilt der Grundsatz, 'τῶν μὲν διὰ τῆς τῶν ἄλλων γενέσεως ἡ φθορὰ ἐπιγίνεται' [*Amb.Io.* 10, 1169BC]. Ja, man kann geradezu sagen, 'εὑρήσει ἐκ φθορᾶς καὶ εἰς τὴν φθορὰν τὴν γένεσιν ἀρχομένην καὶ λήγουσαν' [*Or.Dom.*, 406–7]."

30. *Q.Thal. II*, 65.533–35: "Ὁ δὲ χρόνος, περιγραφομένη καθέστηκε κίνησις, ὅθεν καὶ ἀλλοιωτικὴ τῶν ἐν αὐτῷ καθέστηκεν ἡ κατὰ τὴν ζωὴν κίνησις."

and reflects Maximus' apophatic stance. However, "apophaticism is not a nebulous vagueness of meaning, but our coming together in a common understanding of the signifiers with the knowledge of their cognitive distance from the experience of the signified":[31] it is not the detached, independent linguistic recapitulation and understanding of the Aeon that is attempted through the definition of the Aeon, which is foreign to the direct experience of non-deified persons, but a call to the human person to enter the Aeon, to liberate one's person from the constrains of time as a sequence of motion, of the "before" and "after," of corruption, deterioration, necessity, death, inexistence. A starting point for this liberation is the assurance that the Aeon is not something wholly foreign, distant, and strange, but simply "time deprived of motion"—the world and time as we know it, but liberated from predeterminations, necessities, corruption, distance, and fall.

A pair of similar seemingly contradictory formulations is the στάσις ἀεικίνητος ("ever-moving repose") and the στάσιμος ταυτοκινησία ("stationary movement"),[32] which are also not merely rhetorical devices void of meaning and substance, but signify a reality crucial for Maximus, i.e., the possibility of participating in the fullness that is deification: θέωσις. Maximus writes that the nature/substance, when it resides in God acquires "an ever-moving repose and a stationary movement,"[33] eternally moving around God and God only. What are the implications of the στάσις ἀεικίνητος for the distinction between time and the Aeon?

I have already noted that the Aeon is time itself when it is "deprived of motion," when the motion ceases, when the sequence of the "before" and "after" and the transition from past to future ceases and is no more, making the present, the "now" of that transition, dimensionless and not participating in any numbering of motion—albeit experienceable as Aeon. Maximus testifies the entrance of the human person into the "temporality" of a dimensionless "now," the dimensionless present that constitutes the Aeon, as attainable by the human person when it accepts the reality of deification. The immediacy of the relationship between the uncreated divine person and the created human person *nullifies space*, as the *distance* that constitutes space is being abolished, i.e., the *distance* that makes things and persons

31. Yannaras, Ἕξι φιλοσοφικὲς ζωγραφιές, 126.

32. I have already remarked on the easily discernible influence of Gregory of Nyssa on Maximus concerning the "ever-moving repose," but let me once again refer to Paul M. Blower's "Maximus the Confessor, Gregory of Nyssa, and the Concept of 'Perpetual Progress,'" 157–65.

33. Maximus the Confessor, Q.Thal. II, 65.544–546: "ἐν τῷ θεῷ γινομένη, . . . στάσιν ἀεικίνητον ἕξει καὶ στάσιμον ταυτοκινησίαν, περὶ τὸ ταὐτὸν καὶ ἓν καὶ μόνον ἀϊδίως γινομένην."

known as *objects* (ἀντι-κείμενο, *Gegen-stand*) standing opposite of the subject, thereby *creating space* or *making space known*. In the same way, this relationship nullifies *time* and *temporality* by transforming them into *Aeon, time without motion, time deprived of motion*, as any and every motion or transition between the "before" and "after" is nullified in the directness of the relationship ("it will be joined with the Providence in all directness").[34]

However, *the absence of motion, transition, or change* in the fullness of the relationship's immediacy, in the interpenetration of deification, cannot be characterized as stillness: deification is not a blissful repose, and the encounter of God with his beloved human person is not to be signified as an eternal pause and stillness, but more as a restlessness (ἀεικινησία), a present in a perpetual becoming. Exiting temporality does not need to imply entering stillness and stagnation in the same way that it does not need to imply the nullification of one's existence, but rather the possibility of its fullness and completeness. The limitations of language are exhausted in the effort to signify such possibilities, but Maximus attempts it with στάσις ἀεικίνητος and στάσιμος ταυτοκινησία: the *repose* that is implied by the nullification of time and space (that is, of the distance that is contrary to the fullness of immediacy) is *ever-moving*, thereby signifying a reality beyond motion and repose, movement and stillness as we know them empirically. In the case of time, this describes the possibility that time must not measure our procession towards corruption and deterioration, but that temporality can be liberated by entering the Aeon, i.e., "a time deprived of motion, a time without motion." To be more precise, motion and time are not nullified, but *transformed and transmuted into* a *stationary movement*.

The fact that even the Aeon, commonly translated as "eternity," has a beginning and, as such, an end, generates the question: is there a temporality *without* beginning or end, a *true* "eternity"? We have seen that *infinity* is a property that cannot be attributed to anything else than God. God's "temporality"[35] cannot be the Aeon, as the Aeon has a beginning and, consequently, an end, whereas God, the uncreated, has no beginning or end. Here I would risk to say that in some instances, Maximus employs the words ἀίδιος, ἀίδιον, ἀιδιότης, in order to denote such a "temporality," the "temporality of the uncreated" (as always, a welcome *contradictio in terminis*). However, in other contexts, Maximus uses these words and αἰὼν interchangeably (either as nouns or as epithets), leading me to the conclusion that he does

---

34. *Q. Thal. II*, 65.538–39: "ἀμέσως συναφθῇ τῇ προνοίᾳ."

35. As always, in the relative and apophatic sense of such designations when attributed to the uncreated.

not adopt a systematized distinction of χρόνος–αἰὼν–ἀιδιότης.[36] It would be interesting and very helpful to ponder such a hypothesis, but the Confessor's texts do not provide us with sufficient basis for that.

I will examine each of these three "levels of temporality" in the following chapters.

36. For example, Maximus attributes ἀιδιότης to the λόγοι, something which, seeing that the λόγοι are uncreated and reside in God, makes up a good case for my argument (Cf. *Car.*, 1.100, 2.27). However, in other instances and while attributing ἀιδιότης and infinity to the divine substance, the Confessor writes that ἀιδιότης can be granted to other substances (Cf. *Car.*, 3.28, "Ἡμεῖς δὲ μόνην λέγομεν τὴν θείαν οὐσίαν μὴ ἔχειν τι ἐναντίον, ὡς ἀΐδιόν τε οὖσαν καὶ ἄπειρον καὶ ἀιδιότητος ταῖς ἄλλαις χαριστικήν").

CHAPTER EIGHT

The Fundamentals of Temporality, Spatiality, and Motion: Sections 35–40 from the Tenth "Difficulty"

I HAVE OFFERED AN introductory overview of Maximus' understanding of time (χρόνος) as the numbering of motion and of the similarity of his definition to that of Aristotle, but we will have to delve deeper into Maximus' line of thought and examine his understanding of temporality.[1] In the *Book of Difficulties* (*Ambigua*), in the context of the tenth and longest "Difficulty" of the book (PG91 1105C–1205C)[2] and more specifically in sections 35 to 40,[3]

1. While I will focus on sections from the tenth Difficulty of the *Book of Difficulties* (*Ambigua*), it is true that Maximus' *Mystagogia* also contains many passages illustrating the Confessor's understanding of time and space—primarily as the space of the church and the time of the liturgy. In analyzing Maximus' theory of time, we will not focus on the *Mystagogia* for two reasons, (a) Pascal Mueller-Jourdan has already analyzed Maximus' ideas on spatio-temporality in the *Mystagogia* in his monograph *Typologie spatio-temporelle* comprehensively, offering interesting comparisons with the Aristotelian commentators, and (b) the *Mystagogia* focuses on the church building and the liturgy, offering insights on temporality mainly in this liturgical context, whereas I will focus on Maximus' understanding of time (and, inevitably, space as well) in the context of his ontology and cosmology. Parts of the analysis offered here, particularly concerning sections 36 to 39, have been published in the volume I have edited, *The Fountain and the Flood: Maximus the Confessor and Philosophical Enquiry*.

2. Which, in the distinction between the two books on Difficulties, belongs to the earlier and longer *Ambigua ad Ioannem*.

3. As numbered by Andrew Louth in his *Maximus the Confessor*, following Eriugena's index from his Latin translation of the book (and his shorter section titles). These sections are located in 1176D–1188C, and their translation in 134–39 of Louth's *Maximus the Confessor*. In this chapter, I will quote and refer to this translation of sections 35–40 without further mention of specific page numbers. A general introduction to the tenth Difficulty is offered in 91–93 of Louth's *Maximus the Confessor*.

Maximus offers an in-depth analysis of time, space, infinity, and motion, which I will examine thoroughly in the following pages, focusing on its direct and indirect significance for Maximus' understanding of temporality.[4] I have already cited and quoted crucial passages of these sections in the previous, introductory pages, but to understand Maximus' mind we have to follow closely his train of thought through the flow of the tenth Difficulty's text itself. As Andrew Louth writes, in the tenth Difficulty "we get a glimpse . . . of how Maximus' mind worked. The movement of his mind is that of one who ponders and meditates, patiently drawing together all sorts of apparently diverse concerns. . . . His mind does not move straight ahead in conformity to a linear, logical argument, rather it moves sideways, and gathers together a collection of considerations that are gradually made to converge."[5] Maximus' understanding of the nature of time emerges out of these "apparently diverse concerns."

Section 35:[6] Creation's εὐκοσμία as Disclosing Its Originator

In this section, Maximus offers valuable elucidations concerning the nature of the relationship between created existence and the uncreated Creator. While time measures corruption and decay, i.e., the march of creation towards destruction and death—or, more precisely, while corruption and death manifest in the passage of time, in the "horizon" of time—, time itself is affirmed as very good (just like the totality of creation). Time contributes to the order of creation, to the beauty of the *cosmos* (εὐκοσμία) and manifests it while participating in it.

The saints are the ones who have attained (i.e., who were granted) the capability to discern and behold what is already there to be beheld: the

---

4. While Mueller-Jourdan's *Typologie spatio-temporelle* focuses primarily on the *Mystagogia*, the author has employed these and other parts of the tenth Difficulty as a basis in order to expound Maximus' understanding of spatio-temporality; a synopsis of his conclusions are to be found in his paper "Where and When as Metaphysical Prerequisites for Creation in Ambiguum 10." My analysis of the tenth Difficulty will not depend on Mueller-Jourdan's approach as such (as it has different starting points), and a point-by-point juxtaposition of each element of Mueller-Jourdan's train of thought to ours concerning these specific sections would be most unpractical. Instead, the reader should keep in mind throughout this chapter that Mueller-Jourdan discusses the status of spatio-temporality as discerned in the tenth *Difficulty* mainly in 39–71 of his *Typologie spatio-temporelle*, often arriving at similar conclusions in the analysis of said passages.

5. Louth, *Maximus the Confessor*, 91.

6. *Amb.Io.* 10, 1176BC: Θεωρία φυσική, δι᾽ ἧς τὸν Θεὸν ἐκ τῶν κτισμάτων οἱ ἅγιοι ἐδιδάσκοντο.

nature of creation as being in relation to its source of existence (i.e., a source outside of creation), not as being definitively subject to the incompleteness that results in death and inexistence.[7] This true nature of existence is manifested as the fine order of the world (εὐκοσμία) and as the interconnectedness of everything (τὴν ἀναλογίαν καὶ τὴν χρείαν, ἣν ἕκαστον παρέχεται τῷ παντί). The capability to behold these traits of existence (and existence as being in constant relation with its source) emerges when one is not confined to only discerning created beings as such (i.e., beings in themselves), but discerns the λόγοι according to which they have been fashioned (καθ' ὄν δεδημιούργηνται λόγον δεδημιουργημένα). This discloses beings not merely as objects or things, but simultaneously as intentions and utterances of their Creator and as a channel to the restoration of communion with him.

Maximus asserts that "what has come to be is found to be not otherwise than good beside what now is," that creation needs no "addition or subtraction" in order to be good. Not being the cause of itself, creation is not complete in the sense that God is complete. However, this incompleteness does not constitute a deficit that makes creation "evil" or contrary to the will of its Creator. The motion of the created towards its beginning and end, its source and purpose (a motion that can be clearly discerned by those who can contemplate the λόγοι of beings) amplifies the fact that creation is "good," as it tends to the attainment of completeness.

Through permanence[8] (διαμονή), order (τάξις), position (θέσις), and the "manner of being" (διεξαγωγή), the tendency of the created towards its restored nature (i.e., in communion with its uncreated source) is disclosed.[9]

---

7. Ibid., 1176B: "So therefore when the Saints behold the creation, and its fine order and proportion and the need that each part has of the whole, and how all the perfect parts have been fashioned wisely and with providence in accordance with the λόγος of their fashioning, and how what has come to be is found to be not otherwise than good beside what now is, and is in need of no addition or subtraction in order to be otherwise good, they are taught from the things he has made that there is One who fashioned them." Louth (*Maximus the Confessor,* 134) translates "καθ' ὄν δεδημιούργηνται λόγον δεδημιουργημένα" as "in accordance with reason that fashioned them," but I deem it necessary to stress that Maximus employs the word λόγος here, referring to both one of the everyday meanings of λόγος καθ' ὄν δεδημιούργηνται, "the reason for which they have been fashioned," and the philosophy of the λόγοι.

8. "Permanence" in this sense does not mean, of course, eternal existence/existence without end, but a certain and visible stability in the context of creation's duration in time.

9. *Amb.Io.* 10, 1176C: "So, too, when they see the permanence, the order and position of what has come to be, and its manner of being, in accordance with which each being, according to its proper form, is preserved unconfused and without any disorder; and the course of the stars proceeding in the same way, with no alteration of any kind" (trans. Louth, as is the case for the whole of this chapter).

The reign of corruption and death and the absolutization of createdness' tendency towards nonrelation and inexistence would reveal a world that is devoid of these traits. However, and while the mutability that results in corruption, death, and inexistence is painfully present in the world,[10] creation's laws, its order, its spatiality, and its διαμονὴ reveal createdness as eager to attain its completeness, not as eager to slip towards inexistence. The εὐκοσμία of the universe, "the course of the stars proceeding in the same way," is a perpetual reminder of this aspect of creation.

The importance of temporality in the context of creation's εὐκοσμία is apparent in this culmination of Maximus' argument.[11] The "circle of the year" (κύκλος τοῦ ἐνιαυτοῦ) as stemming from the order and motion of the universe, the motion of the heavenly bodies, also discloses the created world to the ones contemplating the λόγοι (i.e., the saints) as being in constant relationship with its Creator and as revealing his providence. The fact that they, the saints, recognize God as provident (προνοητὴν ἠπίστασαν εἶναι τῶν ὄντων) signifies his being in constant relationship with creation (him as being *in* creation *through* created beings *while* being wholly Other), a relationship that grants creation with fine order and beauty. The use of the word προνοητὴν does not entail binding the created to necessity as in *predetermination*. Maximus' most famous contribution to the development of the ecclesial testimony is the philosophical fortification of the concept of freedom, and human freedom in particular (the will); in Maximus' thinking, *providence* means *care, reference,* and *relation,* not *predetermination* eliminating the possibility of freedom. We come to acknowledge this providence-signifying-presence by beholding the order of the universe in the "equal proportion of the nights and days (with their mutual increase and decrease)," in the orderly passage of time, in the numbering of motion as time (χρόνος).

We have seen in Aristotle's theory of time that it is the human being (the "soul") that numbers motion. It is through human consciousness that motion is manifested as time, that the overall motion is understood and manifested as the transition from past to future, from the "before" to the "after." Without human consciousness, without the "soul," there is no

10. I.e., not the motion according to nature, but the deviation from this natural motion.

11. *Amb.Io.* 10, 1176C: "and the circle of the year proceeding in an orderly manner according to the periodic return of the [heavenly bodies] from and to their own place, and the equal yearly proportion of the nights and days, with their mutual increase and decrease, taking place according to a measure that is neither too small nor too great, they understand that behind everything there is providence, and this they acknowledge as God, the fashioner of all."

numbering of the motion that takes place; there is no time. I have no ground to accept that Maximus' thought differs in this aspect from that of Aristotle's: Maximus never implies that this "measuring" of motion, the "number" by which motion is circumscribed that is time,[12] takes place by itself; a measuring requires the one who measures. In this sense, the human person does not only *behold* the divine order of the universe that is disclosed through the equal distribution of time, but he also *actualizes* it: once again, the human person acts as a *mediator* between createdness and the Creator, as the field in which the vital relationship of these takes place and is realized.

Section 36:[13] Creation's Temporal Beginning

The ancient Greek worldview did not include a definitive beginning of the world; matter itself (although not necessarily in its current form) was thought to be infinite, and a *creatio ex nihilo* would have been considered a folly, thus eliminating the possibility of a created-uncreated distinction. However, notions of a beginningless world have resurfaced in the Christian world at various points, and Maximus devotes this section to annulling that idea. In doing so, he expounds his insights on the relationship of temporal beginning and cause (ἀρχή), end and purpose (τέλος), on motion as characteristic of everything that is created and on the extent up to which the God of ecclesial testimony can be described as the "unmoved mover."

There are two points in the first passage of this section[14] that are of interest to us. First, there is an "understanding" of the uncreated's traces in creation through the "mind," but this cannot possibly be enough. This "intellectual" reference to the Creator (πρὸς αὐτὸν μόνον ἀναδραμεῖται τῇ διανοίᾳ), however powerful it might be, *must* be left behind (ταῦτα ἀφεὶς κάτω), because it cannot suffice for the "transition" that is longed for (ὅτι μηδὲ πέφυκε τῆς διανοίας χωρεῖν τὴν ὅλην διάβασιν); the contemplation of the world in its true nature through the λόγοι produces a yearning, a passion, a strong desire for the personal and direct encounter and relationship (λαβεῖν ποθῶν ἀμέσως) with the one who is traced through these λόγοι, with the person(s) of God. One's tracing of the creative person in his cre-

---

12. *Th.oec.*, PG91 1085A, 1.5.

13. *Amb.Io.* 10, 1176D-1177B.

14. Ibid., 1176D: "For who, seeing the beauty and greatness of God's creatures, does not immediately understand that He has brought all this into being, as the beginning and source of beings and their maker? In his understanding he returns to Him alone, leaving behind all these things. For though he cannot accomplish the complete transition with his mind, or receive without intermediary the object of his desires which he knows through the mediation of its effects . . . ."

ations constitutes an indirect encounter, which nonetheless gives birth to an intense yearning for a real personal encounter in all directness and immediacy (ἀμέσως) with the object of his desire, an encounter that cannot be compromised with intellectual "understanding" (i.e., the grasping of a concept, however profound it might be). This is the second point to be stressed: that, according to Maximus, the absolute otherness of God can be known *through his creations and actions*, through the mediation of its effects (ὃν διὰ μέσων τῶν ἔργων ἐγνώρισε), i.e., through divine activities.[15] The unapproachable substance of the divine person(s) is, of course, completely different from that of created beings (just like the οὐσία of a painter is radically different from the οὐσία of his painting). However, the hypostatic actualization of this unapproachable substance and nature can be encountered "through the mediation of its effects." If by "mysticism" we are to understand radically subjective and "ecstatic" experiences of the individual, then this relationship that Maximus describes has not much to do with "mysticism": it is a distinct approach to the world, a distinct mode for the access to reality pertaining to the primary questions of ontology.

Apart from these points, I should note that, according to Maximus, it is not only creation-as-a-whole that has its "beginning and source" in the uncreated God (meaning that individual beings exists and survive independently inside a self-sufficient and self-sustained creation which, in turn, is their individual "beginning and source"), but each and every *individual being* has its "beginning and source" in the uncreated person(s)[16]—and consequently, as Maximus will go on to say, its end and purpose. As such, striving for the restoration of full communion with the source of existence does not merely characterize the impersonal "totality of creation" as one whole with possibly different internal relations, but each and every individual being. Therefore, the human person's mediating cosmological function refers to each and every individual being, each and every separate otherness that is to be restored as a perfect otherness in perfect communion, and not merely to the aggregate-otherness that is "creation" in comparison and reference to the otherness of the uncreated.

Writing on the erroneous notion that the world could be without beginning, the Confessor analyses important aspects of his philosophy of

---

15. Note that, while God's substance is single and simple, Maximus explicitly affirms the presence of many and different activities (ἐνέργειαι), seeing a substance-activities distinction as obvious. Cf. *Amb.Io.* 22, 1257A: "οἷς ἀπείροις ἐνθεωρῶν ἐνεργείας Θεοῦ . . . τῶν ὧν ἀντιλαμβάνεται θείων ἐνεργειῶν διαφοράς."

16. "τῶν τοῦ Θεοῦ κτισμάτων . . . ὡς ἀρχὴν καὶ αἰτίαν τῶν ὅλων καὶ ποιητήν." God is not merely the cause and the beginning of κτίσις-as-such, but of all the κτίσματα themselves.

motion. Referring to the person that contemplates these subjects, Maximus says:

> [H]e can readily put away the error that the world is without beginning, as he reasons truly that everything that moves must certainly begin to move. No motion is without beginning, since it is not without cause. For motion has a beginning, and a cause from which it is called and an end to which it is drawn. If the beginning of the movement of every moving thing is its motion, and its end the cause to which what is moved is borne (for nothing is moved without cause), then none of the beings is unmoved, except that which moves first (for that which moves first is completely unmoved, because it is without beginning), and none of the beings then is without beginning, because none is unmoved.[17]

Maximus states that (a) everything that is in motion has started being in motion at a certain point (πᾶν κινούμενον πάντως καὶ ἤρξατο τῆς κινήσεως), for there is a first cause for every motion, and the presence of a cause also means that there is also a temporal beginning (πᾶσα δὲ κίνησις οὐκ ἄναρχος, ἐπειδὴ οὐδὲ ἀναίτιος). Note the correlation between temporal beginning and cause: this is not a special theory of the Confessor but a direct implication of the use of the Greek language for philosophical thinking (i.e., the semantic frame of that enquiry), for, as I have noted, ἀρχὴ means both temporal beginning and first cause, i.e., αἰτία. An ἀρχὴ (temporal beginning) without an ἀρχὴ (first cause) would be inconceivable for Greek thought, it would be outside the limits of its world because of it being outside the limits of its language.[18]

The church father then proceeds to clarify that (b) the beginning and first cause of the beings in motion is the one who has set them to motion (ἀρχὴν γὰρ ἔχει τὸ κινοῦν). This first cause is also the beings' end and purpose: it calls and draws them to it (αἰτίαν ἔχει τὸ καλοῦν τε καὶ ἕλκον), and their motion is directed towards it, it being their end and purpose (πρὸς ὃ καὶ κινεῖται τέλος). What has a beginning also has an end, what has a cause also has a purpose (ἀρχὴ-τέλος). Therefore, (c) the end *is* also the cause, for beings in motion move towards their own cause (τέλος ἡ πρὸς ἣν φέρεται τὸ κινούμενον αἰτία).

---

17. *Amb.Io.* 10, 1177A, trans. Louth, as is the case with every quote from *Amb.Io.* 10 in this chapter.

18. Note also Maximus' identification of beginning/cause and end/purpose as well, in *Amb.Io.* 10, 1084A: "καὶ ταυτὸν δείξας [ὁ Θεὸς] τῇ ἀρχῇ τὸ τέλος, καὶ τὴν ἀρχὴν τῷ τέλει, μᾶλλον δὲ ταυτὸν δὲ ταυτὸν ἀρχὴν οὖσαν καὶ τέλος."

Provided that the beginning and cause of the motion of everything that is in motion is that which initiates this motion (εἰ δὲ πάσης κινήσεως παντὸς κινουμένου τὸ κινοῦν ἐστιν ἀρχή), and seeing that nothing moves without a cause and a beginning (οὐδὲν γὰρ ἀναιτίως κινεῖται) and that no being at all is without motion (οὐδὲν δὲ τῶν ὄντων ἀκίνητον—i.e., change, alteration, locomotion, origination, corruption, in short *existence*), Maximus concludes (d) no being is without beginning, as no being is without motion: οὐδὲν δὲ τῶν ὄντων ἀκίνητον.

However, there is an exception[19] to this, which of course is the One who initiates the first motion in the first place (εἰ μὴ τὸ πρώτως κινοῦν). This prime mover is unmoved and motionless, for he has no temporal beginning and no external cause, being the cause of himself (τὸ γὰρ πρώτως κινοῦν πάντως ἀκίνητον, ὅτι καὶ ἄναρχον).[20] If he had an external cause prior to him or a temporal beginning denoting the starting point of his motion, he would by definition not be the prime unmoved mover and the initiator of the first motion. Of course, this syllogism of Maximus' is purely Aristotelian in nature, alluding to Aristotle's prime unmoved mover.[21] A point of interest is Maximus' insistence on correlating this subject to the subject of temporality. For example, while Aristotle writes that everything that is in motion is moved by something/someone,[22] Maximus prefers to focus on the starting point of this motion, on the fact that it has had a beginning[23]—in his attempt to expound that the world as a whole has a beginning, that the world is an outcome of *creatio ex nihilo*.

If everything that has a beginning also has an end, then there can be no eternity in the sense of unlimited duration. Time measures motion, and motion has always a beginning: therefore, it must also have an end, excluding

19. "Exception" is not an accurate choice of words, as for Maximus God is not "one of the beings," for he is beyond being (ὑπερεῖναι). Again, this is not merely a rhetorical or literary device to denote the greatness of the Godhead, but a precise formulation on Maximus' part, respecting and underlining the ontological difference between creation and the uncreated. The implications of the concept of κτίσις instead of, merely, κόσμος are not always apparent, but they are nonetheless vital for the consistence and coherence of ontological enquiry in that context.

20. As we have seen, this logical necessity of the Aristotelian God being motionless and unmoved is transcended in Maximus' worldview involving the possibility of ontological freedom, as the Confessor's God is simultaneously ever-moving and in motion, his distinct actualizations being in constant and perpetual interpenetration (περιχώρησις—cf. Törönen, *Union and Distinction*, 121–24 for this term).

21. As Andrew Louth remarks as well (*Maximus the Confessor*, 207 n. 96), the preconditions for Maximus' train of thought are located in Aristotle's *Physics*, book VIII chapter 5, and *Metaphysics*, 1073a 23–28, 32–34.

22. *Physics*, 256a 13–14: "ἀνάγκη πᾶν τὸ κινούμενον ὑπό τινός τε κινεῖσθαι."

23. *Amb.Io.* 10, 1177A: "πᾶν κινούμενον πάντως καὶ ἤρξατο τῆς κινήσεως."

the possibility of temporal infinity (the existence of infinity *as such* is excluded, as we will see in section 39). Eternity in the sense of unlimited duration cannot be ascribed to the uncreated either (in this sense, the uncreated is *not* eternal): this unending duration would also be the measure/number of a certain motion, but no motion of this sort is to be ascribed to the uncreated.[24] Ever-being (ἀεὶ εἶναι) and ever-well-being (ἀεὶ εὖ εἶναι) are used to describe man's and creation's *redemption* from the cycle of motion that leads to corruption (i.e., they are employed relatively, only in comparison to the current state of temporality), and they are similarly ascribed to the uncreated in the context of an apophatic stance, merely from the viewpoint of humanity. What the Confessor acknowledges as non-sensible realities are created and in motion as well, possessing a distinct type of temporality.[25] *Every* kind of being is moved[26] (while God is not "one of the beings"), but intelligible beings[27] are moved "in accordance with knowledge and understanding,"[28] in accordance with their constituent powers (συστατικαὶ δυνάμεις), i.e., mind (νοῦς) and reason (λόγος).

Section 37:[29] The Motion of Substance, Quantity, and Quality

This section of Maximus' tenth "Difficulty" explains why the expansion and contraction of substance (οὐσία), as well as quantity and quality, must necessarily have a beginning and cause (ἄναρχοι εἶναι οὐ δύνανται). Maximus understands the expansion and contraction of substance as a downward

24. Again, this ever-moving "perpetual interpenetration" stresses that to describe the uncreated as motionless still ascribes characteristics and criteria of createdness to the uncreated. *Beyond* motion would be a more accurate way to formulate this.

25. I will analyze Maximus' concept of the Aeon in the next chapter.

26. *Amb.Io.* 10, 1177A: "πάντα γὰρ κινεῖται τὰ ὁπωσοῦν ὄντα."

27. A detailed analysis of the ontological status of Maximus' sensible/intelligible distinction and of what he means by intelligible realities in the context of philosophical consistency is outside the scope of my study, when encountering these terms, I will be content in integrating them into my analysis and in proceeding onwards. However, I will attempt to approach them as *modes* later in this study.

28. *Amb.Io.* 10, 1177AB, "For every kind of being is moved, except for the sole cause which is unmoved and transcends all things, those beings that are intelligent and rational in a way in accordance with knowledge and understanding, because they are not knowledge itself or understanding itself. For neither is their knowledge or understanding their being, but something they acquire as they consider their being with correct judgment in accordance with mind and reason (what I call their constituent powers)."

29. *Amb.Io.* 10, 1177B-1180A.

and upward motion on an implicit Porphyrian tree,[30] on a scale of the universals, from the most general to the most specific.[31] I have stated that, as there is no οὐσία ἀνυπόστατος, substance is not understood as being a *thing*, "something" residing "somewhere," which excludes a conception of its movement as spatial locomotion in the way that this is experienced by the hypostatic actualization of the substance.[32] However, and as Maximus affirms every created being has a beginning, a cause, and a substance and is in motion, he traces the motion of even the most abstract and general of substances in their "expansion" and "contraction" on the scale of the universals.[33] This motion of the substance, this "expansion" and "contraction" of the substance, has "both a beginning and an end," for it is "not at all capable of being defined by limitlessness."[34] Were the "expansion" and "contraction" of the substances without a beginning and end (i.e., limitless and infinite), both time (the numbering of that expanding and contracting motion) and its cosmological partner, space, would be infinite as well. As we will see in later sections, Maximus excludes the possibility of infinity from creation.

Maximus studiously ascribes (a) temporal beginning, (b) generation, (c) beginning of motion, (d) cause, (e) end, (f) purpose, and, of course, (g) motion to everything created, and the *substances* of everything created, however general and abstract, could not have escaped this attribution, leaving the semantic circumscription devoid of philosophical realism. He proceeds to argue that even general and at times abstract categories like

30. Cf. Louth, *Maximus the Confessor*, 207 n. 98. The concept of the Porphyrian tree (Tree of Porphyry or Arbor Porphyriana) derives from Porphyry's (third-century AD) introduction (Εἰσαγωγὴ) to Aristotle's Categories and is a "scale of being," a division of each substance into *genus* and *differentiae* until no further division is possible.

31. *Amb.Io.* 10, 1177C: "For it is moved from the most universal kind through the more universal kinds to the forms, by which and in which everything is naturally divided, proceeding as far as the most specific forms, by a process of expansion [διαστολή], circumscribing its being towards what is below, and again it is gathered together from the most specific forms, retreating through the more universal, up to the most universal kind, by a process of contraction [συστολή], defining its being towards what is above."

32. I should reiterate here that the substance and the hypostasis are not to be understood as two different "things," but as two different *modes*, the *mode of existence* of homogeneity, the *mode of existence* of the particular.

33. *Amb.Io.* 10, 1177B: "But that which is simply called being itself (ἡ ἁπλῶς λεγόμενη οὐσία) is not only the being (οὐσία) of those things subject to change and corruption, moved in accordance with change and corruption, but also the being of all beings whatever that have been moved and are moved in accordance with the reason and mode of expansion and contraction."

34. *Amb.Io.* 10, 1177C: "ἀρχὴν καὶ τέλος ἔχουσα δείκνυται, τὸν τῆς ἀπειρίας οὐδ' ὅλως ἐπιδέξασθαι δυναμένη λόγον."—"Thus it can be described either way, either from above or from below, and is shown as possessing both beginning and end, not at all capable of being defined by limitlessness."

"substance," "quantity," and "quality" are subject to all the fundamental characteristics of createdness. Expansion and contraction are both a λόγος and a
τρόπος,[35] a (pre)existent "intention" and tendency *and* the distinct mode of
its actual realization. It is not only the substance that is characterized by the
motion of "expansion" and "contraction," but *quantity* and *quality* as well:
"every kind" of quantity can be expanded, without of course attaining infinity, and again contracted, without losing its natural/substantial form, i.e.,
the συμφυὲς εἶδος (which would mean that it would stop belonging to same
substance any more, as there is a strong correlation between οὐσία/φύσις
and εἶδος).[36] The same is true of quality, of *every kind* of quality: the motion
of "expansion" and "contraction" is not only present in cases where such
a thing would be obvious and expected, but in all created things that are
subject to the laws of createdness, τῷ τρεπτῷ τὲ καὶ σκεδαστῷ.[37] Maximus
insists on ascribing the motion of "expansion" and "contraction" to *any* substance, quantity, and quality in order to illustrate that motion is the primary
characteristic of createdness, even in the cases where this is not obvious and
expected, and so even in substances that are not visibly subject to change,
motion, origination, and corruption. For the Confessor, to be in motion is
to have been originated, to have a cause and to have a temporal beginning
(and also to have a spatial status, an end and a purpose).

That is exactly his point and his argument: if substances, qualities, and
quantities are subject to "expansion" and "contraction," then they cannot
be unmoved and motionless, they are by definition in motion (as this "expanding" and "contracting" is a motion in itself). The presence of motion
signifies that there has been a beginning to that motion, and everything
that has had a beginning in its motion has been generated at some point in
time. Everything that is in motion has "received" its motion and its being
(τὸ εἶναί τε καὶ τὸ κινεῖσθαι λαβόν), the implication being that this motion
and being has been received from the One that is ingenerate and unmoved,
i.e., uncreated (ἐκ τοῦ μόνου καὶ ἑνὸς ἀγενήτου τε καὶ ἀκινήτου). Maximus
concludes this section with a wordplay denoting the necessary correlation

---

35. Ibid., 1177B: "τῷ κατὰ τὴν διαστολὴν καὶ συστολὴν λόγῳ τε καὶ τρόπῳ."

36. Ibid., 1177CD: "So it has quantity, not just the quantity of those things subject
to change and corruption which are perceived to increase and decrease in every way
naturally, but also every kind of quantity that can be circumscribed when it is moved
by tightening and loosening and given form according to expansion by partial differences, without however flowing out into limitlessness, and again gathered together as it
retreats in accordance with its kind, without however losing its natural form."

37. Ibid., 1177D: "Similarly with quality which is not just that moved by change
in beings subject to change and corruption, but every kind of quality, moved according to difference in what is changeable and soluble, and receptive of expansion and
contraction."

between (temporal) beginning and cause: he writes that everything that has had a beginning in its existence (τὸ δὲ κατὰ τὴν τοῦ εἶναι γένεσιν ἠργμένον, "ἠργμένον" being the participle perfect of ἄρχω/ἄρχομαι, i.e., ἀρχὴ) cannot possibly be without a cause (οὐδαμῶς ἄναρχον εἶναι δύναται, "ἄν-αρχον" meaning "without an ἀρχή").[38] Essentially, he writes that everything that has had an ἀρχὴ must also have ἀρχή, a tautology that I mentioned earlier and one that illustrates how language *dictates* philosophy (or, adversely, one that illustrates the innate philosophical preciseness of language).[39]

Section 38:[40] Maximus' Space-Time Continuum

In this most interesting section, the Confessor expounds his theory on the correlation of space[41] and time, a view that is far from being taken for granted on the part of his contemporaries: according to him, everything that possesses a spatial status also possesses a temporal one and vice versa, spatiality and temporality being the dimensions of the motion.[42] As the motion of created beings and creation is a continuous one (its cessation causing a collapse into inexistence—with the exception of deification, the στάσις ἀεικίνητος), one would be accurate in describing Maximus' view on spatio-temporality as the space-time continuum of motion. The section's purpose

38. Ibid., 1180A: "For no-one can say that anything that can naturally be scattered and gathered together again either by reason or force can reasonably be thought to be completely unmoved. If it is not unmoved, it is not without beginning. If it is not without beginning, then clearly it is not ingenerate, but just as everyone knows that the motion of what is moved must have had a beginning, so anything that has come into being must have begun to come into being, receiving its being and movement from the sole One who has not come into being and is unmoved. That which has begun to come into being could not in any way be without beginning." As the reader can witness, Andrew Louth translates οὐδαμῶς ἄναρχον εἶναι δύναται as "could not in any way be without beginning," but given that the previous sentence mentioned the origination of being and motion from God, I think that ἄναρχος here should be translated as "without cause." The sentence "That which has begun to come into being could not in any way be without beginning" would be too much of a tautology, even for Maximus.

39. Cf. Maximus' treatment of ἀρχὴ and τέλος in relation to motion in Q.Thal. II, 59.268–83.

40. *Amb.Io.* 10, 1180B–1181A.

41. "Place" would be here historico-philologically more accurate than "space," as space is a modern notion and its application to Maximus could be seen as anachronistic; that being said, for the convenience of this discussion, I will employ the word "space," which is more intelligible today, noting the inadequacy of the term.

42. However, this is only true of the *sensible* creation, as Maximus attributes another form of temporality to intelligible beings, but not exactly spatiality, this is substituted by other forms of ontological *distance*, which I will examine in later chapters.

is to prove that "everything apart from God exists in a place and, therefore, necessarily also in time, as well as that that which exists in a place has necessarily had a temporal beginning."[43]

The Confessor writes that the "being" of beings itself exists "in a certain way and not simply" (καὶ αὐτὸ τὸ εἶναι τῶν ὄντων, τὸ πῶς ἔχον, ἀλλ' οὐχ ἁπλῶς), that every being possesses "howness" in order to exist, it possesses the otherness of its particularity, of its actual realization (i.e., the substance's hypostatization). This is another way of saying that there is no οὐσία ἀνυπόστατος, that every substance (οὐσία) exists insofar as it is to be encountered in particular actualizations (ὑπόστασις). Maximus categorically excludes any other possibility: he accepts the reality of substance and employs it as an ontological category, but explicitly states that the substance does not exist "simply," without the "howness" of an actual realization, of the particular. Without the particular, i.e., the "certain way" of the substance's existence, the substance is but a mere abstraction. This, the particular, is the "first form of the substance's description," and it reveals that the origination of beings entails a temporal beginning in the case of their substances as well (ἦρχθαι κατ' οὐσίαν καὶ γένεσιν τὰ ὄντα).[44] Maximus means (a) the fact that the substances exist insofar as their actual realizations (the particulars) exist and (b) these particulars have been originated in time and possess a temporal beginning entails (c) the substances themselves have originated in time, that they have had a temporal beginning and exist in time (ἐν χρόνῳ, as the title of the section puts it).

Maximus is eager to add that each and every being[45] (except from "the one divine being" who, as the Confessor writes, is not "one of the beings," for it exists beyond being itself, i.e., creation, the mode of creationedness, and creation's inescapable terminology) is in all cases thought of as being *somewhere*, which is always and necessarily bound to being at a certain *point in time*.[46] Maximus does not merely offer an observation; his use of words underlines his insistence on the projected fact. In one short sentence, he repeats four times the inescapable character of the correlation

---

43. *Amb.Io.* 10, 1180B.

44. Ibid., "I should say, too, that the fact that beings exist in a certain way and not simply—that this, indeed, is the first form of circumscription—is a powerful factor in proving that beings have a beginning in respect of being and generation."

45. "Παντὸς τοῦ ὁποσοῦν ὄντος," i.e., each and every being that exists *in a certain way*.

46. *Amb.Io.* 10, 1180B: "Who is ignorant of the fact that every kind of being whatever, apart from the divine and unique being, which properly speaking exists beyond being itself, is already thought of as being somewhere, and that, together with this, it is necessarily thought of as certainly existing at some time?"

of every kind of existence with a spatial and a temporal status: "every kind of being whatever," "in every case" and "certainly," "necessarily" (παντὸς τοῦ ὁπωσοῦν ὄντος—πάντῃ τε καὶ πάντως—ἐξ ἀνάγκης). Spatiality is a precondition of beings, for it does not take place *after* the emergence of beings but is included in their emergence itself; it is "already thought of as being somewhere" (προεπινοεῖται τὸ ποῦ). Something does not first exist and *then, apart from that*, it is located somewhere: the fact of its existence itself necessarily entails its τὸ ποῦ, its "whereness." The same is inescapably and necessarily true of τὸ πότε, every being's temporal status: the existence of every being whatsoever entails it being in time, it possessing "whenness" (πάντῃ τε καὶ πάντως ἐξ ἀνάγκης συνεπινοεῖται τὸ πότε), which is not merely one of the attributes of existing, but an inseparable characteristic thereof. As we can see, the event of existing is itself bound to a continuum of spatio-temporality, a conjunction of spatial and temporal status through which the event of existing is actualized, manifested, and disclosed: without this spatio-temporal continuum of each being, there is "no kind of being whatever," to paraphrase the Confessor.

The reader should note that in the original Greek text, Maximus generally tends to refrain from using the words *space* (τόπος) and *time* (χρόνος) in this section, preferring the use of "*the where*" (τὸ ποῦ) and "*the when*" (τὸ πότε) instead. One would be more accurate in speaking about the "whereness" and "whenness"[47] in Maximus, not about "space" and "time." His choice is in line with his general commitment to write on the *mode* of things, on their "howness," and not to theorize about abstract *objects*. The nouns "space" and "time," in their philosophical context, are mere abstractions; the question concerning the *where?* and *when?* of beings is a much more concrete question, contributing to the realism of Maximus' enquiry and acting as its precondition. Interestingly enough, the Confessor links in his line of thought the "whenness" and "whereness" of beings with their "howness" (τὸ πῶς, τοῦ ὁπωσοῦν ὄντος). He handles these questions as dimensions of the "howness" of things, further intensifying his focus on the *mode of existence*, and not the "whatness" of beings, as the *locus* of ontological enquiry.

Maximus clarifies that the conjunction of spatiality and temporality—of "the where" and "the when"—is not just a matter of coexistence; the one *is* a precondition for the other.[48] These are "simultaneous" (ἅμα) dimensions

47. Mueller-Jourdan and others have also employed the terms "whenness" and "whereness" to describe the notions of ποῦ and πότε in the tenth Difficulty.

48. *Amb.Io.* 10, 1180BC: "For space cannot be thought of, separate from and deprived of time (for they go together and one cannot be without the other), nor can time be separated from and deprived of space, for they are naturally thought of together."

of reality, which would not be conceivable without them; spatio-temporality is necessary for reality (τῶν οὐκ ἄνευ τυγχάνουσιν). It is the very nature of spatiality and temporality to coexist (συνεπινοεῖσθαι πέφυκεν) and it would not be possible to separate them or to deprive the one of the other (οὐδαμῶς διώρισται κατὰ στέρησιν).

It is interesting to note that Maximus' wording consistently subjects these ontological/cosmological axioms and observations to the limitations of human understanding: he speaks of how things are "thought of/already thought of/simultaneously thought of to be," etc. (ἐπινοεῖται, προεπινοεῖται, συνεπινοεῖται), not of how things *are*. Maximus' texts do not allow us to presume he juxtaposes how people *think* things are with how things *really* are, which he would explain elsewhere if this were the case. Instead, his insistence on this wording seems to echo, once again, his apophatic stance. Human persons can understand the world in the measure of their capabilities, "in the measure of their language,"[49] but this understanding will always be unable to exhaust the truth of how things *really are*. However, *this is the only measure we possess*, and it is the only way of understanding we have: language, thinking, and understanding do truly reflect and "circumscribe" the truth of reality—in their measure, according to the limitations of the semantic function's capabilities, which however *do* "iconize" truth.[50] The fact that Maximus insists on this wording does not mean that knowledge is impossible or that our knowledge is false: he simply reminds us to be mindful of this fundamental distinction, to never lose sight of it, and therefore to never abandon the ontological enquiry's prerequisites for realism.

The Confessor proceeds to discuss some definitions of space and time, of "the where" and of "the when." Everything is manifested and disclosed (πάντα δείκνυται) as being subject to spatiality, to "the where" (ὑπὸ τὸ ποῦ), for every created thing exists in space (ὡς εν τόπῳ ὄντα). Everything is "in space," because the totality of everything cannot be greater than the whole

49. *Scholia in De Divinis Nominibus*, CD4.1 189B (p. 122, fn.): τῷ μέτρῳ τῆς ἡμετέρας γλώσσης ἀκολουθῶν, (οὐ γὰρ ὑπερβῆναι ταύτην δυνατὸν ἡμῖν).

50. The reader can find an interesting recent contribution to Maximus' understanding of the notion of truth in Georgi Kapriev's article "Der Wahrheitsbegriff bei Maximus Confessor," in Mensching-Estakhr and Städtler, *Wahrheit und Geschichte*, 137–51, especially in the second part dealing with the *Ambigua*. Kapriev is right in discerning Maximus' threefold approach to truth through his terms, σκιά, εἰκών, and ἀλήθεια (shadow, image/icon, and truth—144f.). The *referring* function of σκιά and εἰκών (they *point* to truth, but they are not truth in themselves) illustrate Maximus' elaborate understanding of the relationship—and, most importantly, the difference—between a *signifier* and its signified *reality*, between an εἰκών and its ἀλήθεια. For an account of Greek patristic thought on the subject, see Zizioulas' *Being as Communion*, 67–122.

of the universe, i.e., the sum of beings cannot exceed the universe itself.[51] As a consequence, no created thing could be *beyond* the universe and not be circumscribed by space. The universe (τὸ πᾶν) cannot but contain everything (τὸ πᾶν); it would be both irrational and impossible to presume that the sum of everything (τὸ πᾶν) is greater than the universe (τὸ πᾶν), that τὸ πᾶν τοῦ παντὸς could be beyond τὸ πᾶν. This is, once more, a clever wordplay expounding philosophical accuracy through semantic/linguistic accuracy.[52] The universe is contained in itself and does not extend beyond itself;[53] the universe "has its circumscription *from* itself and *in* itself." This is the "edge of the universe," the "limit of the universe" (τὸ πέρας ἑαυτοῦ), seen *from the inside*. The notion of the "limit of the universe" *from the outside* (a welcome *contradictio in terminis*), τὸ πέρας ἑαυτοῦ τὸ ἐξώτερον, can only be a reference to what "exists" *beyond* the created, "the infinite power that is the cause of all."[54] The fact that the created universe cannot be infinite and limitless (as I will analyze in section 39) entails that it has a limit, and the notion of the "outer side" of that limit refers the limitations of creation to the created-uncreated distinction, establishing the relationship between the created and the uncreated, creation and its Creator, as the epicenter of existence and as a vital part in the "circumscription" and understanding of existence.

Maximus asserts that this is what space is, i.e., the space of the whole universe (τόπος τοῦ παντός), and confirmingly quotes a definition of

51. *Amb.Io.* 10, 1180C: "By space, we mean that everything is shown as being in a place. For the totality of everything is not beyond the universe (for it is irrational and impossible to conceive of the universe itself as being beyond everything that it is)."

52. *Amb.Io.* 10, 1180C: "οὐ γὰρ ὑπὲρ τὸ πᾶν αὐτὸ τὸ πᾶν τοῦ παντὸς (τοῦτο γάρ πως καὶ ἄλογον καὶ ἀδύνατον αὐτὸ τὸ πᾶν ὑπὲρ τὸ Ἑαυτοῦ πᾶν εἶναι θεσπίζειν)."

53. I cannot adequately stress the independence of philosophical cosmology from physical cosmology and vice versa. The one may inspire the other or reveal aspects of the other as having a relevance or importance not hitherto discerned, but the one may not *substitute* the other, these disciplines attempt to answer different questions and employ different tools and methods in doing so. To mention an example, the theory of the possibility of multiple and parallel universes (multiverse or meta-universe) in the context of physical cosmology would not be a counter-argument to the position of Maximus', in this context, τὸ πᾶν ("everything," "the universe") would be *the sum of all multiple universes*, the sum of creation, and not merely of our "individual universe."

54. *Amb.Io.* 10, 1180C: ". . . but being circumscribed from itself and in itself, in accordance with the infinite power of the cause of all that circumscribes everything, the limit itself is outside itself." Note that Maximus links in another passage the subject of the "limit of the universe" to *time*, and more specifically to the *future*, ibid., 1172A, ". . . the limit of the universe, which is wholly in the future, in which there will no longer be among beings anything bearing or anything borne, nor any kind of motion at all in the ineffable stability which defines the range and motion of what is borne and moved" (trans. Louth).

space as "what surrounds the universe, either the position that is outside the universe, or the limit of the container in which what is contained is contained."[55] This is a definition of space that ultimately derives from Aristotle through Nemesius, as Andrew Louth notes.[56] This could have been a mere philological borrowing, but the attentive reader will have noticed Maximus' "twist" of it. Aristotle's concern is to provide a definition of space (in the context of a cosmology and ontology excluding a created-uncreated distinction), but Maximus attributes this "*limit* of the universe" and this "*outside* of the universe" that "*surrounds* the universe" not to the universe itself, not to creation (albeit it being creation's extreme limit), but to "the infinite power that is the cause of all," to God (an uncreated God beyond motion, spatiality, and temporality). This entails that, for Maximus, space is the *locus* of the relationship between the created and the uncreated, between creation and the Creator. The very definition of space-as-a-whole includes its relation to the divine person(s) and is determined by it. Space signifies a spatial interval and extension, a *distance*, and space-as-a-whole signifies the *distance* between creation and Creator (a distance that is in this case ontological and not spatial)—while simultaneously embodying the hope for the annihilation of this distance.

The Confessor subsequently proceeds to a further discussion of time. It is his previous line of thought on space that similarly and simultaneously proves (συναποδειχθήσεται) that every created thing possesses a temporal status and is subject to "the when" (ὑπὸ τὸ πότε), that everything without exception is "in time" (ἐν χρόνῳ πάντως ὄντα). Maximus links this with modality again, with the *mode of existence*: he repeats that nothing apart from the uncreated exists "simply," without possessing a certain and distinct mode of its existence, without possessing τὸ πῶς εἶναι, its certain "howness." And this "howness" entails that beings have a temporal beginning (and a cause), for the hypostatization (actualization) of the substance *in a certain way* entails its emergence *at a certain point in time*. If it is possible to speak about the "how" of something, Maximus writes, then even if that thing exists now, it is certain that it didn't always exist (οὐκ ἦν),[57] that there was a

55. Ibid., 1180C: "And this is the place of the universe, just as certain people define space, saying that space is what surrounds the universe, either the position that is outside the universe, or the limit of the container in which what is contained is contained."

56. *Physics*, Book IV, chapter 4. See Louth, *Maximus the Confessor*, 207–8 n. 100.

57. Andrew Louth (*Maximus the Confessor*, 208 n. 101) notes here that the use of ἦν (third person singular imperfect of "to be") does not merely denote a past tense, but it is used in an absolute sense meaning eternal existence. Louth explains that this is not a Neoplatonic usage, but a Christian one going back to John 1:1.

time in which it didn't exist.[58] This has to do with the specific "howness" signifying a difference and a distance from mere "whatness" (e.g., the differences of a specific human person in comparison to "humanity" or "human nature"), the *mode of existence* of something manifesting an otherness not found in its *genus*; the motion/change/transition(/origination) from mere nature to the otherness and difference of a being's actual existence cannot but have taken place in the *past*, i.e., in *time*.

In what way does Maximus say that the uncreated does not possess "howness" and what therefore are the implications for the "uncreated's temporality" (insofar as we can use such a term)? In what way does Maximus say that the uncreated does not possess "howness" and which are the implications for the uncreated's temporality, insofar as we can use such a term? In the case of the uncreated and divine, it would be absurd to speak of a "difference" and a "distance" of God's "howness" (τὸ πῶς) and God's "whatness" (τὸ τί), these being categories of createdness. Even the use of the notions of "howness" and "whatness" itself abuses the relative character of language when trying to describe the uncreated with semantic tools forged within createdness. In Maximus' worldview, the three divine persons *are* God's singular "being" and "substance," they are not *different* from it; they do not manifest a *distance* and *difference* from what God *is*: the uncreated's "howness" *is* the uncreated's "whatness." For Maximus and the ecclesial testimony, the three hypostases of God *are* God's one and single "substance." It is not that God's actualization as three persons in otherness and communion *is something different* from God's "being." To say that God's single "substance" is "what" God is and that God's three hypostases are "how" God is does articulate and relatively describe ("circumscribe") the testimony of the ecclesial community's relationship with him, but it cannot exhaust the truth of the uncreated *as such*, a truth that is by definition "beyond words," i.e., words forged to signify beings-in-createdness.[59] This closer examination of the uncreated's freedom from the mode of existence that results in a spatiotemporal status is most relevant to my examination of Maximus' views on time, for it defines and designates the *difference* of created existence from its external and uncreated cause, revealing crucial aspects of this nature.[60]

---

58. *Amb.Io.* 10, 1180CD: "And by time, it is indicated that everything is certainly in time, since everything that possesses existence after God possesses this existence in a certain way and not simply. And therefore they are not without beginning. For if we know how something is, we may know that it is, but not that it [always] was."

59. Cf. Corpus Areopagiticum, *De Mystica Theologia*, 149f.

60. I must here provide a general remark, that such an ontological enquiry attempting to include a created-uncreated distinction (and as such, God/the uncreated) in its line of thought without *reifying* God, without including him within "being" and slipping

I defined "substance" as the mode of participation in being, but God does not "participate in being," for he is not "one of the beings." As a consequence, when we say that God *is* (τὸ θεῖον λέγοντες εἶναι) we are not speaking of *how* God is (οὐ τὸ πῶς εἶναι λέγομεν), which eliminates the need to think of the uncreated as "becoming somehow in time." This reveals the extreme relativity of saying that God "is" or "was," which are both correct and at the same time insufficient, inaccurate. Both can be said "simply, boundlessly, and absolutely," but only if the limitations of signifying the uncreated with the means of the created are respected, as the uncreated cannot be confined into any reason, utterance, meaning, or thought (ἀνεπίδεκτον παντὸς λόγου καὶ νοήματος).[61] "Being" does originate from God, but it is exactly the created-uncreated distinction that does not include God into "being": while he creates "being," he himself is not "being." This independence of the uncreated from either existing "simply" or "in a certain way" further stresses the possession of "howness," of existing "in a certain way" and possessing *a mode of existence* on the part of created beings, as Maximus insists (εἰ δὲ πῶς, ἀλλ' οὐχ ἁπλῶς, ἔχει τὰ ὄντα τὸ εἶναι). He repeats that this "howness" of beings always and in every way (πάντως) entails their "whereness," i.e., their position and limit according to their λόγοι of substance and nature (ὑπὸ τὸ ποῦ διὰ τὴν θέσιν καὶ τὸ πέρας τῶν ἐπ' αὐτοῖς κατὰ φύσιν λόγων), and their "whenness" stemming from the fact that they have had a temporal beginning and cause (ὑπὸ τὸ πότε εἶναι διὰ τὴν ἀρχὴν ἐπιδέξεται). It is the inescapable *modality* of created existence that binds it to *spatio-temporality*.[62]

---

into the premises of ontotheology, verges on being barely possible at all. However, this is exactly the ontological enquiry of the whole of Byzantine civilization (a sweeping but nonetheless accurate generalization) and Maximus the Confessor in particular. In order for such an ontological enquiry to be possible, it is evident that the apophatic epistemological stance is to be employed most emphatically.

61. *Amb.Io.* 10, 1180D: "Thus when we say that the divine is, we do not say how it is. And therefore we say of him that 'he is' and 'he was' simply and boundlessly and absolutely. For the divine cannot be grasped by any reason or thought, nor do we grasp his being when we say that he is."

62. Ibid., 1180D–1181A: "For being is derived from him but he is not being. For he is beyond being itself, and beyond anything that is said or conceived of him, whether simply or in a certain way. But beings possess being in a certain way, and not simply, so that where they are is determined by their position and the natural limit of the λόγοι that are in them, and when they are [is determined] from their beginning."

Section 39:[63] Createdness Excludes the Possibility of Spatio-temporal Infinity

This section of the Confessor's tenth "Difficulty" is devoted to arguing there can be no infinity (both spatial, temporal, or otherwise) and beginninglessness/causelessness within creation; the absence of finitude and of an origination or an originator, i.e., a prior cause, is to be attributed only to the uncreated God. Maximus treats the finitude of created existence as an implication of it having a beginning and cause, being in motion and possessing modality, spatiality, and temporality ("howness," "whereness," "whenness").

The word that Maximus uses to denote finitude is "circumscription" or "delimitation" (περιγραφὴ) and the ability of something to be "circumscribed," i.e., having given limits. He explains both the substances and the hypostases are finite and not limitless. The substance and being of everything cannot be infinite, for its limit is the very sum of everything, a quantity that can be circumscribed. The fact that the substance and being of everything is not infinite nor unbounded stems from both the λόγος of being itself and the λόγος of being's *mode of existence*, of its "howness"[64] and actualization. Consequently the hypostasis, the actual realization of each being, is also subject to circumscription.[65] The hypostases are circumscribed in relation to each other, and this circumscription is effected through *number* and *substance* in accordance with the λόγος[66]—a notion of λόγος that reflects both being and modality, both substance/nature and "howness."[67]

Arriving at the conclusion that nothing is free from circumscription, from being finite, specific, and particular (i.e., from possessing finitude, limits, boundaries), the Confessor links this universal subjection to circumscription to spatio-temporality. He writes that everything, according to its measure, "has received" a spatial and a temporal status, a "whereness" and a "howness." These are reiterated as being absolute prerequisites of existing in creation: without a spatio-temporal limit, nothing can exist, nothing can possess substance (οὐσία), quantity (ποσότης), quality (ποιότης), relation

63. Ibid., 1181A–1184A.

64. Ibid., 1181A: "τόν τε τοῦ εἶναι καὶ τοῦ πῶς εἶναι λόγον."

65. Ibid., 1181B: "Οὐδὲ ἡ τοῦ καθ᾿ ἕκαστον δῆλον ὑπόστασις ἔσται δίχα περιγραφῆς."

66. Ibid.: "ἀλλήλαις τῷ ἀριθμῷ καὶ τῇ οὐσίᾳ κατὰ λόγον περιγεγραμμέναι."

67. Ibid., 1181AB: "And again the being of all the many beings that are in the universe cannot be infinite (for there is a limit to all these things in their multitudinous quantity which circumscribes the λόγος of their being and manner of being, for the being of the universe is not unbounded), nor can the substance of any of them be without circumscription, for they are mutually circumscribed in accordance with their λόγος by number and being."

(σχέσις), action (ποίησις), passion/receptiveness (πάθος), motion (κίνησις), and habit (ἕξις). These are the attributes "with which those who know about these things delimit the universe." In Maximus' thought, the whole spectrum of the characteristics of existing depends on the possession of a given spatio-temporal status, a status that is itself linked with the specificity and otherness of beings, i.e., their "howness."[68]

According to Maximus' argument, due to reason (a reason/λόγος reflecting the principles/λόγοι) the subjection to circumscription and modality dictates a temporal beginning and, in the dual meaning of ἀρχή, a cause—as there is always something that precedes (προεπινοεῖσθαι) each being, both causally and temporally. This means that there was a time when each given being did not exist, thus signifying the beings' generation.[69] Maximus arrives at his core argument concerning infinity: *existing infinitely* (spatially, temporally, or otherwise) and *becoming* without change or alteration cannot coexist.[70] For if something has been generated, then it has been changed into what it has become after its origination and into what it was not before its origination. And everything that can be changed or altered or lacks form has not achieved completeness, it cannot have its end and purpose in itself (αὐτοτελές).[71] This completeness can be achieved or granted

68. Ibid., 1181B: "If none of the beings is free from circumscription, all the beings clearly receive in proportion to themselves both when and where they are. Apart from these, nothing at all can be, neither being, nor quantity, nor quality, nor relation, nor action, nor passion, nor movement, nor habit, nor any other of those attributes with which those who know about these things delimit the universe."

69. *Amb.Io.* 10, 1181B: "Therefore no being is without beginning, if something else can be thought of before it, or uncircumscribed, if something else can be thought of alongside it. If no being is without beginning or uncircumscribed, as follows naturally from the λόγος of the beings, then there was certainly a time when each of the beings was not. And if it was not, it certainly came into being, since [otherwise] it would not be."

70. Ibid., 1181C: "For it cannot receive being and becoming apart from change and alteration. For if it was and [then] became, it changed, going over to what it was not by a process of becoming, or it was altered, receiving an addition to its beauty that it lacked. Nothing that has changed, or altered, or lacked form, can be complete in itself. What is not complete in itself certainly lacks some other thing that will allow it wholeness, and then it is whole, but not complete in itself, since it has wholeness not by nature but by participation. That which needs another for wholeness stands in much greater need when it comes to being itself."

71. This observation does not clash with the content of section 35 (*Amb.Io.* 10, 1176B, "what has come to be is found to be not otherwise than good beside what now is, and is in need of no addition or subtraction in order to be otherwise good"). To be "in need of no addition or subtraction" does not entail containing one's own cause. Created beings can be "very good" without this meaning that creation's cause (and purpose) is not outside of itself. I must note here that when Maximus refers to beings according to the λόγος of nature, either explicitly or implicitly, he refers to the state in which they

only in relation to something that is complete and whole and has its cause and purpose in itself. However, this granted completeness is not the same with perfection, for completeness has been achieved by participation (i.e., through relation and communion), not by its nature. Maximus concludes that if something needs to be in relation and communion with something else in order to achieve completeness, then this is much more so the case concerning its being, its participation in existence.

The Confessor proceeds with one more argument against the notion of the possibility of beginninglessness for created beings (and against the notion of uncreated matter), and specifically an argument concerning substance and form. The notion of *form* contains in itself the realities of generation, change, alteration, and other actualizations of motion. To conceive of a beginningless being (i.e., apart from God) that is only substance without form would be absurd. If substance is superior to form, as was a common affirmation in Maximus' time, then it would not make sense for a being to have achieved the "superior" but to be deprived of the "inferior."[72] Maximus excludes the possibility of the possession of substance or matter without the possession of form, thus binding every created being (possessing substance and form) to spatio-temporality (and, as such, to the possession of a beginning and cause). This is one more variation of the basic affirmation that there is no οὐσία ἀνυπόστατος, an affirmation that acts as a guarantee for the realism of Maximus' ontological thinking. The Confessor hastens to remark that all of this reveals once again that to possess "being itself" (ἁπλῶς εἶναι), i.e., without particularity and modality ("howness"), would be impossible—for substance and matter alike.[73] The cycle of the generation

---

are in perfect communion with the Creator—to their "pre-fallen" or "redeemed" state. The incompleteness of not containing one's cause of existence, of not being αὐτοτελής, fades in the restored full communion with this cause. However, this does not reflect the current state of beings.

72. *Amb.Io.* 10, 1181CD: "For if, as they say, being is established as better than form, any particular being can either grant itself this or possess it simply, as they want to say, but why is it not strong enough to possess simply or grant itself what is worse, that is the form? And if any particular being is not strong enough to grant itself what is worse, or possess it simply, whether those who dare to regard as without beginning beings that are after God and derived from him want to call it being or matter (for they make no distinction), why cannot it possess either simply or from itself what is better, by which I mean being, when it cannot possess what is worse?"

73. Ibid., 1184A: "If matter can in no way possess, either from itself, or simply, what is worse, still less can it possess being itself simply, or from itself. How then can what is too weak to possess, as has been shown, what is worse—that is form—or what is better—that is being—ever possess anything?" It would be interesting to compare Maximus' rejection of the possibility of amorphous matter (in this context, ὕλη without εἶδος) with various ancient Greek views on the subject; however, this would be far

and beginning of substance, being, and form must have its starting point beyond the beings that are subject to generation and beginning themselves (and to substance, being, and form, for that matter). This could have simply been a "prime unmoved mover" logic on the Confessor's part, but his choice of words reveals his insistence on seeing the act of creation not as a mechanical necessity, but as a free act of love, relation, communion: the existence of created beings reveals that every substance, being, and form has been "granted as a gift" (δεδώρηται) from God, establishing the world as a continuous relationship with its Creator, as the *locus* of a relationship that is measured by the primary characteristic of created existence: motion. One could safely say that according to Maximus, to accept the reality of God means accepting creation as spatio-temporally finite, with a given temporal beginning, a spatial limit, and, consequently, a coming end, a *cause* and a *purpose*—and vice versa.[74]

Section 40:[75] Further Elucidations on the Impossibility of Creation's Infinity

Once again, Maximus contradicts here the notion of matter's beginningless-ness and the possibility of uncreated matter. If matter is eternal and has always been,[76] then it follows that it has not been generated, that it is uncreated. If it has not been generated, then it is not in motion and did not begin its being at a certain point in time. If that is the case, then it has no beginning or cause, and it is infinite. Being infinite, it is necessarily motionless, for having achieved infinity and being boundless, there is no space to move into; there is no given greater territory in which its motion could take place. In such a case, there would be two beginningless, infinite, and motionless beings: the uncreated God and uncreated matter.[77] However, this is a *contra-*

---

beyond the scope of this study.

74. Ibid.: "If this is so, then being and form must be given to beings by God, for they exist. If then all being and matter and every form is from God, no-one who is not completely deprived of any sane thought could maintain that matter is without beginning and ungenerate, since he knows that God is the maker and fashioner of the beings."

75. Ibid., 1184BC.

76. The past tense ἦν that is used here signifies eternal/absolute existence, not existence in the past, as I have mentioned earlier. Louth also repeats his previous observation in 208, n. 104 of his *Maximus the Confessor* (the translations in which have been used for the present chapter, as have been noted).

77. *Amb.Io.* 10, 1184B: "And again, if matter was [absolutely], as some say, then it clearly did not come into being; if it did not come into being, it was not moved; if it

dictio in terminis, which Maximus explains by employing the notions of the dyad and the monad. The dyad (infinite/uncreated God and infinite/uncreated matter) cannot possess infinity, beginninglessness, and motionlessness and it cannot be the *cause* of anything,[78] because its mode is the mode of either *union* or *division*—it is circumscribed within this specific territory of these two "functions." *Union*, because the dyad's existence *refers* to the reunion and composition of the two monads from which it is constituted and into which it is disclosed.[79] *Division*, because it is "moved by number": the *division* into a dyad is a *distinction* of the two monads, a distinction described by number, a number signifying division.[80]

Relation is one of the criteria cited by Maximus as signifying the impossibility of "two infinites." The Confessor remarks that nothing that can be divided or can effect division and nothing that can be compounded or can effect composition either by its nature or by its position/arrangement or anything else (i.e., either according to its "whatness" or to its "howness") could ever be infinite. Even division and composition themselves, in the "simple" (i.e., devoid of particularity and modality, "naked") and abstract sense, cannot be infinite. And these cannot be infinite because they are not beyond *relation*: they exist relationally, in relationship to each other. For example, beings under division or composition are in relation to each other by the very fact that they are under division or composition, divided or united, or dividing and composing beings with which they are in relationship (σχέσις). However, the infinite is by definition unrelated to anything,[81] for if it were bound by any relationship to anything, then it would not be

---

was not moved, it did not begin to be; if it did not begin to be, then it is without beginning of any kind; if it is without beginning, then it is infinite; if it is infinite, then it is certainly unmoved (for the infinite is certainly unmoved, for what is not limited can have no place in which to be moved); and if this is the case, then there are assuredly two infinites, unmoved and without beginning, God and matter, which is inconceivable."

78. Maximus uses the word ἀρχὴ here twice in order to stress that he is referring to both beginning and cause, "οὔτε ἄναρχος . . . οὔτε μὴν ἀρχὴ καθόλου τινὸς εἶναι δυνήσεται."

79. *Amb.Io.* 10, 1184BC: "For the dyad could be neither infinite, nor without beginning, nor unmoved, nor the beginning of anything at all, for it is circumscribed in accordance with unity and division. It is circumscribed by unity since it has existence as the composition of monads, which it contains as parts, and into which it can be divided as parts."

80. Ibid., 1184CD: "It [the dyad] is circumscribed by division, since it is moved by number, from which it begins and in which it is contained, since it does not possess being by nature and free from any relationship."

81. Ibid.: "τὸ δὲ ἄπειρον ἄσχετον—οὐ γὰρ ἔχει τι κατὰ σχέσιν συνημμένον παντάπασι."

infinite.[82] A dyad of infinities would be impossible, because this would require being *by nature* beyond relationship[83]—a notion contrary to life and
existence as relation and communion and death and corruption as the cessation of relation and communion. Maximus goes on to argue about the
dyad and the monad, but I will refrain from proceeding with my analysis of
consecutive sections from the *Book of Difficulties*.

Conclusions and Remarks

The reader will have noticed that Andrew Louth's remark on Maximus'
thinking could not have been more accurate when he notes that it is not
linear and systematic but "patiently [draws] together all sorts of apparently
diverse concerns," moving sideways and "gathering together a collection of
considerations that are gradually made to converge."[84] In articulating his
understanding of existence, Maximus often repeats his line of thought,
digresses, and turns to secondary subjects in order to return to his main
argument later, after a "circle" of thought, etc. His thinking is *spiral*, in that
it progresses through the retracing of circles. However, it is this unusual
thinking that reveals his prioritizations, the interconnectedness of the hermeneutic elements of his thought and the preponderance of specific elements in his ontological proposal—or rather, testimony.

In order to proceed to examine Maximus' conception of the Aeon
(αἰών) in the following chapter, I will sum up my conclusions from sections
35–40 concerning time, space, and motion:

i.   Maximus' definition of time as "the numbering of motion"[85] remains
      my primary reference on the nature of time, even if it was not cited in
      these particular sections of the tenth Difficulty. Time *measures* mo-
      tion and is delimited by number.

---

82. Ibid., 1184C: "for nothing that is infinite could be divisible or divided, or
composite or compounded, by nature or arrangement or in any other way, nor could
it simply be division or composition itself, because it is neither sole and simple, nor
numerable, nor numbered, nor co-numbered, nor simply free from any kind of relationship; for all these things are beheld in relationship one to another, but the infinite is
unrelated, for it cannot be held in any kind of relationship at all."

83. Ibid., 1184CD: "οὐ φύσει τὸ εἶναι καὶ ἄσχετον ἔχει." According to the PG, this
is not the ending point of section 40. Andrew Louth, in *Maximus the Confessor*, 208,
n. 106, employs this division from Eriugena's version, which also marks the end of the
section we have examined.

84. Louth, *Maximus the Confessor*, 91.

85. *Th.oec.*, 1085A, 1.5—*Q.Thal. II*, 65.533–34.

ii.   However, "as a consequence, the motion through one's life is alter-
      ing everything in it (ἀλλοιωτικὴ κίνησις)":[86] it follows that time also
      measures corruption, decay, and the march towards annihilation and
      death—just like in Aristotle's theory of time.

iii. Motion is the primary characteristic of existence. Everything created
      is in motion. Everything—whether substances, particulars, qualities,
      quantities, sensible and intelligible (e.g., substance, "quality," etc.)—is
      in motion. The creation and sustaining of existence is the first mo-
      tion, the uncreated's creative motion, and creation's motion has by
      nature the tendency to be a returning motion towards its uncreated
      cause and source, a motion towards the fullness of communion sig-
      nifying completeness.

iv.   Every motion has a beginning and a cause. (Motion emerges from its
      cause and is drawn to it). Nothing within creation is beginningless
      and causeless. Creation itself has had a temporal beginning.

v.   Temporality characterizes everything within creation.[87] In the sen-
      sible world, space and time form a space-time continuum: the one
      presupposes the other, and everything is in space and time. A more
      realistic formulation is that everything possesses a "whereness" and a
      "whenness," a spatio-temporal status.

vi.   Without a spatio-temporal limit, nothing can exist, nothing can
      possess substance (οὐσία), quantity (ποσότης), quality (ποιότης),
      relation (σχέσις), action (ποίησις), passion/receptiveness (πάθος),
      motion (κίνησις), or habit (ἕξις). To sum up: everything created pos-
      sesses (a) temporal beginning, (b) generation, (c) beginning of mo-
      tion, (d) cause, (e) end, (f) purpose, and (g) motion.

vii. Everything created possesses a "howness," a distinct mode of exis-
      tence. This "howness" is closely related with (and a prerequisite of)
      "whenness" and "whereness."

viii. There can be no infinity within existence. Everything has a begin-
      ning, a spatio-temporal status, and a mode of existence (signifying

---

86. Q.Thal. II, 65.534–35.

87. Amb.Io. 67, 1397AB: "For everything that is in motion and has been created
is subject to a beginning, and for this reason is absolutely subject to time, even if it is
a form of time not measurable by motion. For every created thing has a beginning of
its being, since there was a time when it began to exist, and it is subject to extension in
time, from the moment when it began to exist. If, then, every created thing exists and is
in motion, then it is absolutely subject to nature and time, to the one on account of its
existence, and to the other on account of its motion" (trans. Constas).

becoming, γίγνεσθαι, not merely *being*), all of which exclude the possibility of infinity, of escaping circumscription and delimitation. Matter, creation, and the universe; everything is finite.

ix. The fact that there can be no infinity within creation excludes the possibility of eternity in the sense of an unlimited duration of time. Such an understanding of eternity is excluded.

x. The orderly passage of time is an aspect of εὐκοσμία, referring to God. The totality of space, τὸ πᾶν, space-as-a-whole, is referring to God by virtue of its "outer limit."

xi. The synopsis of the above points concerning time is as follows: Maximus speaks of time as the "numbering" of something truly existing (i.e., the motion) or as the "whenness" (τὸ πότε) of something, a mere dimension of existing beings; while he does employ the word χρόνος, he is not very fond of speaking about time as an absolute and independent reality. I am led to the conclusion that the Confessor does not consider time as "something," as an independent reality, but only as a dimension of the motion, a measurement of it by the ones who measure, a status signifying "whenness," i.e., in a quite relative way. It exists by virtue of motion's existence and insofar as motion exists—time does not exist on its own. At the same time and contrary to this observation, time is of paramount importance for creation, for *everything* must necessarily be "in time" (and "in space") in order to exist and every created thing—and creation itself—has had a temporal beginning, a beginning "in time." While time itself exists *relatively*, everything (and creation as a whole itself) is *subject* to time. As the "measuring" of motion, time is also most important and necessary in creation's *overall* motion, i.e., history and creation's progression either towards completeness and redemption or towards annihilation; this overall motion of creation is measured *in time*, and it is measured by humanity, the mediator between creation and the uncreated. Time also measures the change, and consequently also the corruption and decay caused by the motion within creation (ἀλλοιωτικὴ κίνησις); time *numbers* the march towards either death or completeness.

The above are the points found in Maximus' text itself. However, I would also like to provide some conclusions of my own based on Maximus' line of thought and stemming from his syllogisms. As space and time "are naturally thought of together" (συνεπινοεῖσθαι πέφυκεν), one could attempt a paraphrase of Maximus' definition of time in other treatises[88] as "the numbering of motion" and "the circumscription of motion" in the case of space. If (a) motion is the primary and definitive characteristic of created existence, if (b) time is merely the numbering of motion, and (c) if time and space form a continuum that characterizes all created beings while being a dimension of motion themselves, then (d) one would not be far from Maximus' thinking by saying that space is also a "numbering of motion," the numbering of the *distance* that is created by the motion, and the actualization of motion as *distance*[89]—even in the cases where "motion" means change, alteration, corruption, increase, decrease, etc., and not merely spatial locomotion. In this sense, space and spatiality also emerges *as a dimension of the motion*, instead of motion "taking place" in "space." Instead of motion emerging within a preexistent space (and at a given time), motion has an ontological priority over space (and time), as space is one of the motion's dimensions. It is motion that realizes spatio-temporality, for motion is "measured" and "circumscribed" as distance, i.e., as space and time. Space would not then be the numbering of motion with respect to the "before" and "after," but with respect to the "here" and "there." It will become clearer in the course of this study if such a view is seen as a legitimate basis in the Confessor's works.

Space and time alike, constituting an undivided whole (a space-time continuum), emerge as the dimensions of motion, which in all its forms is the primary existential event within creation. A relational existential event simultaneously realizes and discloses creation's relationship with its uncreated source, as the totality of motion is either God's creative motion from the uncreated towards (creating and sustaining) creation or creation's returning motion to its source, cause, purpose, beginning and end.[90] This event discloses existing as being-in-relation. Furthermore, recalling Aristo-

---

88. *Th.oec.*, 1085A, 1.5—*Q.Thal. II*, 65.533–34.

89. "Distance" and "extension" in Greek is usually διάστασις or διάστημα. Note that διάστημα, a word not used by Maximus in this section, means both spatial and temporal *interval*, both spatial and temporal *distance* (Cf. διάστημα in Lampe's *Patristic Lexicon*, 359f., as well as LSJ). Gregory of Nyssa often employs the word with a temporal meaning (*Contra Eunomium* I.1.171: "μηδενὸς διαστήματος χρονικοῦ," I.1.342: "διάστημα χρονικόν"), and this dual meaning of διάστημα-distance as both spatial and temporal distance gives further hints concerning the possibility of defining space as *the numbering of motion in spatial distance*. Distance need not be exclusively *sensible*, but *intelligible* as well—as is the "expansion" and "contraction" of the substance on the Porphyrian tree. On Maximus' use of διάστημα in a temporal sense; see, e.g., *Amb.Io.* 10, 1157A: τοῦ χρονικοῦ τούτου διαστήματος, or *Th.oec.*, 1085A: ὁ αἰὼν πάσχει διάστασιν.

90. Or creation's motion *contrary to nature*, towards nonrelation, annihilation, inexistence.

tle's reservations concerning the autonomous existence and reality of time[91] in which he concludes that time does not exist (or that it exists faintly and obscurely),[92] one might wonder if Maximus is in line with these conclusions. It is clear that both philosophers acknowledge motion (both as the overall motion of existence and each individual motion) as a primary reality. Time is for both of them merely "the numbering of motion," "the circumscription of motion"—something that exists insofar as motion exists and as a numbering and dimension thereof. And while Aristotle separates his doubts concerning time from his acknowledgement of space as an autonomous reality, Maximus' insistence on the absolute and inescapable interrelationship and interdependence of space and time (of "the where" and "the when") would not allow us to presume that he accepts the existence of space as independent of time and motion, as an autonomous reality. It is at least arguable that, in the Confessor's line of thought, both time *and space* exist only insofar as motion exists—with them being motion's dimensions—and do not possess a reality of their own.

If the above syllogisms are true to Maximus' way of thinking, then I could add the following points to the above conclusions:

i. The human person is the one who *numbers* time: it is he who actualizes motion as time. The fact that the human person *actualizes* (motion as) time is one aspect of humanity's mediating function.

ii. Space is a "numbering of motion" as well; it is the disclosure of the *distance* actualized by motion as *space*.

iii. Both time and space exist insofar motion exists; they do not possess an autonomous existence of their own, independently from the motion they are measuring and numbering.

iv. Spatio-temporality emerges as the dual dimension of motion: both of the dimensions of this "space-time continuum" (i.e., spatiality and temporality) are the *numbering* of motion, but the numbering of motion with respect to different types of *distance*.

v. Motion measures a *relation* (σχέσις), both generally within creation and in terms of the created-uncreated distinction. This relation can either end up in the relation's consummation (i.e., fullness of communion-in-otherness) or in the relation's cessation (nonrelation)—both

---

91. It should be noted Aristotle does not have the same reservations concerning the existence and reality of space, as is apparent in his main treatment of the subject in *Physics*, 208a27–213a10.

92. *Physics*, 217b 32–34.

are measured as distance, the annihilation and absolutization of distance respectively.

Sections 35–40 have offered a deep insight into Maximus' understanding of spatio-temporality as τὸ ποῦ and τὸ πότε, as χρόνος and τόπος. Now I will proceed to examine his notion of the Aeon (αἰὼν) as a distinct form of temporality, equally important to time as χρόνος—if not more.

CHAPTER NINE

Inverted Temporality:
The Aeon

WHILE MAXIMUS' NOTION OF the Aeon (αἰών)[1] as a distinct, second form of temporality is clearly expounded in specific passages of his work, the reader is faced with the problem of Maximus' different usage of the term αἰών in different contexts throughout the Maximian corpus.[2] Apart from the meaning illustrated in the dual definition of χρόνος and αἰών in *Amb.Io.* 10, 1164BC, which I hold as the primary definition of the Aeon, Maximus also uses the term in different contexts in order to signify eternity as un-

---

1. I have proposed a reading of Aeon as Maximus' *second* mode of temporality in Mitralexis, "Maximus the Confessor's 'Aeon,'" which consisted in an abridged form of this chapter. A problem with many scholarly accounts of Maximus' understanding of the Aeon is the lack of differentiation between the "eternity" of the Aeon and the "eternity" of the ever-moving repose, resulting in an erroneous and incomplete reading of the Confessor. However, Paul Plass' article "Transcendent Time in Maximus the Confessor" is a valuable contribution. Note Plass' mention of the Maximian and Cappadocian notion of διάστημα (distance, interval, extension) and its relation to temporality in p. 260, as this plays a major role in my treatment of the subject. Plass' article "Transcendent Time and Eternity in Gregory of Nyssa" is a good introduction to these concepts prior to Maximus' renewal of them. In both articles, Plass' contradistinction of the Neoplatonic understanding of eternity and return to the biblical and patristic concept is particularly noteworthy.

2. Which, to different degrees, is also the case with almost any important term Maximus employs, making it exceedingly difficult for the reader to squarely systematize the Confessor's understanding of core notions such as λόγοι, τρόπος (mode), etc. Throughout the secondary literature concerning Maximus, an abundance of attempts at systematizing Maximian terminology can be found (instead, for example, of accepting the fact that only *approaches* to Maximus' thought can be attempted, without claims of definitive answers), often yielding unsatisfactory results and leading to misunderstandings of the Confessor's teachings—a tendency that is gradually being corrected.

limited duration,[3] or a great amount of time/a century,[4] or history, or God's temporality in contrast to our own, etc.[5] This becomes quite pronounced in instances where Maximus uses the word *Aeon* meaning eternity in the sense of unlimited time by employing the word in its plural form αἰῶνες, i.e., the ages.[6] Maximus differentiates between the singular, αἰών, and the plural, αἰῶνες, in a way suggestive of this usage by employing both forms in the same sentence with different meanings[7]—but again, this is not characteristic of the whole of his work and cannot be systematized in such a way. When speaking of the "temporality" of God in contrast to our own, Maximus sometimes refers to it as Aeon or aeonic and sometimes as ἀΐδιος, ἀΐδιον, ἀϊδιότης,[8] in order to contrast God's "temporality" to the Aeon as well[9]—however, as I have noted earlier, the Confessor does not adopt a systematized distinction of χρόνος/αἰών/ἀϊδιότης, whereas he often clarifies that no kind of temporality whatsoever can be applicable to God. And (to make things worse) there are passages in which Maximus refers to ἀϊδιότης simply as eternity without change and alteration,[10] practically equating it

3. E.g. *Q.Thal. I*, 38.52: "πέρας οὐκ ἔχοντος . . . αἰῶνος."

4. E.g. *Q. Thal. II*, 56.140–42: "θεῷ, τῷ πάντας τοὺς ἀπείρους τούς τε προγενομένους καὶ ὄντας καὶ ἐσομένους αἰῶνας προεγνωκότι."

5. *Amb.Io.* 10, 1188B: "But it has been shown that from God, who eternally is [τοῦ ἀεὶ ὄντος] . . ."—*Scholia in De Divinis Nominibus*, CD4.1 229A-C, "Μέτρον ἐστὶ τῶν ὄντων, ἐπειδὴ πάντα ἐν αὐτῷ πεπέρασται, καί αἰὼν μάλιστα δικαίως ἄν λέγοιτο· εἰ γάρ αἰὼν λέγεται, οἷον ἀεὶ ὤν, αὐτός ἐστιν ὁ ἀεί ὤν. . . . Ποιητής δέ αἰώνων, ἅτε τῶν ἀγγέλων ποιητής ὤν, ἀθανασία, παράτασις, ἀειζωῖα, αἰών, ἀλλ᾽ οὐ χρόνος, ἀτελεύτητος καί ἀεί ἐσόμενος λέγεται." Quite logically, due to the numerous different commentators that authored the *Σχόλια*, the differences in the use of the terms αἰὼν and αἰῶνες throughout the *Scholia* can be profound, often offering contradictory illustrations thereof.

6. E.g., *Amb.Io.* 21, 1252B: "φοβερὰν ἐπ᾽ αἰῶσιν ἀπείροις λαβοῦσα κατάκρισιν."

7. *Amb.Io.* 65, 1389D: "Σημαίνει γὰρ καὶ χρόνον, καὶ αἰῶνα, καὶ αἰῶνας."

8. E.g., *Car.*, 2.27.3, as well as 4.3.1: "ἐξ ἀϊδίου δημιουργὸς ὑπάρχων ὁ Θεός." As mentioned earlier, Maximus attributes ἀϊδιότης to the uncreated λόγοι (*Car.*, 1.100, 2.27), thus differentiating ἀϊδιότης from the Aeon, the beings in the Aeon had a beginning and a generation (while the λόγοι had no beginning and no generation).

9. In *Th.oec.*, 1086B-1.6, we find a clear example of the ἀΐδιον attributed to God and the Aeon attributed to the creatures that are not under time: "Οὐκοῦν οὐδὲν αὐτῷ τὸ παράπαν ἐξ ἀϊδίου συνθεωρεῖται κατ᾽ οὐσίαν διάφορον· οὐκ αἰών, οὐ χρόνος, οὐδέ τι τῶν τούτοις ἐνδιαιτωμένων."—"Absolutely nothing that is different from [God] by substance is seen together with him from all eternity [ἐξ ἀϊδίου], neither the Aeon, nor time, nor anything dwelling in them" (trans. Berthold). And, *Amb.Io.* 10, 1188B: "[God] is the maker and fashioner of all Aeon and time and of everything that exists in the Aeon and time, not that they are in any way conceived together with him from eternity [ἐξ ἀϊδίου], for it is known that none of the beings that exist alongside one another from eternity [ἐξ ἀϊδίου] could be creative of any other" (trans. Louth).

10. E.g. Ibid., 1169D: "Nor can it be rightly thought that what does not possess eternity [τὸ μὴ ὡσαύτως ἔχον ἀεί] should appear to any rational understanding as eternal

with the Aeon (as the state of temporality of intelligible realities and "time without motion") and eradicating any hope of a solid χρόνος/αἰὼν/ἀϊδιότης distinction.

However, and apart from this variety in the use of terms, Maximus *does* propose a second form of temporality beyond normal time (χρόνος) and its extensions in duration (extensions that reach up to the "ages of the ages"): a form of temporality that is *inverted time*, as it is time without motion—whereas the main characteristic of time is that it is the numbering of motion.

The Aeon: Time Deprived of Motion

As noted in my general introduction to Maximus' conception of temporality, the Confessor formulates a "dual" definition for both time and the Aeon, intertwining their meanings with each other and constituting the one necessary for defining the other: "The Aeon is time, when its motion ceases, and time is the Aeon, when it is measured in its motion. So the Aeon, to formulate a definition, is time deprived of motion, and time is the Aeon when it is measured while in motion."[11]

In my opinion, this is not a definition mentioned by Maximus in passing, merely rhetorically or as a philosophical loan from Plato in order to elaborate on other matters. It is rather in this definition that the uniqueness of Maximus' conception of temporality is expounded and the prerequisite for understanding the Confessor's notion of the Aeon is provided. The inattentive reader might assume that Maximus' scattered references on temporality are but a patchwork of diverse influences: a definition of time from Aristotle's philosophy, a definition of the Aeon from Plato's dialogues, and so on. However, to arrive at such a conclusion is to refuse to "connect the dots" of Maximus' ontology: his scattered references are unified in his cosmic vision, incorporating elements such as his *returning* motion, deification, and the στάσις ἀεικίνητος, mediation and repose in the ἀεὶ εὖ εἶναι, communion between the absolute othernesses of creation and the uncreated.

It is natural for a Byzantine thinker incorporated into the ecclesial tradition to have no claims of radical originality, but of merely formulating

---

[ἀΐδιον], separate from change and alteration, and not rather scattered and changing in a myriad of ways" (trans. Louth).

11. Ibid., 1164BC. Predecessors to this distinction between αἰὼν and χρόνος are to be located in Plato's *Timaeus* (37d), Plotinus' *Enneads* (3.7.2) and the Areopagite corpus' *De Divinis Nominibus* (CD I, 215–10.3), as Andrew Louth remarks in *Maximus the Confessor*, 207 n. 85.

a given testimony anew, using "tried and tested" semantic tools. However, in the case of ingenious minds like Maximus the Confessor's, this can result in the originality of a philosophical synthesis that transcends the content of its individual constitutive parts. In order to articulate his own philosophical language, Maximus naturally utilizes the languages of others; these are employed as *means* to the *end* of expounding his own cosmic vision, as stepping-stones for the articulation of a Maximian ontology of dialogical reciprocity between createdness and the uncreated. For the ecclesial community, the promised transcendence of the abysmal gap between creation and the uncreated through the hypostasis of Christ is a testimony; to attempt to articulate this testimony and this possibility in a precise philosophical language is to attempt to turn *mystery* into *ontology*—and, notwithstanding the limitations of a consistently apophatic stance, I would say that this is the essence of Maximus' overall exposition when approached through the perspective of philosophy. The study of temporality's nature is a vital part of this undertaking and, in this context, a *renewal* of pre-Christian (or "inadequately Christian")[12] notions thereof is required. We will expound in the following pages how Maximus attempts such a *renewal* through his understanding of the Aeon and, most importantly, through his notion of the ever-moving repose (στάσις ἀεικίνητος).

The first thought that strikes the reader of this definitive formulation is the interdependence and interconnectedness of χρόνος and αἰών: neither of these two terms can be defined without taking into account the other one, and *by defining the one, Maximus is voiding the other*. They describe philosophical terms and realities in a way that they cannot be conceived individually, but only in relation of the one to the other. Χρόνος presupposes αἰών and vice versa, thereby voiding them of individual meaning independent from one another. And either in the context of a contradistinction between νοητὰ (sensible) and αἰσθητὰ (intelligible) or between κτιστὸν (created) and ἄκτιστον (uncreated), this conjoined distinction between χρόνος and

---

12. With this I am referring to early Christian conceptions of various philosophical issues that, when examined closely, prove not to have taken into full account (a) the implications of the created-uncreated distinction or (b) the reality—according to (post-Chalcedonian) Christians—of the full hypostatic union of uncreated and created/human natures/substances in the person of Christ (*inconfusedly, unchangeably, indivisibly, inseparably*, which is a contradiction to (a), and rightly so in the context of Chalcedon, a "foolishness" and "scandal"—1 Cor 1:23). A number of Neoplatonic Christian syntheses would fall under this category. One could perhaps say that, in Chalcedonian Christianity, it is primarily these two criteria that judge whether a given teaching is to be considered a part of the *corpus* of the articulation of the church's testimony or merely a teaching *influenced* by the Christian *Weltanschauung*, if not explicitly non-Chalcedonian.

αἰών implies the interdependence of the broader realities in which they are integrated.

Thus, time is defined as "inverted Aeon" ("the Aeon, when measured in its movement") and the Aeon is defined as "inverted time," the definition of the one referring to the definition of the other—and inverting it. But why does the need arise to incorporate the definition of the Aeon, "time deprived of motion, time without movement," in the definition of time, making it an essential part of the definition of time itself?

Again, the absence of the created-uncreated distinction in pre-Christian Greek worldviews plays an important part here. For Aristotle, the fact that time is the numbering of motion meant that without motion, there is no time, no form of temporality whatsoever. The motion from the "before" to the "after"—from the past to the future—actualizes time, time is but its numbering; no motion means no time, and the νῦν, the "now" of the transition from the "before" to the "after," exists only in the context of that transition and does not possess autonomous existence or measurable dimension. A νῦν that is not part of a temporal motion and transition but exists in itself is inconceivable. Aristotle excludes the possibility of experiencing time as a dimensionless present, of isolating the νῦν from this transition, from the flow of time. As I have previously noted, according to Aristotle the very perception of νῦν on behalf of the subject turns νῦν into past (as it follows νῦν in time) and makes it practically inexperienceable; by trying to grasp/experience the νῦν, we are already in the future/"after" while νῦν has hidden in the past/"before," making it inexistent. However, in the world of Maximus, the absence or cessation of motion does not necessarily signify inexistence.

While God (i.e., the uncreated) is beyond any motion or fixity,[13] the ontological antithetical contradistinction between createdness—perceived as entailing the motion of everything that exists and disclosing being in motion as the prerequisite of existing—and the uncreated leads us to acknowledge God (i.e., the uncreated) as being in *perfect rest, repose, fixity*, as being *completely unmoved*, an "unmoved mover."[14] While acknowledging (being

13. *Amb.Io.* 15, 1221A: "God neither moves nor is stationary (for these are properties of naturally finite beings, which have a beginning and an end); He effects absolutely nothing, nor does He suffer any of those things which are conceived or said of Him among ourselves, since by virtue of His nature He is beyond all motion and rest, and in no way is subject to our modes of existence" (trans. Constas).

14. Simultaneously, it is the same relativity of the language of createdness when attempting to signify, "circumscribe," and "delimit" the uncreated that allows us to speak of God's creative motion, of the internal motion of the divine hypostases' perpetual interpenetration, of God as a lover who is in fierce motion towards the human person, the object of his desire, etc. Cf. *Amb.Io.* 23, 1260A: "[God] providentially draws the things that are in motion back to the limit that it has established for them" (trans.

in) motion as the criterion of (being in) existence, thereby equating motion-lessness to inexistence, Maximus also acknowledges *another* kind of being motionless, in repose and fixity: that which *iconizes* the motionlessness of the uncreated, that which transcends the necessities, predeterminations, and limitations of createdness (i.e., motion), that which is the attainment of "perfection" or achieving the purpose (τέλος→τελείωσις)[15] and the first step towards the transcendence of the ontological gap between creation and the uncreated (further steps being only granted, given, gifts of grace and not attainments of the creature itself). The cessation of motion that leads to inexistence is the παρὰ φύσιν cessation of motion, while the one that leads to perfection is the κατὰ φύσιν development,[16] which could lead to the ὑπὲρ φύσιν ever-moving repose, the gift of deification, of hypostasizing one's otherness through uncreated activities (ἐνέργειαι) on the basis of a created human nature/substance—possibilities of repose spanning from the φεῦ εἶναι (ill-being, being in vain)[17] up to the ἀεὶ εὖ εἶναι (ever well-being).

This means for Maximus, in contrast to the Aristotelian worldview, the absence or cessation of motion does not necessarily entail inexistence; it could also signify the attainment of perfection, of freedom from the cycle of motion, as I will examine. However, according to Maximus, this is not merely a privilege of the Aristotelian "prime unmoved mover" but a possibility granted to creation, to beings that did have a temporal beginning and a generation and exist within temporality, such as humans. In their case, the cessation of motion κατὰ φύσιν does not mean exiting temporality as such: it means entering *a distinct form of temporality,* the Aeon, "time deprived of motion," temporality without motion.

Constas).—Cf. *Amb.Io.* 23, 1260C, Being love and ἔρως, the divine is in motion, while being the object of love and longing it draws towards itself everything that is receptive to love and ἔρως.

15. *Th.oec.,* 1096C–1.35: "Ὅσα μέν ἐν χρόνῳ καί χρόνον δημιουργεῖται, τελειωθέντα ἵσταται, λήγοντα τῆς κατά φύσιν αὐξήσεως."—"All things created in time and accord-ing to time become perfect when they cease their natural growth" (trans. Berthold). Αὔξησις is but one of the aspects of motion. By writing about the things "created in time and according to time," Maximus refers to sensible realities, the intelligible ones being *created in the Aeon and according to the Aeon*—possessing a temporal beginning/generation and a kind of temporality, but the distinct temporality of the Aeon.

16. *Th.oec.,* 1096C–1.35. The reader is reminded, in Maximus, κατὰ φύσιν means according to *pre-fallen* nature, according to a createdness that retains its full commu-nion with its source of existence. In our known and current state of affairs, the κατὰ φύσιν motion is the *returning* motion.

17. *Amb.Io.* 65, 1392C: "If, then, voluntary activity makes use of the potential of nature, either according to nature or against nature, it will receive nature's limit of either well-being or ill-being—and this is eternal being, in which the souls celebrate their Sabbath, receiving cessation from all motion" (trans. Constas).

We *cannot* conclude that Maximus' Aeon is *the temporality of the uncreated*[18] or something similar: the Aeon "has a beginning," Maximus says, it is "not ἄναρχος, not without a beginning" as well as everything "included in it"—however, it cannot be "circumscribed by a number."[19] Despite the lack of identification of the Aeon with the uncreated, or of the Aeon *in* the uncreated, the very distinction between time and Aeon as Maximus formulates it stems from and is implied in the contradistinction between the created and the uncreated, a contradistinction that is not to be found in Aristotle's ontology and generally in Greek philosophy.[20] This explains why the Aristotelian definition of time could not have been merely repeated by Maximus in the context of his ecclesial ontology without change, but only with the inclusion of the Aeon, a temporality deprived of motion.

The fact that the end and purpose of the κατὰ φύσιν motion is the cessation of motion (the completion of the returning motion) accounts for the second part of the Confessor's definition: "Time is the Aeon, when it is measured in its motion."[21] It is not only the cessation of motion that turns time into the Aeon, into a distinct form of temporality: it is time itself that is an actualization of the Aeon in radically different circumstances, when extended in the world of motion and measured within the cycle of motion. The sensible world's motion and the numbering thereof that is time are also a faint *icon* of a world without motion and without the distance (διάστημα/διάστασις) that presupposes it, of a world with no impediments to the fullness of communion between othernesses—and between the absolute othernesses that are creation and the uncreated. The sensible world, its motion and its temporality embody an existential *reference* to that world without existential incompleteness, without corruption and death and with the fullness of communion (i.e., without *the fall*), a reference "through a glass, darkly" (1 Cor 13:12). This referentiality, iconizing function and allusion is

18. There is no temporality of the uncreated whatsoever, *Th.oec.*, 1084A–1.1, "God is one, without beginning, incomprehensible, possessing in his totality the full power of being, fully excluding the notion of time and quality [of whenness and howness]" (trans. Berthold).

19. *Th.oec.*, 1085A–1.5.

20. The Aristotelian "prime unmoved mover" (πρῶτον κινοῦν ἀκίνητον) could be erroneously understood as "uncreated" if we equate the notions of "moved" (κινητὸν) and "born/existing" (γενητὸν) to the notion of "createdness," and as a result understand the "unmoved" Mover as "uncreated." However this would not be accurate. The Aristotelian "prime unmoved mover" does not necessarily reside *outside of the world*, he is *within being/existence* and should not be confused with the Christian notion of uncreatedness, which presupposes a *creatio ex nihilo*.

21. *Amb.Io.* 10, 1164BC: "Χρόνος ἐστὶν ὁ αἰών, ὅταν μετρῆται κινήσει φερόμενος, . . . τὸν δὲ χρόνον αἰῶνα κινήσει μετρούμενον."

articulated in the distinction of two different, yet in a sense antithetical but simultaneously interconnected, types of temporality. If the Aeon were in motion, it would be time: the Aeon's analogous temporal reality in the plane of our sensible world is χρόνος, "time is the Aeon, when it is measured in its motion." In this context, time indeed is, as Plato would say, "a moving *image* of the Aeon."

The Aeon of the νοητά, the Time of the αἰσθητά

While the dimension of spatiality itself, as it is to be encountered within sensible creation, is not a trait of the *intelligible* (νοητά, νοητὴ κτίσις), the intelligible are bound by a form of temporality as well: not time, not temporality "measured by motion," but another mode of temporality,[22] the Aeon. Everything that is created, both sensible and intelligible, is subject to *nature* and *temporality*: "to the one on account of its existence, and to the other on account of its motion."[23]

Apart from being "time without motion," the Aeon signifies also the temporality of the intelligible plane (νοητὰ)—the world of substances, qualities, etc.—in contrast to the created sensible world (αἰσθητά), i.e., creation as perceived solely through the senses.[24] While that which is sensible has been made "in time," in the temporality of the motion's numbering, that which is intelligible has not "received the beginning of its being" within the cycle of numbered motion but in the Aeon and "is eternal" in the sense of Aeonic, αἰώνια.[25] Maximus clarifies that both the sensible and the intelligible realm are different sides of the same created reality and that they are related to each other "through an indissoluble power": they embody *different accesses to the same created reality*, one access defined by sense-perception and the other by the intellect,[26] i.e., the human person's ability to

22. *Amb.Io.* 67, 1397AB.

23. Ibid.

24. *Amb.Io.* 10, 1153A: "Εἰ γὰρ πᾶσα ἡ τῶν ὄντων φύσις εἰς τὰ νοητὰ καὶ τὰ αἰσθητὰ διῄρηται, καὶ τὰ μὲν λέγεται καὶ ἔστιν αἰώνια, ὡς ἐν αἰῶνι τοῦ εἶναι λαβόντων ἀρχήν, τὰ δὲ χρονικά, ὡς ἐν χρόνῳ πεποιημένα, καὶ τὰ μὲν ὑποπίπτει νοήσει, τὰ δὲ αἰσθήσει, διὰ τὴν ταῦτα ἀλλήλοις ἐπισφίγγουσαν τοῦ κατὰ φύσιν σχετικοῦ ἰδιώματος ἄλυτον δύναμιν."—"For the whole nature of reality is divided into the intelligible and the sensible. There is that which is said to be and is Aeonic [αἰώνια], since it receives the beginning of its being in the Aeon, and that which is temporal, since it is made in time; there is that which is subject to intellection, and that which is subject to the power of sense-perception. The entities on each side of this division are naturally related to each other through an indissoluble power that binds them together" (trans. Louth).

25. Ibid.

26. Ibid.

gather the individual stimuli into a *consciousness* that transcends them and to access reality with a fullness beyond the mere perception of individual stimuli and reaction to them.[27]

The intelligible world, creation as perceived beyond the individual stimuli gathered through sense-perception, is also created and finite. It did have a beginning, and it will have an end—as well as everything in it.[28] The presence of beginning, middle, and end signifies the subjection of creatures to temporality—and by temporality I mean both time *and* the Aeon. Created beings, be they "distinguished by time" or "comprehended in the Aeon," possess these definitive marks, which act as criteria for createdness: beginning, middle, and end.[29] To recapitulate, everything that is created does also have a beginning and is subject to temporality[30]—the Aeon being the temporality of the intelligible and time the temporality of the sensible.

While the Aeon is certainly not the temporality of the uncreated but rather the temporality of the created intelligible plane in contrast to the created sensible world, at the same time the reference to the Aeon is also an allusion to the uncreated, to a world without incompleteness. There are several grades of completeness, the highest of which is the full communion between createdness and the uncreated—and of incompleteness, the most existentially grave of which is having lost one's communion to the source and cause of one's existence, risking inexistence. For Maximus, the incompleteness of the sensible world in comparison to the intelligible world is an icon, a reference and a reminder of the incompleteness of the whole of creation in comparison to the uncreated—and the superiority of the Aeon (time without motion) to time (the Aeon in motion) is an icon, a reference and a reminder of the superiority of being granted existence beyond any

27. This grants the human person the ability to become a *creator of otherness* apart from embodying his own otherness, an ability that, among others, differentiates man from the animal kingdom.

28. *Th.oec.*, 1085A-1.5: "Ἡ ἀρχὴ καὶ ἡ μεσότης καὶ τὸ τέλος, τῶν χρόνῳ διαιρετῶν εἰσι γνωρίσματα· εἴποι δ᾽ ἄν τις ἀληθεύων, καὶ τῶν ἐν αἰῶνι συνορωμένων."— "Beginning, middle, and end are characteristics of beings distinguished by time and it can be truly stated that they are also characteristics of beings comprehended in the Aeon" (trans. Berthold).

29. Ibid., Note that this beginning, middle, and end of beings does not only signify the *difference* from the uncreated, but also God's indirect *presence* in them by virtue of being their Creator, *Th.oec.*, 1086Df.-1.10, "God is the beginning, middle, and end of beings in that he is active and not passive, as are all others which we so name. For he is beginning as Creator, middle as provider, and end as goal" (trans. Berthold).

30. *Amb.Io.* 10, 1141B: "Καὶ ὡς πάντα τὰ ὑπὸ χρόνον καὶ αἰῶνα κατὰ τὴν γνῶσιν παρελθών, ὧν τὸ εἶναι χρονικῶς τῆς γενέσεως ἤρξατο τὸ πότε εἶναι οὐκ ἠρνημένης."—". . . transcending everything that is subject to time and the Aeon. For it is not denied that such temporal beings began through generation" (trans. Louth).

kind of temporality in comparison to the temporality of both the sensible and the intelligible world, to both time and the Aeon.

To be more precise: while not constituting the (inexistent) temporality of the uncreated, but of beings that previously had a beginning and generation, the Aeon does in fact function as the equivalent of the uncreated in temporality; it does *iconize* uncreatedness in the field of temporality. The Aeon is described as "time deprived of motion" and as the temporality of existing and created but intelligible realities. However, in Maximus' understanding *everything* that exists within creation is *in motion*, sensible and intelligible realities alike (e.g., substances or qualities, which are in motion as we examined in sections 35–40 of the tenth "Difficulty"). How are we to understand such an apparent inconsistency on the Confessor's part? If that which is "comprehended in the Aeon" is in motion, then how can the Aeon be "time deprived of motion"?

The apparent contradiction is solved when one understands the mindset of thinkers like Maximus, thinkers immersed in a tradition that implicitly holds apophaticism and participation as foundational criteria of knowledge. In speaking of any two given extremities or polar opposites (in this case, perfect motionlessness and constant motion), in making this very distinction, Maximus implicitly emphasizes the middle ground—the region between these two extremities and one's exact position in it—as in a perpetual tug of war, without ending. When a given extremity is not attained or achieved (yet), it can still be *iconized*, in the process of reaching the extremity, a state "in the image of" the extremity can be achieved or granted. However, this does not compromise the *reality* of the extremities, or the reality of the change when one progresses from the one to the other. In Maximian thought, antithetical elements can be united without losing their distinct individuality and otherness, in a markedly Chalcedonian mentality. For a thinker immersed in "Chalcedonian logic,"[31] the incompatibility of polar opposites is transcended in Christ's hypostasis, which transcends the incompatibility of the absolute othernesses, i.e., createdness and the uncreated. The prime example of this Maximian train of thought is to be discerned in the discourse concerning deification, the human person's capability to be granted this very transcendence.[32] Another example is the "perfect

---

31. Which however precedes the Council of Chalcedon, as I have noted and as Törönen has argued in his *Union and Distinction*. I am referring to this mindset of union-in-distinction (συναμφότερον) as "Chalcedonian logic" for purely practical reasons.

32. As we can see, e.g., in Q. *Thal. I*, 22.43–44, humanity can be truly deified in every respect, *except* of an identity of substance with God. This exception does not undermine the *reality* of deification, for Maximus, man *becomes* the uncreated God and his nature

inexistence"[33] and the "dissolution into nonbeing,"[34] which *may* or *may not* be *literal*, without however ceasing to be *real*, as I observed in my discussion of hell and the soul. As it seems, the "fullness that is never fulfilled"[35] and similar formulations are not merely patristic rhetorical *topoi* of apophaticism, but indicative of a pronounced and distinct mentality permeating the totality of *patristic preciseness*. There formulations are not meant to inspire awe in their apparent contradictory vagueness, but to function as concise signifiers of syntheses that are, by their very nature, beyond the coordinates of language. In the context of this semantic extremity, these formulations succeed in *signifying* reality, the price of which is the emptying of the signifier itself from any literal meaning.[36]

In line with these patterns, the Aeon is indicative of true motionlessness and yet, at the same time, absolute motionlessness is reserved solely for the uncreated—without contradicting the former proposition. Created beings can achieve a motionlessness *beyond nature*, but not *natural* motionlessness, for they are not uncreated by nature. In Maximus' mindset (and the patristic mindset in general), *this does not undermine the reality of the achieved motionlessness*—but neither does it undermine the reality of the distinction between natural, "uncreated motionlessness" and the achievable motionlessness attributed to created beings.

The Confessor provides us with another hint in this direction. He says the intelligible creation has had a generation and beginning, as it has passed from nonbeing to being. However, this beginning and generation

---

is hypostasized (actualized) through activities of the uncreated. It is truly a deification *in every respect*—which, in turn, does not annul the *difference* of the fully and truly deified human person's created nature to the uncreated nature. This is not merely a corollary of the difference between substance and hypostasis, in which the hypostatic mode of existence is changed radically and in contrast to the substance's λόγος of nature. This apparently complex peculiarity of Byzantine thought is integrally linked to the distinction between the substance and the *activities* (ἐνέργειαι) of the substance, of the *difference* that Byzantine thought allows to be discerned between these two. It is the possible *difference* between the substance and the activities (ἐνέργειαι) thereof that gives philosophical preciseness to the possibility of a real difference between the substance and its hypostatization/particular actualization, i.e., between the substance's λόγος φύσεως and the hypostasis' τρόπος ὑπάρξεως, which emerges through the activities, through the manifestation of nature's common activities in the particular actualization thereof by the person. Without this substance→activities→hypostasis distinction, the very idea of deification cannot but be, philosophically, non-sense.

33. *Scholia in De Divinis Nominibus*, CD4.1 305B (fn. 309).

34. *Myst.*, 1.67–72.

35. E.g., John of Climacus, Κλίμαξ, PG 88 1148C: "ἀτέλεστος τελειότης."

36. Which is often also the case with the distinct language of poetry; in order for it to *function* as poetry, the emptying of the signifier's literal meaning can be a prerequisite.

of the intelligible creation *is not manifest to human beings* (οὔτε ἀρχὴν γενέσεως ἀνθρώποις κατάδηλον ἔχουσα): from the perspective of humanity (the only perspective that we can have), the intelligible creation *seems* beginningless[37]—and, as such, motionless. This *seeming* beginninglessness and motionlessness is not merely a relative phenomenon, but has a certain reality as well: the intelligible world, it seems, does not "await an end of its existence defined by corruption," it has been gifted with "imperishability by nature."[38] Of course, every created reality is finite, will come to an end and is by nature bound to perish (an axiom of Maximus'); however, some of the intelligible beings have been granted with a partial but direct *participation* in the uncreated, and it is this that accounts for Maximus' reference to an imperishability "by nature"—for only the uncreated can possess imperishability "by nature."

From the sense-perception's perspective, or from the perspective of a person that bases his perception of creation on sense-perception alone, the intelligible world—substances, qualities, etc.—is deprived of motion. From the perspective of the sensible, substances are not in motion, qualities are not expanding and contracting, etc. In this, the intelligible *iconizes* the motionlessness of the uncreated without embodying it, *by participation*. Maximus asserts intelligible realities are in motion, a motion however that is quite stationary in comparison to motion as experienced through sense-perception. The human person's aspiration toward the κατὰ φύσιν and, ultimately, deification is a process of the gradual deprivation of motion, of the gradual annihilation of the distance (διάστημα/διάστασις) that presupposes it. The deprivation of motion and time cannot but also be a deprivation of corruption, φθορά, for it is motion that causes corruption.

With this "imperishability" of certain intelligible things,[39] I do not propose the annulment of previous positions: Maximus is clear on the fact

37. *Amb.Io.* 10, 1165A: "Τοιοῦτον γὰρ καὶ ἡ νοητὴ κτίσις, οὔτε ἀρχὴν γενέσεως ἀνθρώποις κατάδηλον ἔχουσα, κἂν εἰ γεγένηται καὶ ἦρκται καὶ ἐκ τοῦ μὴ ὄντος εἰς τὸ εἶναι παρῆκται, οὔτε τέλος τοῦ εἶναι διὰ φθορᾶς ὡρισμένον ἐκδέχεται. Τὸ γὰρ ἀνώλεθρον φυσικῶς ἔχει λαβοῦσα παρὰ Θεοῦ, τοῦ οὕτως αὐτὴν δημιουργῆσαι θελήσαντος."—"For the intelligible creation is such as to have no beginning of its coming to be that is manifest to human beings, and if it comes to be and commences and passes from non-being to being, it does not await an end of its existence defined by corruption. For it is naturally imperishable, having received this from God who willed to create it such" (trans. Louth).

38. *Amb.Io.* 10, 1165A.

39. For example, the *substance* of beings is not imperishable, should all hypostases of a substance perish, the substance/nature perishes with them. However, the λόγος φύσεως, the λόγος of said substance/nature, cannot perish. The λόγοι are acknowledged by Maximus as truly eternal and imperishable, but they are also uncreated, being the uncreated's *intentions* and *wills*, not the created outcome of activities. At the same

that "the Aeon includes in its existence the category of 'when' and admits of a διάστασις insofar as it began to be: time and the Aeon are not without beginning, so much less are those things which are contained in them"[40]— while both sensible and intelligible beings, both the ones "in time" and the ones "in the Aeon," possess a beginning and an end.[41] It is *participation* that adds a new element to this perspective, and *participation* is directly related to the differentiation between time and the Aeon, i.e., between the beings that have been made in time and the beings that have had their beginning in the Aeon.[42] To cite a relevant passage:

> All beings that participate [τὰ ὄντα μετέχοντα] are works of God that had their beginning in time [χρονικῶς ἠργμένα]—like, for example, the substances of beings. For they have nonbeing before being, as there was a time when the beings that participate did not exist. And there are some works of God which did not have their beginning in time: the participable beings [τὰ ὄντα μεθεκτά], in which the participating beings participate by grace. For example, goodness [ἡ ἀγαθότης] and everything that is included in the λόγος of goodness.[43]

Beings that are not χρονικῶς ἠργμένα "have had their beginning in the Aeon," and it is the participation to them (by grace, κατὰ χάριν, and not by nature, κατὰ φύσιν) that grants some of their attributes to the beings that participate in them. Maximus mentions goodness as an example.[44] However, any imperishability can only be granted directly by the (imperish-

time, they are also acknowledged as *intelligible* in the context of the sensible-intelligible distinction. The problem is that Maximus writes about things that have had a beginning, although not a manifest one, and possess imperishability "by nature." It is not the λόγοι that are meant here, for they have not had a beginning.

40. *Th.oec.*, 1085A–1.5: "Ὁ μὲν γὰρ χρόνος, μετρουμένην ἔχων τὴν κίνησιν, ἀριθμῷ περιγράφεται· ὁ αἰὼν δὲ συνεπινοουμένην ἔχων τῇ ὑπάρξει τὴν πότε κατηγορίαν, πάσχει διάστασιν, ὡς ἀρχὴν τοῦ εἶναι λαβών. Εἰ δὲ χρόνος καὶ αἰὼν οὐκ ἄναρχα, πολλῷ μᾶλλον τὰ ἐν τούτοις περιεχόμενα" (trans. Berthold).

41. Both the sensible and the intelligible, both the ἐν χρόνῳ διαιρετὰ and the ἐν αἰῶνι συνορώμενα, have beginning, middle *and* end. Cf. *Th.oec.*, 1085A–1.5.

42. *Amb.Io.* 10, 1153A.

43. *Th.oec.*, 1100CD–1.48: "Ἔργα μὲν Θεοῦ χρονικῶς ἠργμένα τοῦ εἶναί ἐστι πάντα τὰ ὄντα μετέχοντα· οἷον αἱ διάφοροι τῶν ὄντων οὐσίαι. Τὸ γὰρ μὴ ὄν, ἔχουσι αὐτῶν τοῦ εἶναι πρεσβύτερον. Ἦν γάρ ποτε, ὅτε τὰ ὄντα μετέχοντα οὐκ ἦν. Θεοῦ δὲ ἔργα τυχὸν οὐκ ἠργμένα τοῦ εἶναι χρονικῶς, τὰ ὄντα μεθεκτά, ὧν κατὰ χάριν μετέχουσι τὰ ὄντα μετέχοντα· οἷον, ἡ ἀγαθότης, καὶ πᾶν εἴ τι ἀγαθότητος ἐμπεριέχεται λόγῳ."

44. Here, goodness is not, as opposed, e.g., to Plato, a quality that is wholly identical to God, in another passage Maximus subjugates goodness to truth, inverting a Platonic topos. *Q.Thal. I*, 30.19.19–20, "διὰ τὴν ἀλήθειάν ἐστιν ἡ ἀρετὴ ἀλλ᾽ οὐ διὰ τὴν ἀρετὴν ἡ ἀλήθεια."

able by nature) uncreated and the uncreated's freedom to transcend its own limitations of *being-according-to-uncreatedness*, i.e., by *will* and *intention*: imperishability is "received from God who willed to create [it] such."[45] This entails that even this imperishability and endlessness of intelligible realities that is "natural" insofar as it is actualized *by participation* could be ceased, should God—an acting person, i.e., a communion of three persons with shared *will* and *activity*—intend otherwise; creation would be "terrified" by a choice of God to "hide his face,"[46] risking its inexistence. Even the existence of the uncreated and truly eternal λόγοι (i.e., God's *intentions*) could be threatened by God's *intentions* (a tautology). In this sense (and taking into account that the intelligible *qualities* are "logical," not "things") I would not take Maximus' reference to "*naturally* imperishable"[47] intelligible realities literally, in the sense that we would understand the natural imperishability of the uncreated: were I to do so, this would contradict other Maximian passages in the same book, the second and earlier *Ambigua (Ad Johannem)*.

A Necessary Digression: Is the Intelligible Creation Imperishable or Corruptible?

I need to digress and address this matter further, for we are witnessing an apparent inconsistency.[48] In passages like the aforementioned PG91 1165 A, the "natural imperishability" of intelligible beings is introduced as a reconciliation of the *creatio ex nihilo* with the attested immortality/incorruptibility/imperishability of certain created intelligible beings. However, and while a number of Maximian passages indicate this, the problem is that Maximus still has other passages that directly indicate otherwise.[49] Apart from PG91 1177 B-1180 A, where created intelligible beings (substances, qualities)

45. *Amb.Io.* 10, 1165A.

46. This should have been quite a *topos* in Maximus' Christian education. Cf. Psalm 104:28–29, "when you open your hand, [all creatures] are satisfied with good things. When you hide your face, they are terrified." (Septuagint, "ἀνοίξαντος δέ σου τὴν χεῖρα, τὰ σύμπαντα πλησθήσονται χρηστότητος, ἀποστρέψαντος δέ σου τὸ πρόσωπον, ταραχθήσονται").

47. *Amb.Io.* 10, 1165A: "τὸ γὰρ ἀνώλεθρον φυσικῶς ἔχει λαβοῦσα παρὰ Θεοῦ."

48. I have addressed this inconsistency in Mitralexis, "Maximus the Confessor's 'Intelligible Creation,'" on which I base our treatment of the subject here.

49. This apparent inconsistency is not to be encountered in the case of the sensible creation, which according to Maximus has both a beginning and an end by corruption. Cf. *Amb.Io.* 10, 1164Df., "For the sensible creation is such as to have a beginning known in coming to be, and to look for an end determined by destruction [διαφθορὰ]" (trans. Louth).

move *according to corruption* (excluding natural incorruptibility), we read in other passages that, "to speak truthfully,"[50] beings comprehended in the Aeon as well, not only beings distinguished by time (i.e., intelligible beings as well, not only sensible ones) are characterized by beginning, middle, *and end.* Intelligible beings having "an end" is clearly opposed to Maximus' own assertion in PG91 1165 A that the intelligible creation is incorruptible and imperishable: "it does not await an end of its existence defined by corruption, for it is naturally imperishable." Of course, *Th.oec.* and *Amb.Io.* are different books written in different dates and for different purposes, and one could argue Maximus simply changed his views in the meantime, or was lacking in precision in either of the passages. However, the problem persists. It could simply be an intrinsic inconsistency on Maximus' part, but it is not one of the subjects that the Confessor would treat lightly.

I propose that Maximus uses the term νοητὴ κτίσις with two different meanings, depending on the point of view and the context in which he is using it. According to the first meaning, he refers to the intelligible creation in general, of it as having an end and being able to perish, as populated by beings that "have an end" (PG90 1085 A), that "move according to corruption" (PG91 1177 B-1180 A), etc.—e.g., qualities, substances. In this, the term νοητὴ κτίσις has a literal meaning, for it is referring to a part of κτίσις, creation: created beings. According to the second meaning, he is referring to the νοητὴ κτίσις as populated by uncreated λόγοι as well (λόγοι of substances, but also λόγοι of qualities, in short λόγοι of anything—the λόγοι being intelligible in the sense of not being sensible), which would make it possessing "natural imperishability"[51] insofar as the uncreated activities are concerned. The uncreated λόγοι—God's wills and intentions—as well as the rest of divine uncreated activities are not exactly a part of the intelligible world, as they reside "in God," in the uncreated. However, (a) in the context of a sensible/intelligible distinction they are obviously not to be counted among the sensible beings and (b) while they themselves are uncreated, in their interaction with created realities they emerge, being in relation to them, in the horizon of createdness. For example, while the λόγος of something's substance is uncreated but the substance itself is created and intelligible, the λόγος—exactly by being a λόγος οὐσίας and directly related to the substance—*seems* as being attached to the intelligible created substance and can be erroneously perceived as co-emerging with it. In the uncreated λόγος (divine will, intention, and utterance) being contemplated *through*

---

50. *Th.oec.*, 1085A-1.5: "Ἡ ἀρχή καί ἡ μεσότης καί τό τέλος, τῶν χρόνῳ διαιρετῶν εἰσι γνωρίσματα· εἴποι δ᾽ ἄν τις ἀληθεύων, καί τῶν ἐν αἰῶνι συνορωμένων."

51. *Amb.Io.* 10, 1165A.

the created intelligible substance, it can *seem* as residing in the intelligible
realm, it can *seem* as being a part or principle of the substance and as such
of the νοητὴ κτίσις. Seen that way, imperishability by nature is indeed characteristic of a part of the intelligible creation, i.e., of the uncreated λόγοι
that animate it. Apophatic formulations allow for such seeming inconsistencies: the λόγοι can be characterized as "intelligible," without truly being
"intelligible" but beyond these categories, in the same sense that God can be
characterized as soul, intellect, intelligible, great, powerful, eternal, good,
Father, Son, Spirit—without being anything of these, for all of these are
designations that emerge and are articulated according to the divisions and
distinctions of createdness.[52] These belong to a language, the limits of which
are the limits of the created world.

Thus, the first approach to the νοητὴ κτίσις acknowledges the corruptibility and "end" of the νοητά, while the second one sees it as naturally
imperishable in recognizing the imperishability of the uncreated λόγοι that
are intelligible in the sense of not being sensible. Both approaches coexist without truly manifesting an intrinsic inconsistency, if approached this
way. In essence, this distinction is already there: should all hypostases of
a substance cease to be, their intelligible substance ceases to be as well (as
there is no οὐσία ἀνυπόστατος)—but not the uncreated intelligible λόγος
of that substance, i.e., the intention, will, and utterance of God concerning
it that is the blueprint thereof, which continues to exist "intelligibly." To put
it simply: if one counts the uncreated λόγοι together with the intelligible
beings, by virtue of the λόγοι not being sensible, then the implicit core of
the intelligible realm (i.e., the λόγοι) is indeed "imperishable by nature." If,
however, one does not count the uncreated λόγοι together with the intelligible beings, by virtue of the λόγοι being uncreated and the intelligible
beings created, then the νοητὴ κτίσις is corruptible and, having had a beginning, it will also have an end. Both approaches can be traced in different
Maximian passages. However, the second distinction is a more precise one,
for the uncreated nature of the λόγοι as wills, intentions, and utterances of
God is a characteristic of them that has a priority in significance over them
being intelligible, i.e., not sensible.

In order to return to the motionlessness of the Aeon, the temporality of the moving and created intelligible realm, I need to refer to humanity's ability to *participate* in the Aeon. The human person's gradually fuller
participation in the intelligible realm and in a fuller, deeper perception of
creation is also a gradual entering into the temporality of the Aeon. In this
context, entering the temporality of the Aeon would signify having achieved

52. Cf. Corpus Areopagiticum, *De Mystica Theologia*, CD II, 149f.

a significant but not final step in the *gradual* restoration of the fullness of communion, the *gradual* cessation of motion, the *gradual* annihilation of distance—having progressed from the *practical philosophy* to the *natural contemplation* of the λόγοι to the paving the way for the ultimate step in Maximus' triad, i.e., the *theological mystagogy* or *theological philosophy*.[53] A passage from the Confessor is suggestive of this gradualness: according to Maximus, time does not suffice to serve as the temporality of "those whom it is accustomed to escort to the divine life," time is "not overtaking or accompanying them in their motion."[54] On their way to "the divine life," their temporality becomes the temporality of the Aeon, an Aeon that is a distinct form of temporality but which seems to reside in the future due to it being attainable, but not yet attained.[55] If that is the case, we are to understand the Aeon not only as "time deprived of motion," but also as one's (gradual) "deprivation of motion" (and distance), the temporality of one's gradual liberation from the limitations and necessities of createdness.

Temporality as Disclosure: καιρός, Maximus' νῦν

In my understanding of Maximus' *Weltanschauung*, it is not temporality (be it χρόνος or the Aeon) that functions as the horizon of either being or beings. Relation, the *knowledge* of beings by the person is disclosed as motion,[56] and the *numbering* of motion is time—an icon of the possibility

53. *Amb.Io.* 37, 1296D: "Therefore the first five modes, through the multiform contemplation to which they are subject, are gathered together into practical, natural, and theological philosophy, and these three are further gathered into the modes of present and future, that is, type and truth. Present and future, in turn, are gathered up in the beginning, that is, in the Λόγος who is in the beginning, who enables the worthy to experience and see him" (trans. Constas). The goal is the transcendence of *both* present and future (type and truth) in the Λόγος.

54. *Amb.Io.* 10, 1164B: "For such is time, not overtaking or accompanying in movement those whom it is accustomed to escort to the divine life of the Aeon to come" (trans. Louth). "For it has Jesus as the universal successor of time and the Aeon. And if otherwise the λόγοι of time abide in God . . . ."

55. I.e., this "divine life of the Aeon to come" is not to be exclusively understood as a common cosmic eschatological future, but as the temporality of one's way towards deification as well.

56. And not vice versa. Motion does not merely *take place*, and within it events *happen*; motion is not external and autonomous. *It is the fact that events take place that discloses and actualizes motion as motion.* The act of creation is a motion (is disclosed as a motion), generation is a motion, alteration is a motion, it is not the motion that is disclosed as creation, generation, alteration, etc. *Events have an ontological priority over motion.* I am referring to *knowledge/relation* as analogous to a horizon of being due to the dialectics of communion and otherness, otherness emerges in communion,

of knowledge and communion without motion and distance, an icon of the Aeon, "time without movement."

However, Maximus (along with a number of other Greek church fathers, and based on the text of the Gospels) has a name for this "now" that acts as a disclosure, especially for the disclosure and emergence of truly eternal realities (i.e., the λόγοι) *in time*: it is καιρός, or at least one of the meanings of this word.[57] I will briefly examine an indicative passage:

> God not only knows before the ages [πρὸ τῶν αἰώνων] the things that exist, since they exist in him, in the truth itself, and if all these same things, both the things that are and the things that shall be, did not receive simultaneously being known and actual being on their own, but each thing [receives being] at the proper time [τῷ ἐπιτηδείῳ καιρῷ]—for it is impossible for the infinite to exist simultaneously with things finite—nevertheless also the goal of the disposition of each thing [occurs] according to movement [τὸ τέλος τῆς ἑκάστου κατὰ τὴν κίνησιν διαθέσεως]. For there is neither time nor Aeon separating this [movement] from God. For nothing in him is recent, but the future things are as the present. And if the times and the ages indicate the things that are in God, they do this not for God but for us. For we also must not think that, when God acts, it is then that his knowledge of a thing begins.[58]

The existence of created beings is synonymous with them being known by God (being in a relationship with God, a relationship signified by the word *knowledge*). To exist is to be known by God, i.e., to retain this vital link to the uncreated, to the cause and source of existence. All beings, as their λόγοι, (pre)exist in God atemporally and are *being known* atemporally, beyond any notion of temporal transition. However, there is a distinction between them

---

otherness is realized in the face of the other. In choosing communion and otherness as the foundational *events* of existence, we are accepting *relation* and *knowledge* as their horizon. According to the ecclesial testimony, the human person is not the primary subject of this *knowledge* or the initiator of relation, cf. Gal 4:9, "now that you know God—or rather are known by God" ("νῦν δὲ γνόντες Θεόν, μᾶλλον δὲ γνωσθέντες ὑπὸ Θεοῦ") and 1 Cor 8:2–3, "Anyone who claims to know something does not yet have the necessary knowledge; but anyone who loves God is known by him." Knowledge discloses *any* motion as motion, not only the motion applying to interpersonal relations, for motion is always and by definition a *relational event*.

57. Lampe's *Patristic Greek Lexicon* is not particularly illuminating concerning the philosophically relevant side of καιρός. It gives us the following meanings of the word in 697: apart from *season* and *time*, it also means *fit time*, *opportunity* and can refer to the present age or the age to come, ages of history, time compared with eternity, etc. The meaning of "fit time" stands closer to Maximus' understanding thereof.

58. *Q.Dub.*, 121.3–14 (trans. Prassas).

being known by God (γνωσθῆναι) and acquiring actual being, actualizing their existence (καθ' αὐτὰ εἶναι); this does not happen "simultaneously" (ἅμα), for while the beings' knowledge by God is atemporal, their coming to be takes place within temporality, either in time or in the Aeon: beings, being created, are generated and possess a temporal beginning. They receive their actual being at the right καιρός, at the proper time (τῷ ἐπιτηδείῳ καιρῷ), which is chosen and defined by God. Καιρὸς is not merely the temporal point of generation, it does not simply signify the beginning: καιρὸς is the unique temporality of disclosure, the dimensionless temporal point that manifests potential being as actual being, the dimensionless temporal point in which the actualization of beings and the realization of their λόγοι as beings participating in created reality takes place.

Καιρὸς is not a third kind of temporality along with time and the Aeon, for it is truly dimensionless[59] (while even the Aeon has had a beginning). Καιρὸς takes place *in time* or *in the Aeon*,[60] but it is not time or Aeon itself. Καιρὸς cannot be conceived as having a reality that is independent from the flow of time or the existence of the Aeon, while time and the Aeon themselves are indirectly defined by it: time is the numbering of motion, of beings in motion that came to be in actuality ἐν καιρῷ, while the Aeon signifies the ἐν καιρῷ actualized beings' deprivation of motion (and, of course, the temporality of intelligible beings). In that sense, the Maximian καιρὸς is understood as a *renewal* of the Aristotelian νῦν, as analogous to the νῦν in Maximus' world. These, however, are not identical, καιρὸς is a *renewal* of

59. John Panteleimon Manoussakis offers an interesting account of καιρὸς' dimensionlessness in Greek patristic tradition, "Against this concept of time as χρόνος (the passing of time) stands a different understanding of temporality as καιρός. If chronological time is seen in a horizontal way, that is, as sequence and duration, καιρὸς could be represented as vertical and discontinuous. If χρόνος is measured in seconds, minutes, hours, and years, καιρὸς cannot be measured at all, since it occurs only in the Moment. What is called here 'the Moment'—that is, as we will see, the *Augenblick* or the ἐξαίφνης—is characterized by this dis-continuity through which, according to Heidegger, the world is dis-closed and *Dasein* is faced with his or her de-cision. For even if it were possible to put all the kairological moments together, that still would not give us any measurable sense of καιρός, since each moment of καιρὸς (contrary to different units of time) is, in a unique way, always the same in the sense that it recurs in repetition" (Manoussakis, *God After Metaphysics*, 59). A comparison with the Aristotelian νῦν is inescapable, but their many and substantial differences are to be duly noted.

60. Cf. *Amb.Io.* 42, 1328C: "I am of the opinion that those of pious mind should not think that God knows particular things, the λόγοι of which are eternally contained in His foreknowledge and infinite power, only when they are created and brought into being. For time and the Aeon [alternative translation, the ages and the years] disclose each thing to us as being wisely created at the proper, predetermined moment [κατὰ τὸν προωρισμένον καὶ τὸν εὔθετον ἑκάστου καιρόν], at which point it is brought into being" (trans. Constas).

the νῦν, but not the νῦν itself, for καιρὸς has a much broader meaning. The fact that καιρὸς is a *choice* made by God emphasizes the created-uncreated communion that is intertwined in every facet of temporality: one of the channels that sustains the created world into existence, that retains its vital relationship to the uncreated cause that grants it with existence and prevents it from slipping into nonbeing, is this καιρός, i.e., the fact that each dimensionless point in time, each νῦν that marks the actualization of beings, is a divine *will, intension,* and *presence.* The fact that "the times and the ages [the Aeons] indicate the things that are in God" stresses καιρὸς not only as a disclosure of the individual beings, but seeing that these beings "are in God," καιρὸς reveals the presence of God *through* temporality and *within* temporality.

It is not only the beings' actuality that is given "at the proper time"; it is also the end and goal (τέλος) of each being that is attained at a καιρός, not only according to God's intention but also according to the being's own movement, to its *disposition* according to its motion.[61] In this, the καιρὸς of attaining the goal, end, and purpose is also the temporal equivalent of the goal itself: attaining the right καιρὸς *becomes the goal.* And seeing that καιρὸς is dimensionless and as such its attainment embodies the annihilation of all distance (διάστημα/διάστασις), it is the fulfillment of the Aeon, for it points to the complete cessation of motion by its very dimensionlessness. There is another peculiarity in the concept of καιρός: while it in itself does not possess any dimension, motion, or temporal distance within it, it simultaneously *signifies* a radical motion, be it a being's motion from nonbeing into being (its generation and actualization mentioned above) or a being's motion from being to perfection, the aforementioned τέλος according to its disposition. These profound motions and changes are effected through the καιρός, a unit without any motion, distance, or dimension in itself. There is a great similarity of this to the human person's task of mediation and, ultimately, deification: being in time, man strives to attain the cessation of motion, a motionlessness that is to culminate in ever-moving repose, as I will examine in the next chapter. However, this goal of motionlessness is to be achieved through profound changes, through the radical motions implied in both the cosmic mediation and the deification. The gradualness of the deprivation of motion and of the transition from the contemplation of the λόγοι to an ever fuller participation is not opposed to the momentary character of the καιρός, for the latter is the fulfillment of the former.

---

61. *Q.Dub.*, 121.8: τὸ τέλος τῆς ἑκάστου κατὰ τὴν κίνησιν διαθέσεως.

The reign of καιρὸς is also manifest in the absence of a functional linear progression of time in Scripture.[62] Apart from that, it seems as if the Christian *practices* this καιρὸς-perception of temporality, in resistance to the linear progression of time, within the Byzantine church's liturgical cycle in order to "learn" the temporality of καιρὸς and to be ready for his or her own true καιρὸς—and for the common and collective καιρὸς of the eschatological τέλος. Everything in this liturgical cycle happens *today* and *now*: the commemorated events are referred to as taking place σήμερον, today, and the present tense is used.[63] The "texture" of liturgical time[64] does not merely exert an influence on Maximus' thought: along with the totality of ecclesial life, it is the very frame in which Maximus develops his multifaceted testimony and must be taken into account in order to understand the Confessor's thought.

It has been repeatedly stated here that the human person's goal is to *transcend* time, to abandon the temporality of χρόνος (which is defined by motion) and to enter the Aeon, to aspire for the dimensionlessness of the καιρός. Is there enough basis in Maximus' work for time to be considered as an enemy to man, or at the very least as an obstacle to be overcome? Is temporality so prevalent within creation that its transcendence is to be considered a primary goal?

62. Maximus notes that the tenses used in Scripture are often entangled, with past tenses being used in place of future tenses and vice versa (*Q. Thal. I*, 7.5–9, see also *Amb. Io.* 37, 1293C).

63. Manoussakis proposes that this liturgical presenceness, which he links to the καιρός, is—in the long run of the repetition of numerous liturgical yearly cycles—a repetition that is, in essence, futural and points to a temporality of the promised and the expected, a temporality of the "*to come.*" "This is evident in how the liturgy presents events of the past (such as the birth of Christ, his crucifixion, etc.) as always taking place 'today'—a survey of the hymns used in the church will show that the liturgy knows of no other temporal category than this 'today.' Repetition has become a key philosophical term thanks to the acute analysis of Kierkegaard, who devotes an entire treatise to it. Kierkegaard is right to see in repetition a new temporal category—that is, to be juxtaposed over and against Platonic recollection. Recollection, he writes, allows us to 'enter the eternal backwards', while repetition is decisively futural and in its futural character pushes us to 'enter eternity forwards'. Two different senses of eternity are here contrasted, (a) a preexisting, anterior eternity, what we could call *cosmological* eternity, and (b) an eternity that lies ahead of us and keeps reaching us in the present, what we could call an *eschatological* eternity" (*God After Metaphysics*, 59).

64. In mentioning the liturgical cycle, I must here once more refer to Mueller-Jourdan's study of the understanding of spatio-temporality in Maximus' *Mystagogia* concerning the space and time of the church, a monograph dedicated to the subject (*Typologie spatio-temporelle*).

Temporality as Slavery

Temporality is not merely one of the characteristics of creation; it is inter-twined with the very act of creation's creation and is a vital aspect thereof, either as a *difference* from the uncreated (in that it is an aspect of being generated and divided, i.e., manifesting *distance*) or as a *link* to it (in that it manifests God as cause and maker, as beginning and end): "everything that is after God and has come into being from God, i.e., the nature of beings and time, these appear together, so far as is possible, with God who appears as cause and maker."[65] Time is "cyclical"[66] and, along with all that is in motion, of a "floating, unstable nature" which is to be overcome in order to be able to "receive the divine mysteries."[67] The introduction of temporality marks the emergence of divisions that did not exist "before it,"[68] including the divi-sion between creation and Creator (and, along with it, the division of limit and limitlessness, measure and immeasurability, finitude and infinity, fixity, motion, etc.).[69] This division is to be overcome at the "end of time," in which created beings, being by nature in motion (τὰ κατὰ φύσιν κινούμενα), will be able to cease and abandon all motion (τῆς πρός τε ἑαυτὰ καὶ πρὸς ἄλληλα παντελῶς ἐκβεβηκότα κινήσεως) and truly know the motionless God by experience, transcending corruption.[70] However, temporality is not merely to be overcome in the process of the cessation of motion: it is seen as an *obstacle* and an *enemy*.

According to Maximus, man "is enslaved by time and nature":[71] it would be impossible for humanity to be harmed and damaged without

65. *Amb.Io.* 10, 1164A (trans. Louth).

66. *Opusc.*, PG91 16D.

67. *Amb.Io.* 10, 1120A.

68. The phrase "before the emergence of temporality" cannot signify a temporal priority but rather an ontological one.

69. Cf. *Q.Thal. II,* 60.49–54: "Because of Christ—or rather, the whole mystery of Christ—all the ages [the Aeons] and the beings within those ages have received their beginning and end in Christ. For the union between a limit of the ages and limitless-ness, between measure and immeasurability, between finitude and infinity, between Creator and creation, between rest and motion, was conceived before the ages" (trans. Blowers).

70. *Q.Thal. II,* 60.54–62: "This union has been manifested in Christ at the end of time, and in itself brings God's foreknowledge to fulfillment, in order that naturally mobile creatures might secure themselves around God's total and essential immobility, desisting altogether from their movement toward themselves and toward each other. The union has been manifested so that they might also acquire, by experience, an active knowledge of him in whom they were made worthy to find their stability and to have abiding unchangeably in them the enjoyment of this knowledge" (trans. Blowers).

71. *Exp.Psalm.,* 44–49: "τῷ χρόνῳ καὶ τῇ φύσει δουλώσας τὸν ἄνθρωπον· ἄνευ

those things "that are under the reign of time and nature."[72] Death reigns through temporality by devouring humanity:[73] temporality is not merely one of the characteristics of createdness that are to be overcome along with all other divisions at the completion of the cosmic mediating function of humanity, but the very tool for humanity's enslavement, the enabler of corruption and death—for, being the numbering of motion and every alteration, time is also the numbering of corruption; it is through time that corruption is actualized and disclosed. The aspiration for liberation from corruption is the aspiration for liberation from time:[74] and while the path towards this freedom is the participation in the person who is the hypostatic union of createdness and the uncreated, Christ ("the successor of all time and Aeon,"[75] the "conqueror of the world and perfecter of the Aeon"),[76] Maximus does also mention an example of a human being who attained this freedom. The fact that this person lived *before the incarnation of the Λόγος* makes this example even more noteworthy.[77] For Maximus, the biblical Melchizedek[78]—an icon of Christ himself according to the patristic tradition—"no longer bears within himself temporal life and its motions":[79] such a person "has no experience of what is present to it," for he has become "beginningless" (ἄναρχος) and "without end" (ἀτελεύτητος), he possesses "the sole divine and eternal life of the indwelling Λόγος, a life unbounded by death."[80] It is interesting to note that, according to this passage, a person

---

γὰρ τῶν ὑπὸ φύσιν καὶ χρόνον μάχεσθαι τοῖς ἀνθρώποις παντελῶς οὐ δύναται."

72. Ibid.

73. *Amb.Io.* 10, 1157A: "Death is living on this through the whole of this temporal period, making us his food, and we no longer live, but are eternally eaten up by him through corruption" (trans. Louth).

74. Cf. *Th.oec.,* 1109A—1.70: "The whole world is limited by its own λόγοι and we attribute place and the Aeon to whatever it contains. . . . The one who is saved will be above all worlds, ages/Aeons, and places in which he was once nurtured as a child, and will reach his end in God" (trans. Berthold).

75. *Amb.Io.* 10, 1164B: "Ἰησοῦν γὰρ ἔχει τὸν παντὸς ὄντα καὶ χρόνου καὶ αἰῶνος διάδοχον."

76. Ibid., 1120B: μυστικῶς ἐνέφαινεν ὡς νικητήν τοῦ κόσμου καί συντελεστήν τοῦ αἰῶνος."

77. Maximus usually notes that deification is possible only *after* the incarnation of Christ. Cf. *Q.Thal. I,* 22.31–33, "The other ages—those which are to come about for the realization of the mystical and ineffable deification of humanity—must follow henceforth (i.e., after the incarnation of God)" (trans. Blowers).

78. King and priest mentioned in the fourteenth chapter of the book of Genesis. In Heb 5:6, Christ is identified as "a priest forever, in the order of Melchizedek."

79. *Amb.Io.* 10, 1144C (trans. Louth).

80. Ibid.

who has been born at a certain καιρὸς in time can become not merely imperishable and without end, but even "beginningless"—beginninglessness can be attained by created and originated human beings, fully inverting the coordinates of temporality in cancelling them by their very foundations and not merely from a point onwards. In *Amb.Io.* 10, 1137C–1140D, Maximus uses the example of Melchizedek to stress that it is possible for *any* human being[81] to be granted a state of being without beginning nor end, beyond time, beyond the Aeon, beyond nature.[82] (As Maximus insists that this takes place "in every respect" but without a change in human nature/substance,[83] meaning that only the hypostasis is deified, we are to conclude that he refers to the possibility of the hypostatization/actualization of a created substance/ nature through uncreated activities: the Byzantine toolbox of terminology does not leave us with many other choices.) In the case of Melchizedek, it is "through *knowledge* that the movement of the mind stepped without defilement over properties of time and the Aeon."[84] It is Melchizedek's role in patristic thought as *precursor* to Christ and Old Testament *icon* of Christ that makes his example suitable for such a doctrine of nearly absolute freedom.

For Maximus, man's ascension through the λόγοι, in which he approaches the Λόγος, is a process of knowledge in which time gradually retreats.[85] Man's acquired (i.e., granted) ability to contemplate and *know* reality *as it is*—beyond its constant change in its motion (that is: to gradually come to know the Λόγος through the λόγοι of beings)—effects the gradual

81. Ibid., 1140B, "In accordance with such love the dignity of sonship, the divinely-fitting gift of continual converse with God in his presence, is granted, exhibiting the divine likeness to any who begs for it" (trans. Louth).

82. Cf. ibid., 1140A: "For virtue naturally fights against nature, and true contemplation against time and the Aeon."

83. *Q.Thal. I*, 22.40–44.

84. *Amb.Io.* 10, 1140BC: "Thus I take it that it is probably not from time and nature (μὴ διὰ χρόνου καὶ φύσεως), subject to which the great Melchizedek reached his natural end, that it should be said of those who have already transcended life and reason, that the divine Λόγος justified him, but from and through those things—I mean, virtue and knowledge—he deliberately changed what he is called. Thus the deliberation nobly struggles through the virtues against the law of nature, that is so difficult to fight against, and through knowledge the movement of the mind steps without defilement over properties of time and the Aeon (τὴν χρόνου καὶ αἰῶνος ἰδιότητα). With these it is not right to regard as characteristic the property of what is abandoned, but rather the magnificence of what is assumed, from which and in which alone they are and are known" (trans. Louth). On what *knowledge* as a transformative power means, see the above section on καιρὸς and its footnotes; knowledge signifies a *relation*. Note that even Melchizedek "reached his natural end under time and nature," a point to which I shall return in the next chapter on the ever-moving repose and deification.

85. *Q.Thal. I*, 47.222–24: "ἐπιλείψει τὸν θεωρητικὸν νοῦν ὁ χρόνος τὰς θείας ἀναβάσεις τοῦ λόγου γνωστικῶς ποιούμενον."

subsidence of time, "the numbering and delimitation of motion." Only the one who transcends time and ordinary perception and "discontinues the relationship of his soul to these" can be freed from their "confusion" and ascend.[86] Through this knowledge, the mind "restricts the motion of all time and Aeon."[87] Liberation from time and the Aeon[88] is not merely a by-product of one's contemplation (and knowledge) of reality *as it truly is* and one's ascension towards deification, but a prerequisite for it; liberation from temporality emerges as the very *way* for achieving this. As man's *liberation* from temporality is stressed as the way to his τελείωσις, so is God's absolute *freedom* from all temporality repeatedly stressed: not only is he "beyond present, past, and future"[89] (i.e., the *divisions* of time), but "the very nature of time cannot approach him."[90] While every being is "bound to the categories of time, Aeon and space, by which the universe is enclosed," man's task, iconizing his Creator, is to "transcend everything sensible and intelligible and all time and Aeon and space"[91]—not merely to make the transition from

86. Ibid., 55.115–20: "μόνος ὁ γενόμενος ὑπὲρ αἴσθησιν καὶ χρόνον . . . καὶ τὴν πρὸς ταῦτα τῆς ψυχῆς διακόψας σχέσιν ἐκβαίνει τῆς αὐτῶν συγχύσεως, πρὸς τὴν ἄνω πόλιν ἐπειγόμενος."

87. *Opusc.*, PG91 9A: "νῷ δε, τῆς ἁπλανοῦς ἑνώσεως [γνώσεως] σύστασιν παντὸς αἰῶνος καὶ χρόνου περιορίζων τὴν κίνησιν."

88. The liberation from time and Aeon does not mean the *escape* from time, but rather *traversing the totality thereof* and arriving at the *end of the ages*: Q.Thal. I, 22./4–77, "Existing here and now, we arrive at the end of the ages as active agents and reach the end of the exertion of our power and activity" (trans. Blowers).

89. *Amb.Io.* 37, 1296C: "For the Λόγος, who created all things, and who is in all things according to the relation of present to the future, is comprehended both in type and in truth, in which He is present both in being and manifestation, and yet He is manifested in absolutely nothing, for inasmuch as He transcends the present and the future, He transcends both type and truth, for He contains nothing that might be considered contrary to Him" (trans. Constas).

90. *Th.oec.*, 1165B–2.86.

91. *Amb.Io.* 10, 1153BC: "God is simply and indefinably beyond all beings, both what circumscribes and what is circumscribed and the nature of those [categories] without which none of these could be, I mean, time and Aeon and space, by which the universe is enclosed, He is completely unrelated to anything. Since all this is so, the one who discerns with sagacity how he ought to love God, the transcendent nature, that is beyond reason and knowledge and any kind of relationship whatever, passes without relation through everything sensible and intelligible and all time and Aeon and space" (trans. Louth). Andrew Louth notes on p. 206 n. 57 that in this passage "the Greek word ψυχὴ (translated here 'soul') can equally mean 'life,' as Maximus' comments indicate," which is applicable to a great number of other references to ψυχὴ as well. This is an important point, because this Maximian vocabulary of the "soul" and "mind" (νοῦς) that "knows" is not to be understood as referring to some "incorporeal humanity"— notwithstanding that it certainly introduces a distinction between a person's everyday "bodily" life and the experiences indicated by this vocabulary.

time to the Aeon and from the sensible to the intelligible, but to transcend all of these categories, without remaining in relation to them. The Aeon does not suffice—man must transcend this exalted form of temporality as well.

Conclusions and Remarks

As noted at the beginning of this chapter, Maximus uses the word αἰών with different meanings in different contexts—most notably, he often employs its plural αἰῶνες meaning "the ages," a very long duration in time, history. However, the Aeon as a second mode of temporality beyond time (χρόνος) is clearly to be discerned in Maximus' work and certain characteristics thereof emerge in the Confessor's passages.

i.   The Aeon is "time deprived of motion," in a dual and intertwined definition of temporality in which time is "the Aeon, when measured in its motion."[92] This definition does not merely provide us with an understanding of the Aeon through our more familiar notion of time; rather, the interrelation of the Aeon and time establishes both of them as dependent on one another, as two irreplaceable sides of the same reality.

ii. The Aeon is also defined as constituting the temporality of the intelligible realm, the temporality of intelligible beings. All beings are divided into sensible and intelligible beings, and while time constitutes the temporality of the sensible, the Aeon corresponds to the intelligible. Here, again, both of these (sensible and intelligible, time and the Aeon) are vitally interrelated and interconnected: "The entities on each side of this division are naturally related to each other through an indissoluble power that binds them together."[93]

iii. As expounded in previous chapters, to be created is to have a beginning and to be temporal. Both the sensible and the intelligible are generated, but the sensible have been generated and have their beginning "in time," while the intelligible "in the Aeon." Those that are contemplated "in the Aeon," i.e., intelligible beings, possess beginning, middle, and end as well. To be created is to possess temporality: this elevates temporality to one of the primary criteria and characteristics

---

92. *Amb.Io.* 10, 1164BC.

93. Ibid., 1153A.

of createdness,[94] a status that does not fully apply to spatiality as such, which is only a characteristic of the sensible world.

iv.   The Aeon cannot be described as the temporality of the uncreated, for it has had a beginning, as well as everything in it.[95] However, from humanity's and the sensible creation's point of view, the Aeon *iconizes* the absolute timelessness of the uncreated and *refers* to it. The apparent changelessness of the intelligible—from the perspective of the sensible—reflects the absolute motionlessness of the uncreated. And the temporality of the apparently changeless intelligible world, the Aeon, reflects the absolute timelessness of the uncreated. The human person's ever fuller participation in the Aeon and in the intelligible realm is the first step towards the cessation of motion and deification, due to their function as imperfect icons of the uncreated.

v.   The Aeon is "time deprived of motion" and constitutes the temporality of the intelligible, which, however, are in some varieties of motion. While intelligible beings are in motion ("expansion," "contraction," etc.), the Aeon itself—their mode of temporality—is not susceptible to change. Intelligible beings are beings in motion that is generated and situated within a stable form of temporality, the Aeon. The Aeon is stable in that it cannot be "circumscribed by a number."[96] This is a trait of the Aeon that is in contrast to time's floating and unstable nature.[97]

vi.   In the previous chapter, I stressed the interrelation of time and space, time and spatiality. This is a major difference of time and the sensible to the Aeon and the intelligible, for there is no spatiality, no dimension of space (e.g., in the emergence of "qualities," in the distinction of "substances," etc.) in what Maximus distinguishes as "the intelligible"[98]—which accordingly modifies what motion can

94. *Th.oec.*, 1085A–1.5.
95. Ibid.
96. Ibid.
97. *Amb.Io.* 10, 1120A: "τὴν ῥέουσαν τοῦ χρόνου φύσιν."
98. I must here repeat the sensible/intelligible distinction is a philosophical distinction that does not abscond its delimited realities but "binds them together through an indissoluble power." The intelligible is very far from being "another world" as understood in mystical or esoteric contexts. With the word "intelligible," Maximus denotes all beings and all of reality that are not perceived through sense-perception, while "the entities on each side of this division are naturally related to each other." For example, in the distinction of substance and hypostasis, i.e., of homogeneity and the particular, it is only the particular that is sensible, that is accessible through the sense—not the homogeneity of the particulars itself, which is merely deducted from the hypostases

mean when applied to intelligible beings. While the sensible move and change in space and time, the absence of the dimension of space accounts for the intelligible moving and changing against the background of the changeless Aeon.

vii. If one were to trace a Maximian equivalent to the Aristotelian νῦν, it would be the notion of καιρός. While καιρός has a much wider semantic content in comparison to νῦν, it does also function as the dimensionless unit of temporality in Maximus' thought, like νῦν does in Aristotle's.

viii. Καιρὸς is the "now" that acts as disclosure, the disclosure of God's will and intention to creation in the horizon of temporality. While the λόγος of a being is beyond temporality, its being receives actuality (its existence is actualized) *at the proper time* (τῷ ἐπιτηδείῳ καιρῷ). As such, καιρὸς impregnates the temporality of the created with the indirect presence of the uncreated and gives *meaning* to time.

ix. It is not only the *beginning* and *generation* of something that is marked and actualized in καιρός, but its end, goal, purpose, and perfection as well. In the case of human persons, possessors of free will, this does not take place exclusively according to God's will, but also according to the person's own motion, to its individual *disposition*.[99] The καιρός, being dimensionless, embodies the annihilation of *distance*.

x. Temporality, while being a κατὰ φύσιν characteristic of createdness, is also an obstacle to be overcome, along with all other divisions and "distances." This applies to both time and the Aeon. Even the Aeon must be transcended by humanity in humanity's task as a mediator.

The participation in the atemporality of the uncreated is beyond time and the Aeon, beyond any conception of temporality, which is in itself a delimitation of createdness. However, in speaking about deification Maximus introduces the notion of the *ever-moving repose* (στάσις ἀεικίνητος), which being the end and perfection of motion beyond motionlessness itself, will be expounded in the following chapter as the *third* mode of temporality, i.e., the transcendence and annihilation of *any* temporality.

(or, for those that attain to a fuller access to reality, contemplated as its λόγος οὐσίας). Here, the "substance" is, of course, "intelligible," without this making it less real, merely hypothetical or simply imaginary. The homogeneity of the particulars is neither unreal nor hypothetical nor imaginary; it is as real as the particulars of which it is the substance. However, neither "homogeneities" nor "qualities" (e.g., to be cold, to be new, to be colored, to be moist) occupy spaces. The intelligible is deprived of spatiality.

99. Cf. *Q.Dub.,* 121.8.

CHAPTER TEN

Ever-Moving Repose

The Motion of Deification

ACCORDING TO MY ANALYSIS so far, temporality is a primary characteristic of createdness and is actualized in two different modes, time (χρόνος) and the Aeon (αἰών). Time is the numbering and delimitation of motion, temporality as perceived within sensible creation—as well as the reflection of the Aeon in the world of motion *as we know and perceive it*. The Aeon is time deprived of motion, and the temporality of the intelligible side of creation's delimitation. The uncreated is not merely atemporal in the sense of not being either in time or in the Aeon, but is beyond any conception of temporality and createdness whatsoever—the very notion of a "temporality of the uncreated" is considered as a contradiction in itself.

However, while there is no temporality of the uncreated, one can speak of the temporality of deification, or at least pose the question concerning it. The ecclesial community and Maximus the Confessor as a potent articulator thereof testify that it is possible for the human person to be *deified*,[1] it is

---

1. The subject of deification in general and the notion of deification in Maximus the Confessor in particular is too big of a subject to be exhaustively examined and analyzed here. Even a comprehensive introduction to it would be a major digression and outside the scope of this study. An excellent monograph on the subject is Russell's *Doctrine of Deification,* which dedicates a chapter to Maximus the Confessor's understanding of deification (262–95)—while more or less every major scholar engaged with Maximus has contributed to the subject as well. See also Larchet's *La Divinisation* and Thunberg's *Microcosm and Mediator*, 427–32. The general idea is that while participation in the divine and uncreated *substance* is absolutely impossible, a participation in the uncreated *activities* of that substance is indeed attainable (and always, of course, in its created activities i.e., created beings as well). This participation can result in the (still created) nature of a human person being hypostasized (actualized) through uncreated activities and thus (conjoining a λόγος of created being with a mode of uncreated existence)

possible for created human beings to actualize in themselves (to hypostasize) the *mode* of the uncreated, the *mode* of freedom from every and any limitation of createdness.[2] Man's nature—the λόγος of his substance— remains unchanged in deification, i.e., remains created and human, but his actual realization and hypostasis, his person—the τρόπος (mode) of his existence—is deified, actualized in the mode of the uncreated *in every respect*: "Then God will also completely fulfill the goal of his mystical work of deifying humanity in every respect, of course, short of an identity of substance with God; and he will assimilate humanity to himself."[3] So, while we cannot enquire about the inexistent "temporality of the uncreated," we have to ask: *what happens to temporality in deification*, what is the state of temporality in θέωσις? The Aeon is certainly not the "temporality of deification": it signifies the deprivation of motion, the cessation of movement, the endurance and seeming changelessness of the intelligible—not the hypostatization (actualization) of a created nature in uncreated activities, not the direct partici-

---

being granted uncreatedness, liberation from the constrains and limitations of createdness by participation in the hypostasis of Christ, where a coexistence of created and uncreated nature in one hypostasis has been made possible. This cannot be an achievement of the created human being, but a gift of God, granted by his grace and ἔρως for the human person. In Maximus' own voice, *Amb.Io.* 7, 1076C: "[the human image of God] rather becomes God by deification"— *Amb.Io.* 7, 1084C, "By this blessed inversion, man is made God by deification and God is made man by hominization"— *Amb. Io.* 7, 1088C, "In this way, man as a whole will be divinized, being made God by the grace of God who became man. Man will remain wholly man in soul and body, owing to his nature, but will become wholly God in soul and body owing to the grace and the splendor of the blessed glory of God, which is wholly appropriate to him, and beyond which nothing more splendid or sublime can be imagined" (trans. Constas).—*Q.Thal. I*, 22.35f.: "[God] having completely realized this deification in those who are worthy" (trans. Blowers). Deification does not reflect the restoration of the κατὰ φύσιν, it is not man's restored and perfected nature but is *beyond nature*, ὑπὲρ φύσιν, cf. *Amb.Io.* 20, 1237AB: "For the grace of deification is completely unconditioned, because it finds no faculty or capacity of any sort within nature that could receive it, for if it did, it would no longer be grace but the manifestation of a natural activity latent within the potentiality of nature. And thus, again, what takes place would no longer be marvelous if deification occurred simply in accordance with the receptive capacity of nature. Indeed it would rightly be a work of nature, and not a gift of God, and a person so divinized would be God by nature and would have to be called so in the proper sense. For natural potential in each and every being is nothing other than the unalterable movement of nature toward complete actuality. How, then, deification could make the divinized person go out of himself, I fail to see, if it was something that lay within the bounds of his nature" (trans. Constas).

2. The *mode* of the uncreated being relation, self-transcendence, ἔρως, love (where "God *is* love" [1 John 4,8] is taken as an ontological definition), a "being" that is defined in-relation-to (the *Father* to the *Son*, etc.), and the *mode* of ("fallen") createdness being individual atomicity, nonrelation, death.

3. *Q.Thal. I*, 22.40–44 (trans. Blowers).

pation of the created in the uncreated. The human person does not merely "enter the Aeon" in deification; deification indicates the transcendence of motionlessness and the Aeon, both of which are categories stemming from the perspective of createdness.

Maximus the Confessor does not formulate an elaborate doctrine on the ever-moving repose, nor does he designate the στάσις ἀεικίνητος as the state of motion in deification in the context of a systematic analysis or precise exposition of these matters. However, in searching the Maximian *corpus* for scattered indications on the state of motion and temporality in deification, his references to the "ever-moving repose" and "stationary movement" of the deified human being are most illuminating and characteristic of his perspective on the matter.

A word of caution on the linguistic aspect of my enquiry: as stated repeatedly, Maximus' philosophical language is inherently apophatic (both in cases of negation and affirmation). Formulations and signifiers do not claim to be identical with their signified realities and to exhaust them, language can only *point* to truth, it is not truth itself. However, this is even more the case when Maximus refers to deification and to the uncreated. In referring to them, Maximus attempts to signify something *beyond* the limits of our world, beyond the limits of createdness—and as such, *beyond* the limits of language. The fact that we can only look "through a glass, darkly" (1 Cor 13:12) prompts the Confessor to use a markedly poetic language in order to "circumscribe" and "delimit" the merging of created nature and substance with the mode of the uncreated. In this language, contradictory phrases like "ever-moving repose" or "stationary movement" are not mere rhetorical devices, but an attempt to signify a reality beyond the divisions, dualities, and dichotomies of createdness (in this case: beyond motion and fixity alike). Before examining these passages, what will be required is a clarification of deification as a renewal of the mode of existence and not the λόγος of nature.

Renewing the τρόπος, Retaining the λόγος

Maximus and the patristic tradition insist that θέωσις is a *real* deification of man's hypostasis and actual existence (not an either symbolic or incomplete "elevation" of man to a very high state within createdness), the actualization of a human person through uncreated activities *in every respect*—without, however, an identification *in substance and nature*; man's substance and nature remains created and human,[4] but the human person is hypostasized

4. Note how in *Amb.Io.* 41, 1308BC, Maximus stresses the deified human person

(actualized) according to the *mode* of the uncreated. In explaining this, the Confessor analyses the profound change—and distance from substantial/ natural predeterminations—that can be effected in the actual existence and hypostasis, in the mode of existence (arriving at the "beyond nature," τὸ ὑπὲρ φύσιν)[5] without changing the unchangeable λόγος of substance/ nature. This is not a theory that has been elaborated by Maximus in or- der to explain deification *per se*; it is rather his general view of the λόγος- τρόπος distinction, one application of which is his explication of the state of deification.

According to the Confessor, the renewal or innovation of a being that constitutes a real difference and distance from its nature (from the predeter- minations of its substance) is not only possible, but also capable of reaching beyond the limits of its substance/nature itself.[6] This renewal and innova- tion according to the *mode of existence* is more of a common occurrence than an exception within existence: it is this *mode of existence* that manifests the difference of the hypostasis from its substance as a real difference and not as a superficial phenomenon.[7] Maximus writes:

"becomes completely whatever God is, save at the level of an identity in substance" (simultaneously deifying creation by assimilating it in God, in whom it will be "wholly interpenetrated") by thrice using words signifying wholeness, completeness and total- ity in a row, i.e., "ὅλος, ὅλῳ and ὁλικῶς, ὅλος ὅλῳ περιχωρήσας ὁλικῶς τῷ Θεῷ, καί γενόμενος πᾶν εἴ τί πέρ ἐστιν ὁ Θεός, χωρίς τῆς κατ᾽ οὐσίαν ταὐτότητος."

5. Maximus repeatedly clarifies that deification is not our return to the "pre-fallen" κατὰ φύσιν, but something *beyond* nature. Cf. *Q.Thal.* I, 22.90–92: "We shall become that which in no way results from our ability according to nature, since our human nature has no faculty for grasping what transcends nature (τοῦ ὑπὲρ φύσιν ἡ φύσις καταληπτικὴν οὐ κέκτηται δύναμιν)" (trans. Blowers). This attainment *beyond nature* cannot be an achievement of the created human person, but only a gift from the uncre- ated God, for nature cannot reach to what resides beyond itself, *Q.Thal.* I, 22.94–98, "Intrinsically it is only by the grace of God that deification is bestowed proportionately on created beings. Grace alone illuminates human nature with supernatural light, and, by the superiority of its glory, elevates our nature above its proper limits in excess of glory" (trans. Blowers).

6. Maximus' understanding of the innovation through the *mode of existence*, tran- scending the substance while leaving it intact, reminds us of existentialism's distinction between *being* and *existing*.

7. For example, in the case of humanity we term *mode* the way in which the com- mon human nature is actualized (ἐνεργεῖται) into a specific human person, manifesting change and otherness without modifying nature itself, *Amb.Io.* 42, 1341D: "Now the λόγος of human nature is that it consists of soul and body, and this nature consists of a rational soul and body, whereas its mode is the order whereby it naturally acts and is acted upon (τρόπος δὲ ἡ ἐν τῷ ἐνεργεῖν καί ἐνεργεῖσθαι φυσικῶς τάξις ἐστίν), fre- quently alternating and changing, without however in any way changing nature along with it" (trans. Constas).

> Every innovation, generally speaking, takes place in relation to the mode of whatever is being innovated [περὶ τὸν τρόπον τοῦ καινοτομουμένου πράγματος], not in relation to its λόγος of nature, because when a λόγος is innovated it effectively results in the destruction of nature, since the nature in question no longer possesses inviolate the λόγος according to which it exists. When, however, the mode is innovated—so that the λόγος of nature is preserved inviolate—it manifests a wondrous power, for it displays nature being acted on and acting outside the limits of its own laws [ὡς τὴν φύσιν ἐνεργουμένην τε καὶ ἐνεργοῦσαν ὑπὲρ τὸν ἑαυτῆς ἀποδεικνὺς δηλονότι θεσμόν].[8]

The mode is innovated by the very existence of the being of which it is a mode of existence,[9] for it is actualized in otherness; the question that remains is how far-reaching this innovation is in any given case. Maximus asserts this innovation/actualization can even "display nature being acted on and acting outside the limits of its own laws," thereby manifesting "wondrous power." However, even in that case, the λόγος of nature and nature itself remain intact,[10] for the subsistence of nature and of its inviolate λόγος is a prerequisite for the existence of a being *as itself*, for the existence of a being as participating in a given mode of natural homogeneity. This general principle applies to deification as well, the difference being that it is the existence of the hypostasis of Christ (the actualization of created and uncreated natures in one person and hypostasis) that enables such a far-reaching innovation of the *mode* to take place.

This, the λόγος-τρόπος distinction, is the hermeneutic basis of Maximus' explication of deification: the τρόπος is granted divine uncreatedness, the λόγος remains created and human. To be more precise: the *mode* of the uncreated is actualized (ἐνεργεῖται) on the basis of a created and human

---

8. Ibid.

9. Cf. *Amb.Th.*, 5.117–19: "We know that the λόγος of being (ὁ τοῦ εἶναι λόγος) is one thing, and the mode of existence (ὁ τοῦ πῶς εἶναι τρόπος) is another; the λόγος is confirmed with respect to nature, while the τρόπος is confirmed with respect to the economy."

10. The λόγοι cannot change, for they are motionless, being uncreated and beyond temporality as intentions and wills of God. However, they are perceived as being in motion in their disclosure through the beings of which they are the λόγοι, created beings which are of course in motion. In relation to the actualization of their corresponding creatures in motion, they emerge as being in motion themselves. Cf. *Amb.Io.* 17, 1228BC: "What human being, as I have said, can know the intelligible λόγοι of beings as they are in themselves, and how they are distinct from each other? Who can grasp how they have an immovable, natural rest, and a natural movement that prevents them from being transformed into one another? Or how they have rest in motion, and—what is even more paradoxical—their motion in rest?" (trans. Constas).

nature. However, the reader would do well to resist the temptation of reifying either the λόγος or the τρόπος. A contradistinction of these two is only conceivable in the case of λόγος οὐσίας and τρόπος ὑπάρξεως, i.e., principle/λόγος of substance and mode of existence, pertaining to the substance and the hypostasis respectively. Apart from this specific context, and given that Maximus utilizes these terms with differences in meaning that are not always subtle, I would even say that the concept of the τρόπος in general is a λόγος of relations: an outcome of relations like the λόγος/ratio of a mathematical division. And that each λόγος[11] is also a τρόπος: a mode of existing as a divine utterance and intention. Both the λόγος and the τρόπος are equally indispensable, equally vital in disclosing truth, and the importance of neither of them is to be underestimated.[12] The substance and the hypostasis, their λόγος and τρόπος as well as the crucial role of created and uncreated activities (ἐνέργειαι) alike provide the semantic frame in which the possibility of deification is ontologically described. However, this does not suffice to provide us with the necessary explanation concerning the state of motion and temporality in deification: we must examine the notion of στάσις ἀεικίνητος, the "ever-moving repose."

A Third Mode of Motion and Temporality: στάσις ἀεικίνητος

The notion of στάσις ἀεικίνητος emerges primarily in two questions of Maximus' Πρὸς Θαλάσσιον,[13] in passages concerning deification or the process towards deification. In both cases, it is explicitly related not only to motion, but to temporality as well.

Maximus' reasoning unfolds with the assertion that motion is changing the beings that are in motion, and that this change is a fundamental trait of createdness. However, when nature will be conjoined with the Λόγος in

11. The λόγοι are not only λόγοι of natures/substances, but λόγοι of everything: *Amb.Io.* 17, 1228D: "What, in turn, is the λόγος that underlies each particular substance, nature, species, form, compound, potential, actuality, and passivity?" (trans. Constas).

12. Cf. *Amb.Io.* 10, 1136BC: "Thence they are taught the divinely-perfect and saving meaning concerning the Father and the Son and the Holy Spirit, according to which they are hiddenly illuminated that the meaning of the cause is not simply that of being but are reverently initiated about the mode of existence" (trans. Louth).

13. *Q.Thal. II*, 59.122–59 and 65.509–53. It is also mentioned in *Opusc.*, PG91 185A, as the state following the motionlessness resulting from the *completion of yearning*, a state in which death is conquered: πόθου τε πλήρωσιν εἰληφώς, τὴν ἐφ᾽ ἑαυτῷ τοῦ ποθουμένου τελείαν ἐκνίκησιν, καὶ παύλαν κινήσεως τὴν ἀεικίνητον στάσιν, καθ᾽ ἣν ὁ πάλαι τῆς φύσεως κρατήσας ἐξαφανίζεται θάνατος, οὐχ ἡττωμένης τούτῳ διὰ παραβάσεως.

motionlessness, this change will cease along with the motion that is causing it.[14] The relative and finite repose that signifies the completion of the beings' motion is to take place within the "presence of the boundless fixity" signifying the uncreated; it is within this fixity that the beings' repose naturally occurs.[15] The difference between the motionlessness of creatures and the motionlessness of the uncreated is that creatures (i.e., beings that are finite by nature) possess a motion that changes what they are, and it is the cessation of that motion that results in their kind of motionlessness—while we cannot know any changing motion in the uncreated (for it is not finite), resulting in an "absolute" motionlessness or rather a kind of motionlessness beyond the mere cessation of motion.[16] It is in this context that Maximus formulates his definition of time, according to which creation is "a finite space and a circumscribed fixity, while time is the circumscription of motion: as a consequence, life's motion changes the beings that are subjected to it"[17]—linking life, motion, and time to *change*, which can either be the change of corruption or the change of transformation. Up to this point, Maximus describes the state of motion and time within creation and as subjected to createdness; however, he goes on to describe the ὑπὲρ φύσιν state and the transformation that it effects on motion and temporality.

    Maximus writes that when nature transcends space (τόπον) and time (χρόνον), i.e., the dimensions of createdness comprised of the finite motion and repose *by activity* (κατ' ἐνέργειαν), it will be joined with divinity ("the Providence") in all immediacy and directness (ἀμέσως συναφθῇ τῇ προνοίᾳ). In doing so, divinity (the πρόνοια, Providence) will be encountered and disclosed as a naturally simple, single, and motionless λόγος, completely devoid of any circumscription and motion.[18] The first thing to be noted here is that the absolute immediacy and directness of the described union, as well as the disclosure of divinity as devoid of any motion and delimitation whatsoever, point to the annihilation of *distance*.[19] The absence

---

14. Q.Thal. II, 65.522–24.

15. Ibid., 65.525–28.

16. Ibid., 65.528–32.

17. Ibid., 65.532–35.

18. Ibid., 65.535–41.

19. The annihilation of *distance* is described by Maximus as follows, *Th.oec.*, 1165B-2.86, "It is the fulfillment of those who are moved by a longing for the ultimate object of desire. When they reach it they receive a special kind of repose from all movement, *because they will require no further time or period to go through* (ὡς μηκέτι χρόνου τινός ὄντος αὐτῶν ἢ αἰῶνος τοῦ διαβαθῆναι ὀφείλοντος) since at the completion of these they arrive at God who is before all Aeons and whom the very nature of time cannot approach" (trans. Berthold).

of *any* delimitation whatsoever and the absence of motion beyond its mere cessation do not merely signify an annulment of *distance*, but an existential annihilation thereof, *transforming* both motion and temporality. Neither motionless nor the Aeon are applicable signifiers for this state, for it transcends their constitutive definitions and delimitations.

Maximus proceeds to make this distinction himself: "Because of that, as long as nature exists *in time* (ὑπάρχουσα χρονικῶς) within creation, it possesses a motion capable of effecting change due to the finite fixity of creation and the corruption that is caused by the passage of time."[20] However, "when nature arrives at God, because of the natural singularity of the One in whom it was created, *it will acquire an ever-moving repose and a stationary movement* eternally actualized in conjunction with the One and Single and Same. This ever-moving repose and stationary movement is known by the Λόγος as a direct and permanent firmness around the first cause of everything that has been created by the first cause"[21]—the use of πεποιημένων[22] indicating a *personal* first cause, a person that creates. Maximus clarifies this notion of the infinity *around* God in a passage from the *Ambigua ad Ioannem*, in which he notes that "infinity is around God, but it is not God himself, for he incomparably transcends even this."[23] Describing the ones united with God as being *around* God can be understood as describing their non-dissolution in divinity, i.e., the fact that they retain their otherness even when enjoying the fullness of communion with divinity. Back in Πρὸς Θαλάσσιον, the Confessor goes on to clarify that in this union of created nature with the Λόγος and divine Providence *in all immediacy and directness* "there is nothing at all that manifests generation and time."[24] The beings that are conjoined with the uncreated and thereby transformed are

20. *Q.Thal. II*, 65.541–44: "Διόπερ ἐν μὲν τῷ κόσμῳ ὑπάρχουσα χρονικῶς ἡ φύσις ἀλλοιωτὴν ἔχει τὴν κίνησιν διὰ τὴν τοῦ κόσμου πεπερασμένην στάσιν καὶ τὴν καθ᾽ ἑτεροίωσιν τοῦ χρόνου φοράν."

21. Ibid., 65.544–49: ἐν δὲ τῷ θεῷ γινομένη διὰ τὴν φυσικὴν τοῦ ἐν ᾧ γέγονε μονάδα, στάσιν ἀεικίνητον ἕξει καὶ στάσιμον ταυτοκινησίαν, περὶ τὸ ταὐτὸν καὶ ἓν καὶ μόνον ἀϊδίως γινομένη, ἣν οἶδεν ὁ λόγος ἄμεσον εἶναι περὶ τὸ πρῶτον αἴτιον τῶν ἐξ αὐτοῦ πεποιημένων μόνιμον ἵδρυσιν. Note the use of ἀϊδίως, not αἰωνίως.

22. Participle stemming the verb ποιέω-ποιῶ, "I create."

23. *Amb.Io.* 15, 1220C: "[which is known only to] the One who grants this ineffable grace to the worthy, that is, it is known only to God, and to those who in the future will come to experience it, when all things will be free from all change and alteration, when the endless, multiform movement of beings around particular objects will come to an end in the infinity that is around God, in which all things that are in motion will come to rest. For infinity is around God, but it is not God Himself, for He incomparably transcends even this" (trans. Constas).

24. *Q.Thal. II*, 65.549–53, and particularly: "καθ᾽ ἣν οὐδεμία τὸ παράπαν ἐστὶ χρόνου καὶ γενέσεως ἔμφασις."

not merely liberated from time, but also from something that has already happened, i.e., their generation: while retaining their otherness and not dissolving into divinity, they become liberated even from the fact that they have had a generation, a Maximian statement that greatly emphasizes the reality of the freedom from predeterminations thus attained.[25]

Maximus chooses to construct a terminology pertaining to motion when describing deification and union with God and when writing about the *ever-moving repose* and the *stationary movement* of the ones that will be joined with divinity in all immediacy and directness. It is this terminology that describes the created-uncreated communion as an event *beyond* motion (or even beyond the cessation/negation of motion) and *beyond* temporality in both its modes as time and the Aeon. As every definition of the Maximian modes of temporality has motion (or the absence of motion) as its component, it follows that the concept of the ever-moving repose is to be considered as the distinct mode of both motion and temporality in deification. If time is "the numbering of motion," "the Aeon, when measured in its movement" and the Aeon is "time deprived of motion," then the ever-moving repose and stationary movement around God is the "immediacy and directness" of their communion, the annihilation of *distance*—and not merely its cessation. Describing this state as a "direct and permanent firmness" around God entails that it is not a fleeting event or a temporary phenomenon, but an existential possibility that is a vital component of the ontological totality of existence as encompassing both created reality and its uncreated source and cause.

Furthermore, Maximus repeatedly locates this transformation in the *future*,[26] stressing the implicit transcendental temporality of this state, both when referring to the possibility of the person's deification and when referring to the common eschatological "end of the ages." Truth, both as the arrival at the κατὰ φύσιν and its transcendence towards the ὑπὲρ φύσιν, resides in the *future*, not in the present or past. I will examine what this entails in the subsection concerning the "eighth day," as the very notion of *future* is relevant and applicable only in one of the three modes of temporality, i.e., time (χρόνος); neither in the Aeon nor in the utterly transcendental ever-moving repose.

---

25. Reminding us of Maximus' reference to Melchizedek.

26. For example, see the above mentioned passage *Amb.Io.* 15, 1220C: "to those who in the future will come to experience it . . . ."

The Ever-Moving Repose of Acquiring Uncreatedness by Participation

In another passage,[27] Maximus attempts to describe this transformation beyond the limits of language with a torrent of descriptions and definitions that he equates with one another, literally trying to "circumscribe" and point towards what cannot be *defined*. In doing this, the interrelation of his descriptions and definitions is truly revealing, with the concept of the ever-moving repose and stationary movement providing the basis of an understanding of deification in the context of motion as a primary characteristic of existence. Maximus begins by writing that the salvation and fulfillment (σωτηρία) of the souls is the end, goal, and completion of faith, which in turn is the true disclosure of the object of faith.[28] The true disclosure of the object of faith is the ineffable interpenetration of the believer by the object of faith, according to the measure of the believer's faith.[29] This interpenetration is the return of the believer to his cause and beginning at the end and goal of his journey[30]—which, in turn, is described as the fulfillment of desire.[31] *And the fulfillment of desire is the ever-moving repose of those that desire around the object of desire.*[32] This ever-moving repose is the perpetual, eternal, dimensionless (and, as such, devoid of distance) enjoyment of the object of desire, which in turn is *the participation in divinity beyond nature.*[33] This participation constitutes the likeness of the ones that participate to the one that is participated, i.e., the attainable identification of the ones that participate with the one that is participated *through the activities* (κατ᾽ ἐνέργειαν) due to this likeness.[34] This is the *deification* of those that are worthy thereof.[35] Maximus hastens to link this to temporality:

27. *Q. Thal. II*, 59.122–59.

28. *Q. Thal. II*, 59.122–24.

29. Ibid., 59.124–26.

30. Which in itself has connotations concerning temporality, as it signifies the liberation from the flow and progression of time and from the flow and progression of events as well.

31. *Q. Thal. II*, 59.126–30.

32. Ibid., 59.130–31: "ἐφέσεως δὲ πλήρωσίς ἐστιν ἡ περὶ τὸ ἐφετὸν τῶν ἐφιεμένων ἀεικίνητος στάσις."

33. Ibid., 59.131–34: "ἀεικίνητος δὲ στάσις ἐστὶν ἡ τοῦ ἐφετοῦ διηνεκής τε καὶ ἀδιάστατος ἀπόλαυσις· ἀπόλαυσις δὲ διηνεκὴς καὶ ἀδιάστατος ἡ τῶν ὑπὲρ φύσιν θείων καθέστηκε μέθεξις."

34. Ibid., 59.134–38: "ἡ δὲ πρὸς τὸ μετεχόμενον τῶν μετεχόντων ὁμοίωσίς ἐστιν ἡ κατ᾽ ἐνέργειαν πρὸς αὐτὸ τὸ μετεχόμενον τῶν μετεχόντων δι᾽ ὁμοιότητος ἐνδεχομένη ταυτότης."

35. Ibid., 59.138–41: "ἡ δὲ τῶν μετεχόντων ἐνδεχομένη κατ᾽ ἐνέργειαν δι᾽

he goes on to say deification is, "and let me stress my words," the completion of all "times" and all "Aeons," of all years and all ages (πάντων τῶν
χρόνων καὶ τῶν αἰώνων) and of everything that is included in them.³⁶ This
completion of all χρόνοι and αἰῶνες and of everything that is included in
them constitutes the unceasing and dimensionless (i.e., devoid of *distance*)
unity of the true cause and beginning of those that are saved, completed,
fulfilled, and deified, with their purpose and end.³⁷ And so on—concluding
that this union of the uncreated God with the created human nature by far
transcends any conceivable thought or formulation that can be arrived at
within createdness.³⁸

The third and ultimate mode of motion and temporality is the very
transcendence and completion thereof. This ever-moving repose in deification is described as the completion of every possible mode of motion and
temporality, "completing time and the Aeon and everything that is included
in them." The whole of creation is recapitulated in the deified person that
embodies the completion of communion; the totality of existence is returned
to its uncreated source, completing, recapitulating, and transcending the
fundamental components of createdness: beginning, end, motion, and temporality. Humanity's mediating task is to annihilate all existential divisions
(*distances*) and to restore communion "so that they all may be one":³⁹ Maximus notes "the human person is to make the whole of creation perceived
through the senses one with itself and undivided [ταὐτότητα μίαν ποιήσειεν
ἀδιαίρετον], not dividing it spatially by intervals [τοῖς διαστήμασι] in any
way."⁴⁰

The Confessor does not describe this as a subjective and mystical event
that is contained and exhausted in the individual, but as a distinct possibility for reality's mode of existence apart from the mode of the uncreated and
the mode of createdness. The possibility of created nature's hypostatization
(actualization) in the mode of the uncreated (*without natural confusion,
change, division, or separation*) is not merely a "merging" of existential mo-
dalities, but a third, distinct mode of being. By its very definition, it does not
take place within time (i.e., at a certain time), for it *transforms* time: as such,
both the "individual" ever-moving repose of the deified person and the

---

ὁμοιότητος πρὸς τὸ μετεχόμενον ταυτότης ἐστὶν ἡ θέωσις τῶν ἀξιουμένων θεώσεως."

36. Ibid., 59.141–43: "ἡ δὲ θέωσίς ἐστι καθ' ὑπογραφῆς λόγον πάντων τῶν χρόνων
καὶ τῶν αἰώνων καὶ τῶν ἐν χρόνῳ καὶ αἰῶνι περιοχὴ καὶ πέρας."

37. Ibid., 59.143–46.

38. Ibid., 59.156–59.

39. Cf. John 17:21: ἵνα πάντες ἓν ὦσιν.

40. *Amb.Io.* 41, 1305D (trans. Louth).

"collective" ever-moving repose of creation itself are not wholly different,[41] but nonetheless seemingly situated in a distant and eschatological future[42]— for such a mode of temporality cannot be perceived as time's "now" by those who do not participate in it. For all intents and purposes, it takes place *at the end of time itself*—i.e., beyond temporality. However, to encounter a deified person is to participate in the presence of this "future" in the present—and to suspect that this "future" is the expected dimensionless present that, in absence of an existential *distance* between the related othernesses in communion, actualizes the νῦν as the hidden reality of temporality by annihilating the transition from the "before" to the "after."[43] (By definition, these explications can be as precise as phrases like "stationary movement" and "ever-moving repose," for they are attempts at signifying that which cannot be delimited, residing outside the limits of our world and language. They can only function as hints and indications.)

My conclusion is that in the light of the ever-moving repose, the world's overall motion is disclosed not as an impersonal cosmological process and function, but as a relationship (between the uncreated and creation in all its "logical" manifestations) that can be either affirmed as returning motion or rejected in a deviation thereof. Temporality *measures* this relationship,

41. Maximus notes in *Amb.Io.* 50, 1368C–1369A that human persons are actualized in three different states, the present life, the state after death, and the future age to come. The difference is that in this last state "we will partake without any mediation of the most sublime Λόγος of Wisdom, and being transformed in accordance with Him, we will become Gods by grace." Each of these states can be seen as an icon of the other and a referral to it: "εἰκονισθῆναι τῶν εἰρημένων τόπων τόν ἰδιότητα."

42. Cf. Plass' "Transcendent Time in Maximus the Confessor," 268: "In the incarnation of the timeless Λόγος the perfecting of human nature which lies in the future is also present. . . . But 'future' also means the cessation of time, and Maximus can also see the future as the divine plan complete and present as a whole."

43. Note also Maximus' reference to the whole of time and history as "God's year," as a singular temporal unit which is only actualized in its completion, *Amb.Io.* 46, 1357AB: "The year acceptable to the Lord (as Scripture calls it), when understood allegorically, is the entire extension of the ages, beginning from the moment when God was pleased to give substance to beings, and existence to what did not exist" (trans. Constas) up to the "completion of the ages," the "end of the λόγος of everything that is in motion" and the granting of the promised deification, as Maximus goes on to say. In *Q.Thal. I*, 9.8–12, Maximus notes, referring to John the Evangelist, that we do not know the exact *mode* of this future deification (τὸν τρόπον τῆς μελλούσης θεώσεως ἠγνοηκέναι λέγει). However, even this distant future, this *completion of all ages* is already present, simultaneously *expected* and *already here* (a typical Christian notion on eschatological time, as Oscar Cullmann has demonstrated in his *Christ and Time*), Cf. *Q.Thal. I*, 22.60–65, "Or rather, since our Lord Jesus Christ is the beginning [ἀρχή], middle [μεσότης] and the end [τέλος] of all ages, past and future, [it would be fair to say that] *the end of the ages*—specifically that end which will actually come about by grace for the deification of those who are worthy—*has come upon us* in potency through faith" (trans. Blowers).

the completion of which is the transformation of temporality into an ever-moving repose (the fullness of communion) and the refutation of which is measured as gradual corruption leading to death and inexistence. The complete affirmation of the returning motion, the full actualization of motion as κατὰ φύσιν, cannot be understood as resulting in a static motionlessness: this does not describe our experiences of its faint reflections accurately. The fullness of communion[44] and the proximity of the related "logical" othernesses, while presupposing the annihilation of distance and, as such, the ceasing of motion, catapults motion beyond nature and nature beyond motion, ὑπὲρ φύσιν: this can only be circumscribed in language as a motion beyond fixity and a fixity beyond motion, as an "ever-moving repose" and a "stationary movement." The deified person is accounted as being "beyond the Aeon, time, and space, having God as his space."[45] I have noted that motion is the primary ontological characteristic of creatures together with their createdness. However, motion is manifested as a component of *relation* and *distance*, and it is motion that counts/discloses/actualizes this *relation* and *distance*, time being the *number, numbering, circumscription, and delimitation* thereof. Time *measures* either communion or distance, which are disclosed as motion: but the consummation of communion cannot be described as mere timelessness or motionlessness, for it cannot but be, in a sense, *active*. I am referring to an *ever-moving repose* that is a *stationary movement*; the dimensionless present of the fullness of communion; a radically transformed νῦν, eternal by the very fact that it does not possess duration, i.e., temporal *distance*.

---

44. Maximus employs a language of ἔρως when describing this union, *Amb.Io.* 7, 1073C–1076A: "If it [the νοῦς, i.e., the human person beyond its mere perception of the sensible] loves, it certainly suffers an ecstasy [ἔκστασις] toward it as an object of love. If it suffers this ecstasy, it obviously urges itself onward, and if it urges itself onward, it surely intensifies and greatly accelerates its motion. And if its motion is intensified in this way, it will not cease until it is wholly present in the whole beloved, and wholly encompassed by it, willingly receiving the whole saving circumscription by its own choice, so that it might be wholly qualified by the whole circumscriber, and, being wholly circumscribed, will no longer be able to wish to be known from its own qualities, but rather from those of the circumscriber, in the same way that air is thoroughly permeated by light, or iron in a forge is completely penetrated by the fire, or anything else of this sort" (trans. Constas). Cf. *Q.Thal. I*, 10.92–95 and 54.145–49.

45. *Th.oec.*, 1108C–1.68: "The Aeon, time, and place belong in the category of the relative [τῶν πρός τι]. Without them nothing of what is included in them exists. God is not of the category of the relative because he does not have anything at all included in him. If, then, the inheritance of those who are worthy is God himself, the one who is rendered worthy of this grace will be above the Aeon, time and place. He will have God himself as a place" (trans. Berthold).

Death and Relation

I have repeatedly referred to relationality and self-transcending love as the mode of life and the mode of the uncreated, and to nonrelation and individual onticity as the mode of death, the mode of "fallen" createdness. It must be stressed that this is not an *a posteriori* analysis imposed by my hermeneutical approach: it is Maximus himself who makes that distinction. According to the Confessor's definitive formulation, "Death is, primarily, separation from God"[46]—and, consequently, from everything that God is, from everything created in which God is present through its λόγος: death is defined as the choice of nonrelation, and primarily as the refusal to be in communion with the *person* behind creation. Maximus continues: "and life is, primarily, the one who says, *I am the life*":[47] life is defined as a *person* (the person of the Λόγος), and participation in life is the participation in that person, the relationship with that person—a relationship that is also forged through the relationship with the ones who are made "in the image and likeness" of that God, i.e., human persons (and the whole of creation in its "logical" quality), a relationship manifested by *actualizing* the uncreated's mode of existence, the mode of relationality, self-transcendence, ἔρως, love. Humanity's mediating function, i.e., the personalization of creation, is also an actualization of this mode. To actualize this mode of existence is to *possess God*: "the one who possesses love possesses God himself, since *God is love*."[48]

However, there is a limit to how fully a human person can actualize this mode of existence while he himself is actualized through created activities inevitably dictating a distinct individual atomicity (and not merely an otherness)—for example, the natural atomicity of the human body. As long as this individual atomicity is preserved, the fullness of relationality, self-transcendence, and communion cannot be achieved. According to Maximus,

> [S]o long as one is in the present time of this life even if he be perfect in his earthly state both in action and in contemplation, he still has knowledge, prophecy, and the pledge of the Holy Spirit only in part, but not in their fullness. He has yet to come at the end of the ages to the perfect rest which reveals face to face to those who are worthy the truth as it is in itself. Then one will

---

46. *Car.*, 2.93.1: "Θάνατος μέν ἐστι κυρίως ὁ τοῦ Θεοῦ χωρισμός."

47. *Car.*, 2.93.4: "Ζωὴ δὲ κυρίως ἐστὶν ὁ εἰπών· Ἐγώ εἰμι ἡ ζωή."

48. *Car.*, 4.100.5–6: "Ὁ οὖν κτησάμενος τὴν ἀγάπην, αὐτὸν τὸν Θεὸν ἐκτήσατο, ἐπειδὴ ὁ Θεὸς ἀγάπη ἐστίν" (trans. Berthold).

possess not just a part of the fullness but rather acquire through participation the entire fullness of grace.[49]

I suspect that what Maximus implies is if life is communion and death is nonrelation, then biological death need not necessarily be the severance of the created basis for the actualization of the person, but perhaps also the severance of our ultimate *resistance* to the fullness of communion and life, the annihilation of the ultimate frontier of individual atomicity preventing the fullness of relation and otherness: matter, the body.[50] The hope that the Confessor articulates is that if man's whole life constitutes an affirmative an-swer to God's continuous call from nonbeing into being, then the *Other* of that relationship could grant the uncreated hypostatization (actualization) of the person to those who are receptive to it:

> For I do not think that the limit of this present life is rightly called death, but rather release from death, separation from cor-ruption, freedom from slavery, cessation of trouble, the taking away of wars, passage beyond confusion, the receding of dark-ness, rest from labours, silence from confused buzzing, quiet from excitement, a veiling of shame, flight from the passions, the vanishing of sin, and, to speak briefly, the termination of evils. By achieving these things through voluntary mortifica-tion, the Saints commend themselves as strangers and exiles from this life.[51]

Man's *receptiveness* to this divine, uncreated life and grace that consti-tutes the person even without its created and natural activities (i.e., matter) is of paramount importance to Maximus: "each partakes according to his ability,"[52] it is the "quality of disposition [ποιότητα τῆς διαθέσεως] found in

---

49. *Th.oec.*, 1165BC–2.87 (trans. Berthold).

50. *Q.Thal. I*, 42.26–28: "τὸ τέλος τοῦ παθητοῦ τῆς φύσεως, φημὶ δὲ τὸν θάνατον, τῆς κατὰ φύσιν πρὸς ἀφθαρσίαν μεταποιήσεως ἀρχὴν ποιησάμενος."—"[he] turned the end of our nature's passibility—which is death—into the beginning of our natural transformation to incorruption" (trans. Blowers).

51. *Amb.Io.* 10, 1157CD (trans. Louth).

52. *Q.Dub.*, 102.5–14: "Rather, it is necessary to suppose this, that just as we have optical, auditory and respiratory ability, and these things do not receive all the air or the light or the voice—since there will then be no partaking of these things left for anyone else—but in proportion to the power that is present in each, each partakes according to their ability; thus, also the mercy of God grants both forgiveness and grace according to the quality of the underlying disposition of each one, e.g., when someone repented completely, he is also forgiven completely. One who repented partially is also forgiven partially. And the same thing also holds true for the one who loves" (trans. Prassas).

each one"[53] that prepares the person—or leaves him unprepared—for the ultimate unification and communion. This is promised to take place "at the end of the ages" (κατὰ τὸ πέρας τῶν αἰώνων). However, what could this mean, given that we are referring to uncreated existence, i.e., existence beyond any conception of temporality? How could that reside in the "future" in a context where the category of time is not applicable at all? This leads us to Maximus' passages concerning the biblical "eighth day," the promised ultimate eschatological "future."

The Eighth Day

A common or at least closely related vocabulary is used for both the deification of a human person and the common completion/salvation and deification of a part of humanity *at the end of the ages*, the future described in theology with the term *eschatology*. However, to say this eschatological transformation will take place *in the future, in a future time* seems to be contrary to the fact that the described reality is clearly beyond the realm of temporality as χρόνος, i.e., the mode of temporality in which the very notion of *future* has a semantic content and sense. Future and past, the "before" and the "after," characterize time as the numbering of motion: they are neither applicable to the Aeon of intelligible creation nor to the implicit temporality of deification, i.e., the ever-moving repose. As such, we can understand the notion of "future" concerning the "age to come" and the "eighth day" only in the general and relative sense of *what has not yet become a reality*, of the coming, of the expected, the hoped-for and the soon-to-be. It is a "future" insofar as it does not reside in humanity's perceived present or its past, but our understanding thereof would be erroneous if we would constrain it in the semantic context of "past" and "future": in the Maximian worldview, "the age to come" is not merely another occurrence in a linear progression of time—although it is expected to be the end and completion of all occurrences in the linear progression of time, "the end of history."

Maximus differentiates between a human person's deification and the "age to come"—he does not consider them as being the same.[54] As we ex-

53. *Q.Thal. II*, 59.165–70: "Κατὰ γὰρ τὴν ὑποκειμένην ἑκάστῳ ποιότητα τῆς διαθέσεως ὁ θεός, τοῖς πᾶσιν ἑνούμενος ὡς οἶδεν αὐτός, τὴν αἴσθησιν ἑκάστῳ παρέχεται καθὼς ἐστιν ἕκαστος ὑφ' ἑαυτοῦ διαπεπλασμένος πρὸς ὑποδοχὴν τοῦ πάντως πᾶσιν ἑνωθησομένου κατὰ τὸ πέρας τῶν αἰώνων."

54. Cf. *Amb.Io.* 50, 1368C–1369A. A substantial difference is also the expectation of the common *resurrection of the dead*, which is expected as *one, singular, common* event innovating creation and not merely as an occurrence in the person's path to deification.

amined in the previous subsection, there is a substantial difference between the completion that can be achieved in human life and the completion that requires the completion of human life itself. However, the Confessor often blurs the lines between these different states himself, suggesting that these are not to be understood as states that follow one another in a linear progression. For example, he refers to the eschatological "eighth day" of Christian theology both in terms of a person's deification and of the "collective" end of the ages, the end of time itself. The *"eighth day"* is both the expected historical event of the end of history, the transformation of creation, *and* the person's deification and completion.[55] In attempting to understand how these are both different and essentially the same,[56] the reader should bear in mind that both events take place beyond the realm of χρόνος. As such, one could not say that the first takes place "at some point," while the second "at some other point": their difference, priority, and sequence is an *ontological* one, *not* a temporal one. Apart from that, in the context of the human person's mediating function, his own ὑπὲρ φύσιν completion and participation in the uncreated *is* the mediation for the cosmos' completion and participation in the uncreated.

Maximus treats the "sixth," "seventh," and "eighth day" as states and modes of existence, not as "days" or as events bearing a primarily temporal connotation. He compares and parallels this triad to a number of his

---

55. Maximus does consistently position deification in the *future*, in the *age to come*, at the *end of the ages*, e.g., *Q.Thal. I*, 22.77–82: "But in the ages to come we shall undergo by grace the transformation unto deification and no longer be active but passive; and for this reason we shall not cease from being deified. At that point our passion will be supernatural, and there will be no principle restrictive of the divine activity in infinitely deifying those who are passive to it" (trans. Blowers). However, this future is *beyond* motion and, as a consequence, distance, see *Q.Theop.*, PG90, 1393A, where deification (ἡ μετὰ χάριν ἐκθέωσις) *follows* the "delimitation of motion by fixity." In fact, Maximus explicitly links the deification of humanity (a possibility founded by Christ's self-abasement) with the "limits of all history," *Or.Dom.*, 42–44, ". . . the mysterious self-abasement of the only-begotten Son with a view to the deification of our nature, a self-abasement in which he holds enclosed the limits of all history [πάντων τῶν αἰώνων τὸ πέρας περιγραφόμενον]" (trans. Berthold). The deification and salvation of humanity is, by divine purpose, the end of all ages itself and a purpose conceived before all ages (*Opusc.*, PG91 25A: "ἡ σωτηρία τῶν σωζωμένων· σκοπὸς ὑπάρχουσα θεῖος, ὡς τέλος πάντων προεπινοηθὲν τῶν αἰώνων").

56. Plass notes in "Transcendent Time in Maximus the Confessor," 271: "The 'Lord's Day' need not be simply the specific date on which the present world will come to an end; it can be any point of time that is shaped by (i.e., both anticipates and participates in) the divine purpose embracing the whole of history. . . . In eschatological perspective the end of time penetrates the whole of time; since there is a pattern of history, events separate in time are drawn together and superimposed on each other to make up a series all of whose moments coexist simultaneously."

other triads, but the main idea underlining his conception thereof is that the number seven "signifies time, the Aeon, ages, motion, place/containment, measure, limit and providence,"[57] and as such the "eighth day" is the transcendence of all these. "According to Scripture, the sixth day brings in the completion of beings subject to nature. The seventh limits the movement of temporal distinctiveness. The eighth indicates the mode of existence above nature and time."[58] These "days" signify the progression towards eternal well-being (ἀεὶ εὖ εἶναι) as well: "The sixth day reveals the λόγος of the being of beings, the seventh indicates the manner of the well-being of things, the eighth communicates the ineffable mystery of the eternal well-being of things."[59] Apart from that, the progression from the sixth to the "eighth day" signifies the transition from the completion of natural activities (κατὰ φύσιν ἐνεργειῶν) to the deification of those, to whom deification can be granted: "The sixth day is the full accomplishment of the natural activities of those who practice virtue. The seventh is the fulfilment and rest of the natural activities of those who are worthy. The eighth is the promotion and transition to deification of those who are worthy."[60]

The "eighth day" does not merely signify the being's rest and cessation of motion (which is described as the Sabbath, the "seventh day"), but the state beyond that, i.e., the "Sabbath of Sabbaths," *true* immobility beyond the duality of motion and motionlessness (exactly what Maximus terms *ever-moving repose* and *stationary movement* in other passages). For this,

57. *Amb.Io.* 65, 1389D: "According to sacred Scripture, the number seven, when taken simply as a number, by its nature contains within itself a wealth of mystical contemplation for those who love to labor for divine things. For it signifies time, the Aeon, ages, motion, as well as containment, measure, limit, and providence [χρόνον, καὶ αἰῶνα, καὶ αἰῶνας, κίνησίν τε καὶ περιοχὴν καὶ μέτρον, καὶ ὅρον καὶ πρόνοιαν], and many other things when it is properly contemplated according to the λόγος of each" (trans. Constas).

58. *Th.oec.*, 1101C–1.51 (trans. Berthold).

59. Ibid., 1104C–1.56: "Ἡ ἕκτη ἡμέρα, τὸν τοῦ εἶναι τῶν ὄντων λόγον ὑποδηλοῖ· ἡ δὲ ἑβδόμη, τὸν τοῦ εὖ εἶναι τῶν ὄντων τρόπον ὑποσημαίνει· ἡ δὲ ὀγδόη, τὸ τοῦ ἀεὶ εὖ εἶναι τῶν ὄντων ἄρρητον μυστήριον ὑπαγορεύει" (trans. Berthold).

60. *Th.oec.*, 1104BC–1.55: According to the rest of the passage, "the Lord has perhaps never allowed a more mystical glance at these seventh and eighth days than in referring to them as the day and the hour of fulfillment, since it encloses the mysteries and the λόγοι of all things. Absolutely no heavenly or earthly power can know these days before experiencing the passion, only the blessed divinity which created them" (trans. Berthold). Here, Maximus expresses what I have termed (in a Wittgensteinian way) the inability to accurately articulate in language realities residing beyond the limits of our world, for they simultaneously reside beyond the limits of our language, as the described realities pertains to the uncreated as well, "absolutely no heavenly or earthly power can know these days before experiencing the passion, only the blessed divinity which created them."

a language pertaining to ἔρως and self-transcendence is employed: κατ' ἐρωτικὴν ἔκστασιν.[61] After an analysis of the being/well-being/ever-being triad,[62] the Confessor writes that eternal being (ἀεὶ εἶναι) is:

> [T]he mystically blessed Sabbath, the great day of rest from divine works, which, according to the account of the world's creation in Scripture, appears to have neither beginning, nor end, nor created origin, since it is the manifestation of realities beyond limit and measure, sequent to the motion of whatever is limited by measure, and the infinite identity of realities that are uncontained and uncircumscribed, sequent to the quantity of things contained and circumscribed.[63]

The Sabbath, the "seventh day," is also the completion of the *returning motion*, the restoration of the beings' κατὰ φύσιν. "The Sabbath of God is the full return to him of all creatures whereby he rests from his own natural activity toward them, his very divine activity which acts in an ineffable way."[64] However, this is not enough; there is a state, a mode of existence beyond that, the "eighth day" or ever well-being (ἀεὶ εὖ εἶναι). It is:

> the eighth and the first, or rather, the one and perpetual day, is the unalloyed, all-shining presence of God, which comes about after things in motion have come to rest; and, throughout the whole being of those who by their free choice have used the λόγος of being according to nature, the whole God suitably abides, bestowing on them eternal well-being by giving them a share in himself, because he alone, properly speaking, is, and is good, and is eternal.[65]

---

61. *Th.oec.*, 1097C–1.39: "Sabbaths of Sabbaths (Σάββατα Σαββάτων) are the spiritual peace of the rational soul which, having withdrawn the mind even from all the more divine λόγοι which are in beings, dwells entirely in God alone in a loving ecstasy (κατ' ἐρωτικὴν ἔκστασιν), and has rendered itself by mystical theology totally immobile (παντελῶς ἀκίνητον) in God" (trans. Berthold).

62. *Amb.Io.* 65, 1392AB.

63. Ibid., 1392C (trans. Constas).

64. *Th.oec.*, 1100BC–1.47 (trans. Berthold). This return is a matter of *activities*, ἐνέργειαι. Maximus continues, "For God rests from his natural activity in each being by which each of them moves naturally. He rests when each being, having obtained the divine energy in due measure, will determine its own natural activity with respect to God." As it is God's natural activity that causes the natural, returning motion of beings, the completion of their returning motion in achieving their return is also God's *rest* from this activity.

65. *Amb.Io.* 65, 1392CD (trans. Constas). The passage continues with an analysis of the "ever ill-being" (ἀεὶ φεῦ εἶναι): "but to those who have willfully used the principle of their being contrary to nature, he rightly renders not well-being but eternal ill-being,

To have completed the "sixth day" (to have accomplished its mode of existence) is to proceed to the "seventh day," the "Sabbath," i.e., beyond "the existence of what is subject to nature and to time" in the contemplation of eternity.[66] Further, to be granted the "eighth day" is to be granted deification and resurrection from the dead—the dead being "what is less than God."[67] Again, the uncreated is defined as *proper, true* life, everything beyond that being essentially "dead," i.e., confined to the mode of death, the mode of nonrelation.

Conclusions and Remarks

According to my examination of Maximus' passages, I have come to the following conclusions:

i. There is no motion or temporality of the uncreated, for the uncreated is by definition beyond these categories and divisions. To say God is "motionless" or "timeless/eternal" bears meaning only in a relative manner, in contradistinction and comparison to the motion and temporality of creation.

ii. However, (and while there is no motion or temporality of the uncreated), the state of motion and temporality in the complete participation of created nature in the uncreated, in deification, constitutes a third and distinct mode of motion and temporality; a mode beyond motion and motionlessness, beyond time and Aeon, beyond the division of sensible and intelligible. According to the Confessor, this third mode of motion and temporality is testified as being experienceable by human beings, which has been made possible by the incarnation

---

since well-being is no longer accessible to those who have placed themselves in opposition to it, and they have absolutely no motion after the manifestation of what was sought, by which what is sought is naturally revealed to those who seek it."

66. *Th.oec.*, 1104AB-1.54: "The one who has divinely accomplished in himself the sixth day by appropriate works and thoughts, and who has with God nobly brought his works to an end, has crossed by comprehension all the ground of what is subject to nature and to time. He is transported to the mystical contemplation of the immortal ages, and in an unknowable manner he makes Sabbath in his mind in leaving behind and totally surpassing beings" (trans. Berthold).

67. *Th.oec.*, 1104AB-1.54: "The one who has become worthy of the eighth day is risen from the dead, that is, from what is less than God, sensible and intelligible things, words, and thoughts; and he lives the blessed life of God, who alone is said to be and is in very truth the Life, in such a way that he becomes himself God by deification [γενώμενος τῇ θεώσει θεός]" (trans. Berthold).

and resurrection of the Λόγος, the existence of the person and hypostasis of Christ.

iii. The most fitting, although apophatic, characterization of this third mode of motion and temporality in deification is its description as the *ever-moving repose* (στάσις ἀεικίνητος) and *stationary movement* (στάσιμος ταυτοκινησία) around God, in a union in all directness and immediacy (ἀμέσως συναφθῆ τῇ προνοίᾳ).

iv. By deification, I am referring to the human person being granted *real* identity with God in every respect except of an identity in substance/nature. According to Maximus, in deification the hypostasis of the human person is divine and uncreated, but his substance remains human and created: the mode of existence (τρόπος ὑπάρξεως) is fundamentally changed and innovated, but the λόγος of substance and nature, along with substance/nature itself, remains unchanged. This is described with the language of *activities* (ἐνέργειαι), the hypostatically manifested activities of the substance. In deification, the human person's nature is granted to be actualized through divine, uncreated activities, actualizing an uncreated, divine hypostasis. These descriptions are, by definition, *at the edge of language.*

v. Deification fulfills humanity's mediating task of restoring the union of everything, so that they all may be one. This is achieved by annihilating all divisions, including the created-uncreated division, the full communion of which it restores. To annihilate divisions is to annihilate *distance*—ontological distance, temporal, spatial, or otherwise.[68] Again: this cannot be an individual achievement of the natural person alone, but a fruit of communion, a *gift*; it must be granted to the person (i.e., "by grace") by the one who possesses it.

vi. Apart from the ever-moving repose, Maximus also refers to the "eighth day" in describing deification: while the transcendence of the *natural* "sixth day" (i.e., the "seventh day"/Sabbath), is already a state where the returning motion has been completed and motionlessness has been achieved, the human person aspires to the "eighth day," the Sabbath of Sabbaths, where all divisions and distinctions will have ceased (a motionlessness beyond the cessation of motion and related formulations signifying uncreatedness). In signifying both the human person's deification and the end of history itself, the

---

68. The use of the term ἀδιάστατος in Maximus' passages denote exactly what its etymological information conveys, i.e., a state without διάστασις, dimension, distance, etc.

eschatological end of the ages and the renewal of creation, the Confessor stresses the interconnectedness of these two events.

vii. The ever-moving repose describes a radical *transformation* of temporality by the annihilation of its constitutive parts, i.e., by the annihilation of *distance*.

viii. In doing this, the ever-moving repose is disclosed as the dimensionless "now" of a relationship, in which the related persons are in so complete a communion that they manifest their *otherness* without actualizing *distance*.

ix. This completes the reconstruction of Maximus' implicit vision concerning temporality: the primary characteristic of creation is its *motion*, which can either be the *returning* motion towards the full communion with its uncreated source and cause, or a deviation from this returning motion, i.e., a motion resulting in nonrelation, individual onticity, corruption, and death. Time *measures* this motion, and as such time *measures* this relationship. When this relationship is fulfilled and consummated in the actualization of existence as communion (i.e., in the mode of the uncreated), there is no *distance* to be measured by time or to be manifested in the Aeon[69]—and temporality is transformed into an *ever-moving repose* and a *stationary movement*.

---

69. The Aeon does not measure a motion, but the motion (and distance) of intelligible creation takes place against the background of the temporality of the Aeon.

Concluding Remarks:
Reconstructing Maximus the Confessor's
Theory of Time

MAXIMUS THE CONFESSOR'S THEORY of time, as it has been reconstructed in this study, constitutes a conception of temporality that is beyond the usual contradistinction between presentism, possibilism, and eternalism,[1] and it is substantially different from other theories of time that have been developed in late antiquity, e.g., Augustine's or Boethius'[2]—notwithstanding, of course, the presence of similarities, which however do not lead to an identical or similar vision of temporality.

To sum up Maximus' theory of time, I must first stress that in the background of his *Gedankenwelt* stands a foundational narration concerning ontology and cosmology, namely the existence of *divisions, dualities,* and *distances* that are to be overcome through the mediation of humanity—a mediation that has been made possible by the hypostasis of Christ.

1. Eternalism holds that the past, present, and future are all real; possibilism holds that the past and the present is real, but not the future; and presentism is the belief that only the present is real. See Callender, *The Oxford Handbook of Philosophy of Time*, 3. Were I compelled to include Maximus' theory in one of these categories, I would categorize it under presentism and not eternalism, since only the "now" of dimensionless presence measures the reality of communion. However, such a categorization would be a misreception of the Confessor's thought, as Maximus' understanding of temporality is quite different from that and does not constitute an answer to the question that would categorize time theories under eternalism, possibilism, and presentism—it derives from a distinct *Gedankenwelt*, where temporality measures the reality of *relation*.

2. For a comparison between Eastern Christian and Western theories of time, see Bradshaw's article "Time and Eternity in the Greek Fathers." While a similarity between notions such as *nunc stans* or *semper praesens aeternitas* and some of Maximus' formulations is to be observed, the substantial difference lies exactly in temporality's function as a *measurement of relation/communion* in Maximus' case, which changes the semantic frame of otherwise seemingly comparable notions and expounds their differing foundations. For an overview of Augustine's theory of time, see Gloy's *Philosophiegeschichte der Zeit*, 97–122.

Maximus' vision of the human person as a cosmic mediator is not solely a matter of philosophical anthropology, or, even less, of mystical experience, but a vital part of his ontology: of his understanding of being and existence *as such*. The *purpose* of existence is the *truth* of existence, and this purpose is the transcendence of divisions and distances by the mediation of humanity and through the grace of God, "so that it may all be one" in the restoration of communion—a communion that does not engulf otherness, but one that brings it to light and discloses its reality. The divisions that are most relevant to this enquiry are (a) the created-uncreated distinction, separating God from creation and (b) the distinction between the sensible and the intelligible.[3]

The primary ontological characteristic of creation is *motion* (which, in part, is what we commonly name *change*). Creation has come to be through God's creative motion, and motion is the manner in which creation is actualized. Creation, as well as everything in it, has had a beginning; and everything that has had a beginning is in motion. There are two general modes of motion, two ways in which each and every motion can be actualized:[4] (1) motion "according to nature," which is the *returning* motion of creation towards its Creator, beginning, cause, purpose, and end, i.e., creation's attempt to restore the life-giving communion; and (2) motion "contrary to nature," which is every deviation from the above mentioned *returning* motion, i.e., a motion yearning to achieve individual onticity, nonrelation, and death; a tendency towards inexistence.

This discloses the world's motion as the manifestation of a relationship: God's call to his creatures can either be freely[5] affirmed or freely rejected. The actualization of motion as *returning* motion manifests the affirmative response to God's call for communion; the deviation thereof manifests the

---

3. Maximus presents five cosmological divisions (influenced by Gregory of Nyssa), the first two of which are of vital importance for the present study (in contrast to the last three), *Amb.Io.* 41, 1304D, "They say that the substance of everything that has come into being is divided into five divisions. The first of these divides from the uncreated nature the universal created nature [τὴν διαιροῦσαν τῆς ἀκτίστου φύσεως τὴν κτιστὴν καθόλου φύσιν], which receives its being from becoming . . . . The second division is that in accordance with which the whole nature that receives being from creation is divided by God into that which is perceived by the mind and that perceived by the senses [διαιρεῖται εἰς νοητὰ καὶ αἰσθητά]" (trans. Louth).

4. These are not two irreconcilable extremities, but *modes* that are encountered as intertwined with one another within creation.

5. This freedom primarily characterizes those that have freedom of choice and a free will, i.e., human beings, and *through them* nature and creation as a whole, which is thereby "personalized," it is exactly this that is humanity's function and task of *mediation*.

refusal to enter this relation and especially humanity's striving for individual onticity, deprived of the life-giving Other's fellowship.

Time (χρόνος), in Maximus as well as in Aristotle, is the numbering, circumscription, and delimitation of motion. It is motion that exists, and time is the numbering of this existing reality: time exists insofar as motion exists. Being a manifestation of motion, time is conjoined with space (which also emerges from the reality of motion) in a coherent spatio-temporality within the sensible world, i.e., within the world as it can be perceived by the senses. Given creation's failure to actualize its overall motion as a solely *returning* motion, time measures and actualizes *corruption* as well. Our (i.e., creation's and humanity's) motion "contrary to nature," our deviation from the yearning of communion is actualized and manifested as *corruption*. Time *measures* this corruptive motion as well: time *measures* corruption as our existential failure.

The Aeon (αἰὼν) is "time, when it is deprived of motion," as well as the temporality of sensible creation, of the world as perceived by the mind: the realm of substances, qualities, etc. These are in motion as well, although not in a motion entailing spatiality in any way. This motion takes place in the temporal background of the Aeon, which *seems* motionless and eternal; however, it has had a beginning—along with everything in it.[6] The Aeon is a distinct *mode* of temporality which is not merely defined in contradistinction to time, but *defines* time as well: time is "the Aeon, when measured in its movement." Ordinary time, the temporality of the sensible, is (as Plato would say) a moving icon of the Aeon; the seemingly eternal and unchanging temporality of the Aeon is reflected, and simultaneously distorted, in our sensible world as time. Time is eternity in motion, eternity subjected to the transition from the "before" to the "after," to the constant flow from the past to the future, casting the present moment to inexistence. The purpose of beings in motion is described as an arrival at their rest and repose: the Aeon iconizes the temporality of this repose as a "time without motion."

The human person has been granted with the ability to pierce the veil of createdness by iconizing Christ's mode of existence, by existentially participating in a hypostasis that actualizes both created (human) and un-created (divine) natures in one person, the hypostasis of Christ. The human person can participate in uncreatedness and restore the fullness of his communion with the person(s) of God. Man's affirmative response to God's erotic call can be granted to result in a divine-human communion that actualizes man's created nature through uncreated activities, thereby *deifying*

---

6. Unless, of course, if we imprecisely take the λόγοι as residing in the intelligible creation (in contrast to creation as perceived by our senses) as well, and not solely beyond createdness.

him, transforming him into an uncreated God *in every respect* except of an
identity in nature/substance—for the mode of existence (τρόπος ὑπάρξεως)
can be radically innovated, but not the λόγος of nature (λόγος οὐσίας/
φύσεως) and nature itself. This deification fundamentally transforms motion and temporality. The uncreated God is not merely "motionless" (an
Aristotelian "prime unmoved mover"), in a contradistinction with creation's
"motion," for both of these are merely categories stemming from createdness. (That is why God can be signified as being in perpetual motion and
interpenetration as well.) The uncreated is *beyond* the categories of motion
and motionlessness, time and timelessness, etc. As a consequence, the mode
of existence in deification[7] cannot be merely signified through a language
describing the end of motion in repose or the end of temporality in its cessation: it is beyond that. Maximus uses the terms "ever-moving repose"
(στάσις ἀεικίνητος) and "stationary movement" (στάσιμος ταυτοκινησία)
to denote this third state of motion beyond movement and fixity and temporality beyond time and the Aeon. The "ever-moving repose" describes a
reality without ontological, spatial, or temporal *distance*: it describes the
fullness of communion-in-otherness. Both man's deification and the overall
transformation of creation in an expected and promised *future* without corruption and death are signified by a phrase bearing an obvious temporal
connotation, the "eighth day".

This threefold exposition of temporality (as χρόνος, αἰών, and στάσις
ἀεικίνητος) completes the present understanding of reality's motion as the
manifestation of a *relationship*. Time *measures* this relationship: it measures
it either as existential failure, refusal, and *distance* (i.e., as corruption, death,
and inexistence) or as communion, nearness, and immediacy. In annihilating all *distances* in a "union with the Providence in all directness and
immediacy," in liberating temporality from its transition from the past to
the future, deification discloses temporality as the dimensionless present
of the fullness of communion, as the transcendence of division and dualities, as the completion of a relationship that actualizes otherness as communion and not difference as division. This is not merely described by
Maximus as our return to the κατὰ φύσιν, but as our attainment of the ὑπὲρ
φύσιν—and it cannot be delimited as an idle rest and fixity, but as a vibrant
ever-moving repose. Temporality is not annihilated; it is *transformed* and
liberated from its predeterminations and necessities. It does not measure a
distance any more, a distance from the "before" to the "after," but discloses

---

7. I.e., a possible mode of existence for, indirectly, the whole of creation through
man's mediation. Therefore, this mode of existence is not merely a matter concerning
humanity—a matter of philosophical anthropology or mystical experience—but a matter of *ontology*, of existence and reality's mode of existence *as such*.

the dimensionlessness of a presence, the reality of a communion, the consummation of a relationship.

It would be fascinating to explore the implications of such an understanding of temporality in a comparative manner, not only within the framework of philosophy but beyond, e.g. in a comparison with today's natural sciences, psychology, and other contemporary approaches to the nature of time. However, such an endeavor is to be reserved for a study dedicated to the examination of that particular subject. In exploring Maximus the Confessor's understanding of time, we have examined only one of the aspects of his rich philosophical personality. I express here the hope that Maximus' work will continue to be researched as a *corpus* of high *philosophical* significance, and that Maximus the Confessor will find his place in the *European history of philosophy*, in the shared philosophical legacy of the European continent.

Bibliography

This is a selective bibliography, as a number of Maximian bibliographies have been published over the decades. The most comprehensive bibliography is Mikonja Knežević's *Maximus the Confessor (580–662) Bibliography* (Belgrade: Institute for Theological Research, Bibliographia Serbica Theologica 6, 2012), comprising of over 3,000 titles—monographs, articles, papers, critical editions, translations, etc. Concerning all available primary sources up to 2012, a comprehensive list of all editions of Maximus' texts and many translations is to be found in pp. 81–125 of the aforementioned book.

Editions of Maximus the Confessor's Works and Related Material

Patrologia Graeca

Migne, Jacques Paul, ed. *Patrologiae Cursus Completus*. Series Graeca—161 vols. Paris: Migne, 1857–66.
Volumes 90, 91: Maximi Confessoris Opera Omnia, 1865.
Volumes 3, 4: Corpus Areopagiticum, Scholia

Critical Editions of Maximus the Confessor's works:

Along with critical editions in print form, the *Thesaurus Linguae Graecae* has been used as well in order to access them. For the reader's convenience in tracing back relevant passages, I have employed the citation information of the TLG, which varies from *chapter and line number* to *page number* according to each particular critical edition. The *Corpus Christianorum Series Graeca* has been abbreviated as CCSG and the other critical editions as *Ceresa-Gastaldo, Cantarella* and *Constas / DOML* respectively.

Corpus Christianorum Series Graeca (CCSG). Turnhout: Brepols

Quaestiones ad Thalassium I. Quaestiones I–LV, una cum Latina Interpretatione Ioannis Scotti Eriugenae. Edited by Carl Laga and Carlos Steel, 1980 (CCSG 7).

Quaestiones et dubia. Edited by José H. Declerck, 1982 (CCSG 10).

Ambigua ad Iohannem iuxta Iohannis Scotti Eriugenae latinam interpretationem. Edited by Edouard Jeauneau, 1988 (CCSG 18).—i.e., no original Greek text, only Eriugena's Latin translation.

Quaestiones ad Thalassium II. Quaestiones LVI–LXV, una cum Latina Interpretatione Ioannis Scotti Eriugenae. Edited by Carl Laga and Carlos Steel, 1990 (CCSG 22).

Opuscula exegetica duo: Expositio in Psalmum LIX—Expositio orationis dominicae. Edited by Peter Van Deun, 1991 (CCSG 23).

Liber asceticus. Edited by Peter Van Deun Steven Gysens 2000 (CCSG 40).

Ambigua ad Thomam una cum Epistula secunda ad eundem. Edited by Bart Janssens, 2002. (CCSG 48).

Mystagogia. Una cum Latina interpretatione Anastasii Bibliothecarii. Edited by Christian Boudignon, 2011 (CCSG 69).

Sources chrétiennes. Paris: Les Éditions du Cerf. Maxime le Confesseur

Questions à Thalassios—Tome 1, Questions 1 à 40. Edited by Jean-Claude Larchet and Françoise Vinel, 2010 (Sources chrétiennes 529).

Questions à Thalassios—Tome 2, Questions 41 à 55. Edited by Jean-Claude Larchet and Françoise Vinel, 2012 (Sources chrétiennes 554).

Other Critical Editions

Cantarella, Raffaele. *S. Massimo Confessore. La mistagogia ed altri scritti.* Florence: Testi Cristiani, 1931.

Ceresa-Gastaldo, Aldo. *Massimo Confessore—Capitoli sulla caritá. Ed. criticamente con introd., versione e note.* Rome: Ed. Studium (Verba Seniorum, collana di testi e studi patristici, n.s. 3), 1963.

Constas, Nicholas. *Maximos the Confessor: On Difficulties in the Church Fathers—The Ambigua* (two volumes). Cambridge: Harvard University Press (Dumbarton Oaks Medieval Library 28 & 29), 2014.

Other Editions and Translations of Maximus the Confessor's works:

Allen, Pauline, and Bronwen Neil. *Maximus the Confessor and His Companions. Documents from Exile.* Oxford: Oxford University Press, 2002.

Berthold, George C. *Maximus the Confessor: Selected Writings.* New York: Paulist, 1985.

Blowers, Paul M., and Robert Louis Wilken. *On the Cosmic Mystery of Jesus Christ: Selected Writings from St. Maximus the Confessor.* Crestwood, NY: St. Vladimir's Seminary Press, 2003.

Lollar, Joshua. *Maximus the Confessor: Ambigua to Thomas and Second Letter to Thomas.* Turnhout: Brepols (Corpus Christianorum in Translation 2), 2010.

Louth, Andrew. *Maximus the Confessor.* London: Routledge, 1996.

Prassas, Despina. *St. Maximus the Confessor's Questions and Doubts.* DeKalb, IL: Northern Illinois University Press, 2009.

Sherwood, Polycarp. *St. Maximus the Confessor: The Ascetic Life—The Four Centuries on Charity.* Westminster, MD: Newman, 1955.

Shoemaker, Stephen J. *Maximus the Confessor: The Life of the Virgin.* New Haven: Yale University Press, 2012.

Bibliography

Aichele, Alexander. *Ontologie des Nicht-Seienden: Aristoteles' Metaphysik der Bewegung.* Neue Studien zur Philosophie, 21. Göttingen: Vandenhoeck & Ruprecht, 2009.

Allen, Pauline. "Life and Times of Maximus the Confessor." In *The Oxford Handbook of Maximus the Confessor,* edited by Pauline Allen and Bronwen Neil, 3–18. Oxford: Oxford University Press, 2015.

Allen, Pauline, and Bronwen Neil, eds. *The Oxford Handbook of Maximus the Confessor.* Oxford: Oxford University Press, 2015.

Antoine Lévy, Pauli Annala, Olli Hallamaa, and Tuomo Lankila, eds. *The Architecture of the Cosmos: St. Maximus the Confessor. New Perspectives.* Helsinki: Luther-Agricola-Society, 2015.

Archer-Hind, R. D., ed. *The Timaeus of Plato. With Introduction and Notes.* Salem, NH: Ayer, 1988.

Aryeh L. "Aristotle's Definition of Motion." *Phronesis* 14 (1969) 40–62.

Balthasar, Hans Urs von. *Cosmic Liturgy: The Universe according to Maximus the Confessor.* Translated by Brian E. Daley. San Francisco: Ignatius, 2003.

———. *Kosmische Liturgie: Das Weltbild Maximus des Bekenners.* Einsiedeln: Johannes Verlag, 1961.

Bathrellos, Demetrios. *The Byzantine Christ: Person, Nature, and Will in the Christology of Saint Maximus the Confessor.* Oxford: Oxford University Press, 2004.

Baun, Jane, Averil Cameron, Mark Edwards, and Markus Vinzent, eds. *Papers presented at the fifteenth International Conference on Patristic Studies held in Oxford 2007— From the Fifth Century: Greek Writers, Latin Writers, Nachleben.* Studia Patristica 48. Leuven: Peeters, 2010.

Beck, H. G. *Kirche und theologische Literatur im Byzantinischen Reich.* München: Beck, 1959.

Benevich, Grigory. "Maximus' Heritage in Russia and Ukraine." In *The Oxford Handbook of Maximus the Confessor,* edited by Pauline Allen and Bronwen Neil, 460–79. Oxford: Oxford University Press, 2015.

Betsakos, Vasileios. *Στάσις ἀεικίνητος: ἡ ἀνακαίνιση τῆς ἀριστοτελικῆς κινήσεως στὴ θεολογία Μαξίμου τοῦ Ὁμολογητοῦ.* Athens: Armos, 2006.

———. *Ψυχὴ ἄρα ζωή: ὁ ἀποφατικὸς χαρακτήρας τῆς ἀριστοτελικῆς κινήσεως τῆς ψυχῆς.* Athens: Armos, 2007.

Blowers, Paul M. *Exegesis and Spiritual Pedagogy in Maximus the Confessor.* South Bend, IN: University of Notre Dame Press, 1991.

———. "Maximus the Confessor, Gregory of Nyssa, and the Concept of 'Perpetual Progress." *Vigiliae Christianae* 46 (1992) 151–71.

———. *Maximus the Confessor: Jesus Christ and the Transfiguration of the World.* Oxford: Oxford University Press, 2016.

Böhme, Gernot. *Zeit und Zahl: Studien zur Zeittheorie bei Platon, Aristoteles, Leibniz und Kant.* Frankfurt am Main: Klostermann, 1974.

Bostock, David. *Space, Time, Matter, and Form. Essays on Aristotle's Physics.* Oxford: Oxford University Press, 2006.

Bradshaw, David. *Aristotle East and West—Metaphysics and the Division of Christendom.* Cambridge: Cambridge University Press, 2004.

———. "Time and Eternity in the Greek Fathers." *The Thomist* 70 (2006) 311–66.

Brague, Rémi. "Aristotle's Definition of Motion and Its Ontological Implications." *Graduate Faculty Philosophy Journal* 13:2 (1990) 1–22.

Breidert, Wolfgang. *Das aristotelische Kontinuum in der Scholastik.* Beiträge zur Geschichte der Philosophie und Theologie des Mittelalters: Neue Folge, 1. Munster: Aschendorff, 1970.

Brock, Sebastian. "An Early Syriac Life of Maximus the Confessor." *Analecta Bollandiana* 91 (1973) 299–346.

Burnet, John. *Platonis Opera,* vol. 4. Oxford: Clarendon, 1902.

Callender, Craig, ed. *The Oxford Handbook of Philosophy of Time.* Oxford: Oxford University Press, 2013.

Carrier, Martin. *Raum—Zeit.* Grundthemen Philosophie. Berlin: De Gruyter, 2009.

Celia, Francesco. "Il λόγος κεφαλαιώδης dello ps.-Gregorio il Taumaturgo: uno status quaestionis e un primo approccio al problema delle fonti." *Adamantius* 17 (2011) 164–89.

Conen, Paul F. *Die Zeittheorie des Aristoteles.* Zetemata, 35. München: Beck, 1964.

Constas, Maximos (Fr. Maximos Simonopetrites). "St. Maximus the Confessor: The Reception of His Thought in East and West." In *Papers Presented at the Fifteenth International Conference on Patristic Studies held in Oxford 2007—From the Fifth Century: Greek Writers, Latin Writers, Nachleben,* edited by Baun, Jane, Averil Cameron, Mark Edwards and Markus Vinzent, 25–53. Studia Patristica 48. Leuven: Peeters, 2010.

Coope, Ursula. *Time for Aristotle. Physics IV.10–14.* Oxford Aristotle Studies. Oxford: Oxford University Press, 2005.

Cooper, Adam G. *The Body in St. Maximus the Confessor: Holy Flesh, Wholly Deified.* Oxford: Oxford University Press, 2005.

Cornford, Francis Macdonald. *Plato's Cosmology: The 'Timaeus' of Plato Translated with a Running Commentary.* London: Routledge & Kegan Paul, 1956.

Cullmann, Oscar. *Christ and Time: The Primitive Christian Conception of Time and History.* London: SCM, 1967.

Cvetkovic, Vladimir. "St. Gregory's Argument Concerning the Lack of *Diastema* in the Divine Activities from *Ad Ablabium.*" In *Gregory of Nyssa: the Minor Treatises on Trinitarian Theology and Apollinarism: Proceedings of the 11th International Colloquium on Gregory of Nyssa (Tübingen, 17—20 September 2008),* edited by Volker Henning Drecoll and Margitta Berghaus, 369–82. Leiden: Brill, 2011.

———. "St. Maximus on Πάθος and Κίνησις in *Ambiguum 7.*" In *Papers Presented at the Fifteenth International Conference on Patristic Studies held in Oxford 2007—From the Fifth Century: Greek Writers, Latin Writers, Nachleben,* edited by Baun, Jane,

Averil Cameron, Mark Edwards and Markus Vinzent, 95–104. Studia Patristica 48. Leuven: Peeters, 2010.

Dalmais, Irénée Henri. *Théologie de l'église et mystère liturgique dans la Mystagogie de s. Maxime le Confesseur.* Berlin: Akademie-Verlag, 1975.

Elders, Leo. *Aristotle's Theology: A Commentary on Book Λ of the Metaphysics.* Assen: Von Gorcum, 1972.

Elser, Konrad. *Die Lehre des Aristoteles über das Wirken Gottes.* Münster: Aschendorff, 1893.

Epsen, Edward: "Eternity is a Present, Time is its Unwrapping." *The Heythrop Journal* 52 (2010) 417–29.

Garrigues, Juan Miguel. *Maxime le Confesseur. La charité, avenir divin de l'homme.* Théologie historique, 38. Paris: Beauchesne, 1976.

Gatti, Maria Luisa. *Massimo il Confessore. Saggio di bibliografia generale ragionata e contributi per una ricostruzione scientifica del suo pensiero metafisico e religioso. Metafisica del Platonismo nel suo sviluppo storico e nella filosofia patristica.* Studi o testi, 2. Milan: Vita e Pensiero, Pubblicazioni della Università Cattolica del Sacro Cuore, 1987.

Gersh, Stephen E. *Κίνησις Ἀκίνητος—A Study of Spiritual Motion in the Philosophy of Proclus.* Leiden: Brill, 1973.

Gigon, Olof: "Die Theologie der Vorsokratiker." In *La notion du divin depuis Homer jusqu'à Platon Platon. Entretiens sur l' Antiquité Classique,* edited by Herbert Jennings Rose, 127–55. Genève: Vandoeuvres, 1952.

Gloy, Karen. *Philosophiegeschichte der Zeit.* Paderborn: Fink, 2008.

Graham, Daniel W. "Aristotle's Definition of Motion." *Ancient Philosophy* 8 (1988) 209–15.

Grigoropoulou, Evaggelia. "The Early Development of the Thought of Christos Yannaras." PhD, Durham University, 2008. Available at Durham E-theses Online: http://etheses.dur.ac.uk/1976/.

Harvey, Susan A., ed. *The Oxford Handbook of Early Christian Studies.* Oxford: Oxford University Press, 2008.

Heil, Gunter, and Adolf Martin Ritter, eds. *Corpus Dionysiacum II: Pseudo-Dionysius Areopagita. De coelesti hierarchia, de ecclesiastica hierarchia, de mystica theologia, epistulae.* Berlin: De Gruyter, 1991.

Heinzer, Felix. *Maximus Confessor, Actes du Symposium sur Maxime le Confesseur, Fribourg, 2—5 sept. 1980.* Edited by Christoph Schönborn. Fribourg, Suisse: Éd. Universitaires, 1982.

Hörz, Herbert. *Philosophie der Zeit: Zeitverständnis in Geschichte und Gegenwart.* Berlin: Deutscher Verlag der Wissinschaften, 1989.

Hovorun, Cyril. *Will, Action, and Freedom. Christological Controversies in the Seventh Century.* Leiden: Brill, 2008.

Huber, Johannes. *Die Philosophie der Kirchenväter.* München: Cotta, 1859.

Hussey, Edward. *Aristotle's Physics. Books III and IV.* Oxford: Clarendon, 1983.

Ierodiakonou, Katerina, and Börje Bydén. "Byzantine Philosophy." In *The Stanford Encyclopedia of Philosophy.* Winter 2008 ed. Edited by Edward N. Zalta. URL = <http://plato.stanford.edu/archives/win2008/entries/byzantine-philosophy/>, retrieved 07 April 2013.

Ierodiakonou, Katerina, ed. *Byzantine Philosophy and Its Ancient Sources.* Oxford: Oxford University Press, 2002.

Jaeger, Werner. *The Theology of the Early Greek Philosophers*. Oxford: Clarendon, 1947.

Jankowiak, Marek, and Phil Booth: "An Updated Date-List of the Works of Maximus the Confessor." In *The Oxford Handbook of Maximus the Confessor*, edited by Pauline Allen and Bronwen Neil, 19–83. Oxford: Oxford University Press, 2015.

Janssens, Bart. "Does the Combination of Maximus' *Ambigua ad Thomam* and *Ambigua ad Iohannem* Go Back to the Confessor Himself?" *Sacris Erudiri* 42 (2003) 281–86.

Kapriev, Georgi T. *Philosophie in Byzanz*. Würzburg: Königshausen & Neumann, 2005.

Kapsimalakou, Christina. Ἐλευθερία καὶ ἀναγκαιότητα κατὰ τὸν Μάξιμο τὸν Ὁμολογητή: πρὸς μιὰ Ὀντολογία τοῦ Προσώπου. Patras: University of Patras (Diss.), 2012.

Karamanolis, George. *The Philosophy of Early Christianity*. Durham: Acumen, 2013.

Karayiannis, Vasilios. *Maxime le confesseur: Essence et énergies de Dieu*. Théologie historique, 93. Paris: Beauchesne, 1993.

Kattan, Assaad Elias. *Verleiblichung und Synergie. Grundzüge der Bibelhermeneutik bei Maximus Confessor*. Supplements to Vigiliae Christianae, 63. Leiden: Brill, 2003.

Kaulbach, Friedrich. *Der philosophische Begriff der Bewegung. Studien zu Aristoteles, Leibniz und Kant*. Münstersche Forschungen, 16. Köln: Böhlau, 1965.

Khoperia, Lela. "The Georgian Tradition on Maximus the Confessor." In *The Oxford Handbook of Maximus the Confessor*, edited by Pauline Allen and Bronwen Neil, 439–59. Oxford: Oxford University Press, 2015.

Knežević, Mikonja. *Maximus the Confessor (580–662) Bibliography*. Bibliographia Serbica Theologica vol. 6. Belgrade: Institute for Theological Research, 2012.

Knight, Douglas H., ed. *The Theology of John Zizioulas: Personhood and the Church*. Farnham, UK: Ashgate, 2007.

Kosman, Aryeh L. "Aristotle's Definition of Motion." *Phronesis* 14 (1969) 40–62.

Lampe, Geoffrey W. H., ed. *A Patristic Greek Lexicon*. Oxford: Clarendon, 1961.

Larchet, Jean-Claude. *La Divinisation de l'homme selon saint Maxime le Confesseur*. Paris: Éditions du Cerf, 1996.

———. *Maxime le Confesseur, médiateur entre l'Orient et l'Occident*, Paris: Éditions du Cerf,1998.

———. *Saint Maxime le Confesseur*, Paris: Éditions du Cerf, 2003.

Le Guillou, Marie-Joseph. *Le Christ et l'église. Théologie du mystère*. Paris: Éditions du centurion, 1963.

———. *L'expérience de l'Esprit saint en Orient et en Occident*. Saint-Maur, Les Plans-sur-Bex: Editions Parole et silence, 2001.

Leiss, Pekka. *Die aristotelische Lehre von der Zeit. Ihre Aporien und deren Auflösung*. AKAN-Einzelschriften, 5. Trier: Wiss. Verl, 2004.

Lévy, Antoine. *Le Cree Et L'incree: Maxime Le Confesseur Et Thomas D'Aquin*. Paris: Librairie Philosophique Vrin, 2006.

Liddell, Henry G., Robert Scott, and Henry S. Jones, eds. *A Greek-English Lexicon (with a Revised Supplement)*. Oxford: Clarendon, 1996.

Lollar, Joshua. *To See into the Life of Things: The Contemplation of Nature in Maximus the Confessor and his Predecessors*. Turnhout: Brepols, 2013.

Lossky, Vladimir. *The Mystical Theology of the Eastern Church*. Cambridge: James Clarke, 1991.

Loudovikos, Nikolaos. *Church in the Making: An Apophatic Ecclesiology of Consubstantiality*. Translated by Norman Russell. Crestwood, NY: St. Vladimir's Seminary Press, 2016.

———. *A Eucharistic Ontology: Maximus the Confessor's Eschatological Ontology of Being as Dialogical Reciprocity.* Translated by Elizabeth Theokritoff. Brookline: HC, 2010 [a substantially revised translation of Ἡ Εὐχαριστιακὴ Ὀντολογία].

———. Ἡ εὐχαριστιακὴ ὀντολογία: τὰ εὐχαριστιακὰ θεμέλια τοῦ εἶναι ὡς ἐν κοινωνίᾳ γίγνεσθα, στὴν ἐσχατολογικὴ ὀντολογία τοῦ ἁγίου Μαξίμου τοῦ Ὁμολογητῇ. Athens: Domos, 1992.

Louth, Andrew. *Denys the Areopagite.* London: Continuum, 2001.

———. "Maximos the Confessor." In *The Wiley Blackwell Companion to Patristics,* edited by Ken Parry, 251–63. Chichester, UK: Wiley-Blackwell, 2015.

———. *The Origins of the Christian Mystical Tradition: From Plato to Denys.* Oxford: Oxford University Press, 2007.

———. "St. Maximos' Doctrine of the Logoi of Creation." In *Knowing the Purpose of Creation through the Resurrection—Proceedings of the Symposium on St. Maximus the Confessor, October 18–21, 2012,* edited by Maxim Vasiljević, 77–84. Georgetown, CA: Sebastian, 2013.

Luibheid, Colm, and Paul Rorem. *Pseudo-Dionysius: The Complete Works.* Mahwah, NY: Paulist, 1987.

Mainzer, Klaus. *Zeit: von der Urzeit zur Computerzeit.* München: Beck, 1996.

Manoussakis, John Panteleimon. *God After Metaphysics. A Theological Aesthetic.* Bloomington, IN: Indiana University Press, 2007.

Manuwald, Bernd. *Studien zum Unbewegten Beweger in der Naturphilosophie des Aristoteles.* Mainz: Akademie der Wissenschaften und der Literatur, 1989.

Marion, Jean-Luc. *God Without Being—Hors-Texte.* Translated by Thomas A. Carlson. Chicago: University of Chicago Press, 2012.

Marquardt, Udo. *Die Einheit der Zeit bei Aristoteles.* Epistemata/Reihe Philosophie, 127. Wurzburg: Konigshausen & Neumann, 1993.

Matsoukas, Nikos. Κόσμος, Ἄνθρωπος, Κοινωνία κατὰ τὸν Ἅγιο Μάξιμο τὸν Ὁμολογητή. Athens: Grigoris, 1980.

Maudlin, Tim. *Philosophy of Physics—Space and Time.* Princeton: Princeton University Press, 2012.

McLure, Roger. *The Philosophy of Time: Time before Times.* London: Routledge, 2005.

Mensching-Estakhr, Alia, and Michael Städtler, eds. *Wahrheit und Geschichte. Die gebrochene Tradition metaphysischen Denkens. Festschrift zum 70. Geburtstag von Günther Mensching.* Würzburg: Königshausen & Neumann, 2012.

Mesch, Walter. *Reflektierte Gegenwart: eine Studie über Zeit und Ewigkeit bei Platon, Aristoteles, Plotin und Augustinus.* Frankfurt am Main: Klostermann, 2003.

Mitralexis, Sotiris. "Aspekte der Philosophischen Anthropologie Maximus' des Bekenners: Seele und Hypostase als ontologische Voraussetzungen." In *Ommasin allois. Festschrift für Professor Ioannis E. Theodoropoulos zum 65. Geburtstag,* edited by Vasileios E. Pantazis and Michael Stork, 283–93. Essen: Oldib, 2014.

———, ed. *The Fountain and the Flood: Maximus the Confessor and Philosophical Enquiry.* Studia Patristica. Leuven: Peeters, 2017.

———. "Maximus the Confessor's 'Aeon' as a Distinct Mode of Temporality." *Heythrop Journal* 57 (2016). DOI: 10.1111/heyj.12319

———. "Maximus the Confessor's 'Intelligible Creation'. Solving Contradictions on Imperishability and Corruptibility." *Forum Philosophicum* 19:2 (2014) 241–49.

———. "Maximus' 'Logical' Ontology: An Introduction and Interpretative Approach to Maximus the Confessor' Notion of the λόγοι." *Sobornost* 37:1 (2015) 65–82.

———. "Maximus' Theory of Motion: Motion κατὰ φύσιν, Returning Motion, Motion παρὰ φύσιν." In *Maximus the Confessor as a European Philosopher*, edited by Sotiris Mitralexis et al. Eugene, OR: Cascade, forthcoming 2017.

———. "A Note on the Definition of χρόνος and αἰὼν in St. Maximus the Confessor through Aristotle." In *Knowing the Purpose of Creation through the Resurrection—Proceedings of the Symposium on St. Maximus the Confessor, October 18-21, 2012*, edited by Maxim Vasiljević, 419–26. California: Sebastian, 2013.

———. "Person, Eros, Critical Ontology: An Attempt to Recapitulate Christos Yannaras' Philosophy." *Sobornost* 34:1 (2012) 33–40.

———. "Relation, Activity and Otherness in Christos Yannaras' Propositions for a Critical Ontology." In *Christos Yannaras: Polis, Philosophy, Theology*, edited by Andreas Andreopoulos and Mary B. Cunningham. London: Ashgate, forthcoming 2017.

———. "Temporality in Aristotle's Philosophy: Motion, Time and Decay." *Φιλοσοφεῖν* 11 (2015) 149–74.

———. "Transcending the Body/Soul Distinction through the Perspective of Maximus the Confessor's Anthropology." In *The Resounding Soul: Reflections on the Metaphysics and Vivacity of the Human Person*, edited by Eric Austin Lee and Samuel Kimbriel, 135–48. Eugene, OR: Cascade, 2015.

Mitralexis, Sotiris, Georgios Steiris, Marcin Podbielski, and Sebastian Lalla, eds. *Maximus the Confessor as a European Philosopher*. Eugene, OR: Cascade, forthcoming 2017.

Mueller-Jourdan, Pascal. "Where and When as Metaphysical Prerequisites for Creation in Ambiguum 10." In *Knowing the Purpose of Creation through the Resurrection—Proceedings of the Symposium on St. Maximus the Confessor, October 18-21, 2012*, edited by Maxim Vasiljević, 287–96. Georgetown, CA: Sebastian, 2013.

———. *Typologie Spatio-Temporelle de l'Ecclesia Byzantine: La Mystagogie de Maxime le Confesseur*. Supplements to Vigiliae Christianae, 74 Leiden: Brill, 2005.

Müller, Thomas, ed. *Philosophie der Zeit. Neue analytische Ansätze*. Frankfurt am Main: Klostermann, 2007.

Neil, Bronwen, and Pauline Allen, eds. *The Life of Maximus the Confessor. Recension 3*. Strathfield, NSW: St. Paul's, 2003.

Nesteruk, Alexei V. *The Universe as Communion. Towards a Neo-Patristic Synthesis of Theology and Science*. London: T. & T. Clark, 2008.

Nichols, Aidan. *Byzantine Gospel: Maximus the Confessor in Modern Scholarship*. Edinburgh: T. & T. Clark, 1993.

Oehler, Klaus. *Antike Philosophie und Byzantinisches Mittelalter*. München: Beck, 1969.

———. *Der Unbewegte Beweger des Aristoteles*. Frankfurt am Main: Klostermann, 1984.

Perl, Eric David. "Metaphysics and Christology in Maximus Confessor and Eriugena." In *Eriugena—East and West: Papers of the Eighth International Colloquium of the Society for the Promotion of Eriugenian Studies*, edited by Bernard McGinn and Willemien Otten, 253–79. South Bend, IN: University of Notre Dame Press, 1994.

———. "Methexis: Creation, Incarnation, Deification in Saint Maximus Confessor." PhD diss., Yale University of Chicago, 1991.

———. "St. Gregory Palamas and the Metaphysics of Creation". *Dionysius* 14 (1990) 105–30.

———. "Symbol, Sacrament, and Hierarchy in St. Dionysios the Areopagite." *Greek Orthodox Theological Review* 39 (1994) 311–55.

———. *Theophany: The Neoplatonic Philosophy of Dionysius the Areopagite*. New York: State University of New York Press, 2007.

Plass, Paul. "'Moving Rest' in Maximus the Confessor." *Classica et Mediaevalia* 35 (1984) 177–90.

———. "Transcendent Time and Eternity in Gregory of Nyssa." *Vigiliae Christianae* 34 (1980) 180–92.

———. "Transcendent Time in Maximus the Confessor." *The Thomist* 44:2 (1980) 259–77.

Podskalsky, Gerhard. *Theologie und Philosophie in Byzanz. Der Streit um die theologische Methodik in der spätbyzantinischen Geistesgeschichte (14./15. Jh.), seine systematischen Grundlagen und seine historische Entwicklung*. München: Beck, 1977.

Ray, Christopher. *Time, Space and Philosophy*. London: Routledge, 1991.

Renczes, Philipp Gabriel. *Agir de Dieu et liberté de l'homme, Recherches sur l'anthropologie théologique de saint Maxime le Confesseur*, Paris: Éditions du Cerf, 2003.

Riou, Alain. *Le monde et l'Eglise selon Maxime le Confesseur*. Théologie historique, 22. Paris: Beauchesne, 1973.

Roark, Tony. *Aristotle on Time: A Study of the Physics*. Cambridge: Cambridge University Press, 2011.

Rolt, Clarence Edwin. *Dionysius the Areopagite: On the Divine Names and the Mystical Theology*. London: SPCK, 1920.

Rorem, Paul, and John C. Lamoreaux. *John of Scythopolis and the Dionysian Corpus*. New York: Oxford University Press, 1998.

Rudolph, Enno, ed. *Zeit, Bewegung, Handlung. Studien zur Zeitabhandlung des Aristoteles*. Evangelische Studiengemeinschaft: Forschungen und Berichte der Evangelischen Studiengemeinschaft, 42. Stuttgart: Klett-Cotta,1988.

Russell, Norman. *The Doctrine of Deification in the Greek Patristic Tradition*. Oxford: Oxford University Press, 2006.

———. "Modern Greek Theologians and the Greek Fathers." *Philosophy & Theology* 18:1 (2006) 77–92.

Sarnowsky, Jürgen. *Die aristotelisch-scholastische Theorie der Bewegung. Studien zum Kommentar Alberts von Sachsen zur Physik des Aristoteles*. Münster: Aschendorff, 1989.

Sattler, Barbara. "The Emergence of the Concept of Motion: Aristotle's Notion of *Kinesis* as a Reaction to Zeno's Paradoxes and Plato's *Timaeus*." PhD diss., Freie Universität, Berlin, 2006.

Savvidis, Kyriakos. *Die Lehre von der Vergöttlichung des Menschen bei Maximos dem Bekenner und ihre Rezeption durch Gregor Palamas*. St. Ottilien: EOS-Verl., 1997.

Scheffel, Wolfgang. *Aspekte der platonischen Kosmologie: Untersuchungen zum Dialog "Timaios."* Leiden: Brill, 1976.

Schmidt, Ernst A. *Platons Zeittheorie: Kosmos, Seele, Zahl und Ewigkeit im "Timaios."* Frankfurt am Main: Klostermann, 2012.

Sherwood, Polycarp. *An Annotated Date-list of the Works of Maximus the Confessor*. Romae: Herder, 1952.

———. *The Earlier Ambigua of Saint Maximus the Confessor and His Refutation of Origenism*. Romae: Herder, 1955.

Shields, Christopher John. *Aristotle*. London: Routledge, 2007.

Skliris, Dionysios. "Le concept de tropos chez Maxime le Confesseur" ["The Notion of Mode in the Philosophy of Maximus the Confessor," in French]. PhD diss., University of Paris IV–Sorbonne, 2015.

———. "'Hypostasis', 'Person', 'Individual': A Comparison between the Terms that Denote Concrete Being in St. Maximus' Theology." In *Knowing the Purpose of Creation through the Resurrection—Proceedings of the Symposium on St. Maximus the Confessor, October 18-21, 2012*, edited by Maxim Vasiljević, 437–50. Georgetown, CA: Sebastian, 2013.

Soppa, Wilhelm. *Die Diversa Capita unter den Schriften des heiligen Maximus Confessor in deutscher Bearbeitung und quellenkritischer Beleuchtung*. Dresden: Saxonia-Buchdr., 1922.

Suchla, Beate Regina, ed. *Corpus Dionysiacum I: Pseudo-Dionysius Areopagita. De Divinis Nominibus*. Berlin: de Gruyter, 1990.

———. *Corpus Dionysiacum Band 4,1. Ioannis Scythopolitani prologus et scholia in Dionysii Areopagitae librum 'De divinis nominibus' cum additamentis interpretum aliorum*. Berlin, Boston: de Gruyter, 2011.

Suchla, Beate Regina. *Dionysius Areopagita. Leben—Werk—Wirkung*. Freiburg i. Br: Herder, 2008.

———. *Die sogenannten Maximus-Scholien des Corpus Dionysiacum Areopagiticum*. Göttingen: Vandenhoeck & Ruprecht, 1980.

Tatakis, Basil. *Byzantine Philosophy*. Translated by Nicholas J. Moutafakis. Indianapolis: Hackett, 2003. (English translation of *La Philosophie Byzantine*.)

———. *Christian Philosophy in the Patristic and Byzantine Tradition*. Rollinsford, NH: Orthodox Research Institute, 2007.

———. *La Philosophie Byzantine*. Fascicule supplémentaire No II of Émile Bréhier's Histoire de la Philosophie. Paris: Presses Universitaires de France, 1949.

Taylor, Alfred E. *A Commentary on Plato's Timaeus*. Oxford: Clarendon, 1928.

Thomson, Iain. "Ontotheology? Understanding Heidegger's *Destruktion* of Metaphysics." *International Journal of Philosophical Studies* 8:3 (2000) 297–327.

Thunberg, Lars. *Man and the Cosmos. The Vision of St. Maximus the Confessor*. Crestwood, NY: St. Vladimir's Seminary Press, 1985.

———. *Microcosm and Mediator: The Theological Anthropology of Maximus the Confessor*. Chicago: Open Court, 1995.

Tollefsen, Torstein. *Activity and Participation in Late Antique and Early Christian Thought*. Oxford: Oxford University Press, 2012.

———. "Causality and Movement in St. Maximus' *Ambiguum 7*." In *Papers Presented at the Fifteenth International Conference on Patristic Studies held in Oxford 2007—From the Fifth Century: Greek Writers, Latin Writers, Nachleben*, edited by Baun, Jane, Averil Cameron, Mark Edwards and Markus Vinzent, 85–93. *Studia Patristica* 48. Leuven: Peeters, 2010.

———. *The Christocentric Cosmology of St. Maximus the Confessor*. Oxford: Oxford University Press, 2008.

———. "St. Maximus' Concept of a Human Hypostasis." In *Knowing the Purpose of Creation through the Resurrection—Proceedings of the Symposium on St. Maximus the Confessor, October 18-21, 2012*, edited by Maxim Vasiljević, 115–27. Georgetown, CA: Sebastian, 2013.

Törönen, Melchisedec. *Union and Distinction in the Thought of St. Maximus the Confessor*. Oxford: Oxford University Press, 2007.

Tredennick, Hugh. *Aristotle: Metaphysics, Volume I: Books I–IX, with an English translation by Hugh Tredennick*. Cambridge: Harvard University Press, 1933.

Tredennick, Hugh and G. Cyril Armstrong. *Aristotle: Metaphysics, Volume II: Books X–XIV, translated by Hugh Tredennick, Oeconomica, Magna Moralia, translated by G. Cyril Armstrong*. Cambridge: Harvard University Press, 1935.

Tsikrikas, Zenon. *Der Sohn des Menschen. Theodizee oder Theogonie des christlichen Gottes?* Paderborn: Schöningh, 2012.

Vargas, Antonio. "Proclus and the Metaphysics of Time." PhD diss., Humboldt Universität zu Berlin, 2016.

Vasiljević, Maxim, ed. *Knowing the Purpose of Creation through the Resurrection—Proceedings of the Symposium on St. Maximus the Confessor, October 18–21, 2012*. Georgetown, CA: Sebastian, 2013.

Vletsis, Athanasios V. *Τὸ προπατορικὸ ἁμάρτημα στὴ θεολογία Μαξίμου τοῦ Ὁμολογητοῦ: ἔρευνα στὶς ἀπαρχὲς μιᾶς ὀντολογίας τῶν κτιστῶν*. Thessaloniki: Tertios, 1998.

Völker, Walther. *Maximus Confessor als Meister des geistlichen Lebens*. Wiesbaden: Steiner, 1965.

Wagner, Michael F. *The Enigmatic Reality of Time: Aristotle, Plotinus, and Today*. Leiden: Brill, 2008.

Wicksteed, Philip H., and Francis M. Cornford. *Aristotle: Physics, with an English translation by Philip H. Wicksteed and Francis M. Cornford*. 2 vols. Cambridge: Harvard University Press, 1957.

Williams, Rowan. *Arius: Heresy and Tradition*. Grand Rapids: Eerdmans, 2002.

Wittgenstein, Ludwig. *Tractatus Logico-Philosophicus*. Translated by Brian McGuiness and David Pears. London: Routledge, 2011.

Yannaras, Christos. *Against Religion: The Alienation of the Ecclesial Event*. Translated by Norman Russell. Brookline MA: Holy Cross, 2013.

———. "Ὁ ἀποφατικὸς Ἀριστοτέλης." *Diavazo* 135 (1986) 14–16.

———. *Elements of Faith: An Introduction to Orthodox Theology*. Translated by Keith Schram. Edinburgh: T. & T. Clark, 1991.

———. *The Enigma of Evil*. Translated by Norman Russell. Brookline, MA: Holy Cross, 2012.

———. *The Freedom of Morality*. Translated by Elisabeth Briere. Crestwood, NY: St. Vladimir's Seminary Press, 1984.

———. *The Meaning of Reality: Essays on Existence and Communion, Eros and History*. Edited by Herman A. Middleton and Gregory Edwards. Los Angeles: Sebastian & Indiktos, 2011.

———. *On the Absence and Unknowability of God: Heidegger and the Areopagite*. Edited by Andrew Louth, translated by Haralambos Ventis. London: T. & T. Clark, 2005.

———. "The Ontological Realism of Our Hopes Hereafter: Conclusions from St. Maximus the Confessor's Brief References." In *Knowing the Purpose of Creation through the Resurrection—Proceedings of the Symposium on St. Maximus the Confessor, October 18–21, 2012*, edited by Maxim Vasiljević, 379–86. Georgetown, CA: Sebastian, 2013.

———. *Orthodoxy and the West: Hellenic Self-Identity in the Modern Age*. Translated by Peter Chamberas and Norman Russell. Brookline, MA: Holy Cross, 2006.

————. *Person and Eros*. Translated by Norman Russell. Brookline, MA: Holy Cross, 2007.

————. *Postmodern Metaphysics*. Translated by Norman Russell. Brookline, MA: Holy Cross, 2004.

————. *Relational Ontology*. Translated by Norman Russell. Brookline, MA: Holy Cross, 2011.

————. *The Schism in Philosophy*. Translated by Norman Russell. Brookline, MA: Holy Cross, 2015.

————. *Variations on the Song of Songs*. Translated by Norman Russell. Brookline, MA: Holy Cross, 2005.

————. *Ἕξι φιλοσοφικὲς ζωγραφιές*. Athens: Ikaros, 2011.

————. *Ὀρθὸς λόγος καὶ κοινωνικὴ πρακτική*. Athens: Domos, 2006.

————. *Προτάσεις κριτικῆς ὀντολογίας*. Athens: Domos, 1985 & Ikaros, 2010.

————. *Σχεδίασμα εἰσαγωγῆς στὴ φιλοσοφία*. Athens: Domos, 1988.

————. *Τὸ πραγματικὸ καὶ τὸ φαντασιῶδες στὴν Πολιτικὴ Οἰκονομία*. Athens: Domos 2006.

————. *Τὸ ρητὸ καὶ τὸ ἄρρητο: τὰ γλωσσικὰ ὅρια ρεαλισμοῦ τῆς μεταφυσικῆς*. Athens: Ikaros, 1999.

Zimmerli, Walther Ch., ed. *Klassiker der modernen Zeitphilosophie*. Darmstadt: Wissenschaftliche Buchgesellschaft, 2007.

Zizioulas, John D. *Being as Communion: Studies in Personhood and the Church*. London: Darton, Longman and Todd, 1985.

————. *Communion and Otherness: Further Studies in Personhood and the Church*. London: T. & T. Clark, 2006.

————. *L'Etre ecclésial*. Genève: Labor et Fides, 1981.

————. *The One and the Many: Studies on God, Man, the Church and the World Today*. Los Angeles: Sebastian, 2010.

————. "Person and Nature in the Theology of St. Maximus the Confessor." In *Knowing the Purpose of Creation through the Resurrection—Proceedings of the Symposium on St. Maximus the Confessor, October 18–21, 2012*, edited by Maxim Vasiljević, 85–113. Georgetown, CA: Sebastian, 2013.

Zizioulas, John D., and Douglas H. Knight. *Lectures in Christian Dogmatics*. London: T. & T. Clark, 2008.

Index

GREEK WORDS

Made in the USA
Monee, IL
10 February 2020

21576112R00150